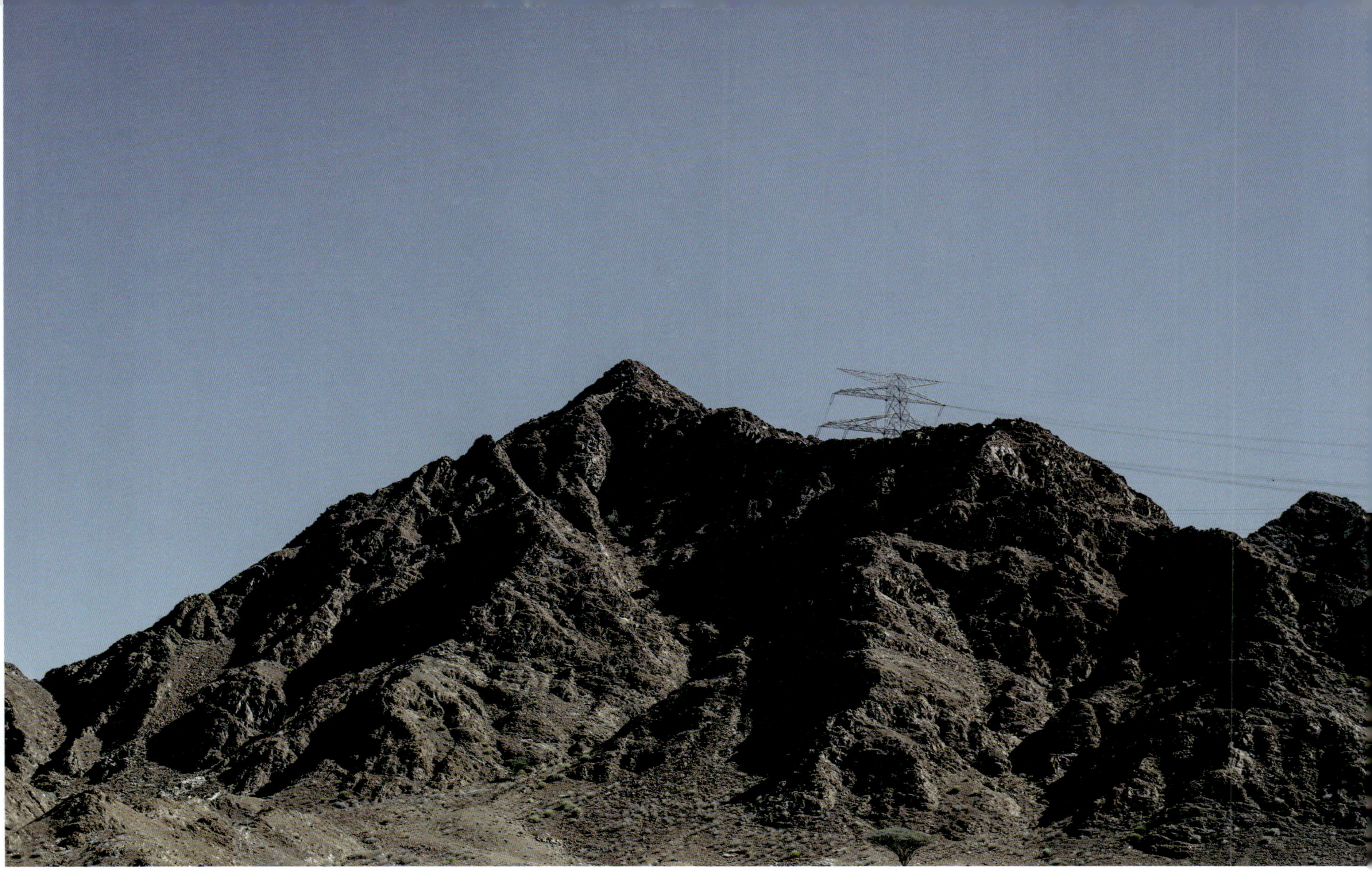

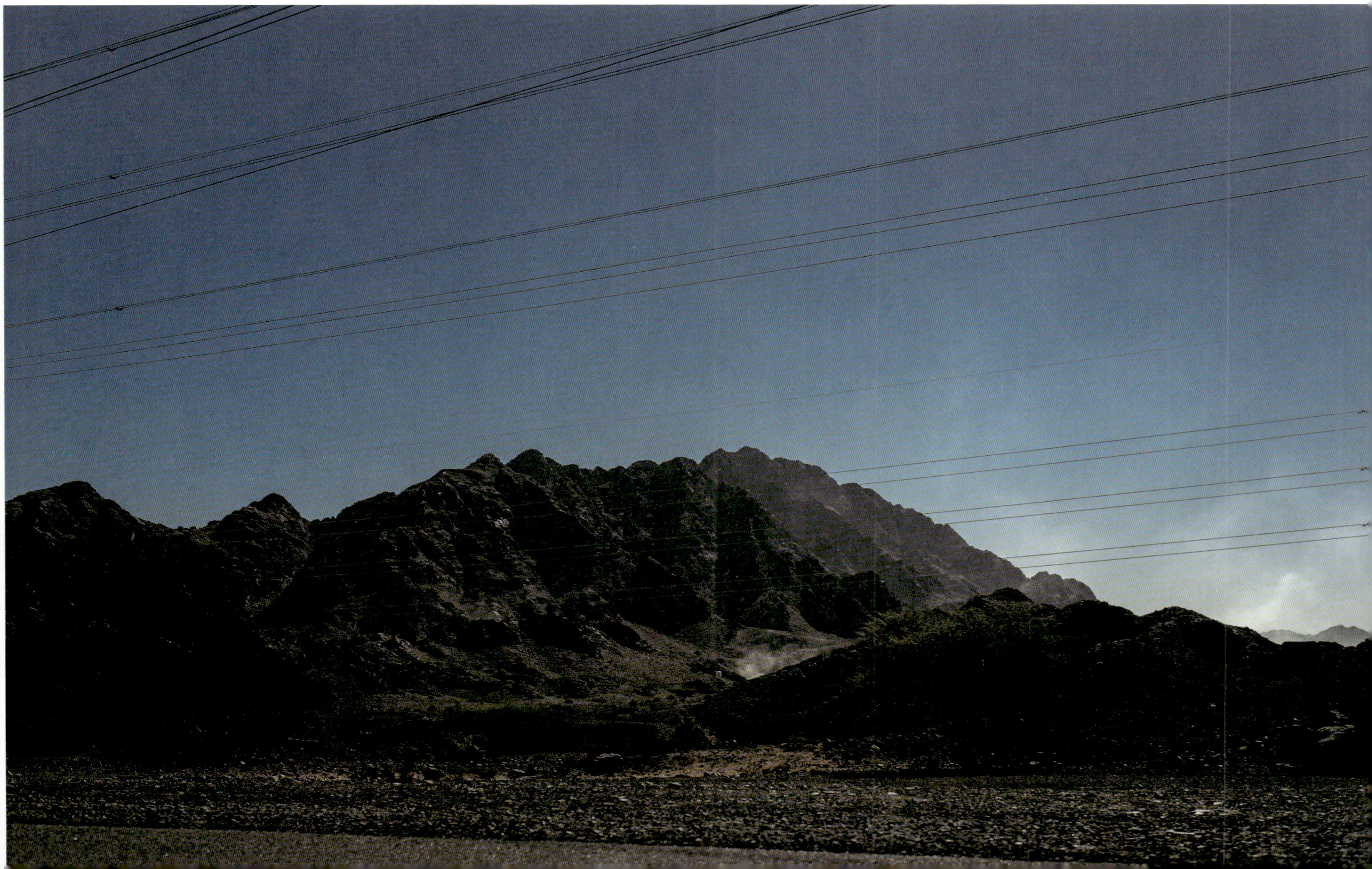

STOP

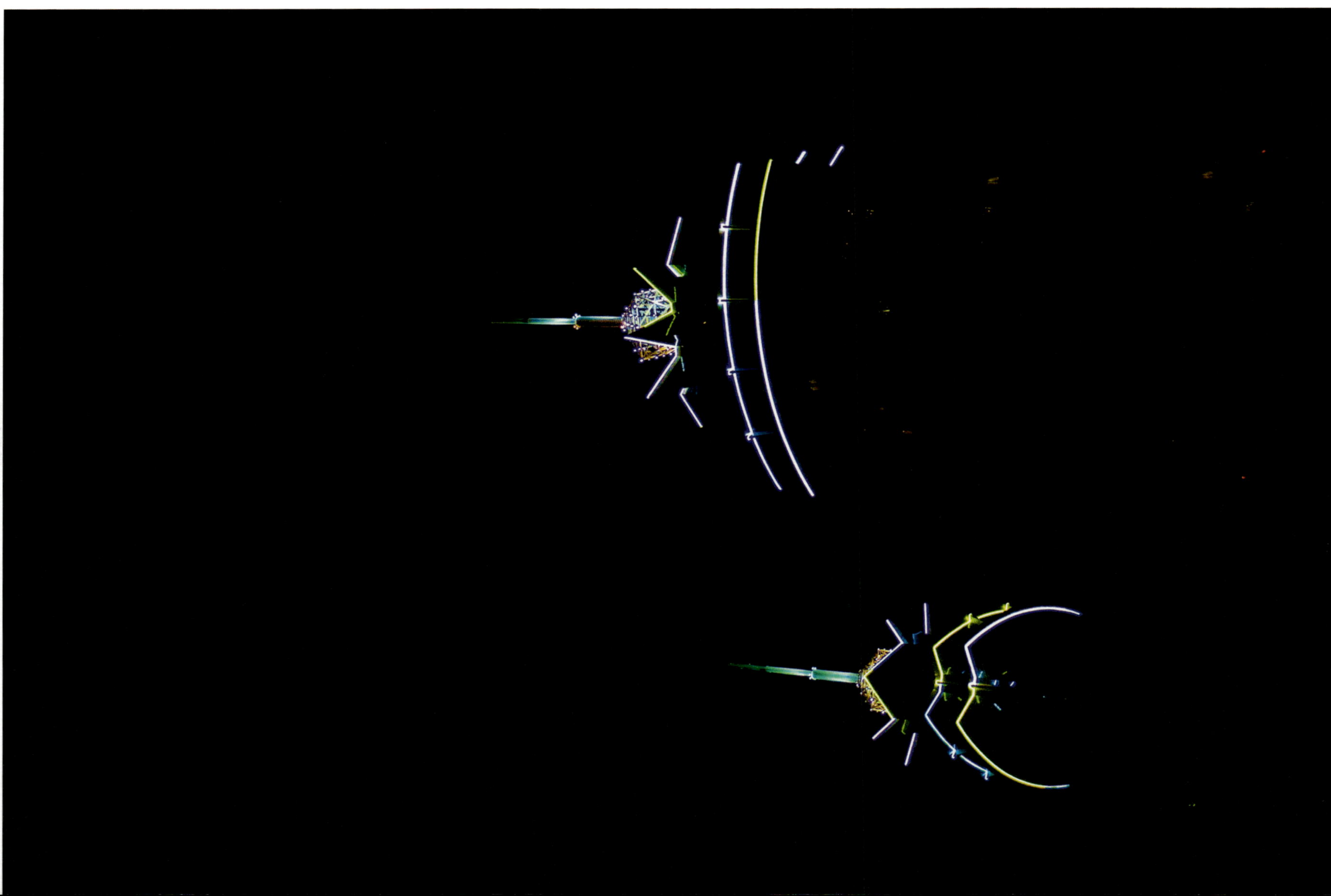

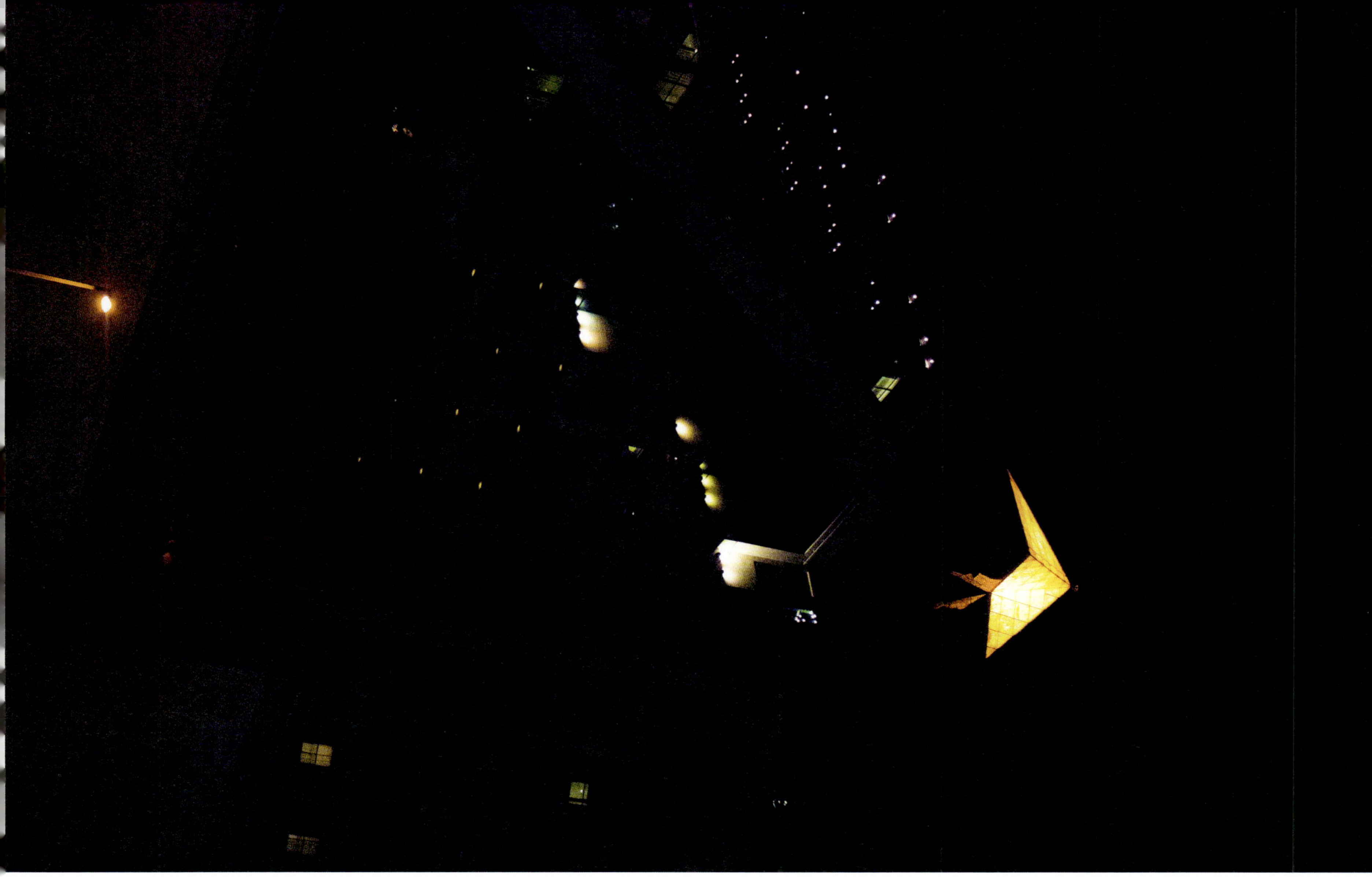

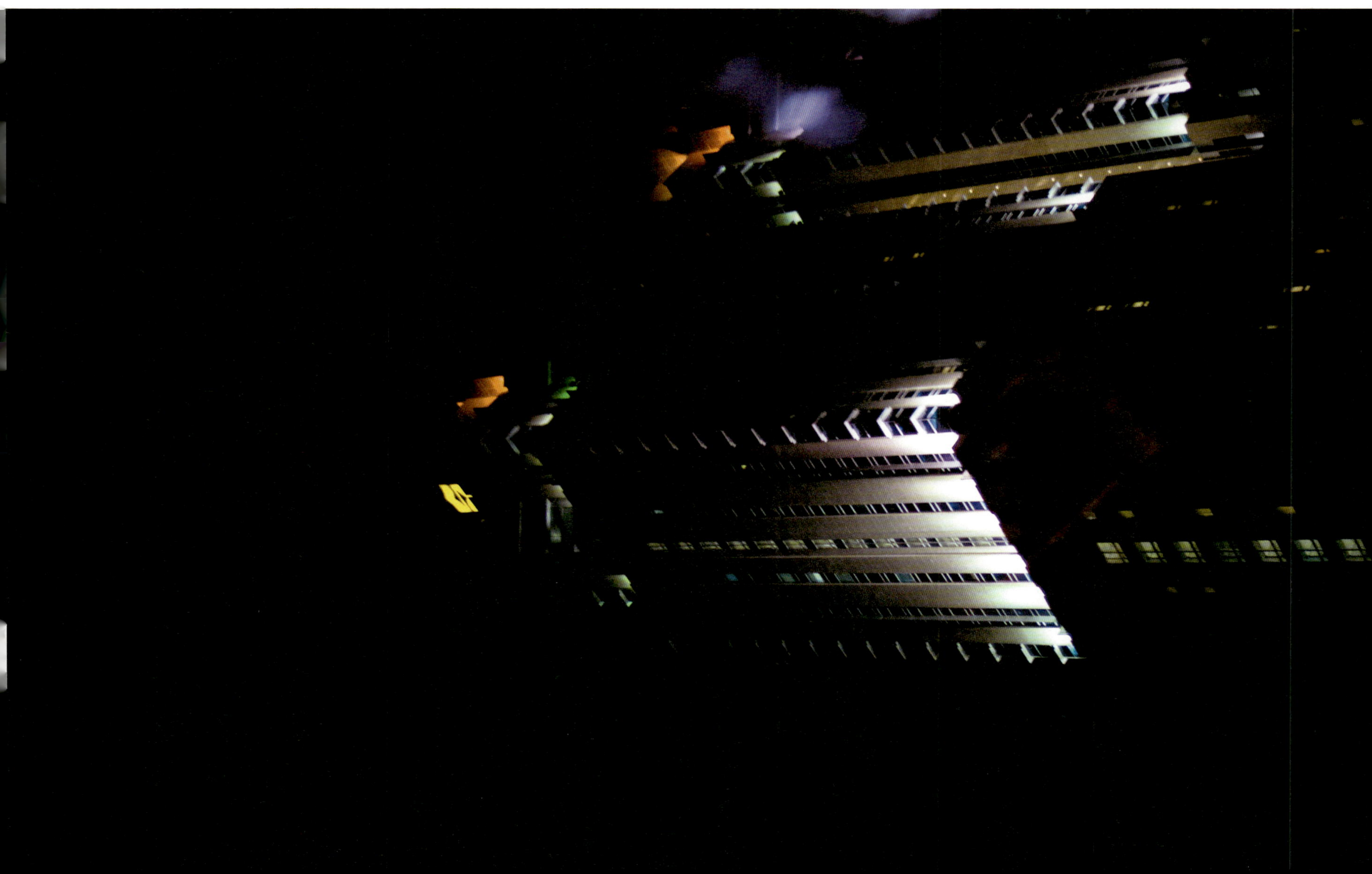

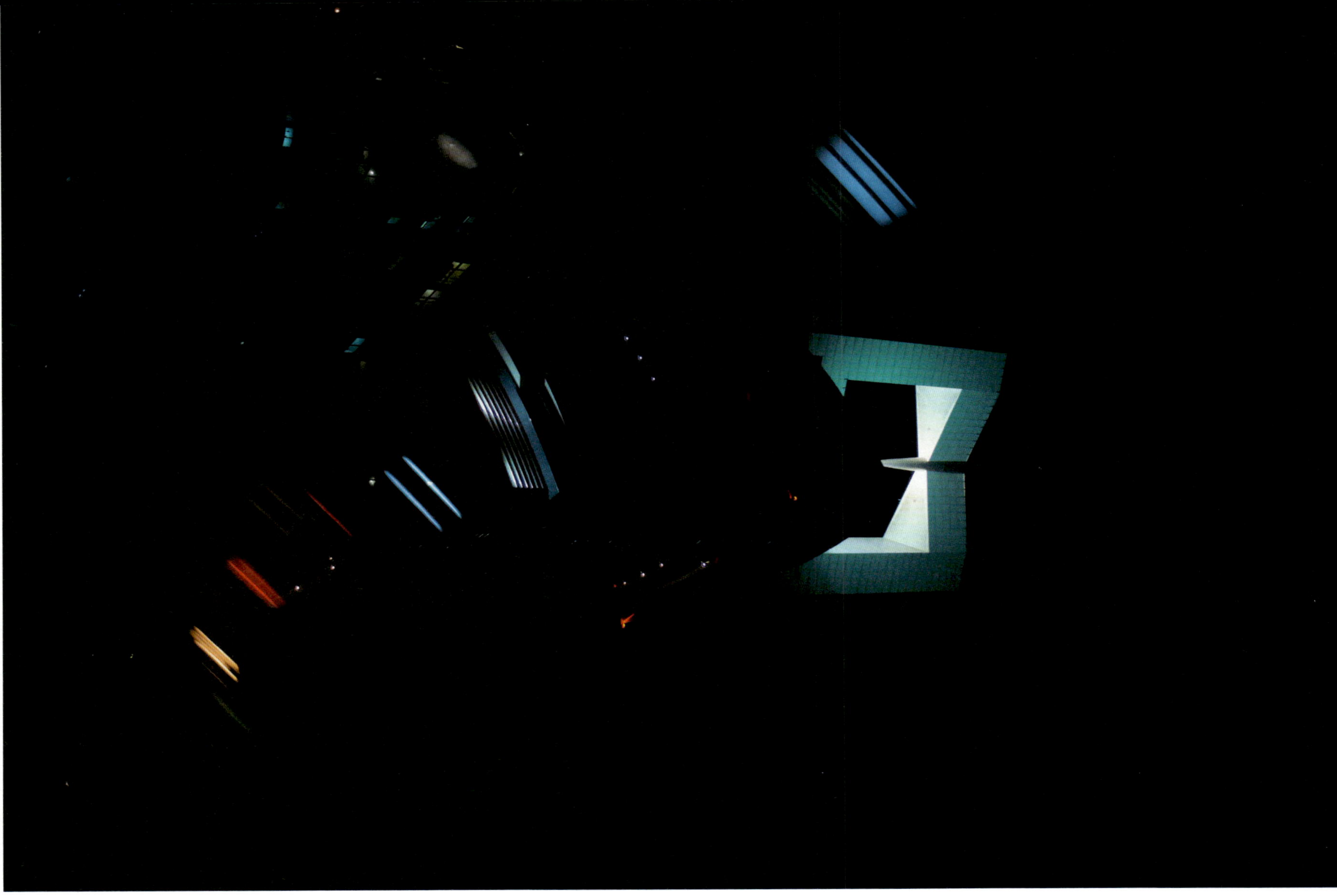

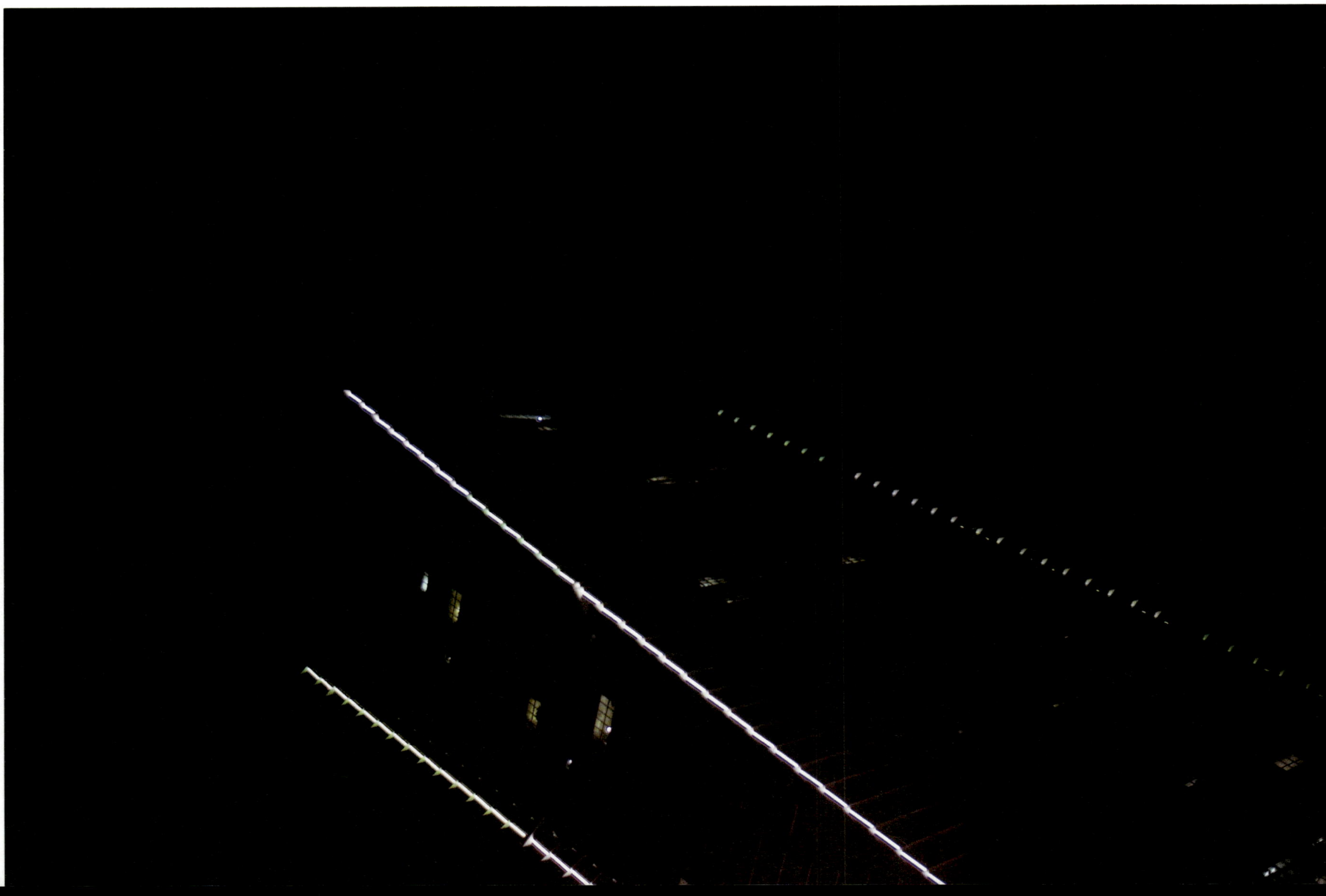

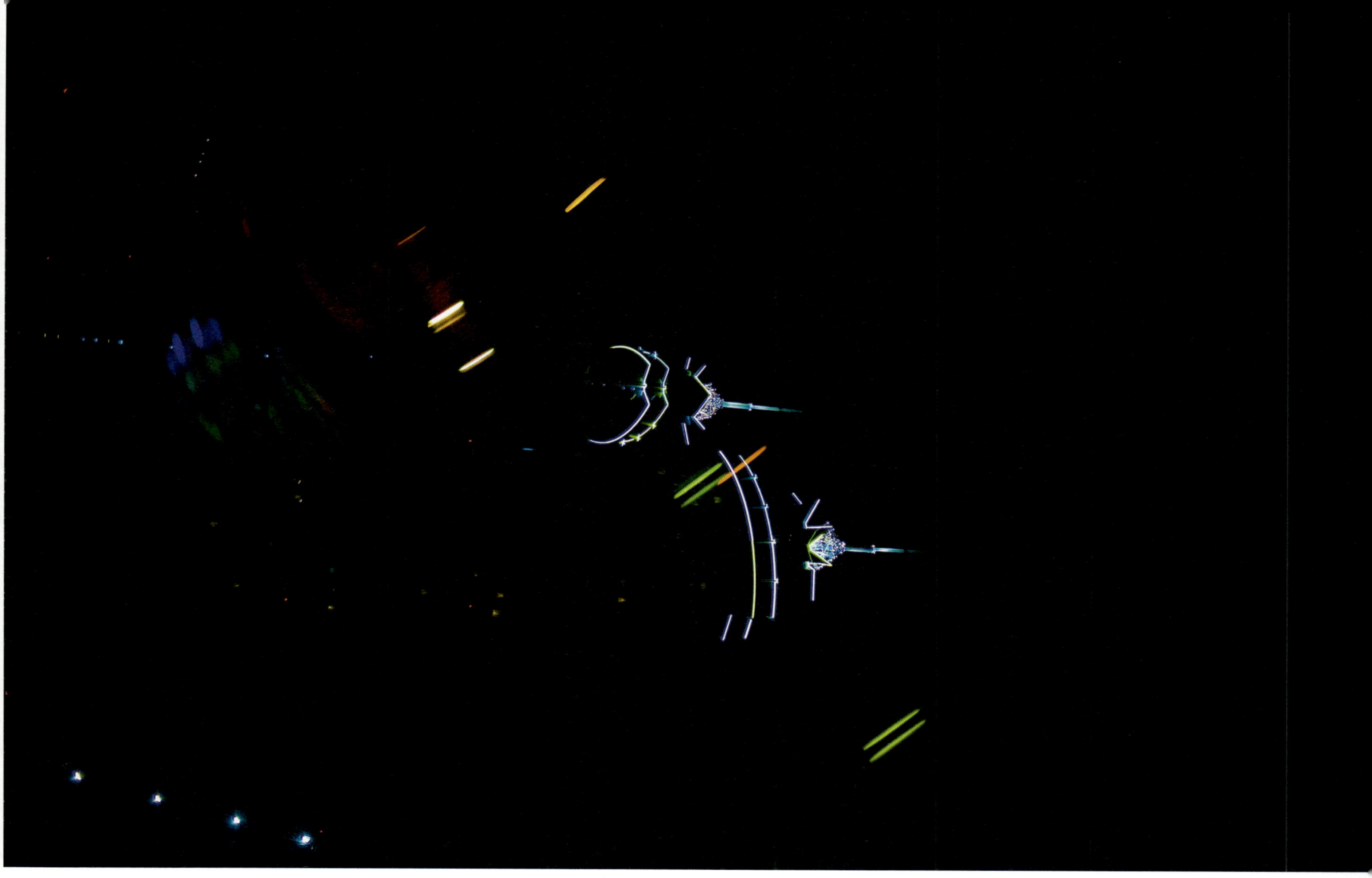

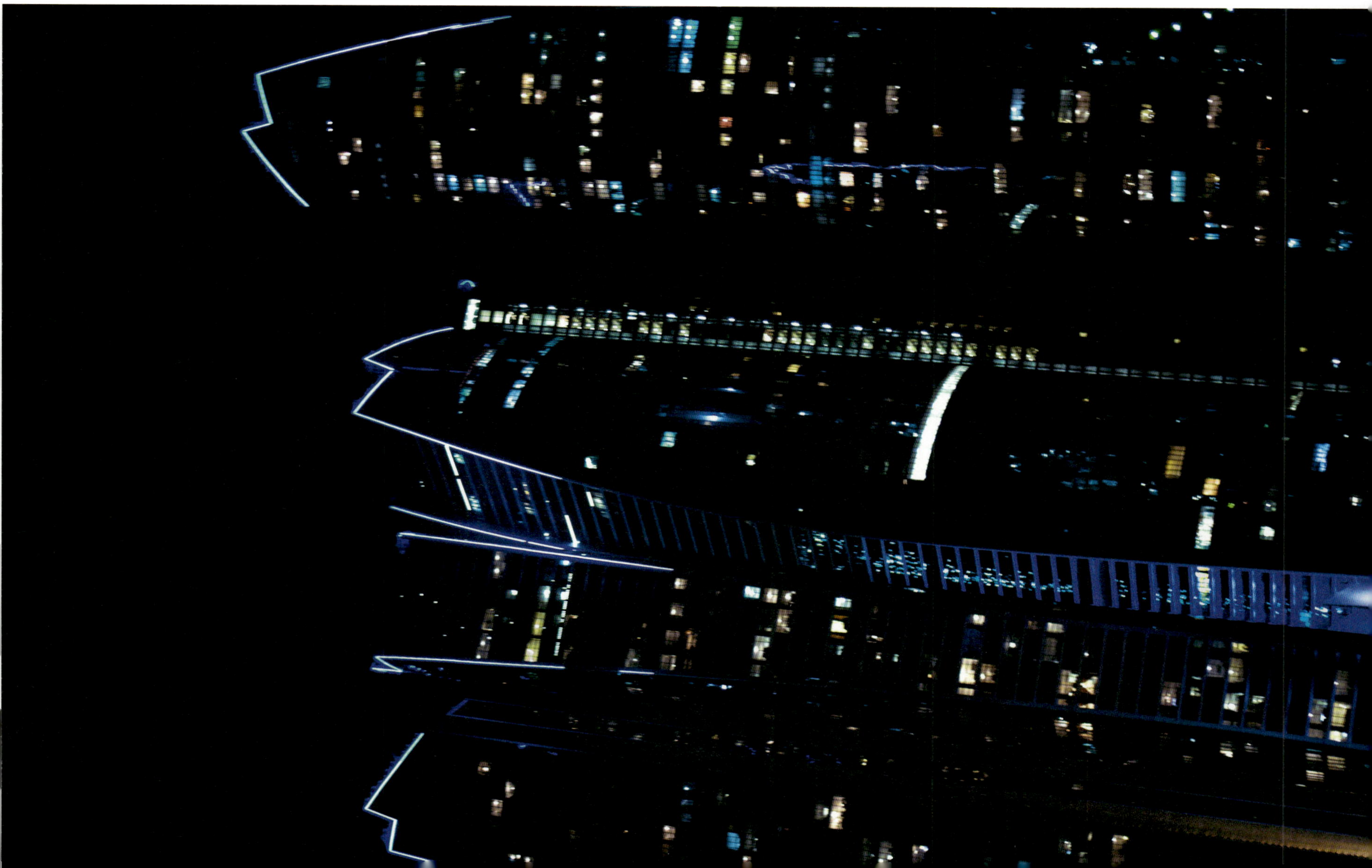

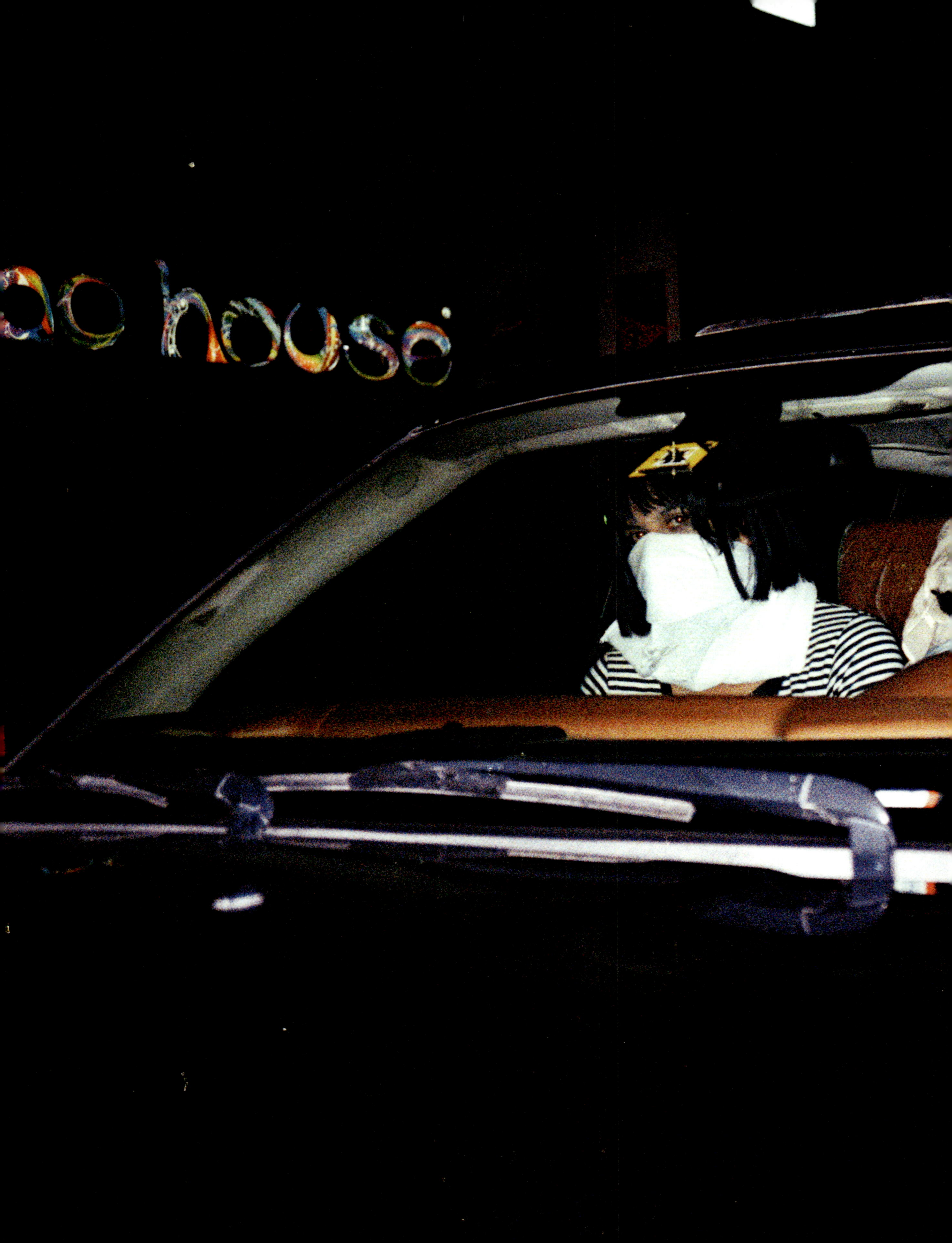
house

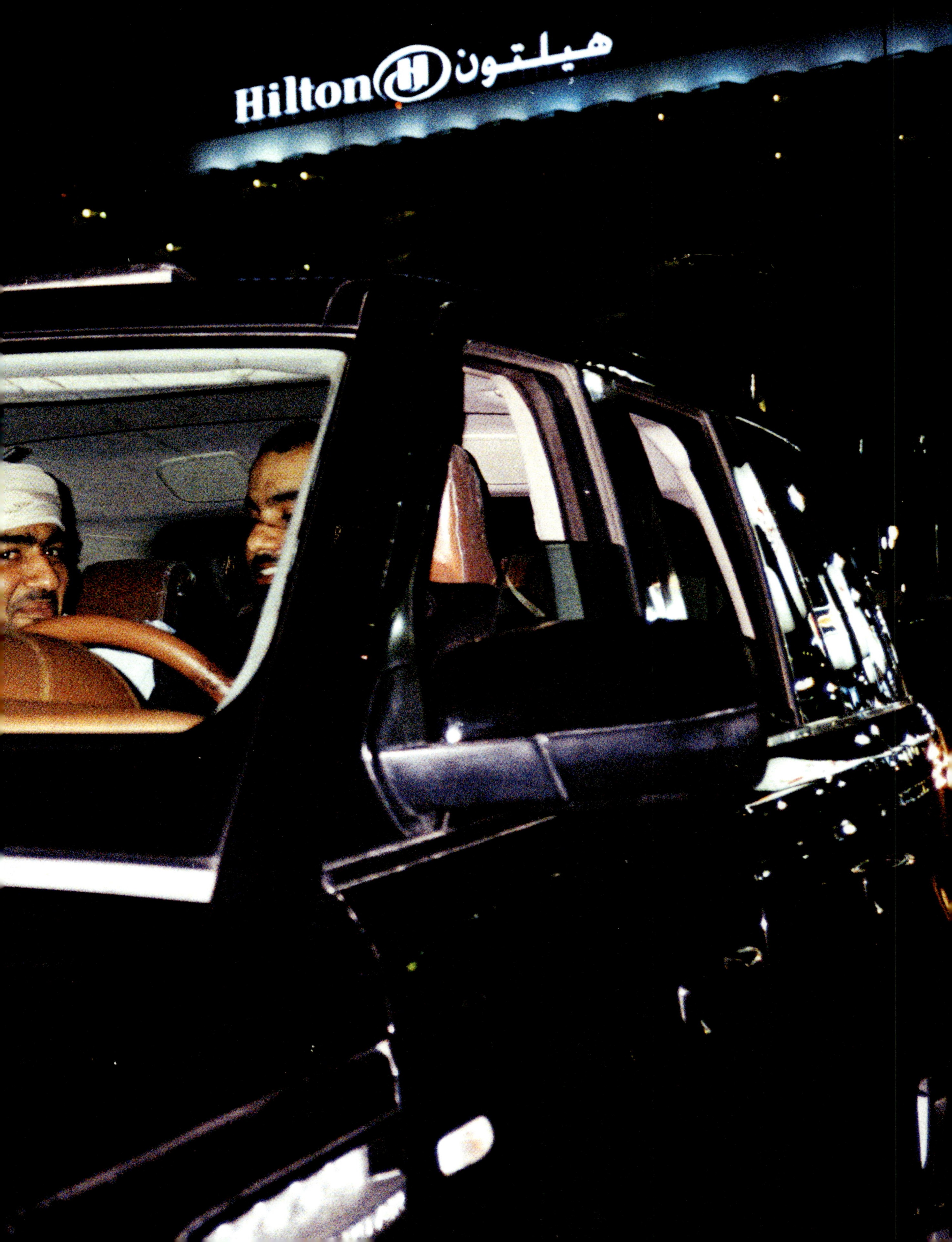
Hilton هيلتون

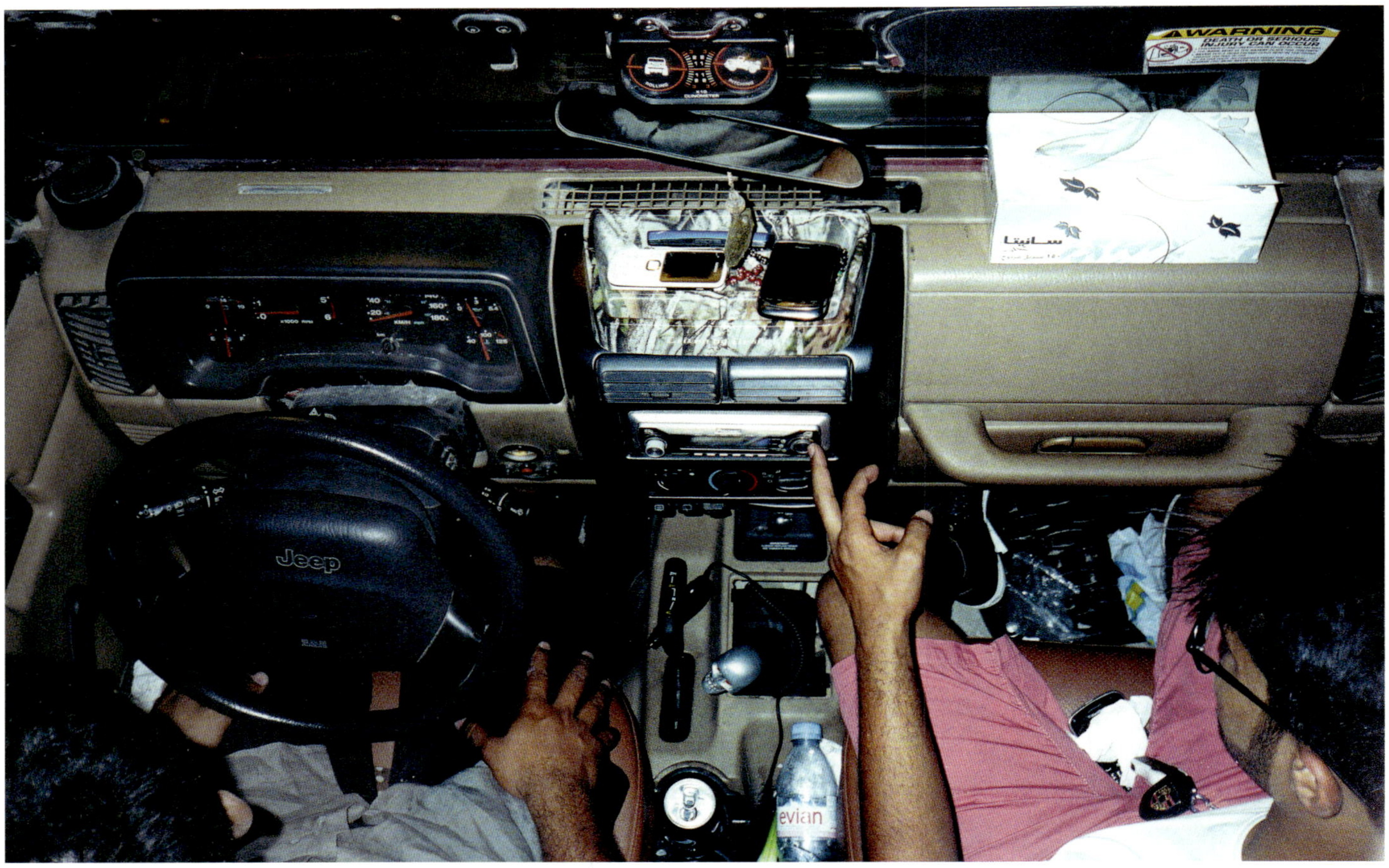
WARNING
Jeep
evian

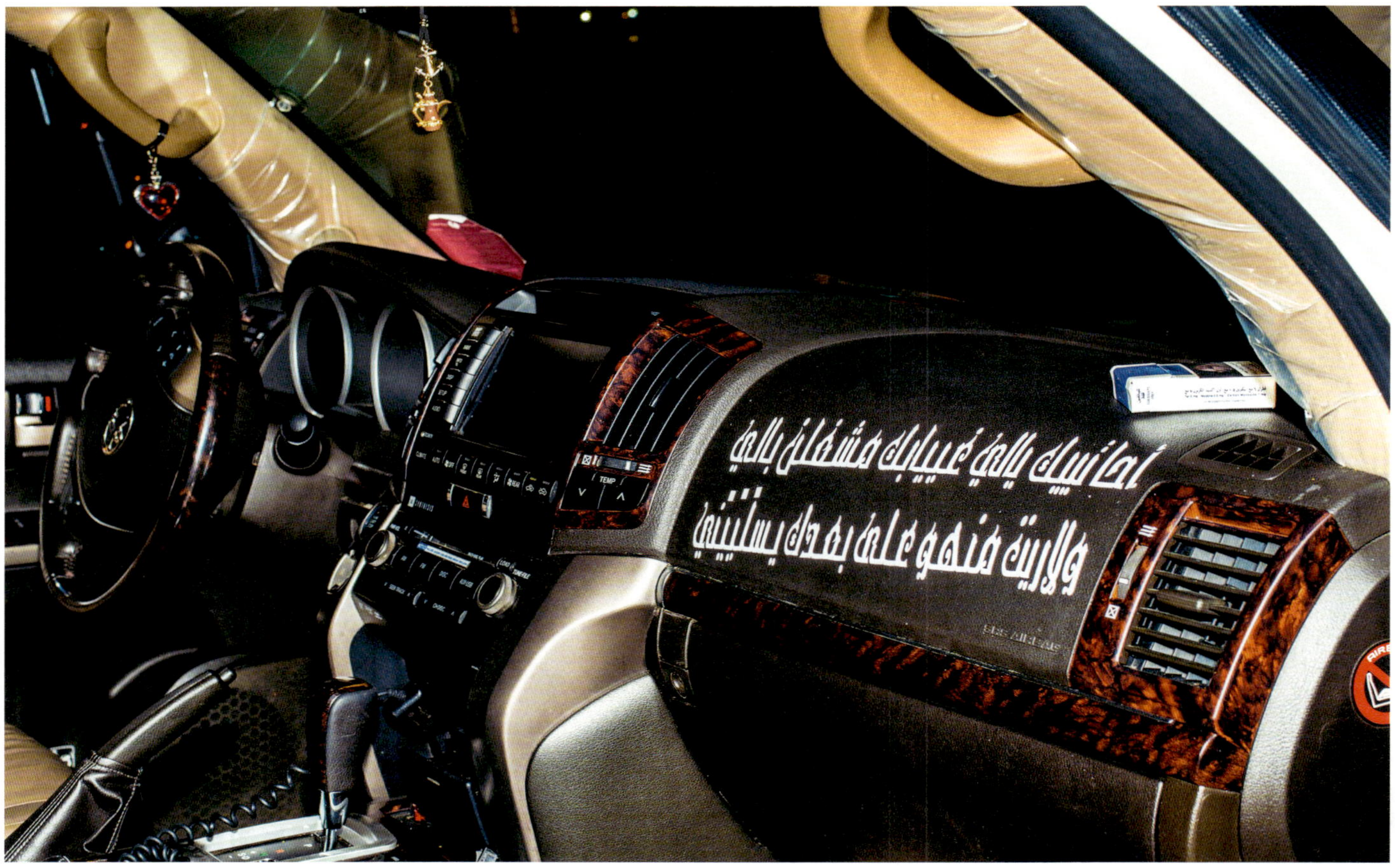
أحاتيك يالي غيابك مشغلني بالي
ولاريت منهو على بعدك يسليني
SRS AIRBAG

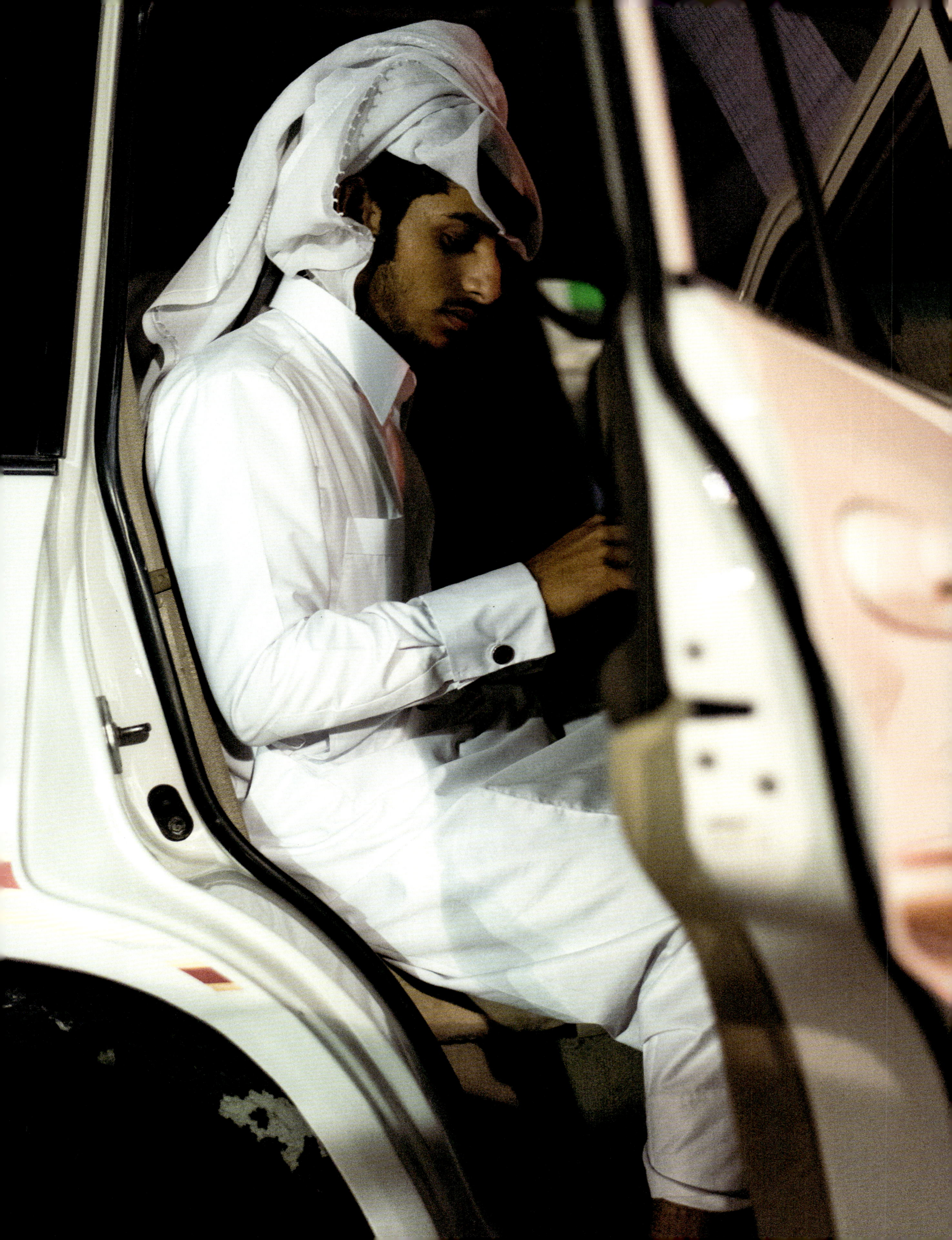

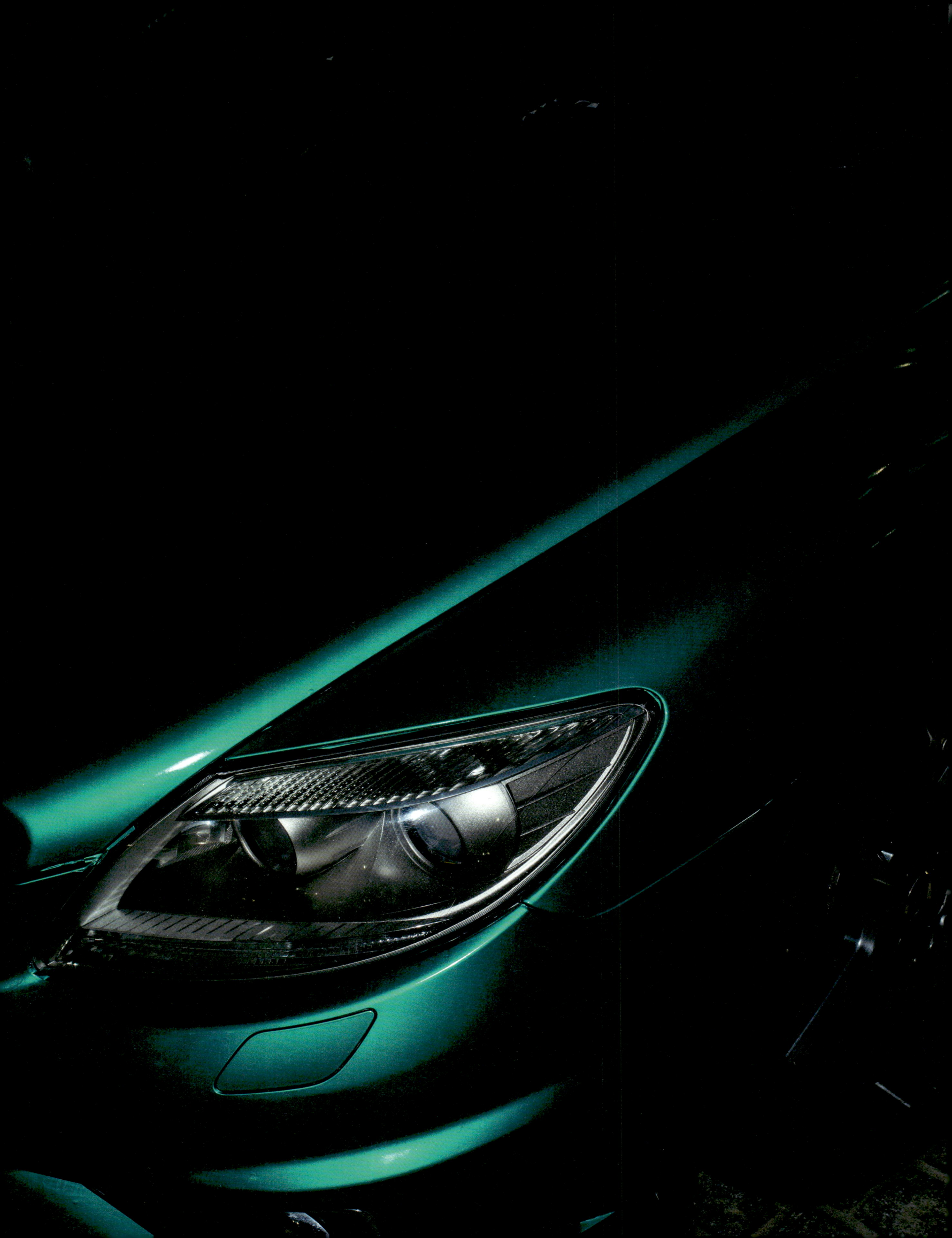

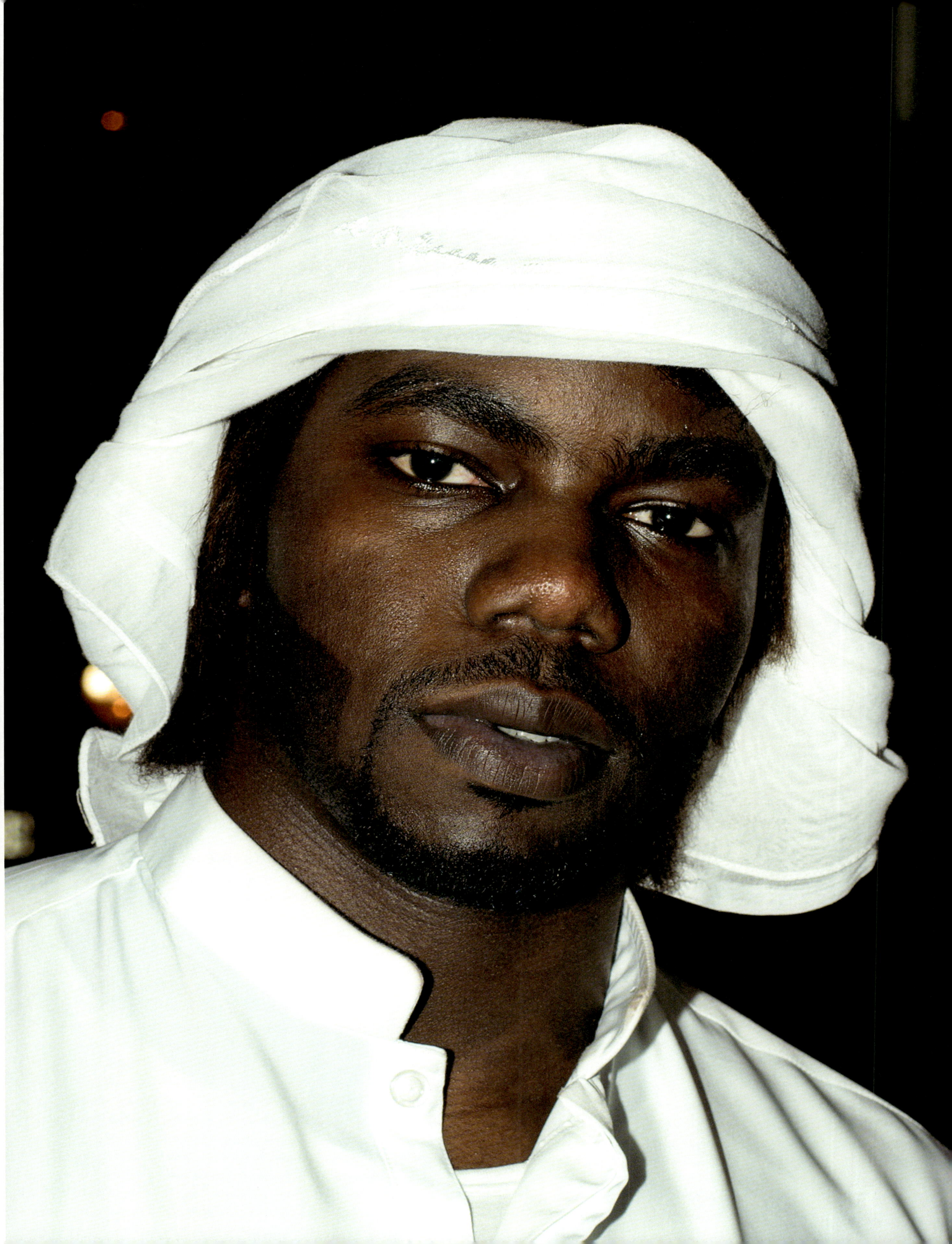

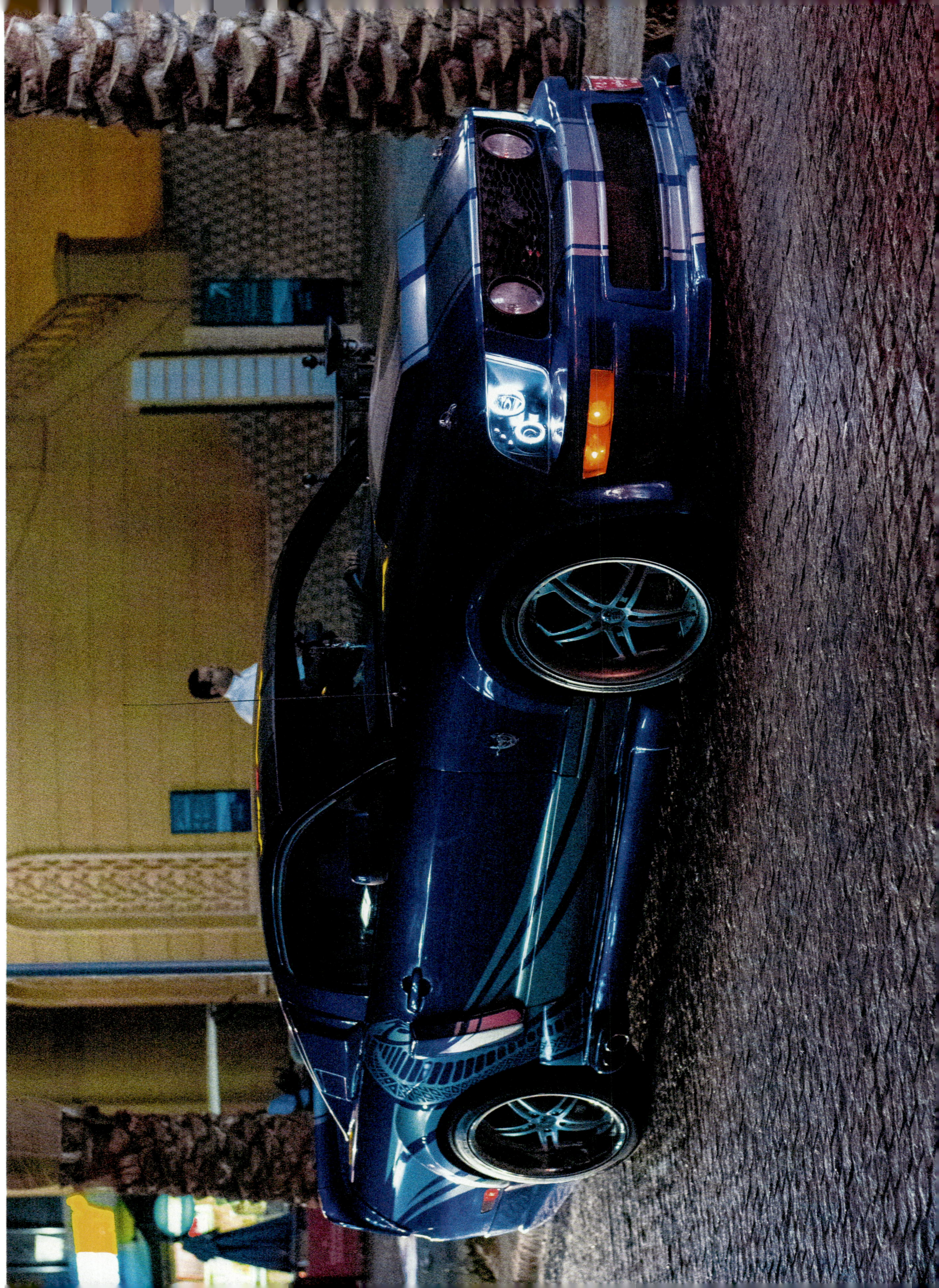

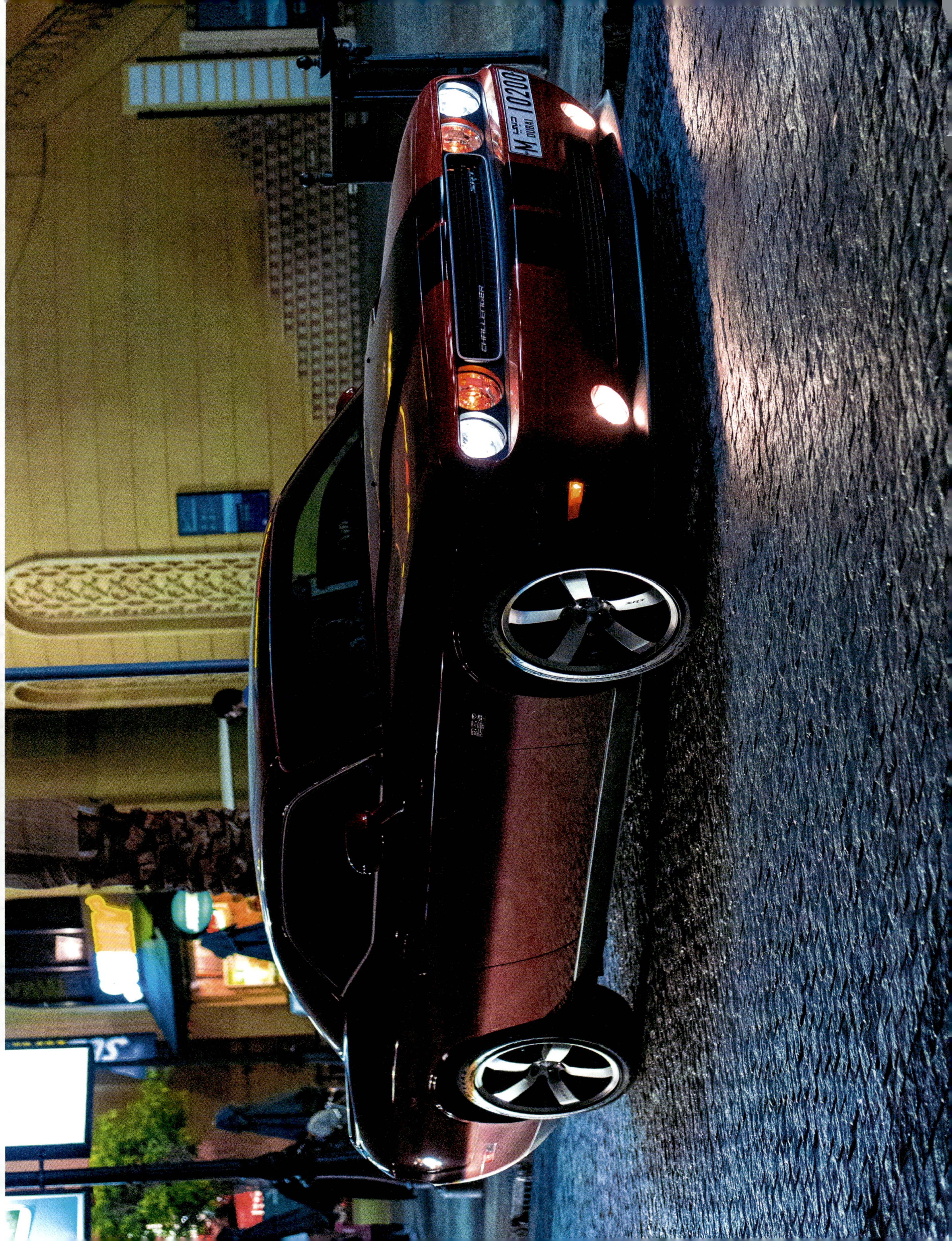
M 10200
DUBAI
CHALLENGER

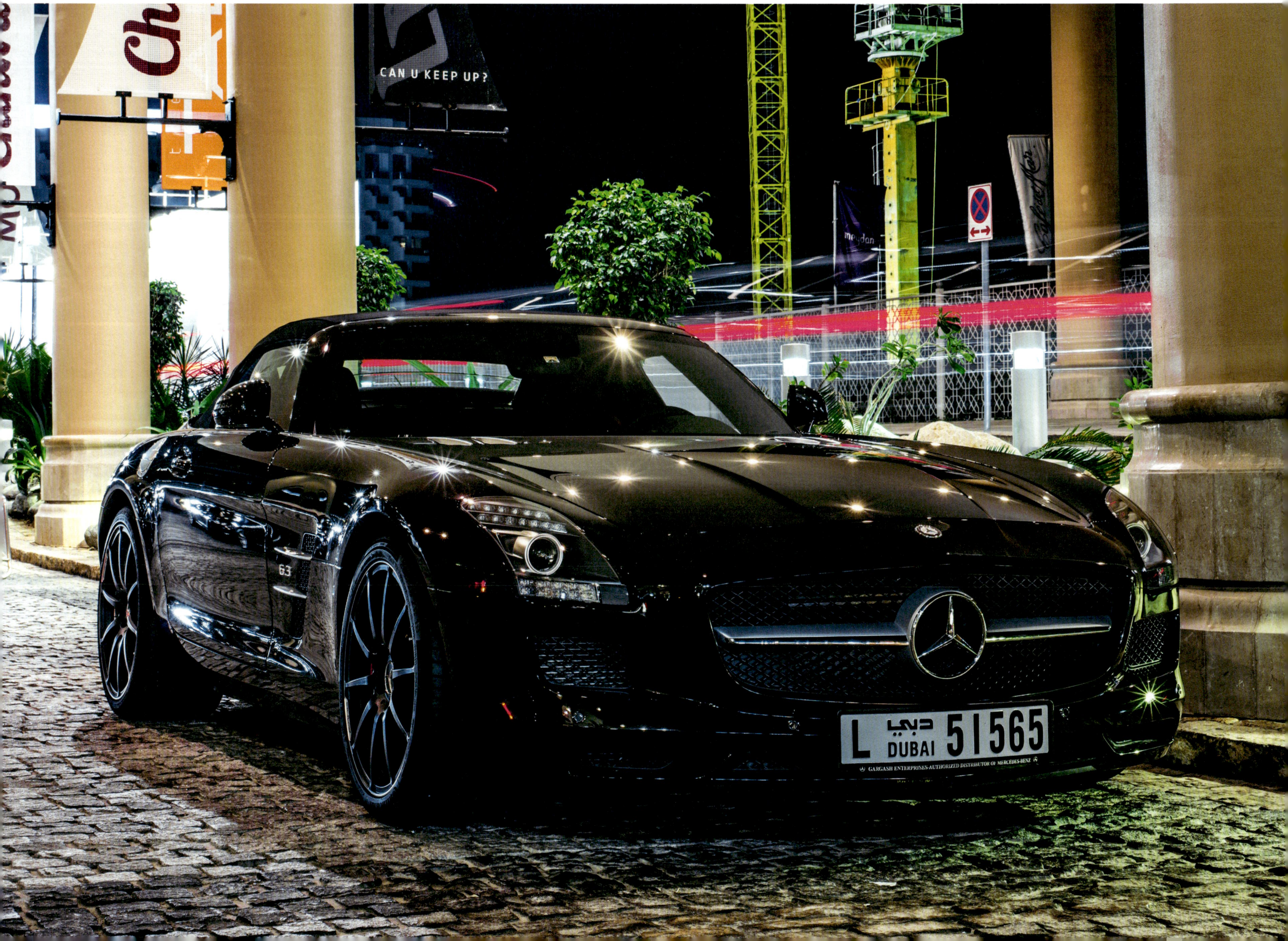
CAN U KEEP UP?
L دبي DUBAI 51565

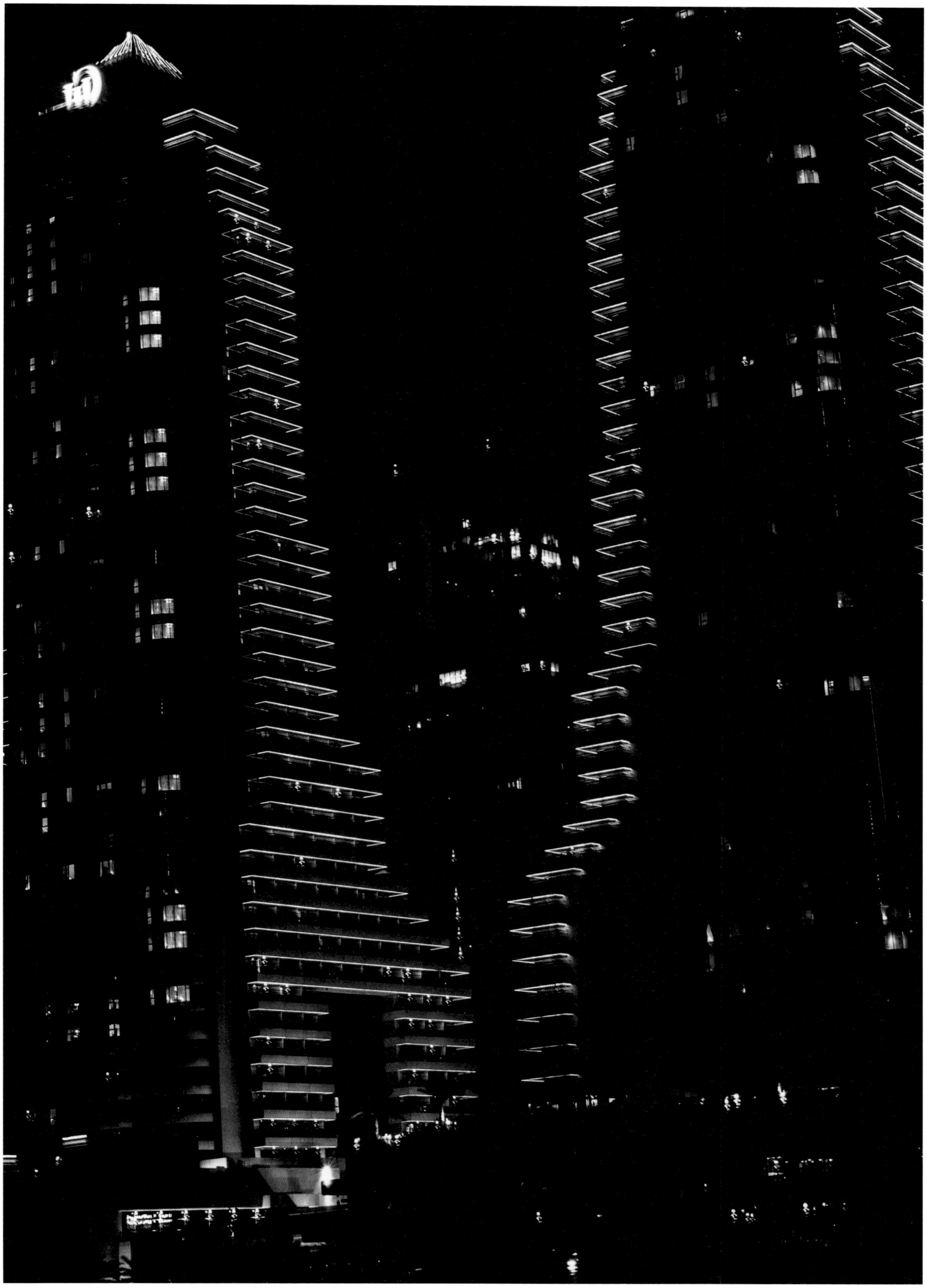

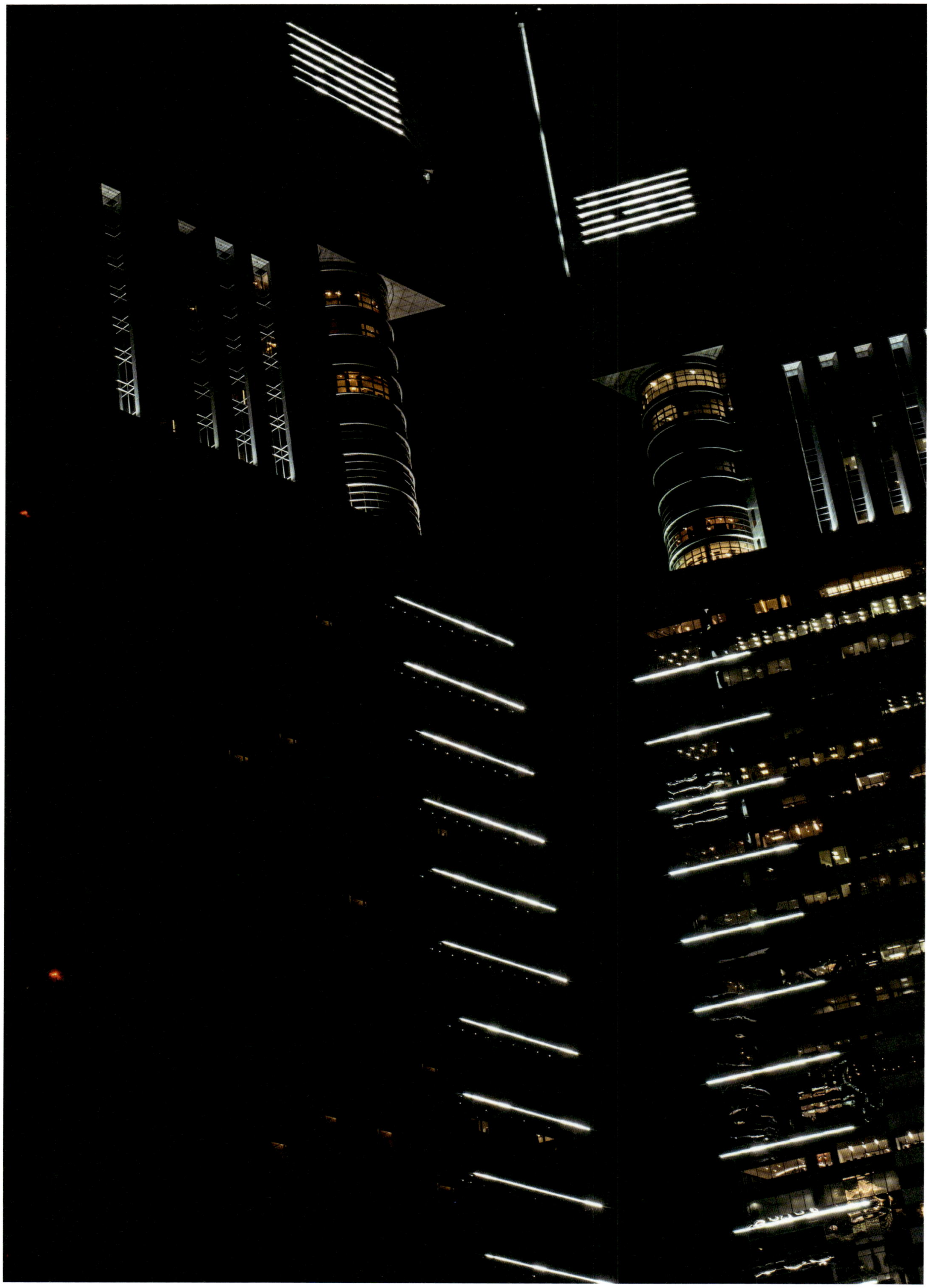

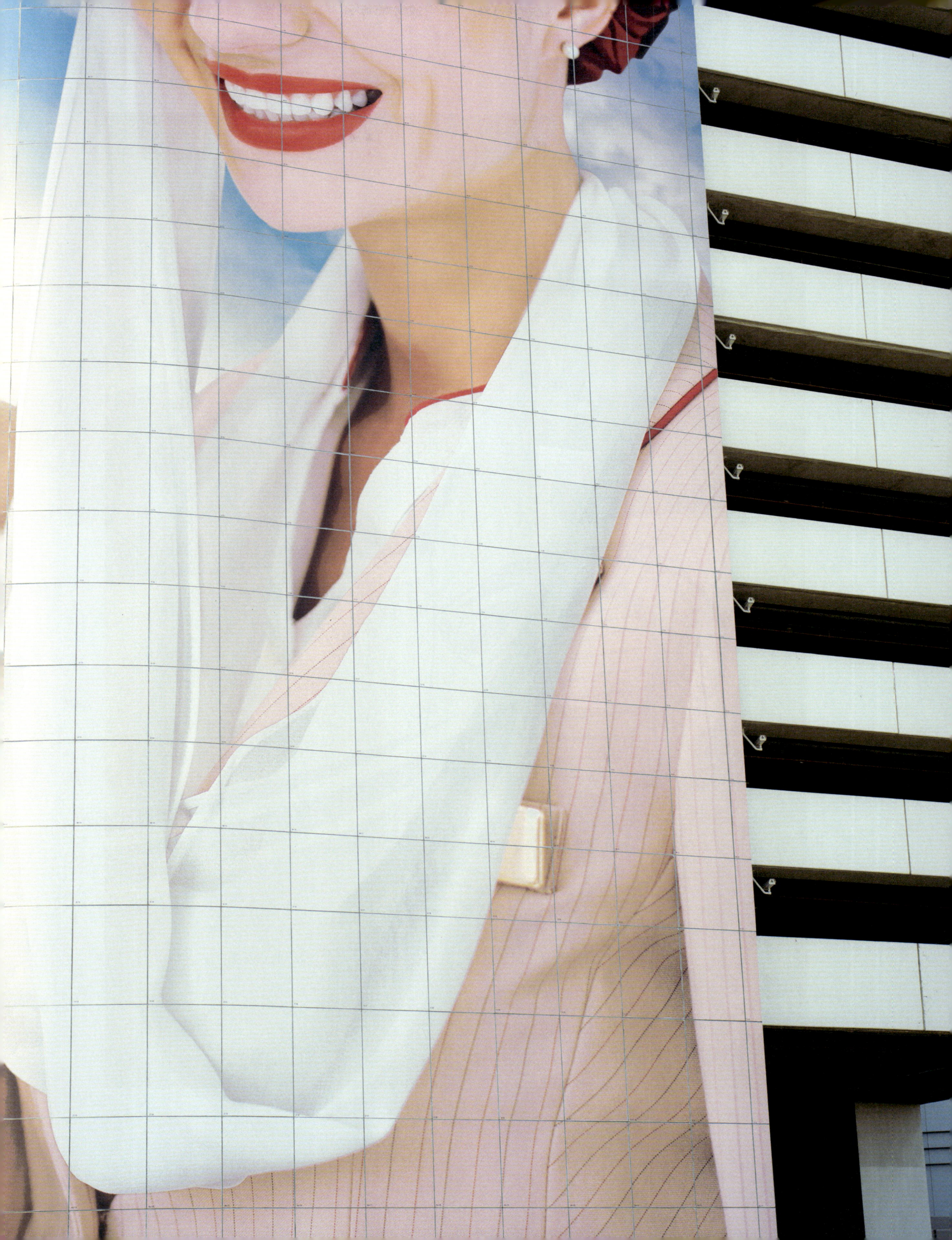

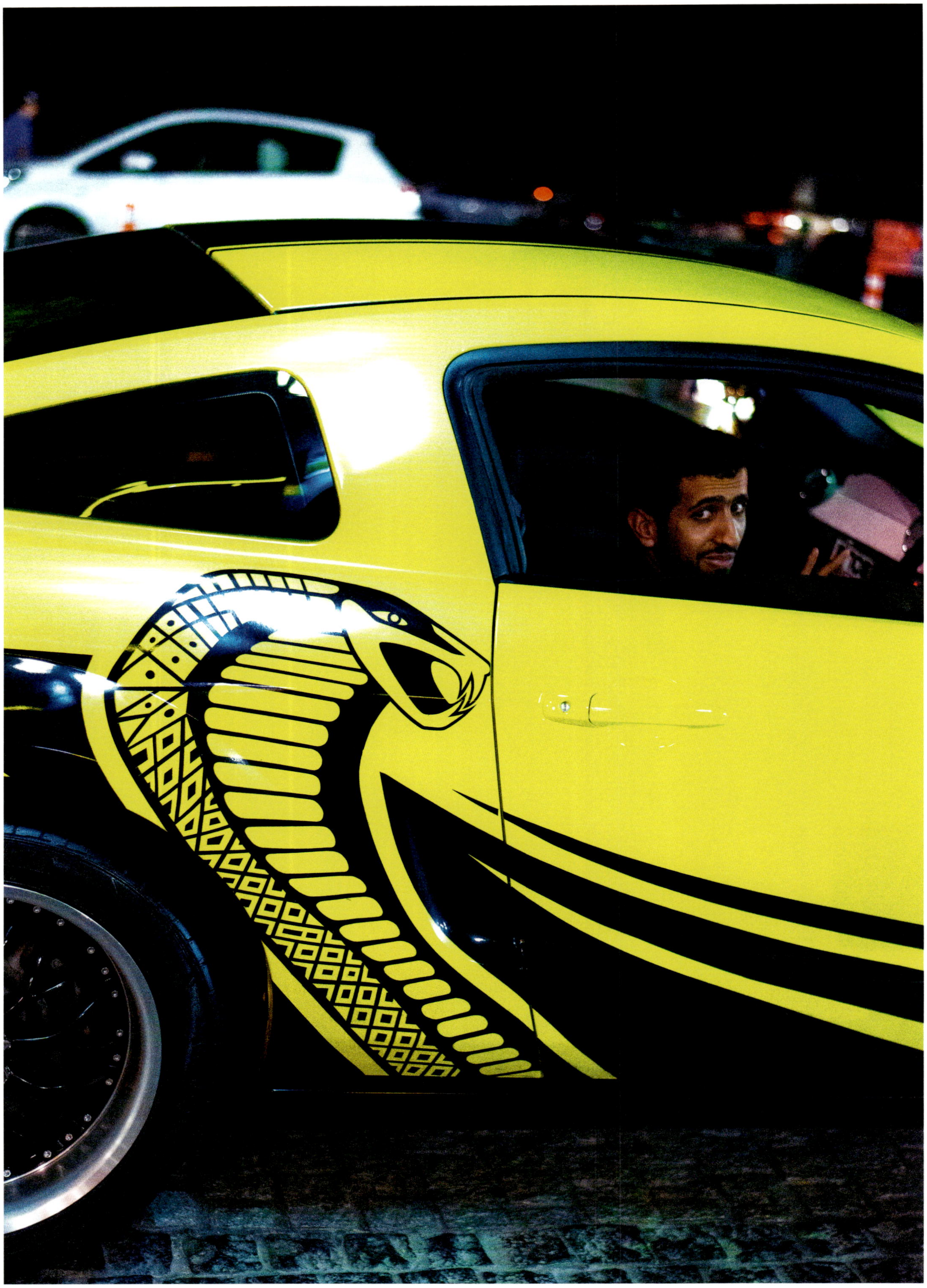

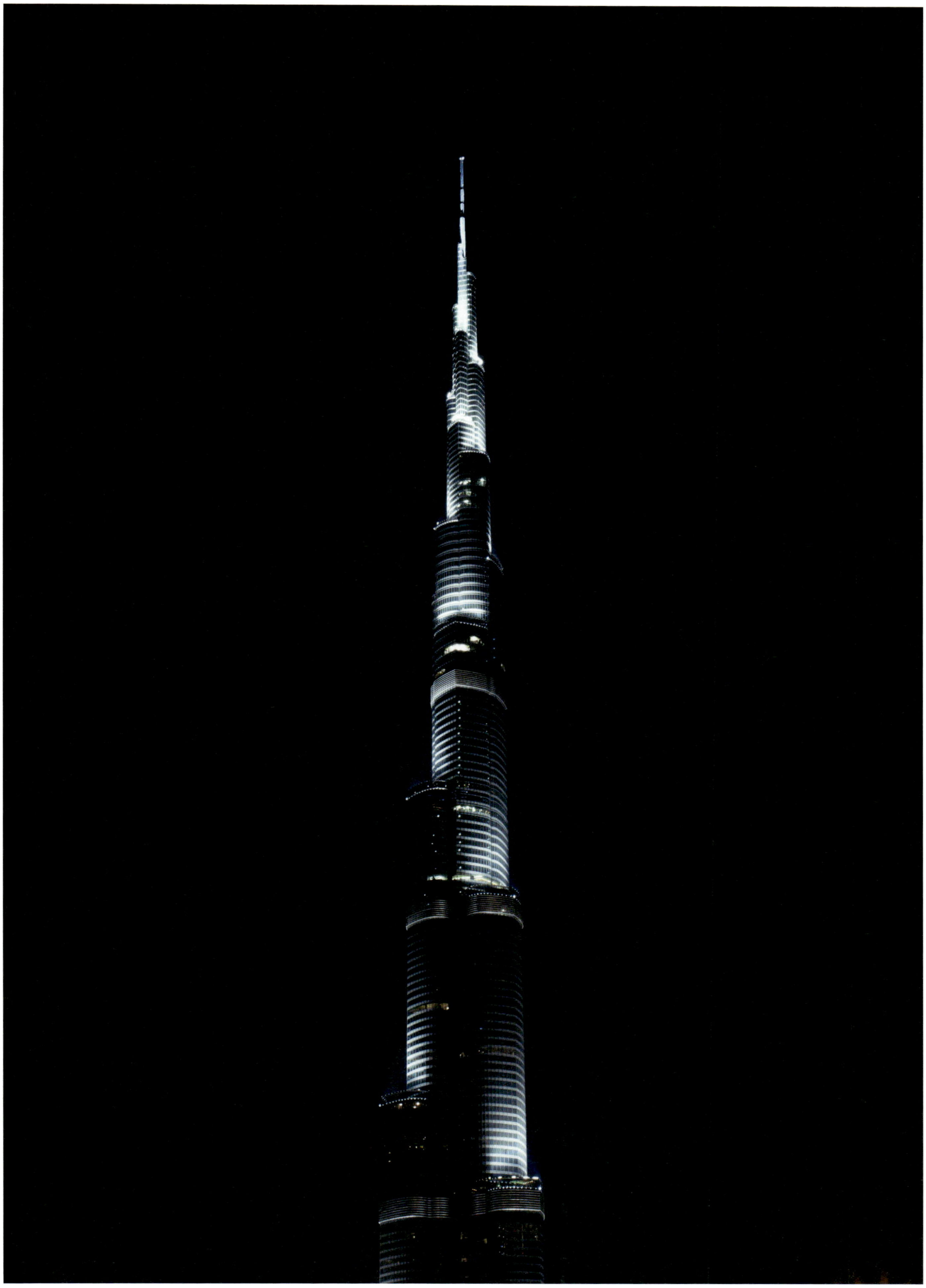

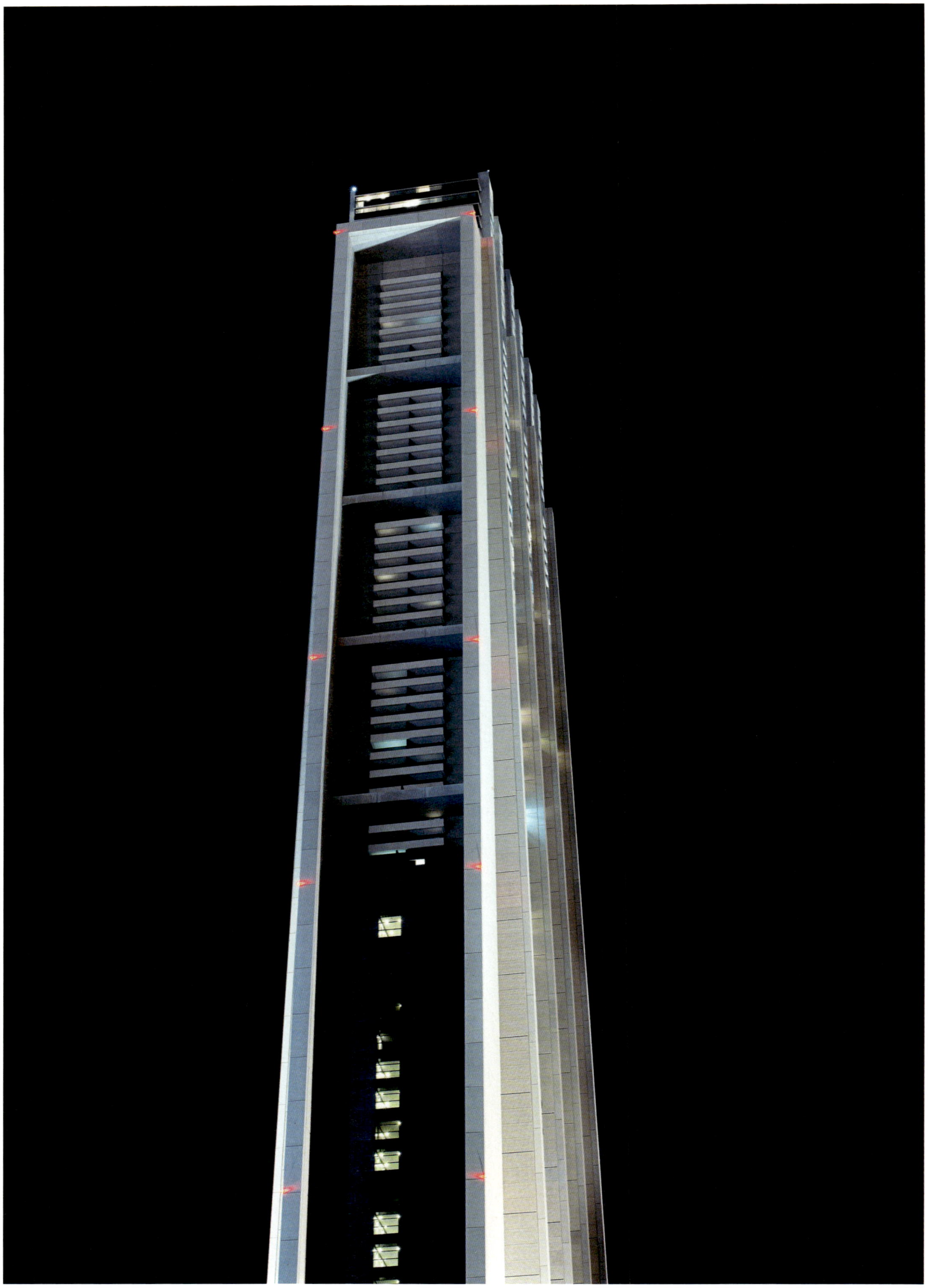

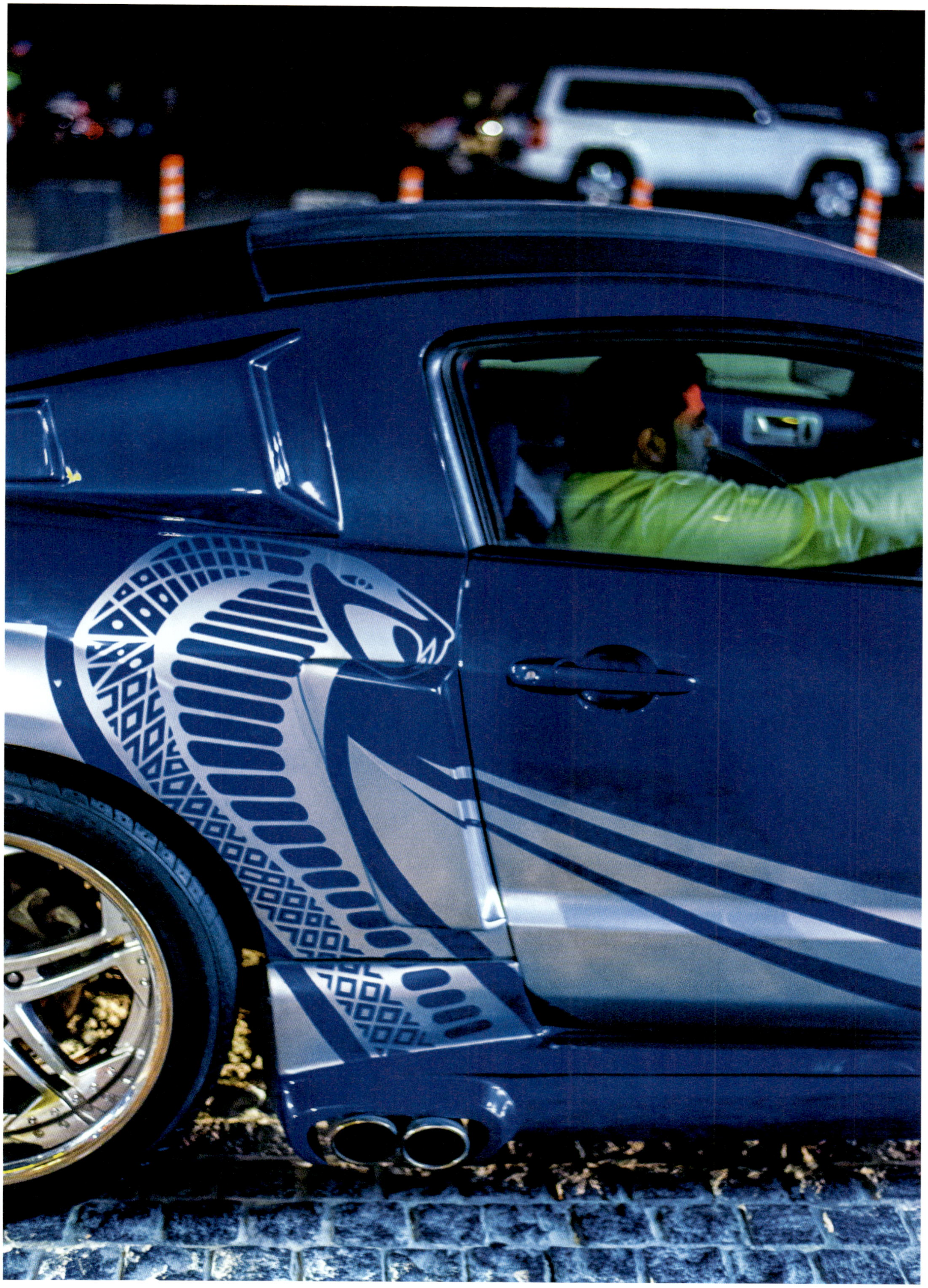

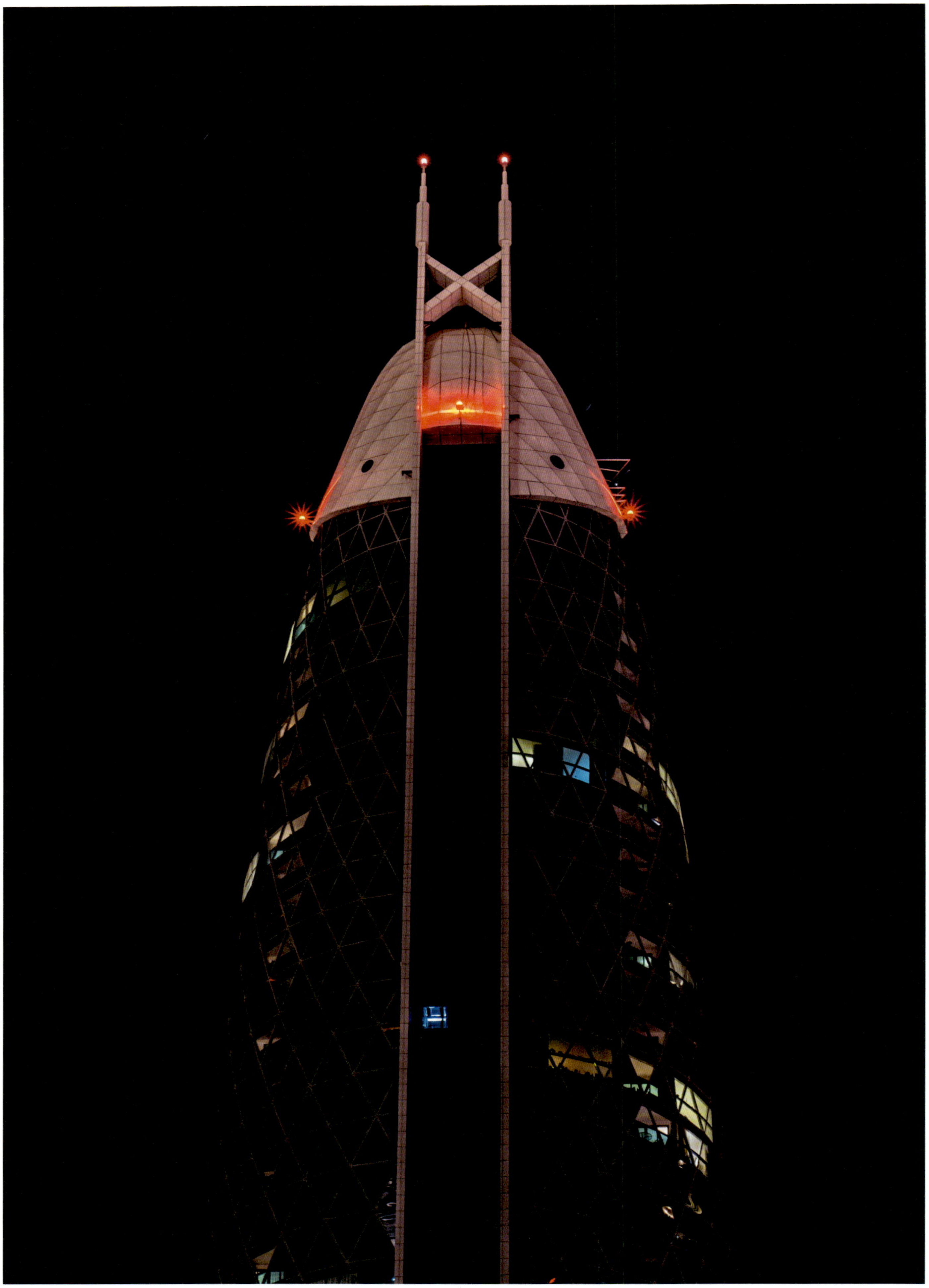

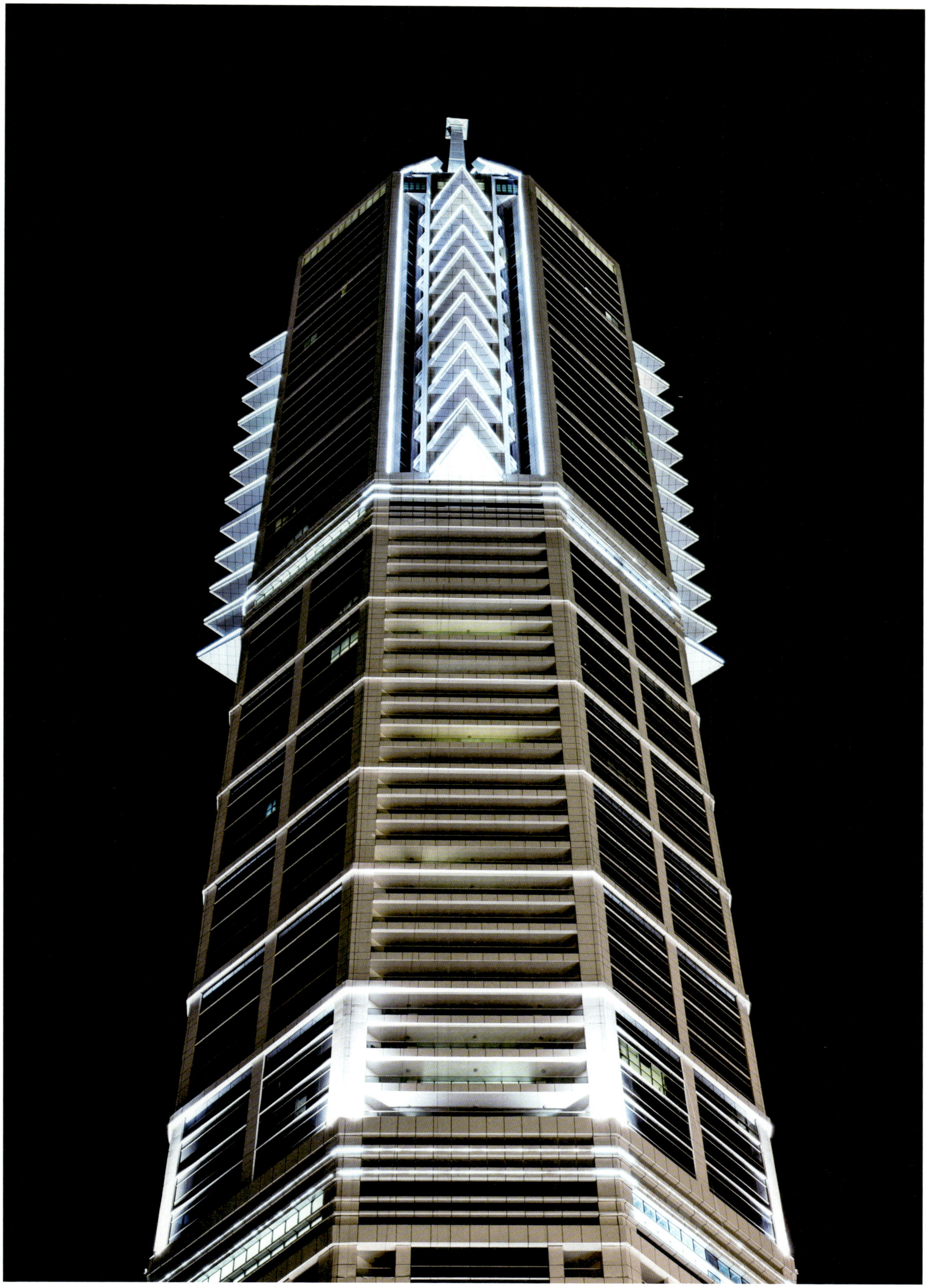

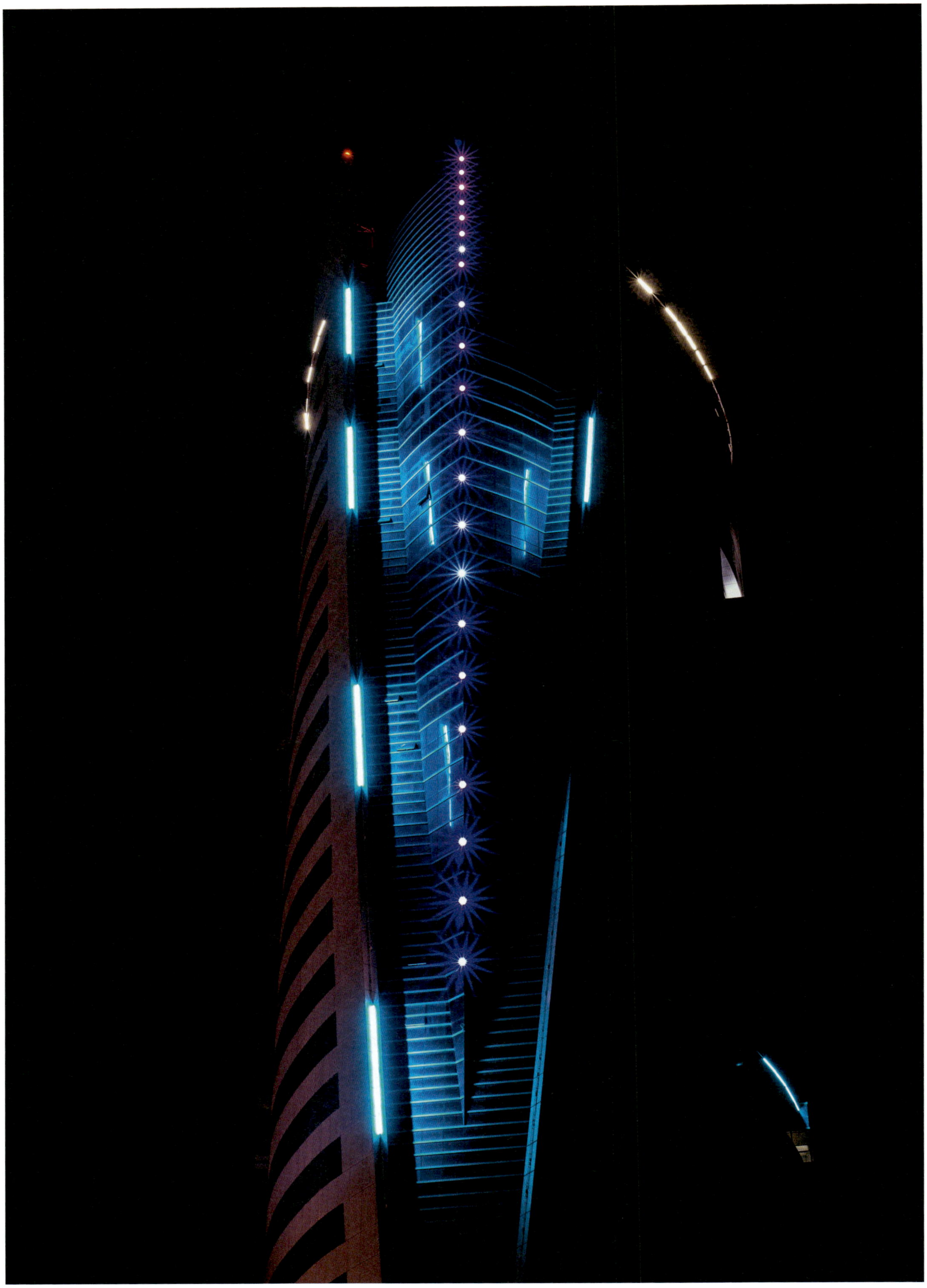

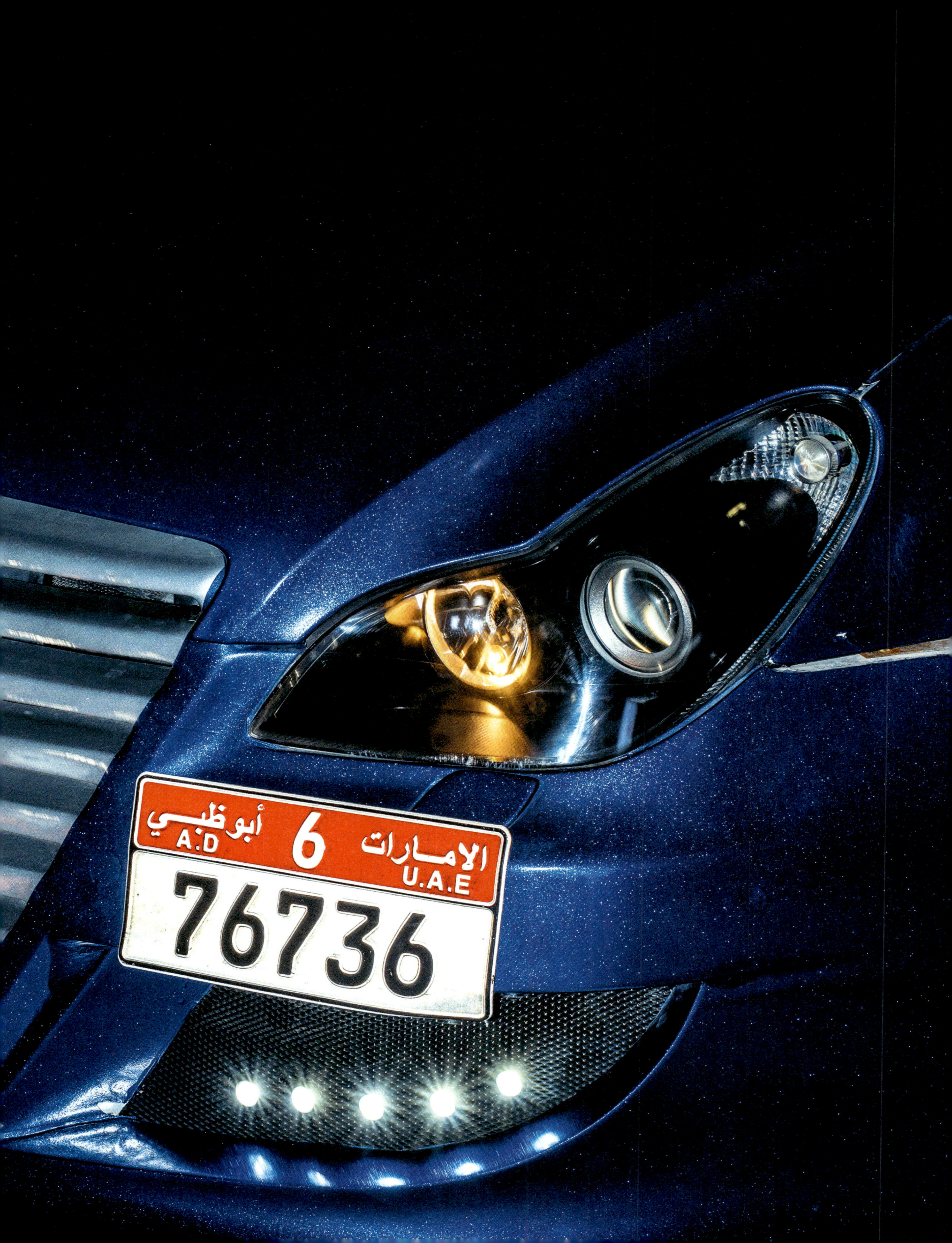
أبوظبي
A.D
6
الامارات
U.A.E
76736

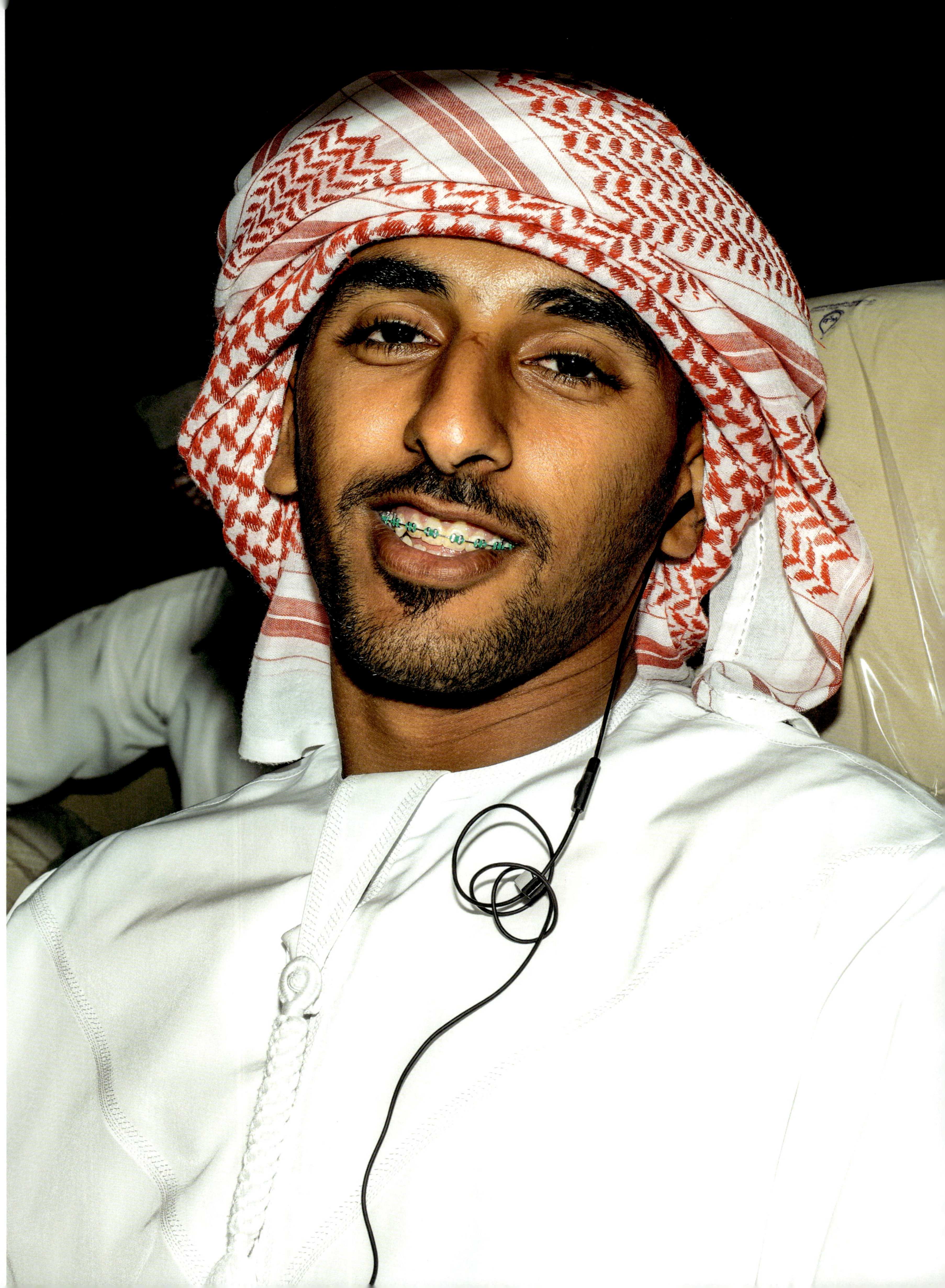

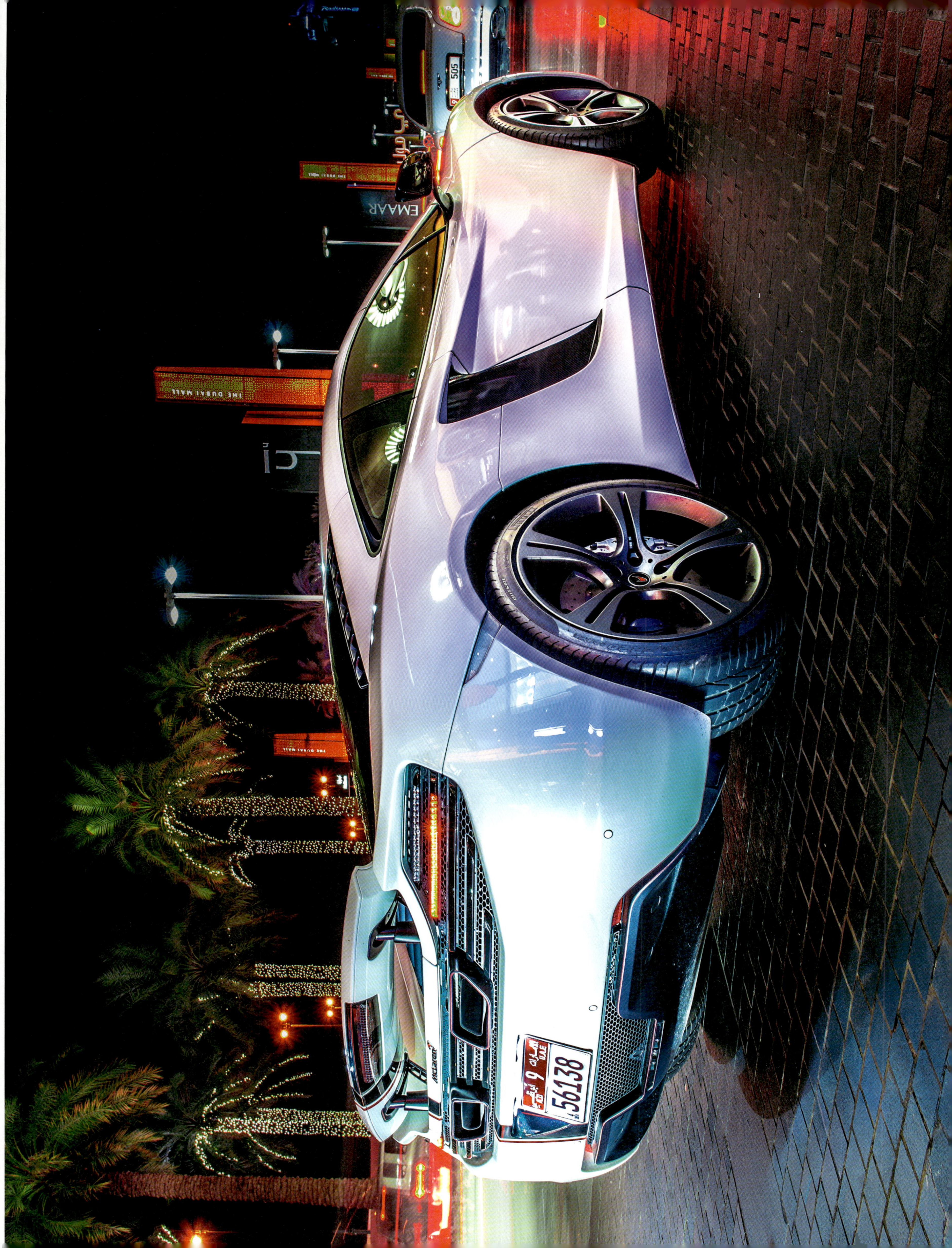
THE DUBAI MALL
EMAAR
56138

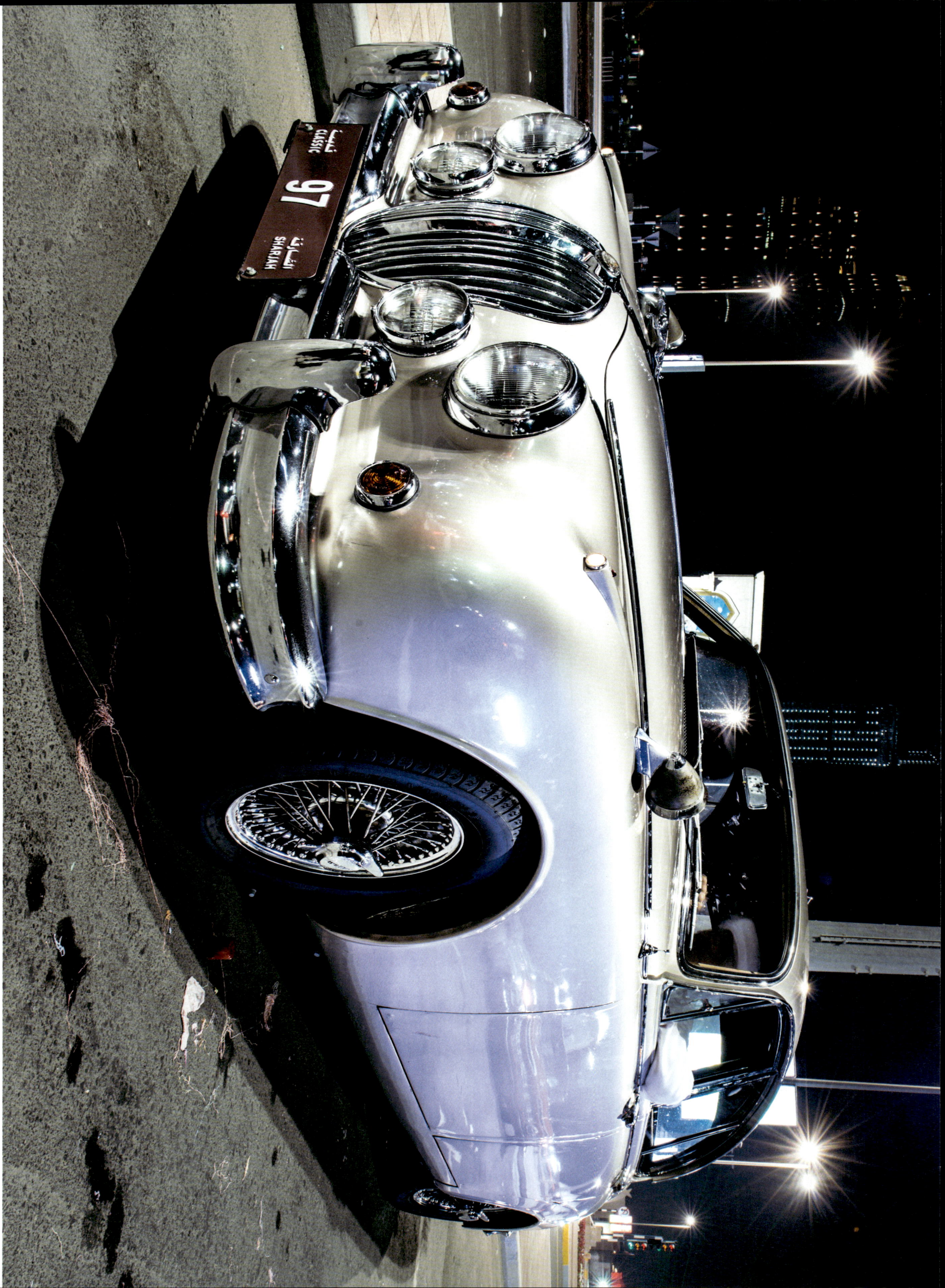
CLASSIC
97
SHARJAH

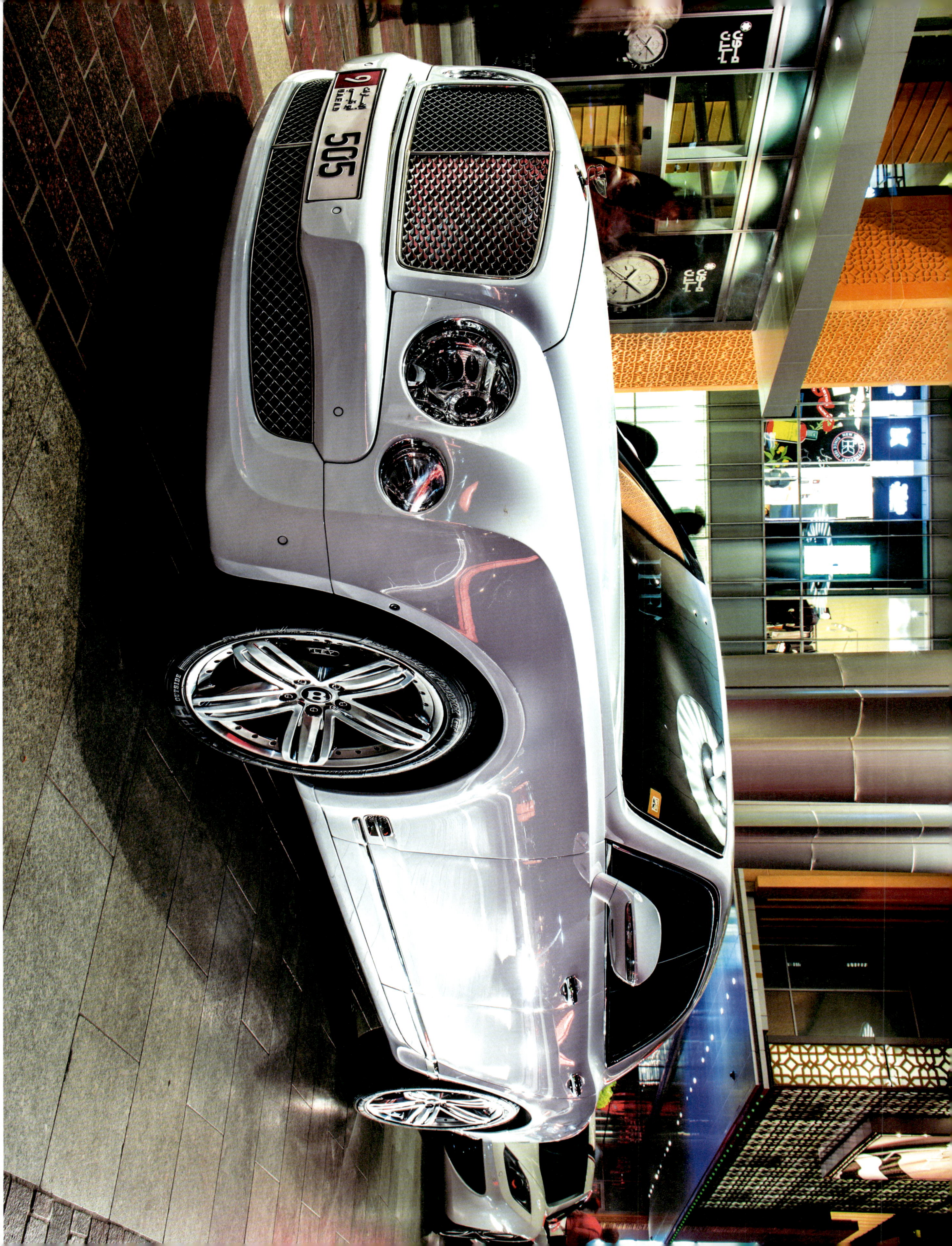

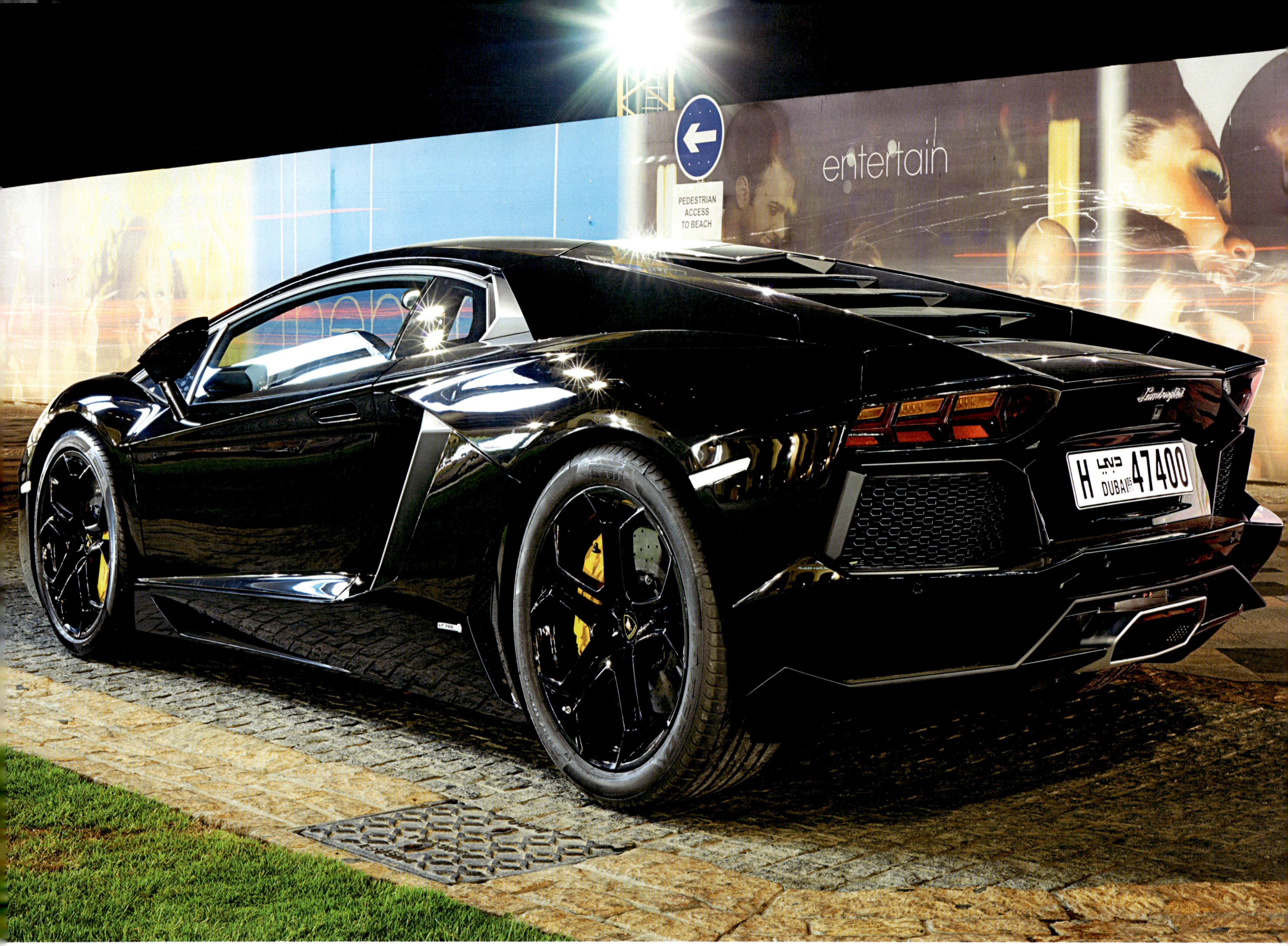
PEDESTRIAN
ACCESS
TO BEACH
entertain
H دبي DUBAI 47400

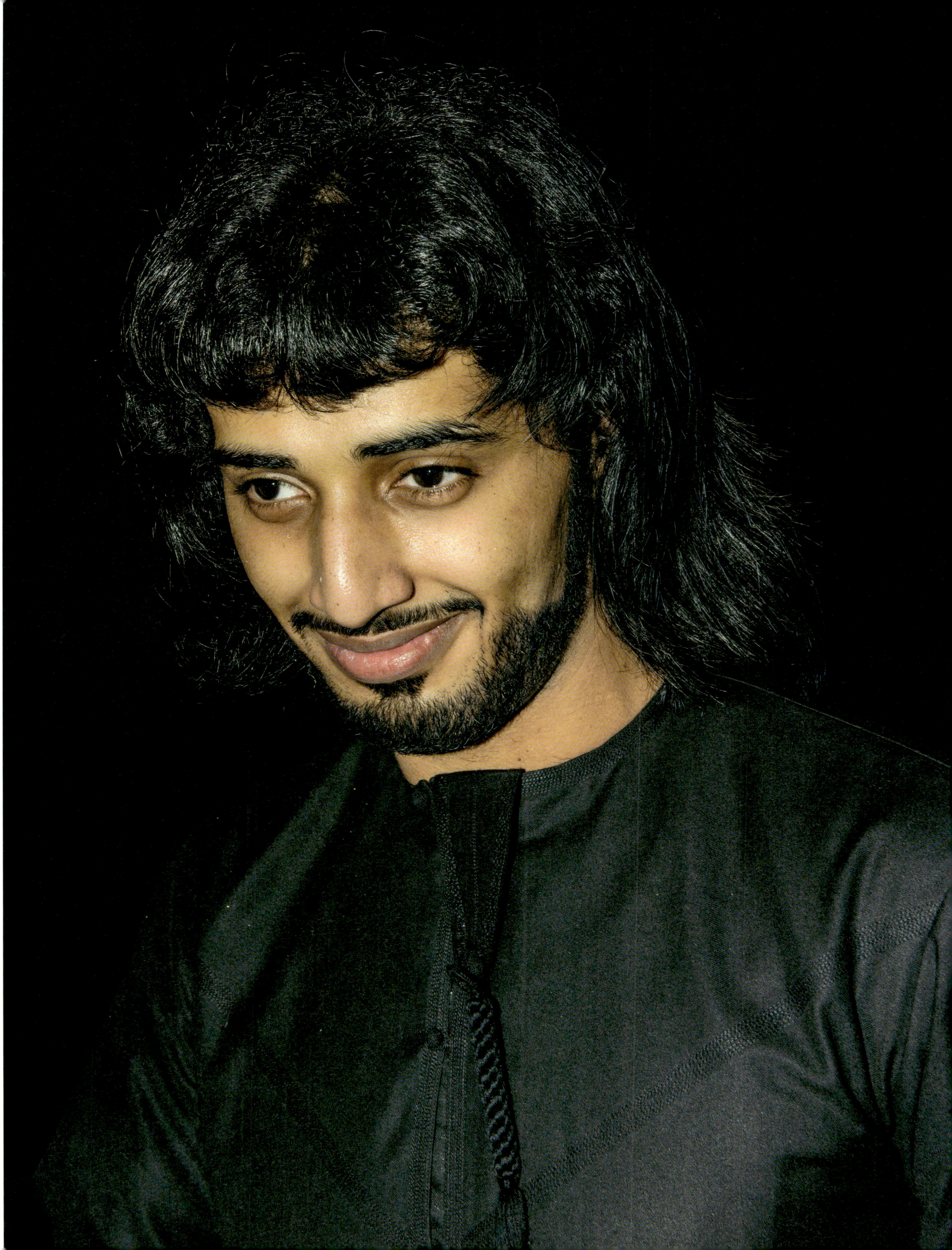

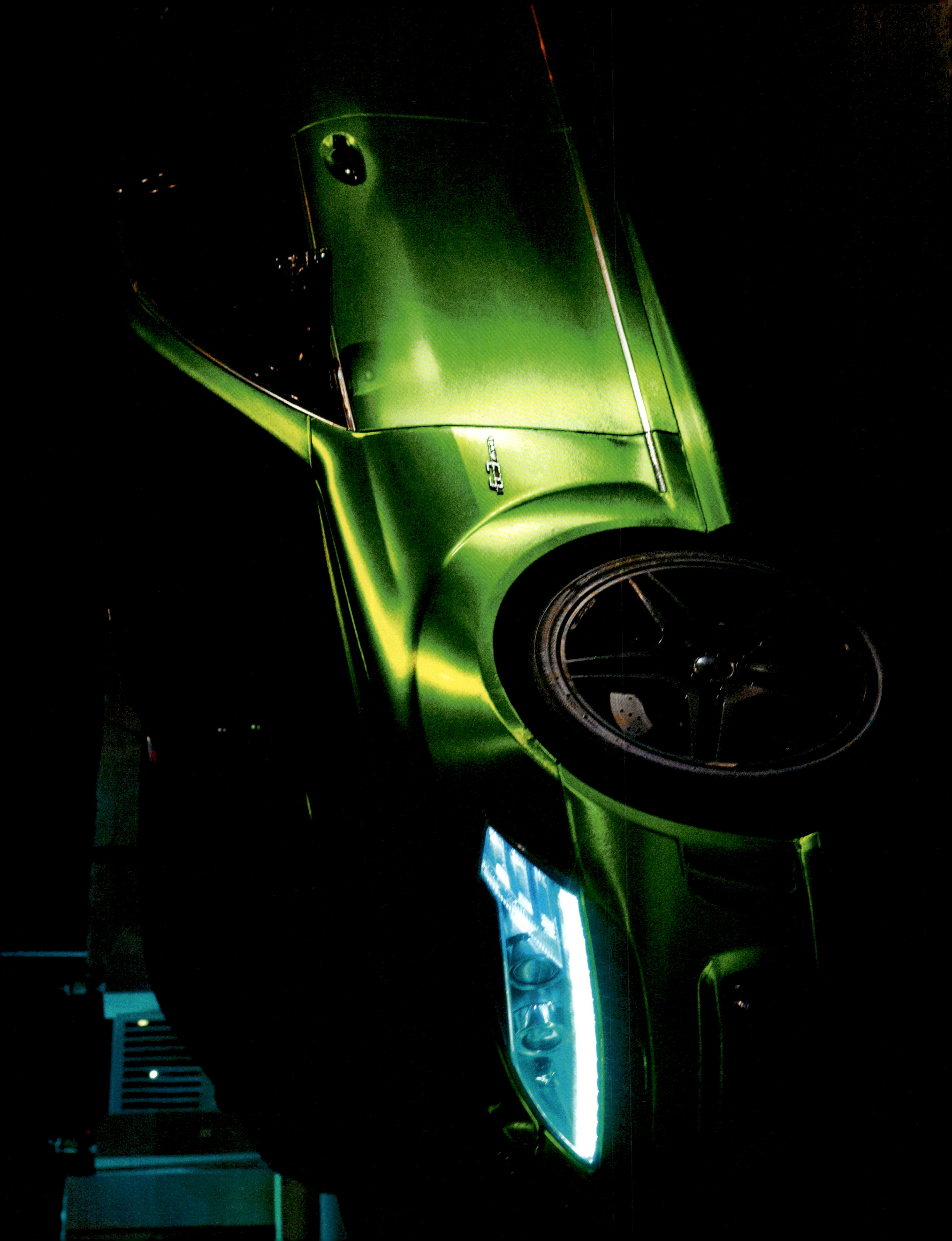

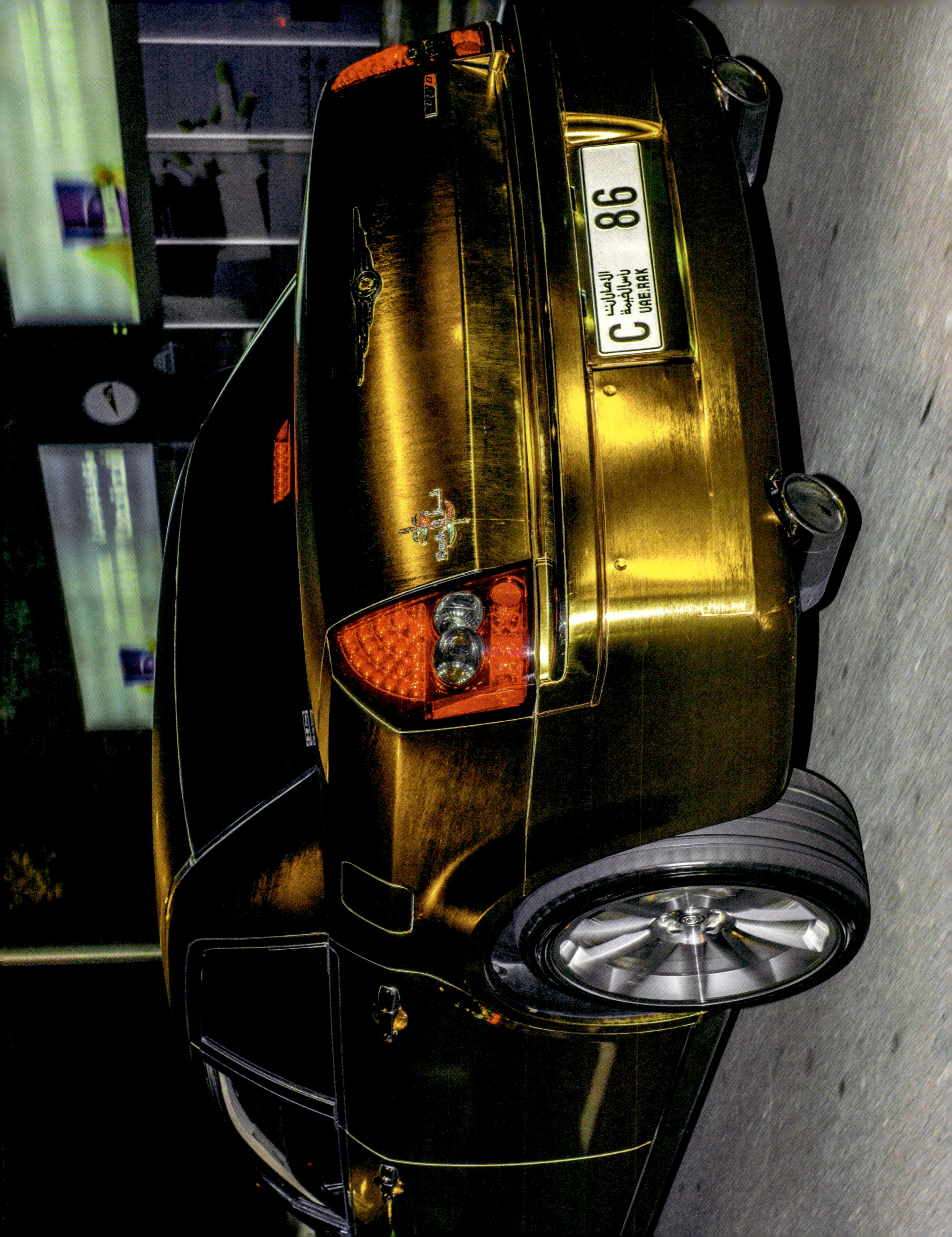
C 86
UAE.RAK

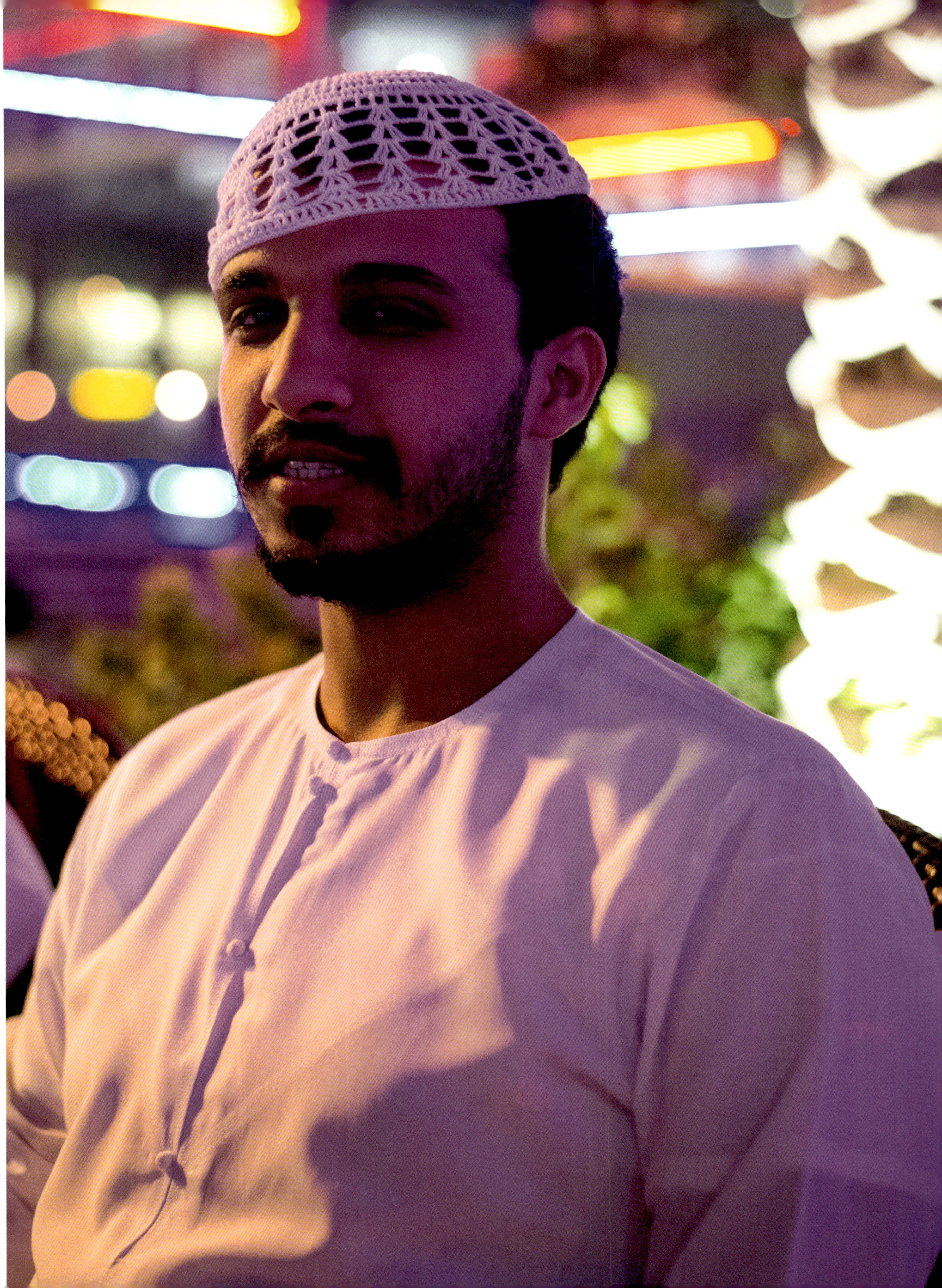

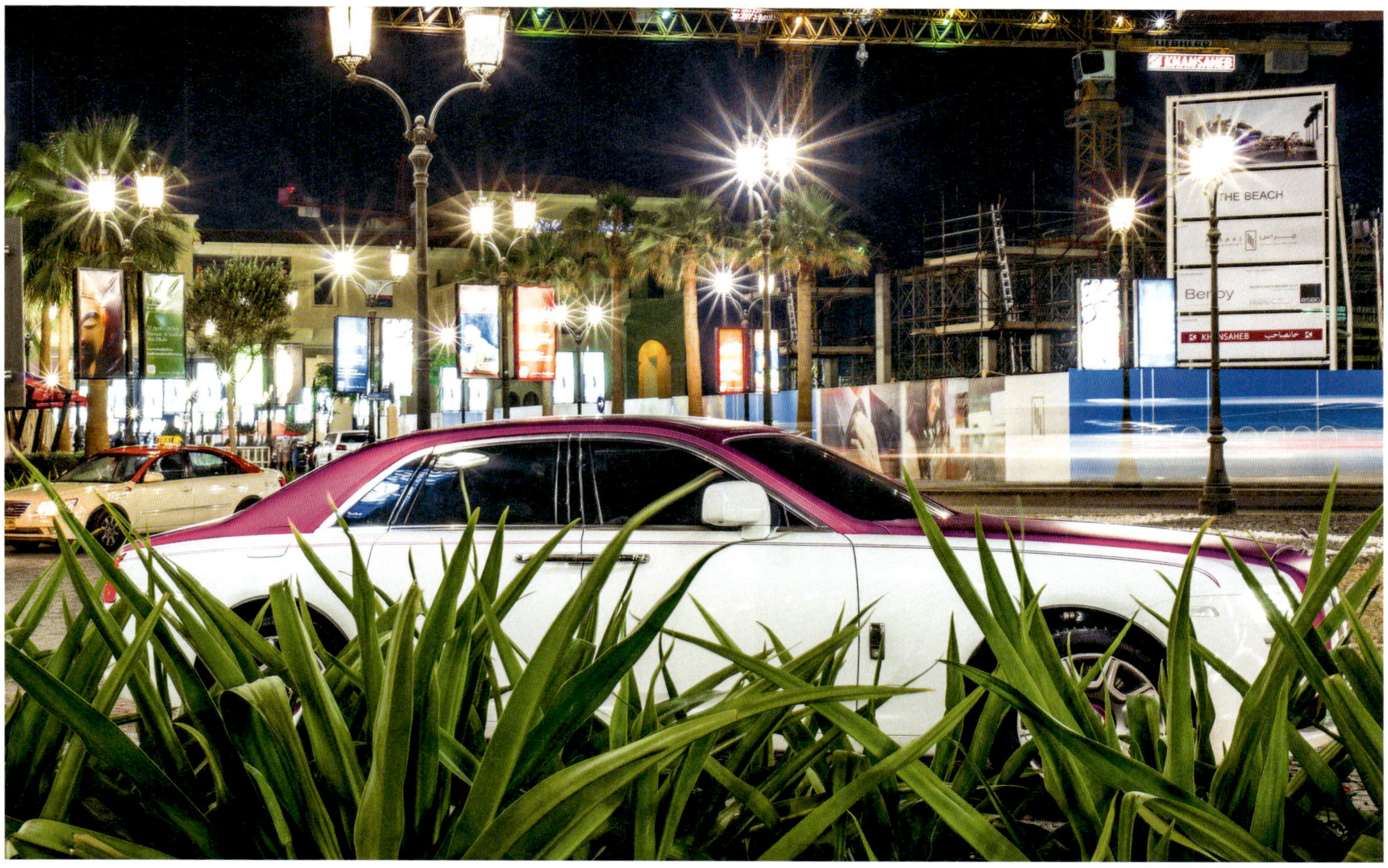
KHANSAHEB
THE BEACH

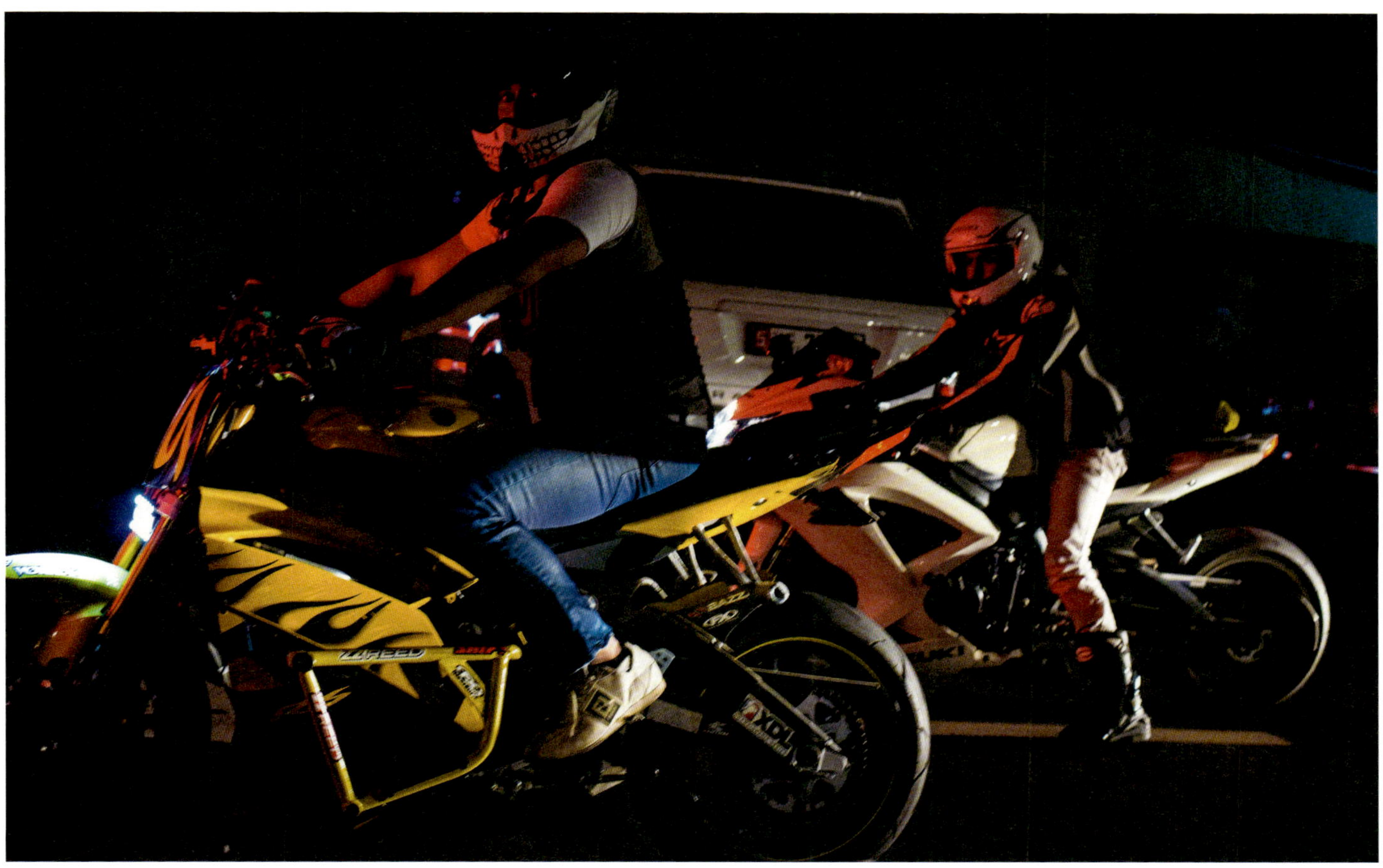

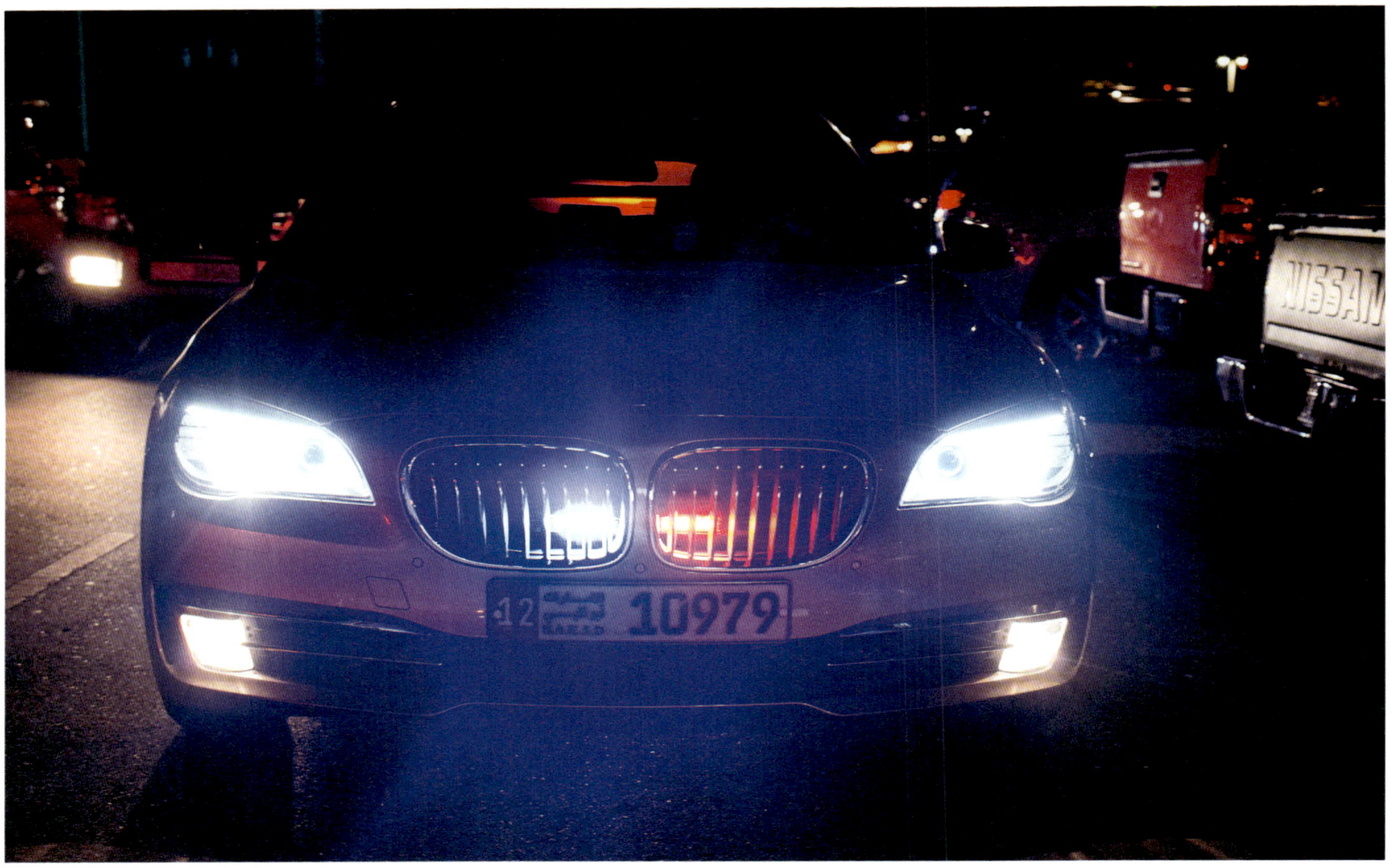
10979

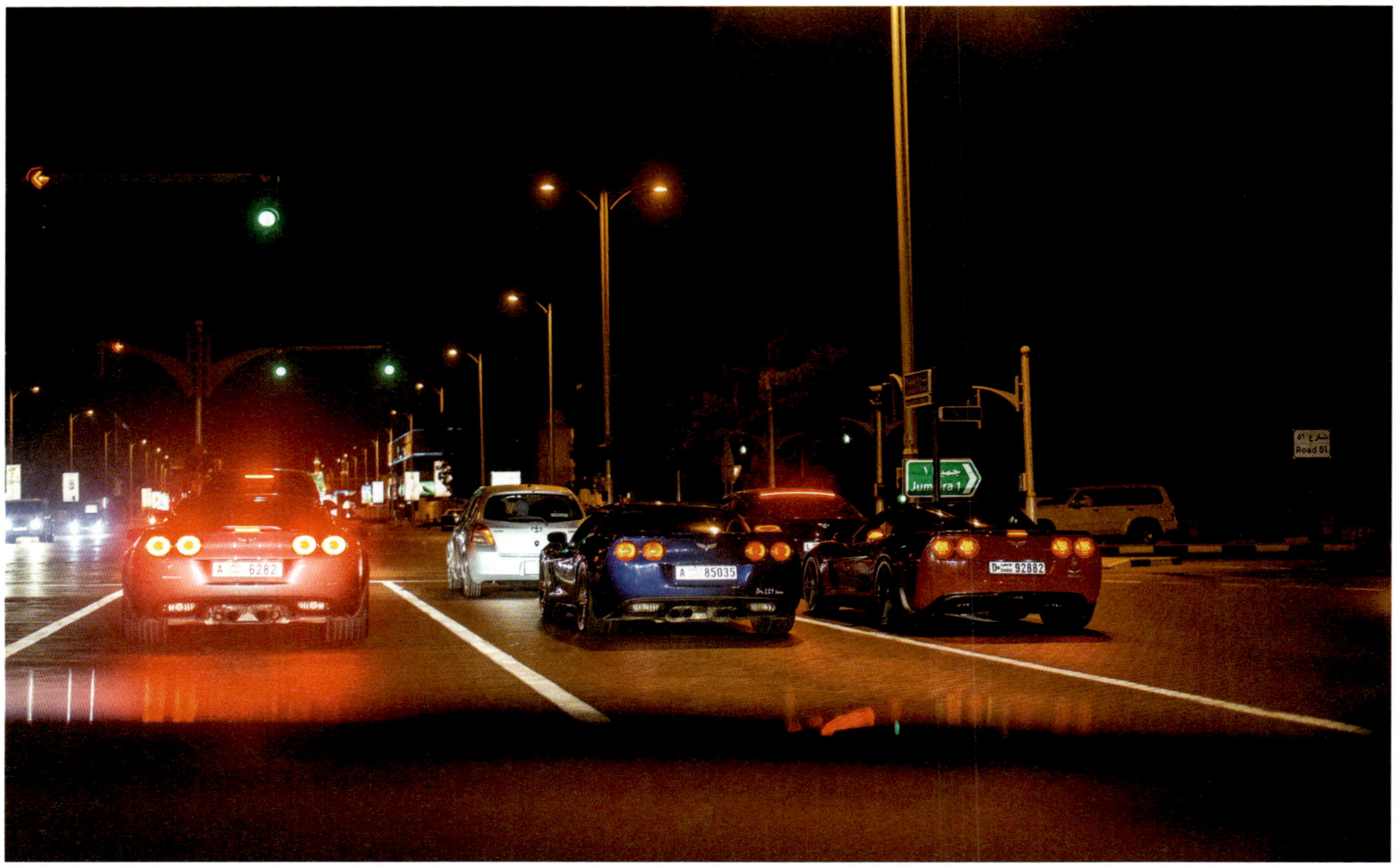

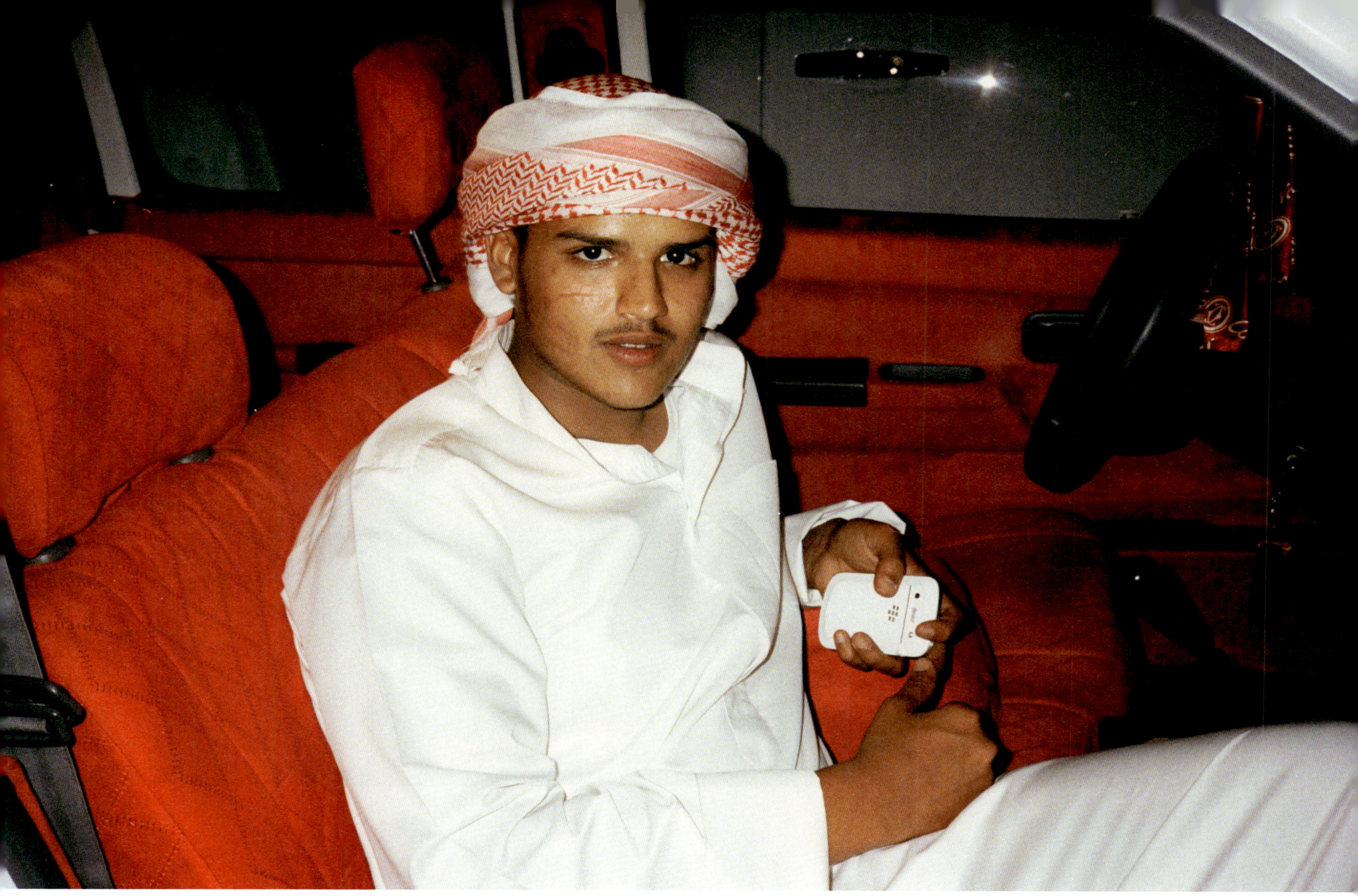

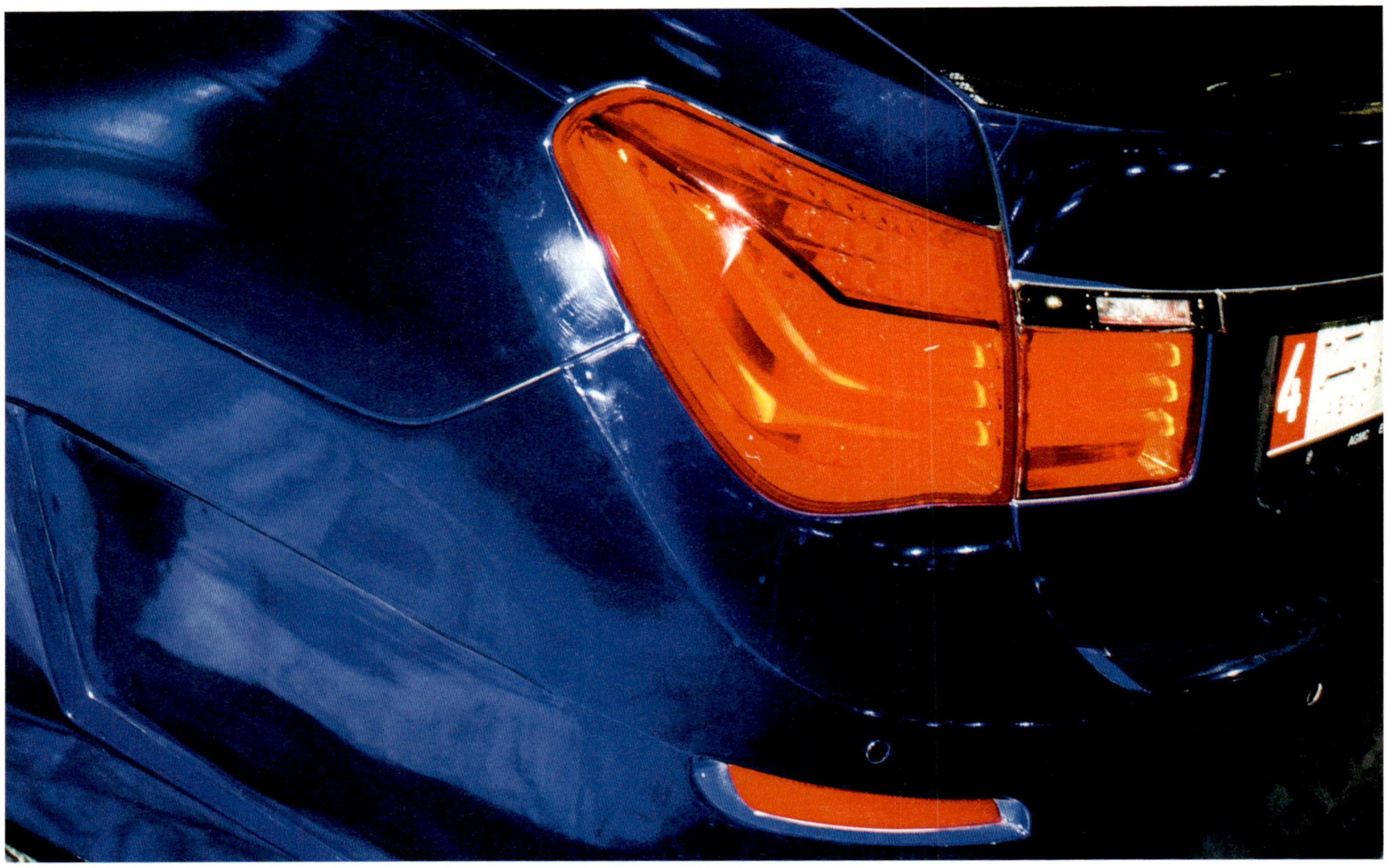

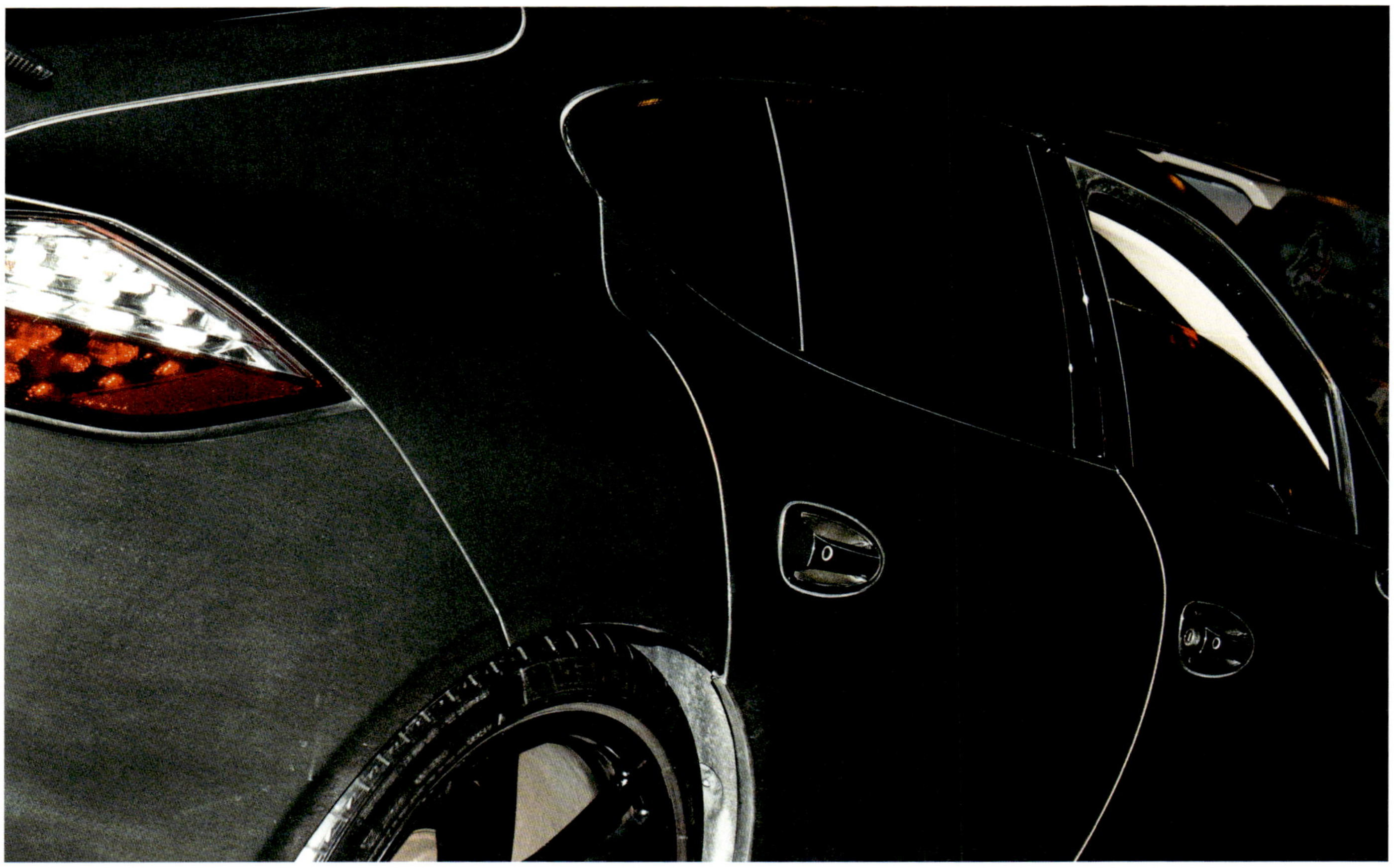

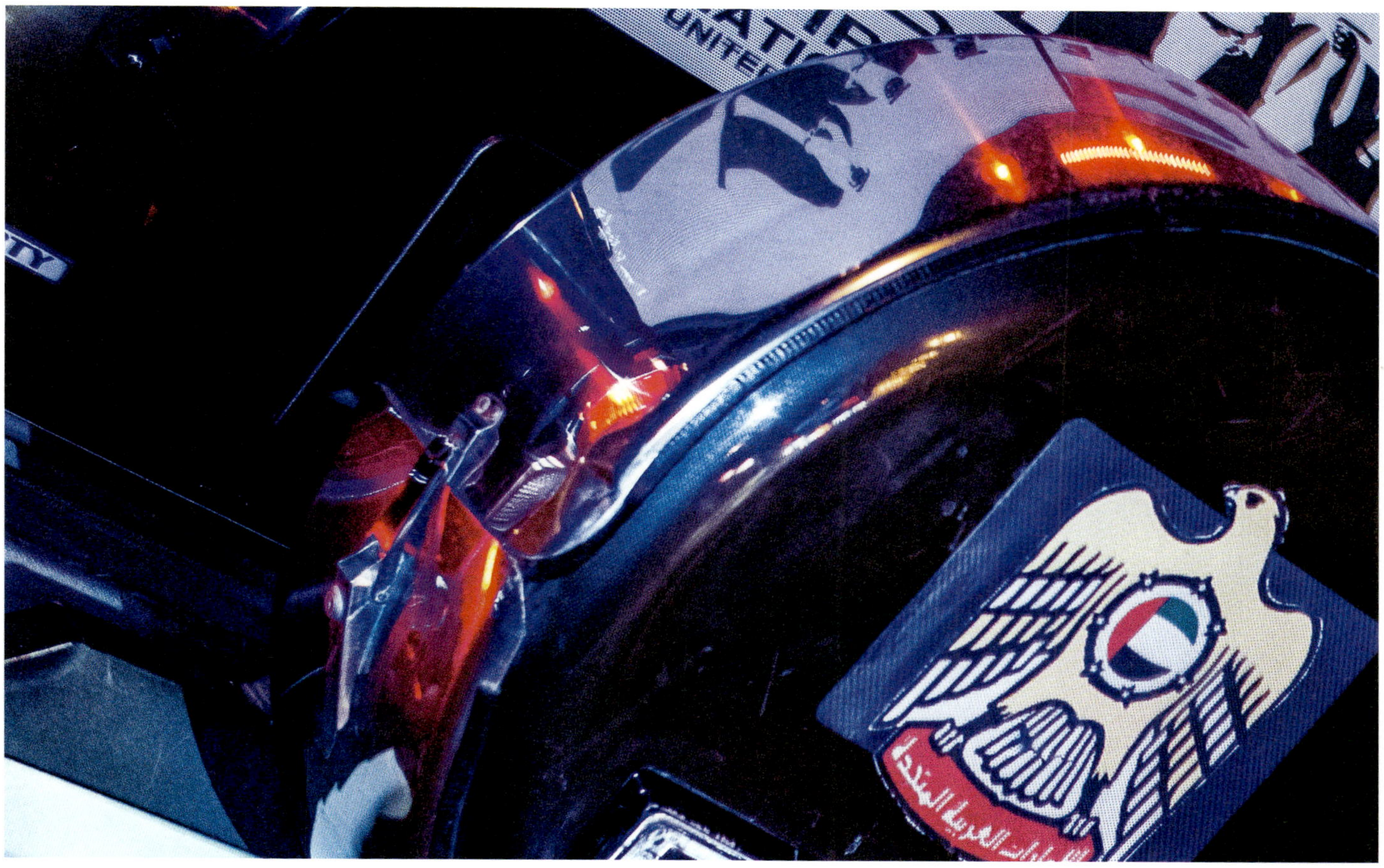

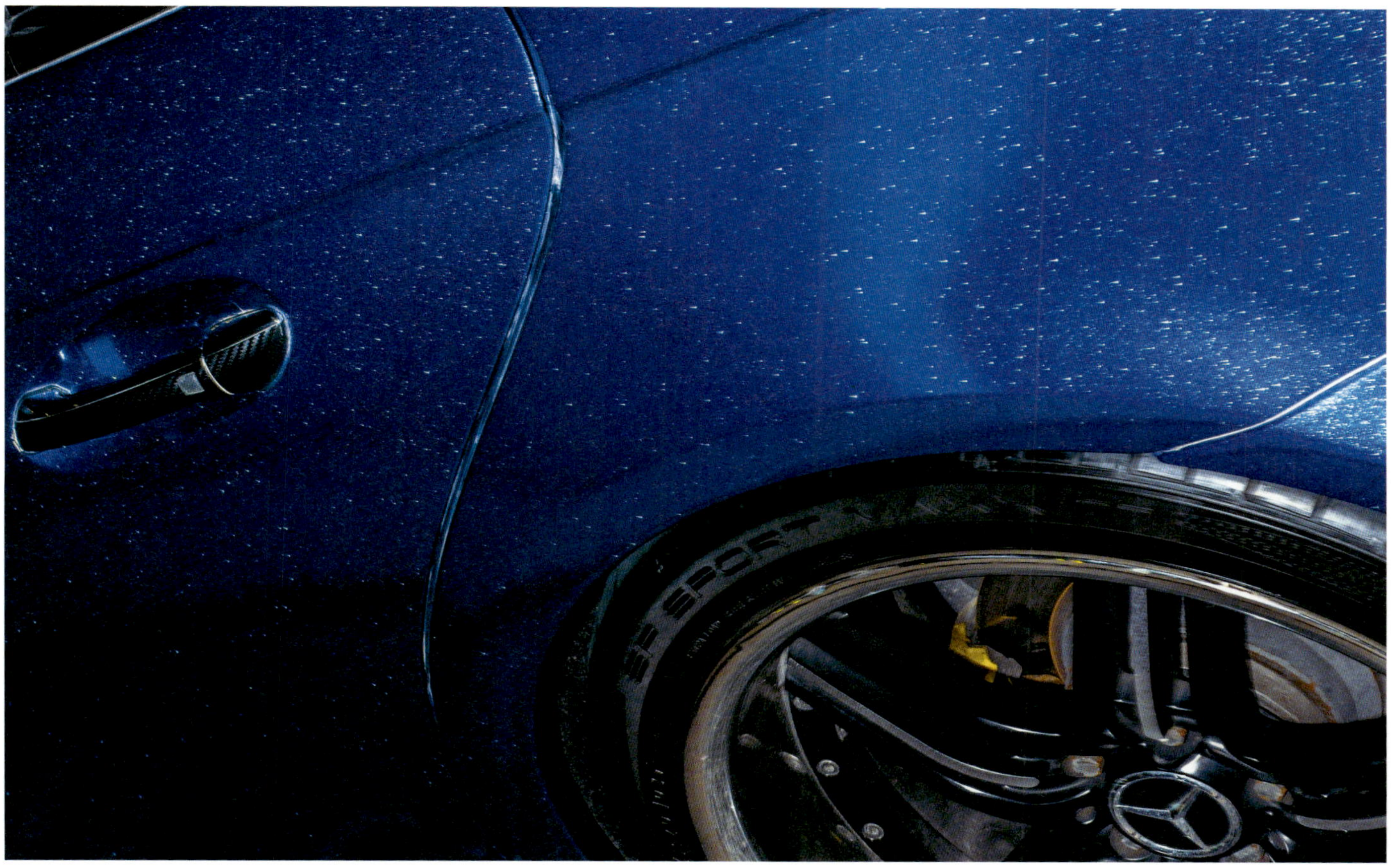

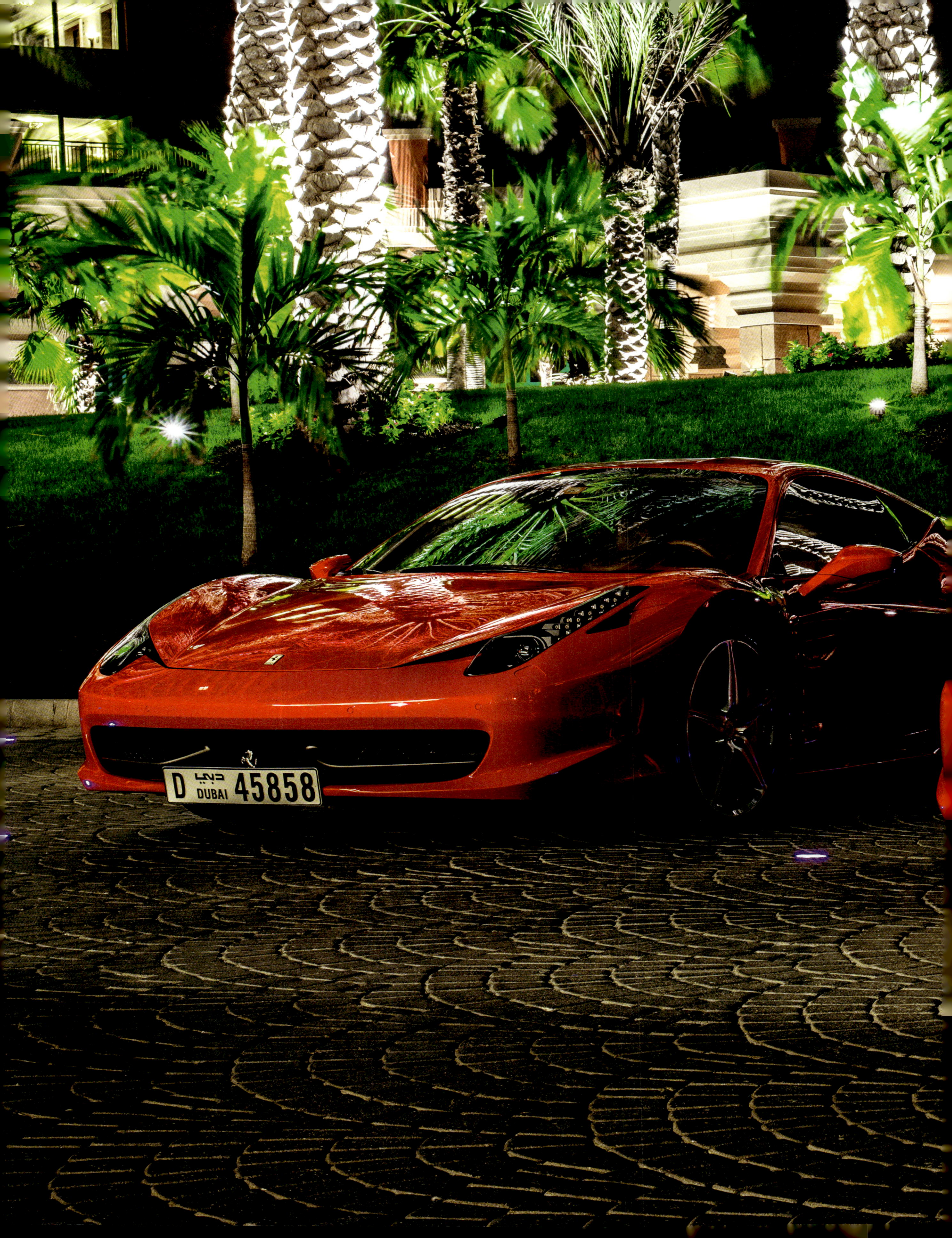
D دبي DUBAI 45858

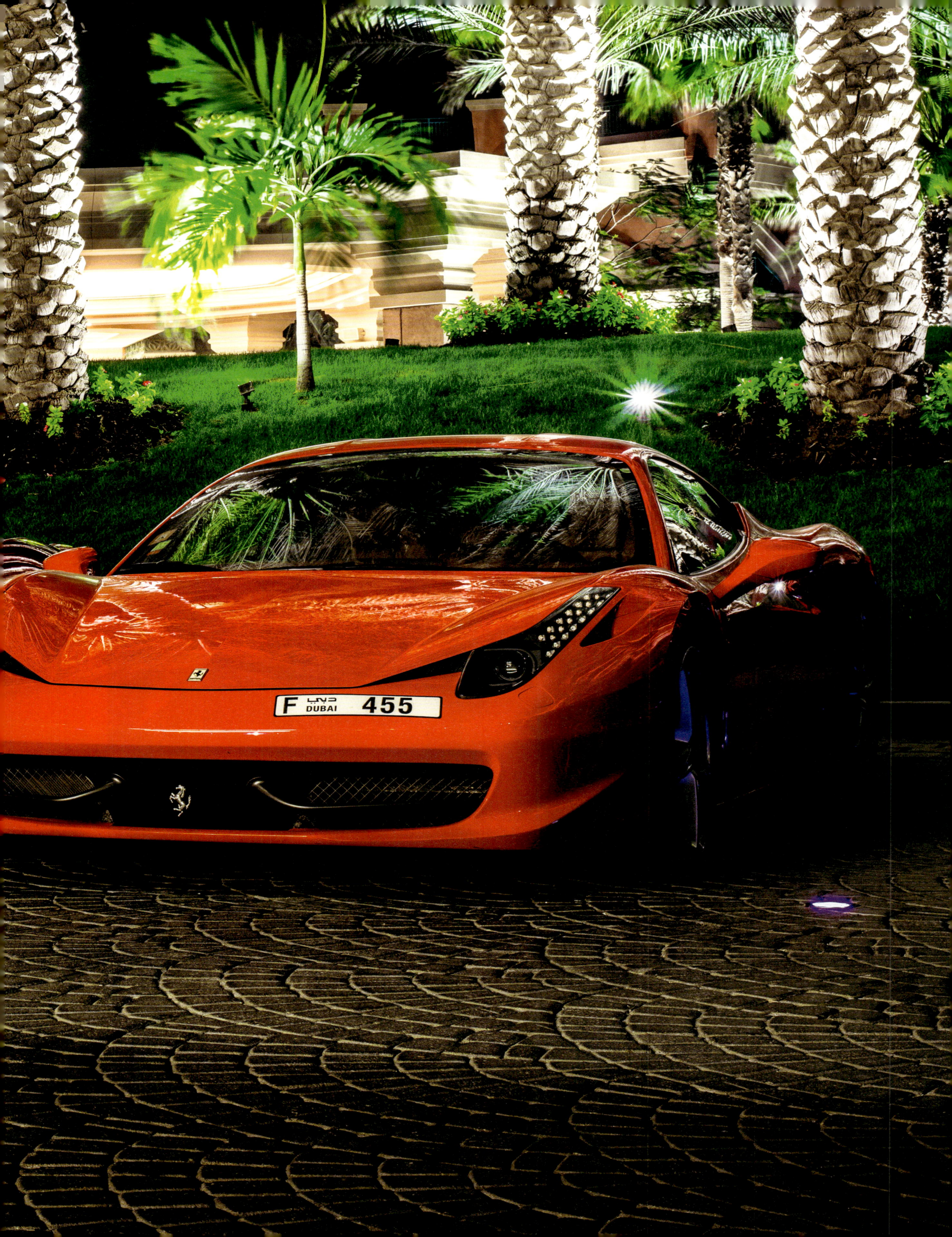
F دبي DUBAI 455

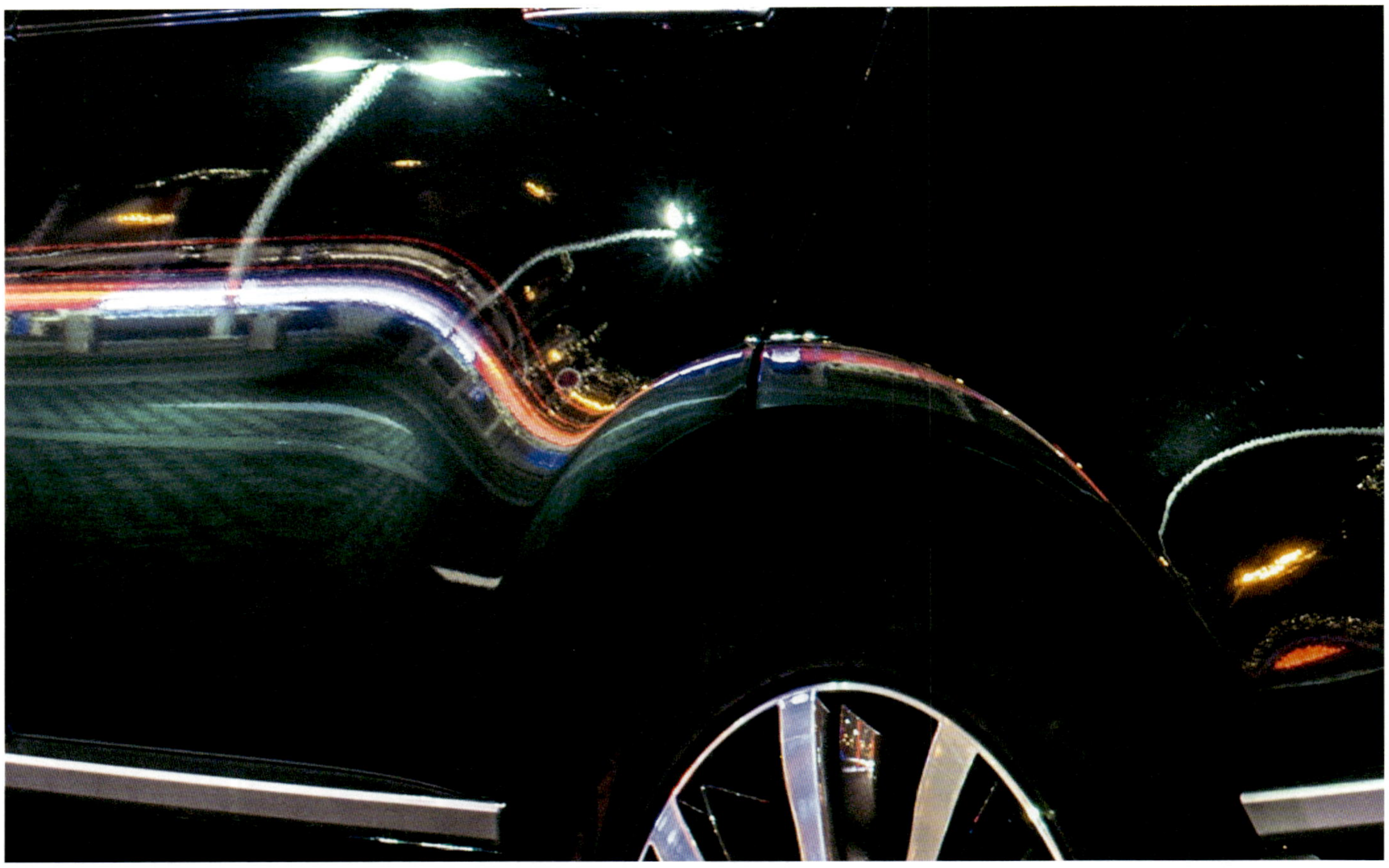

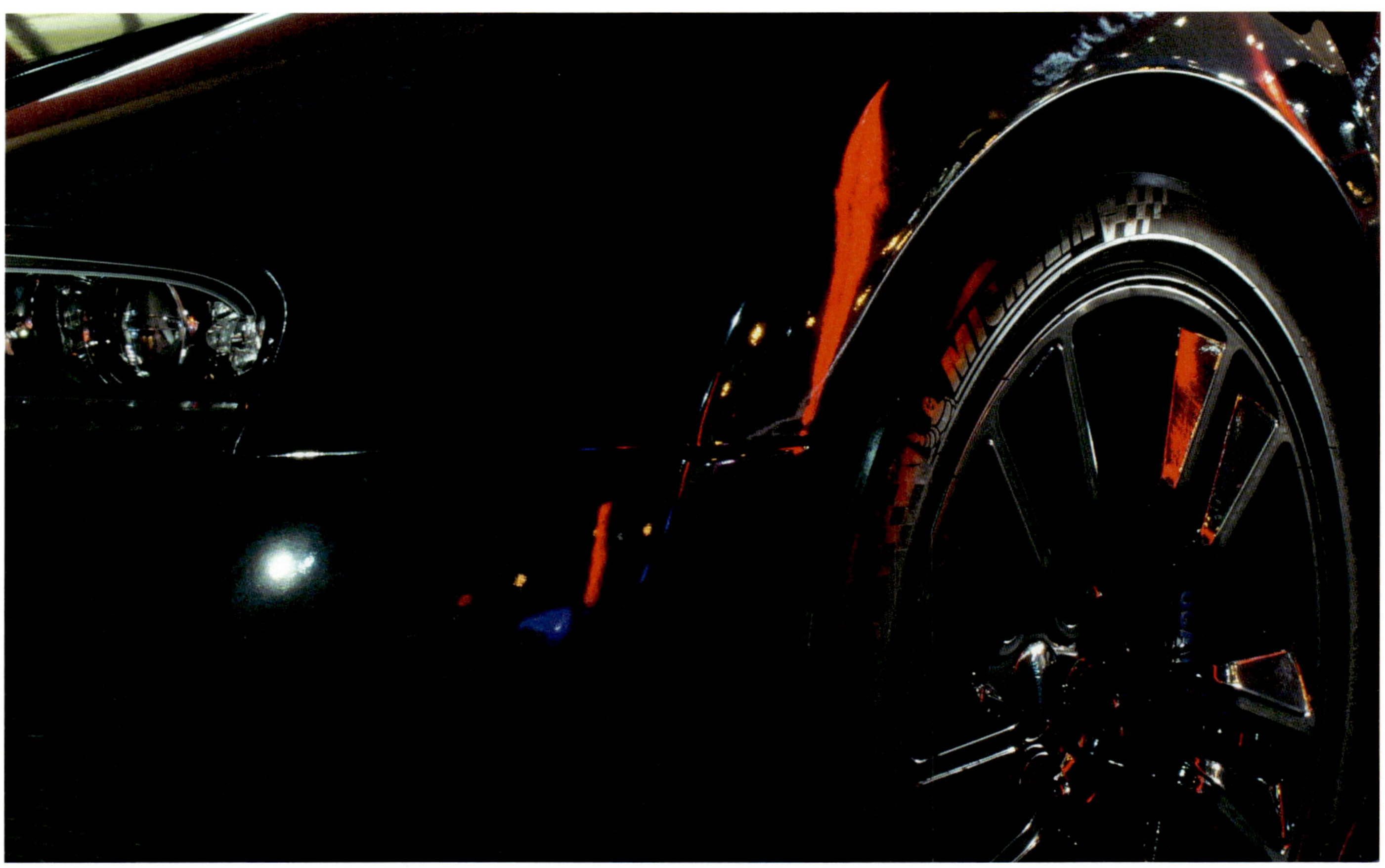
MICHELIN

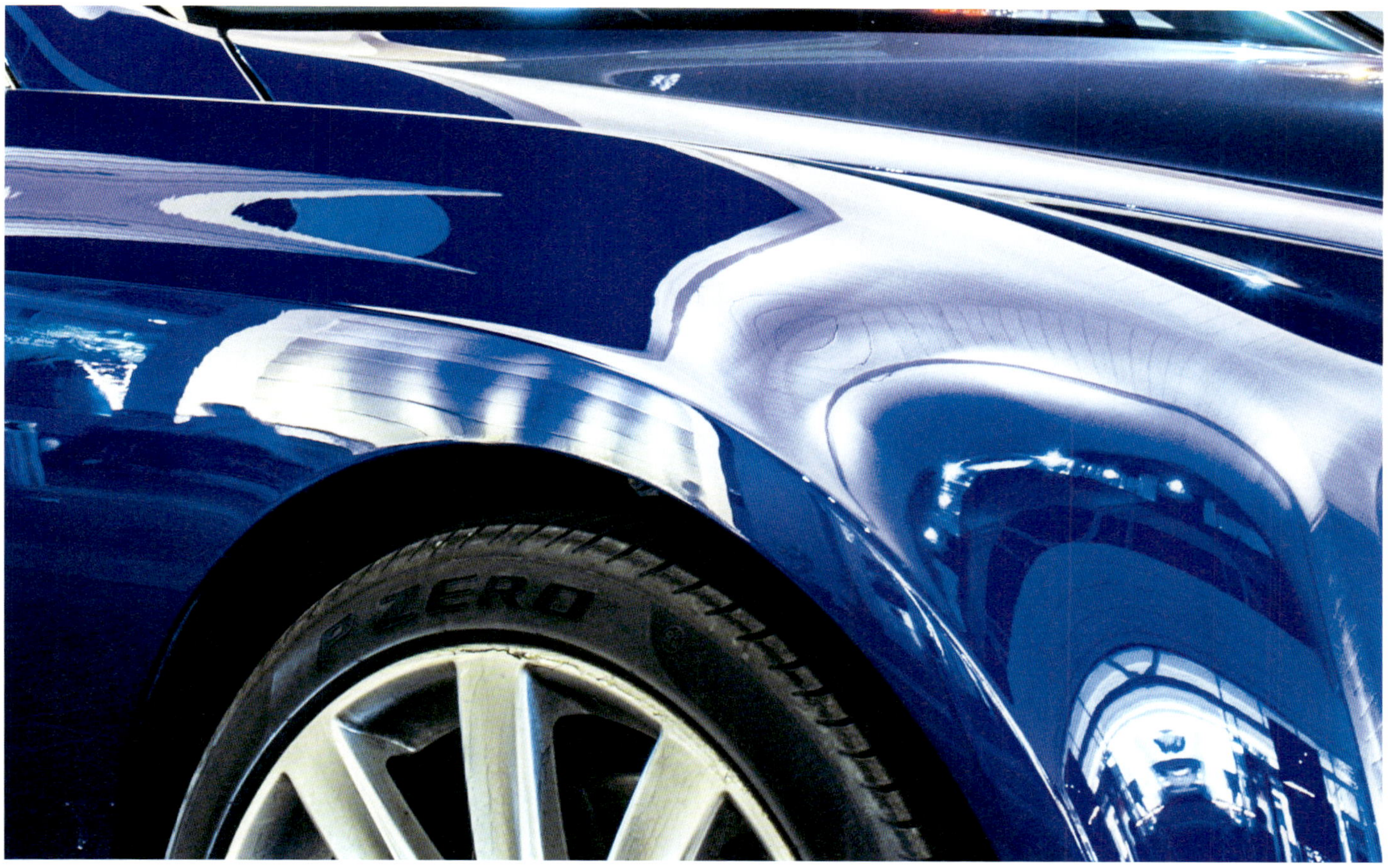
P ZERO

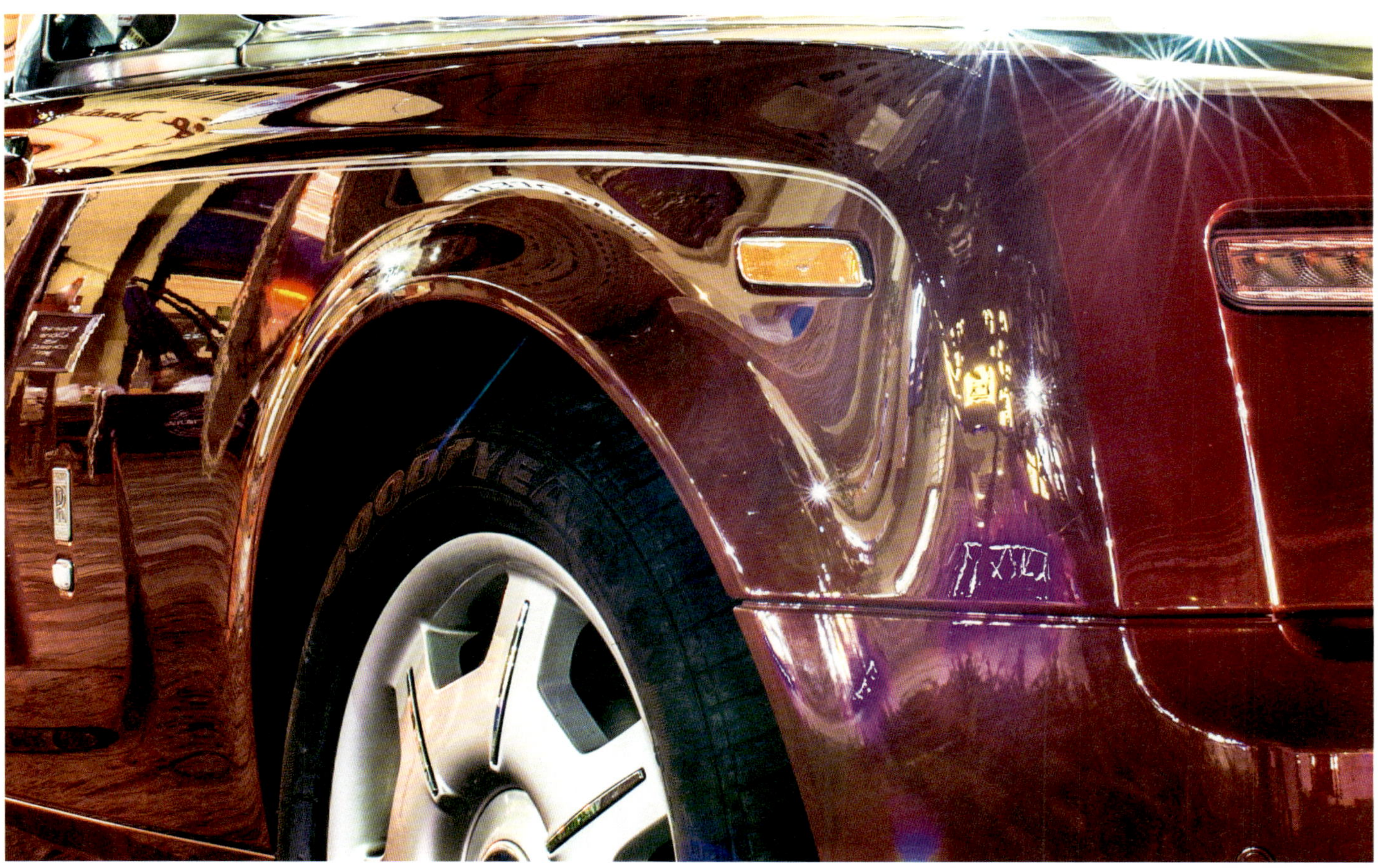
GOODYEA

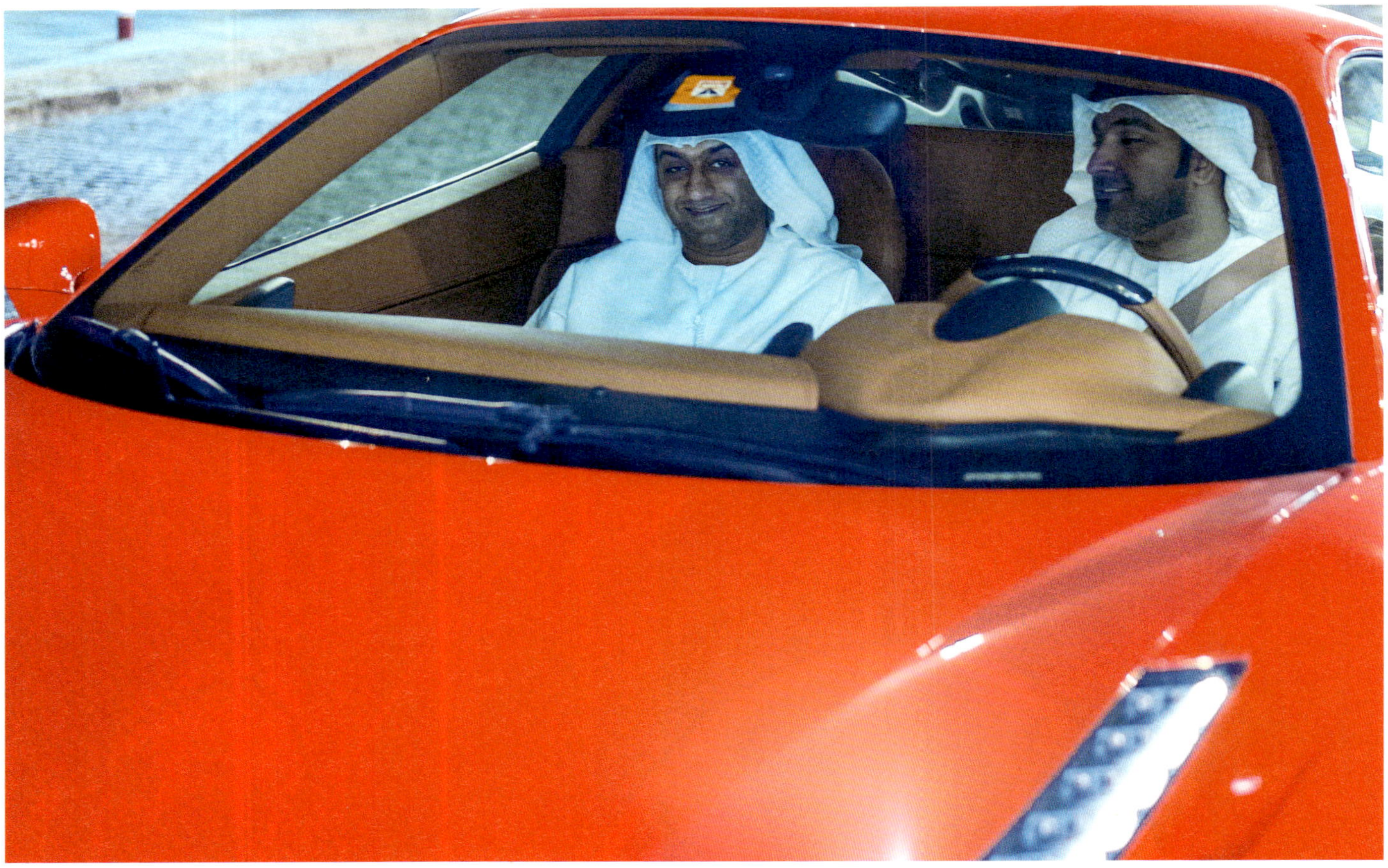

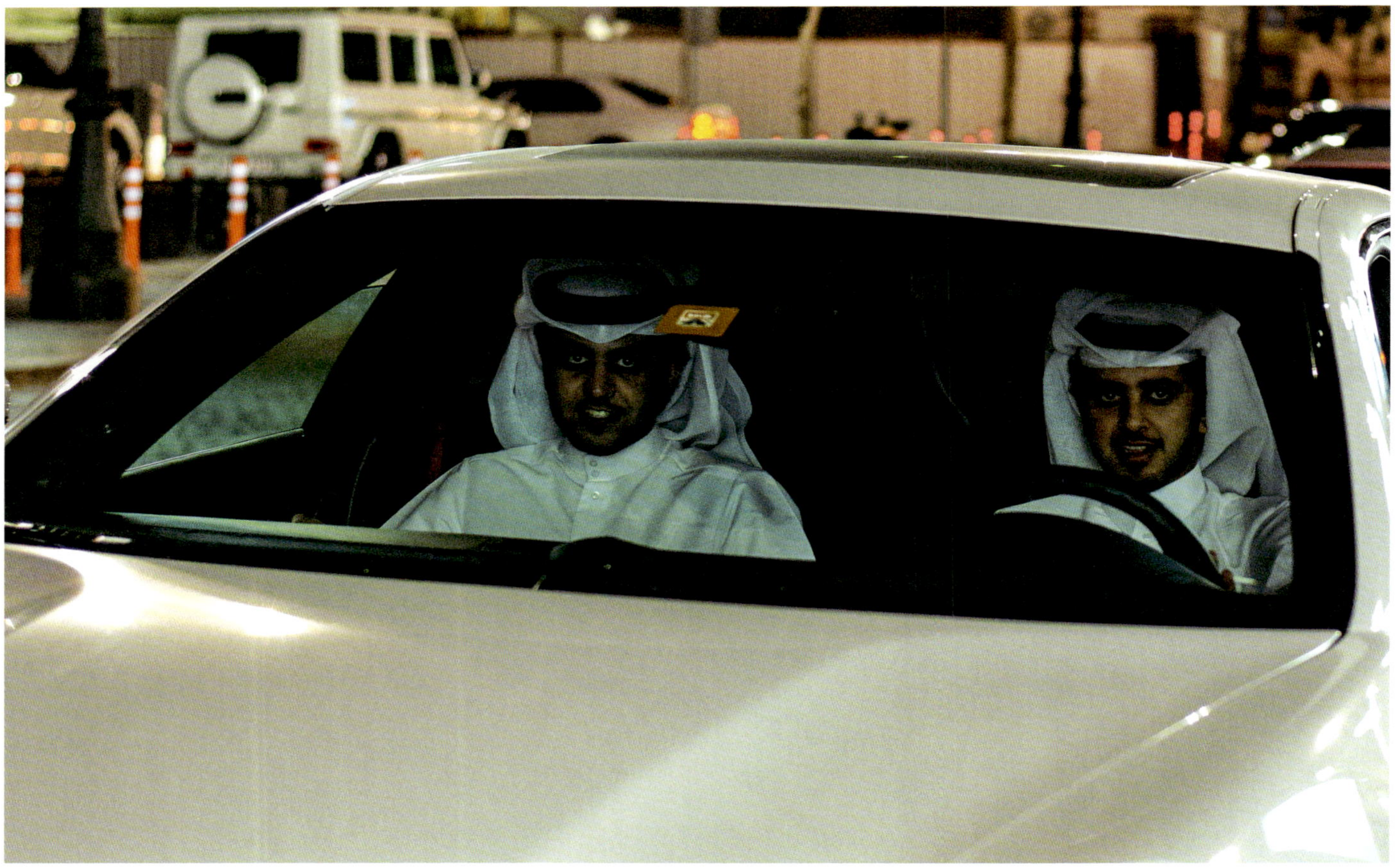

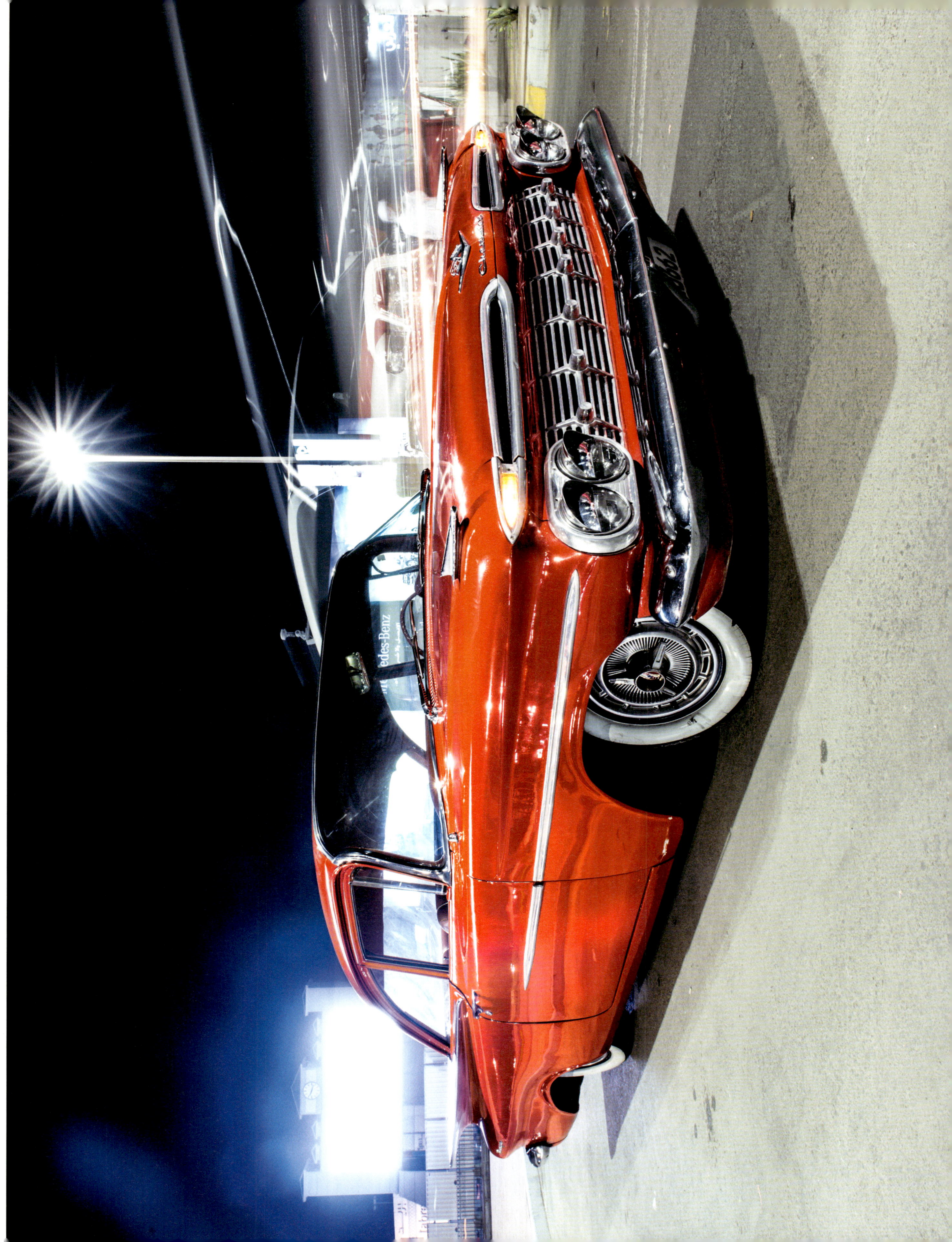

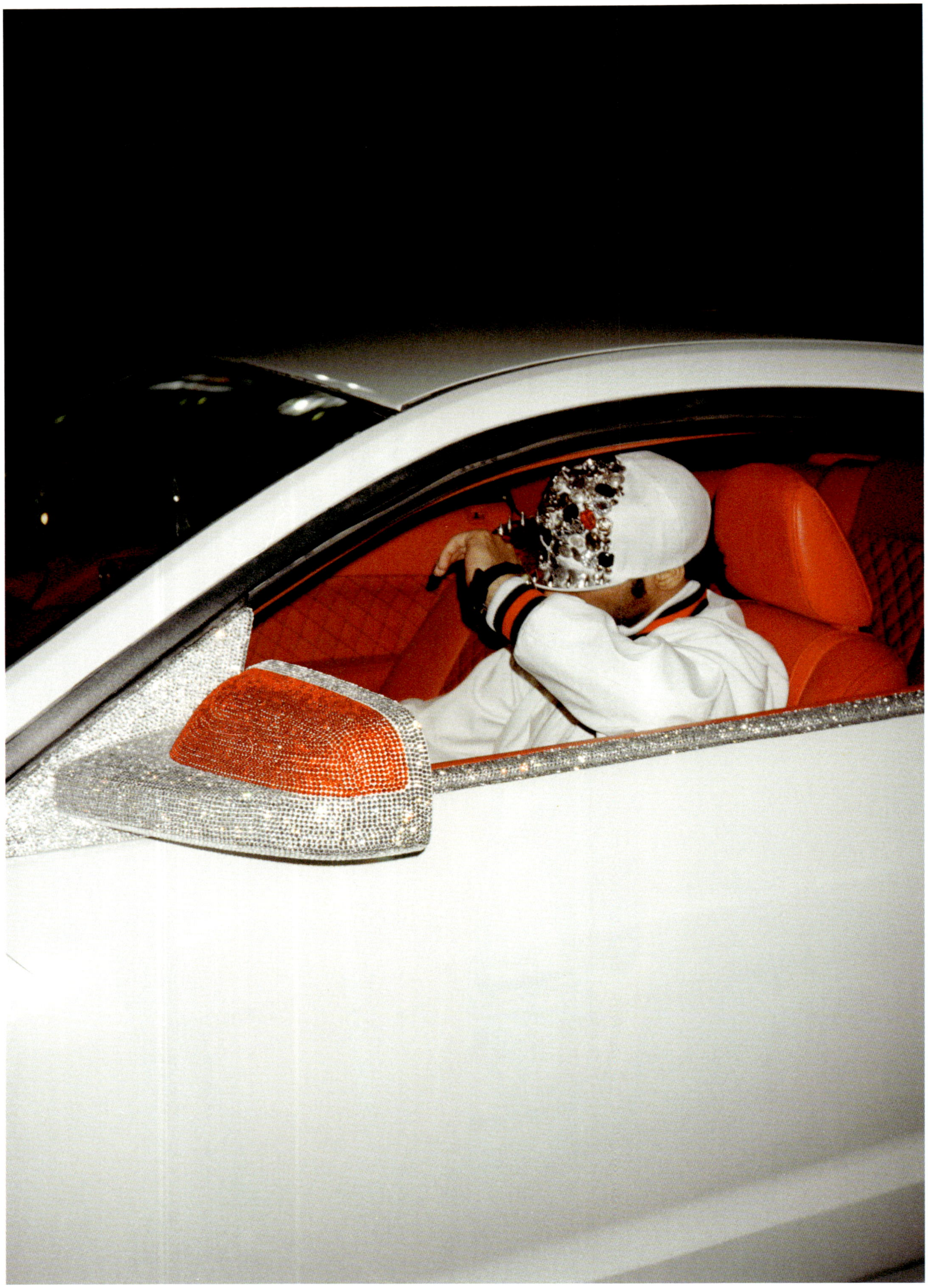

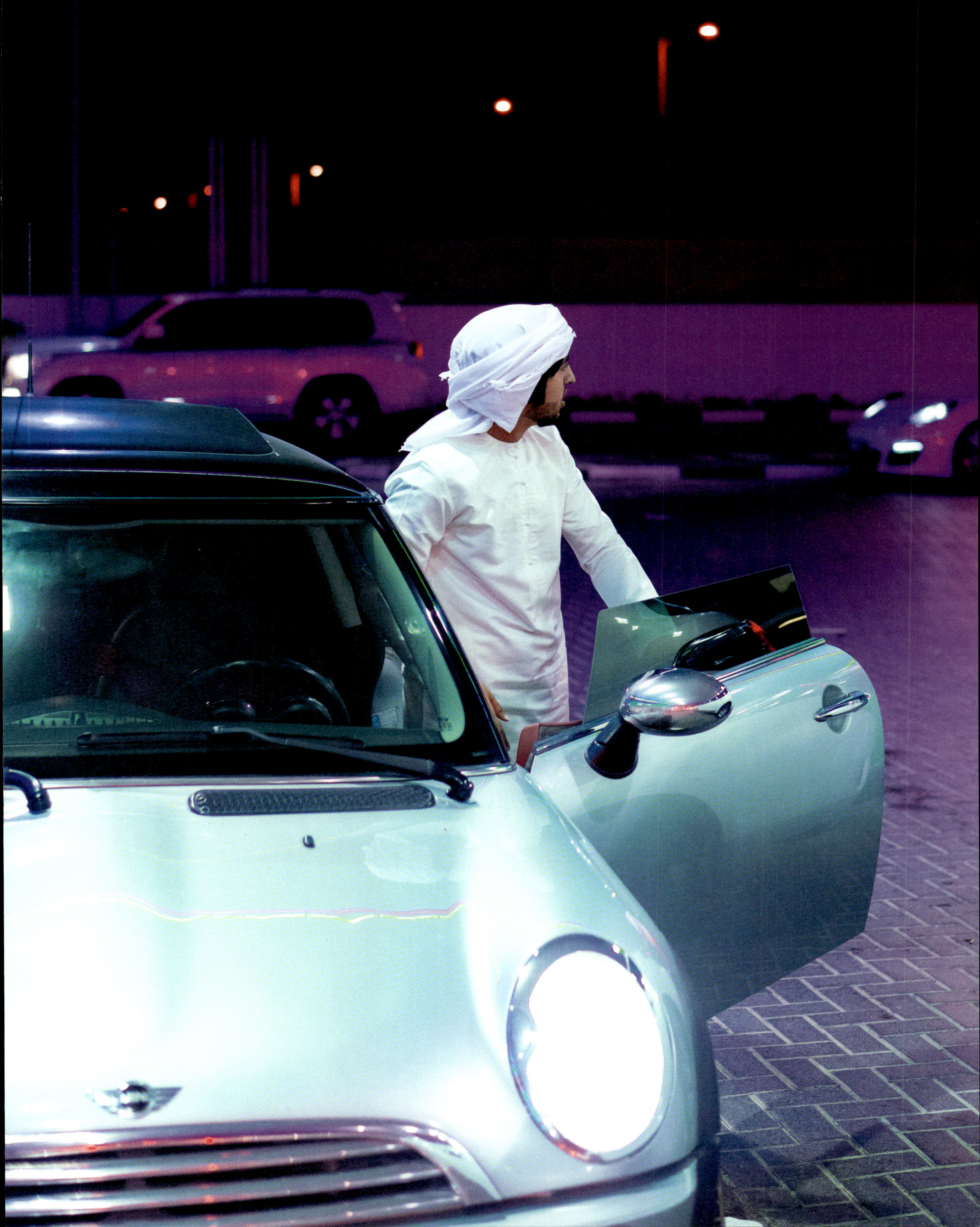

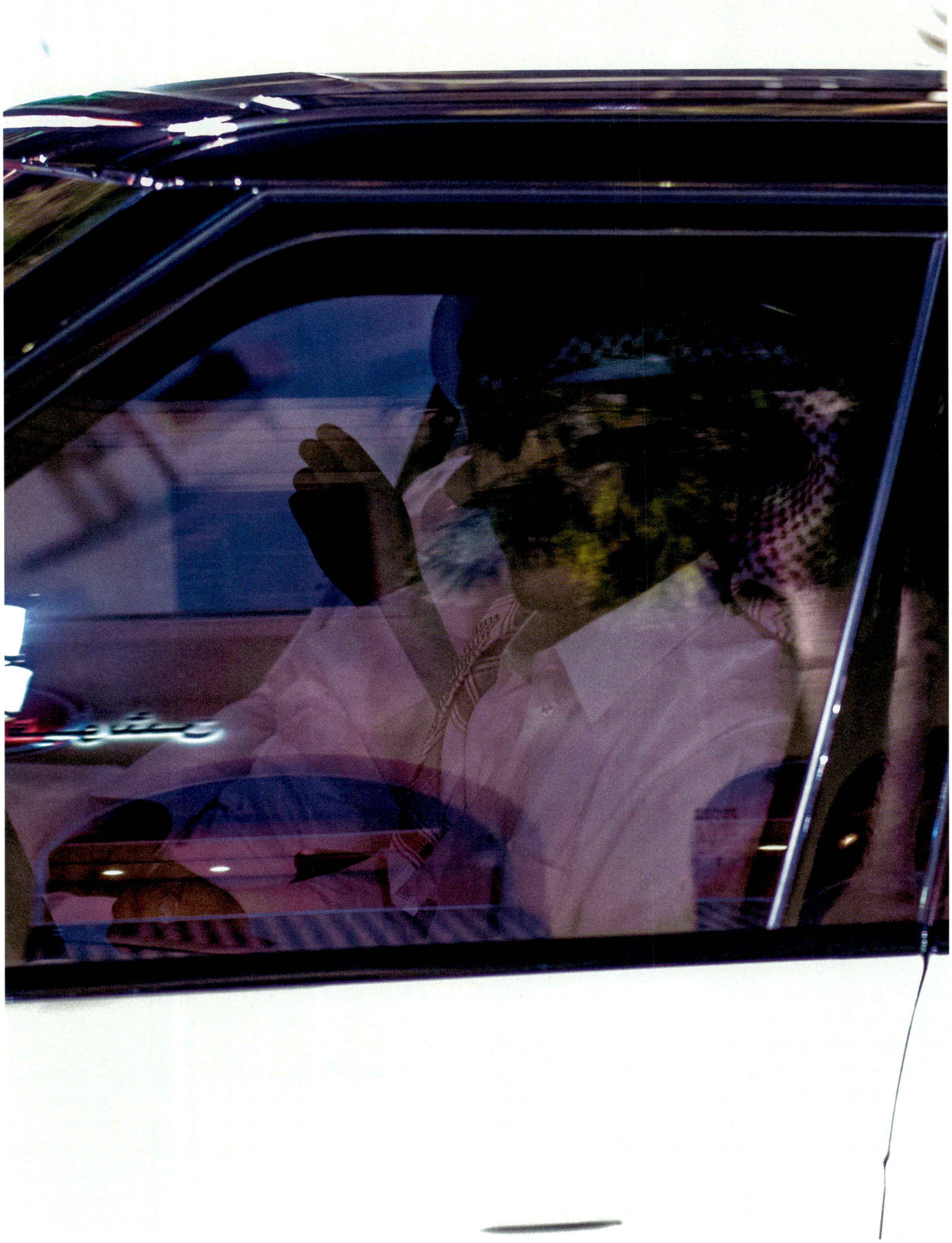

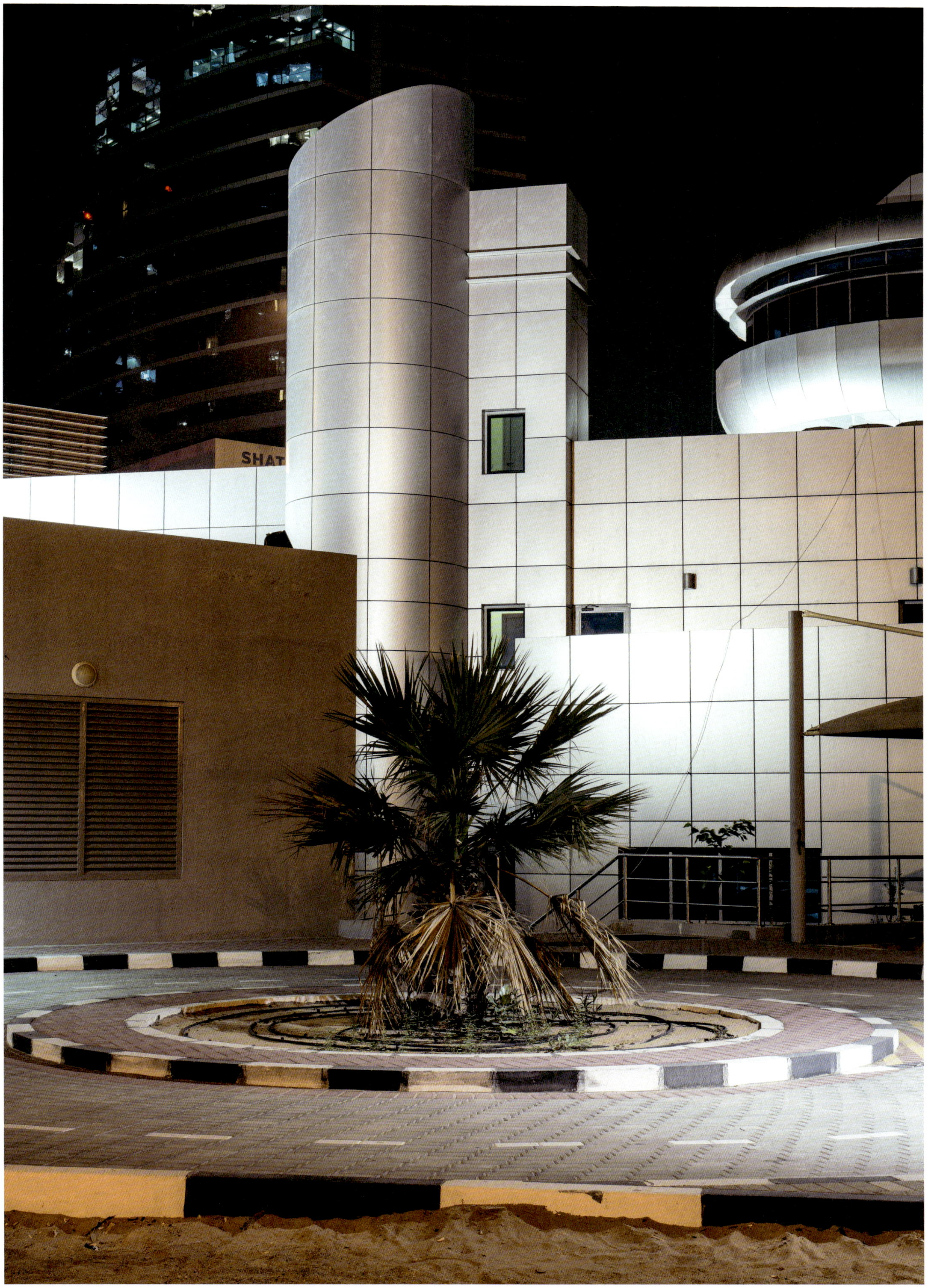

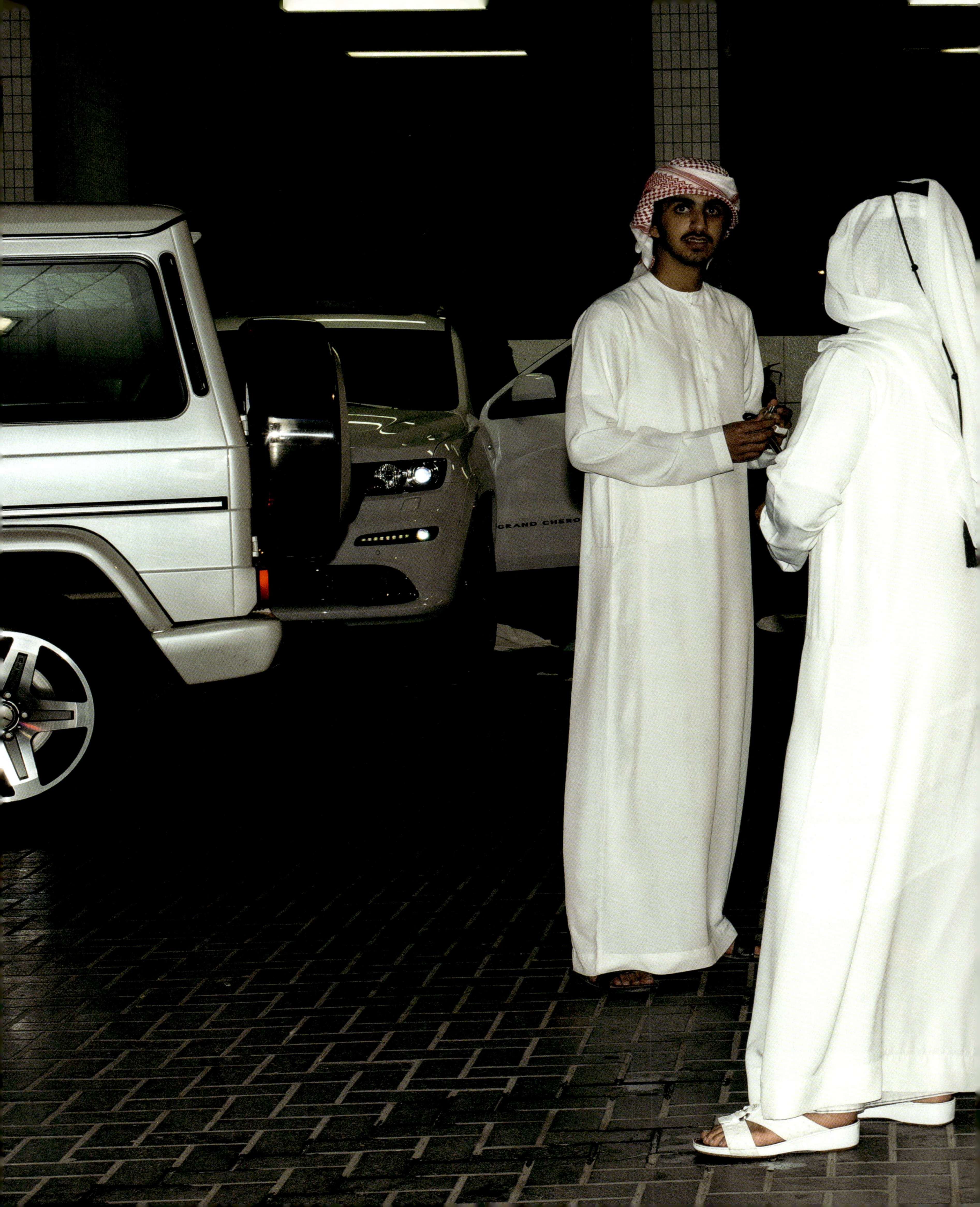

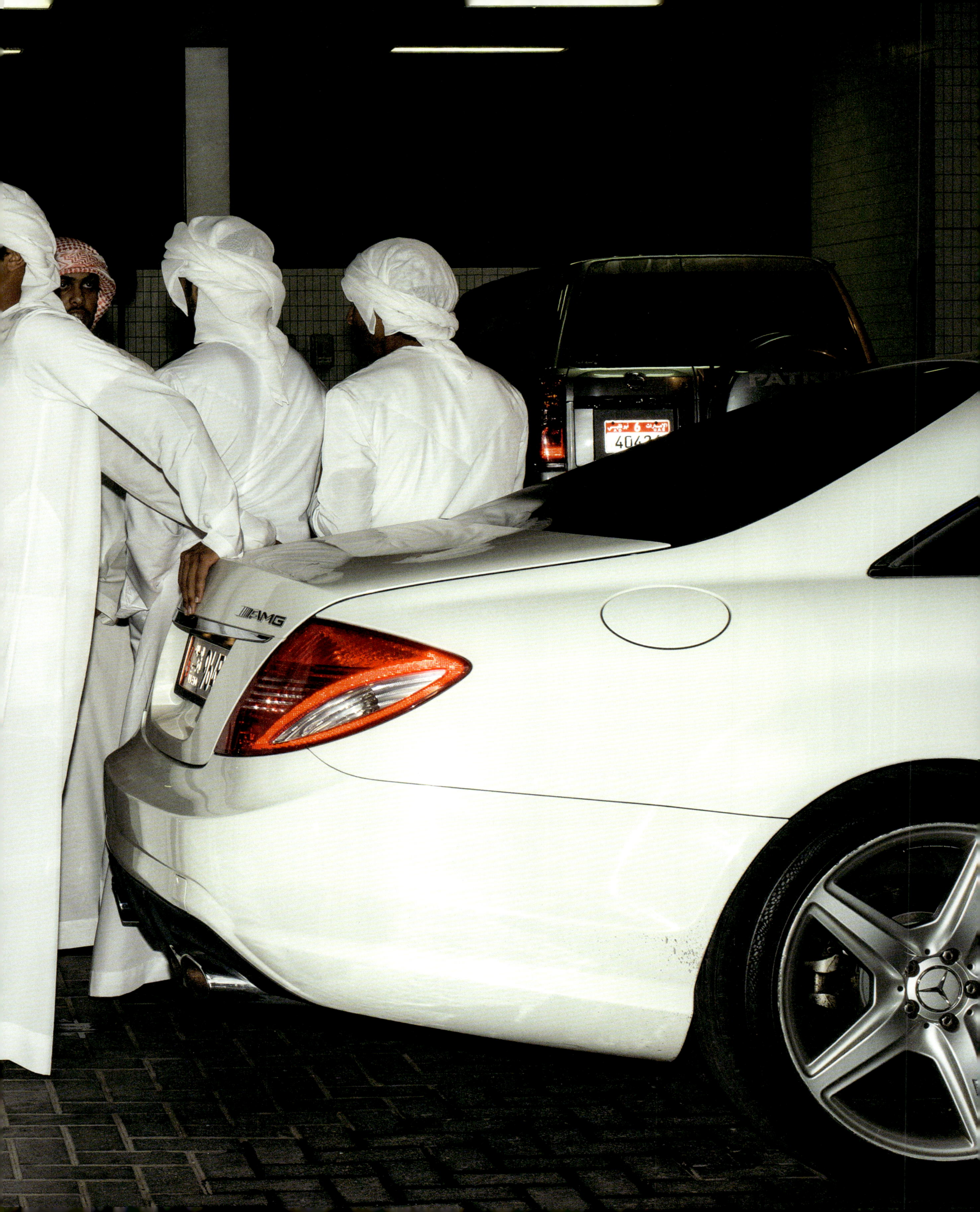
AMG

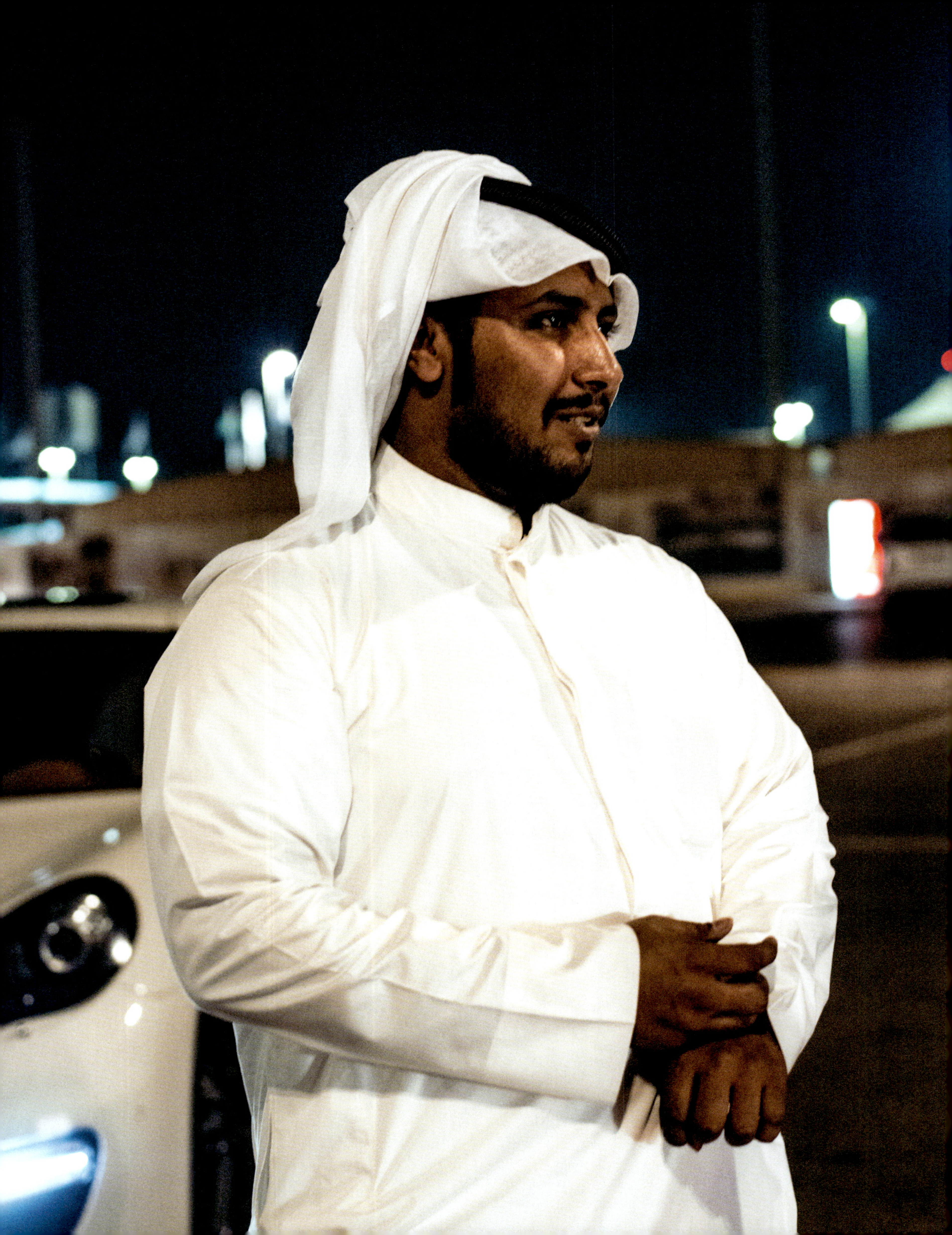

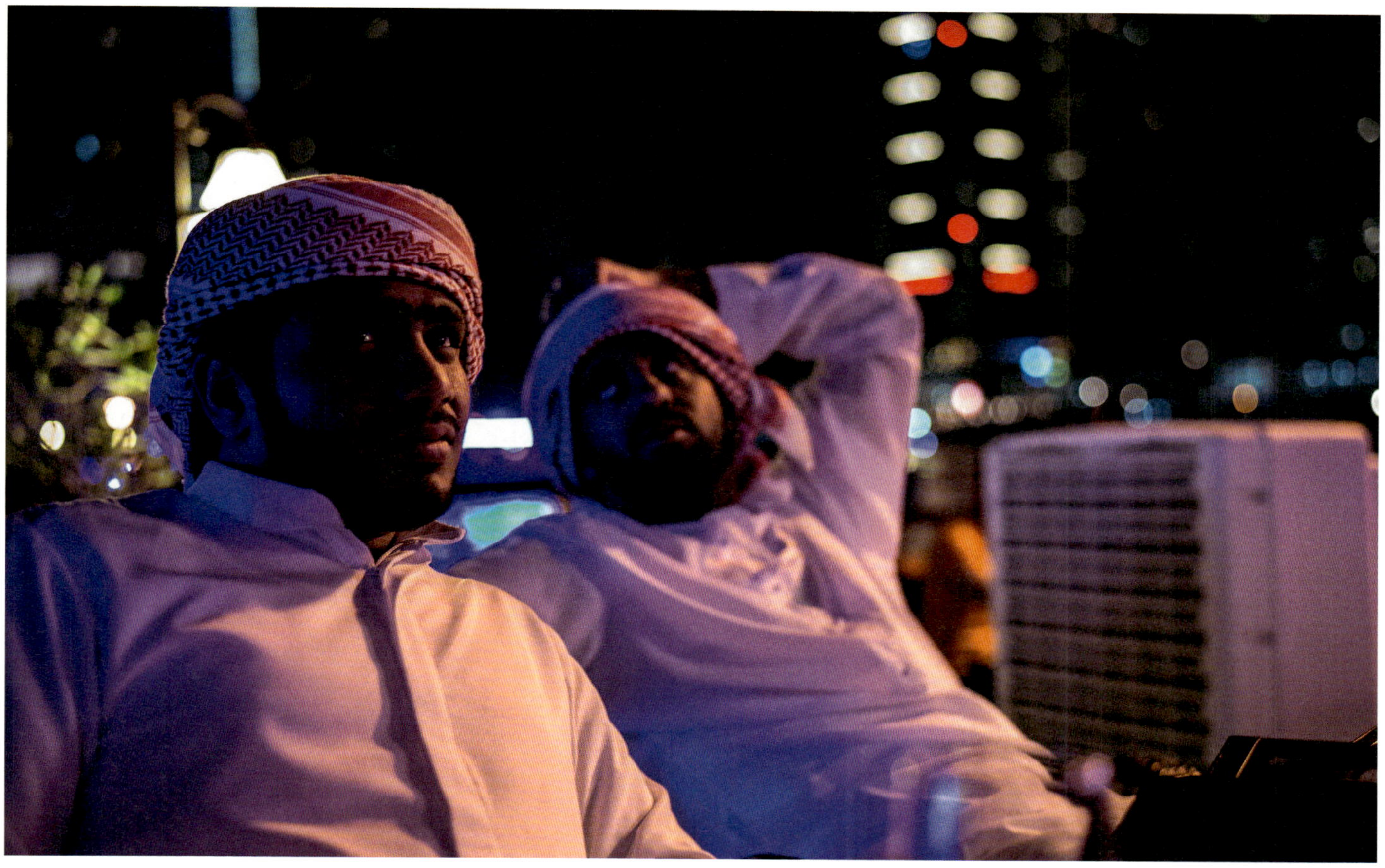

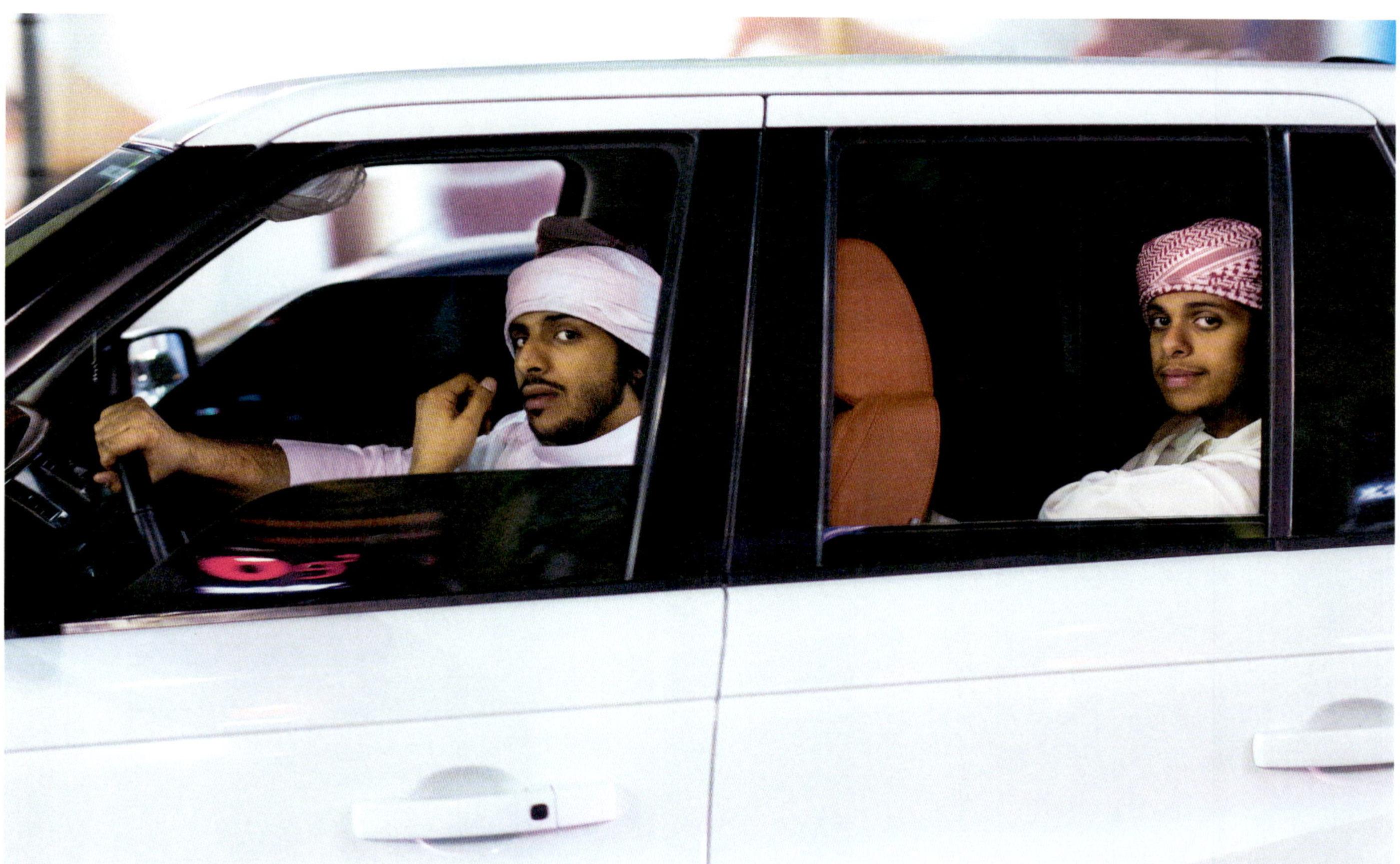

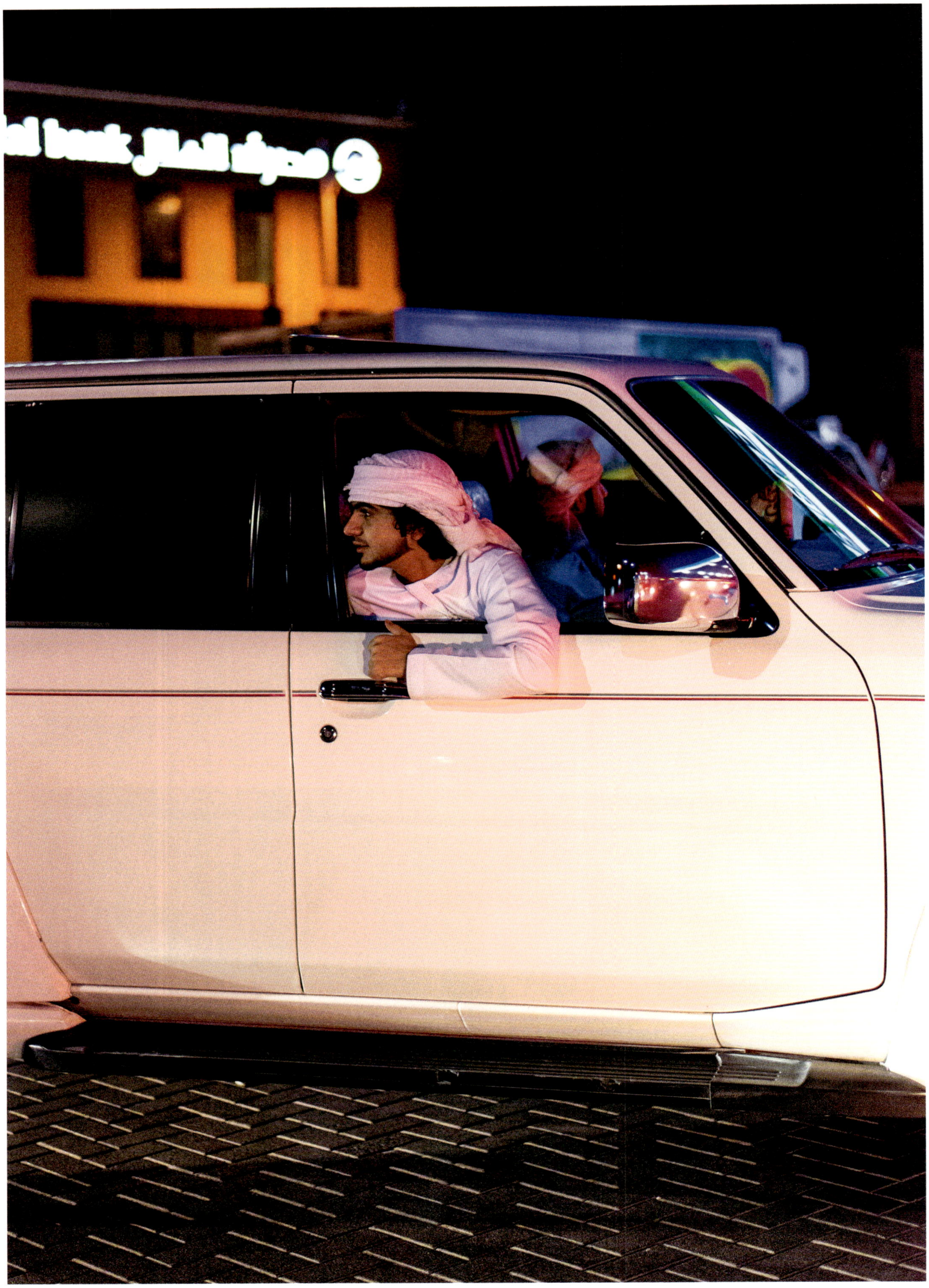
al bank مصرف الهلال

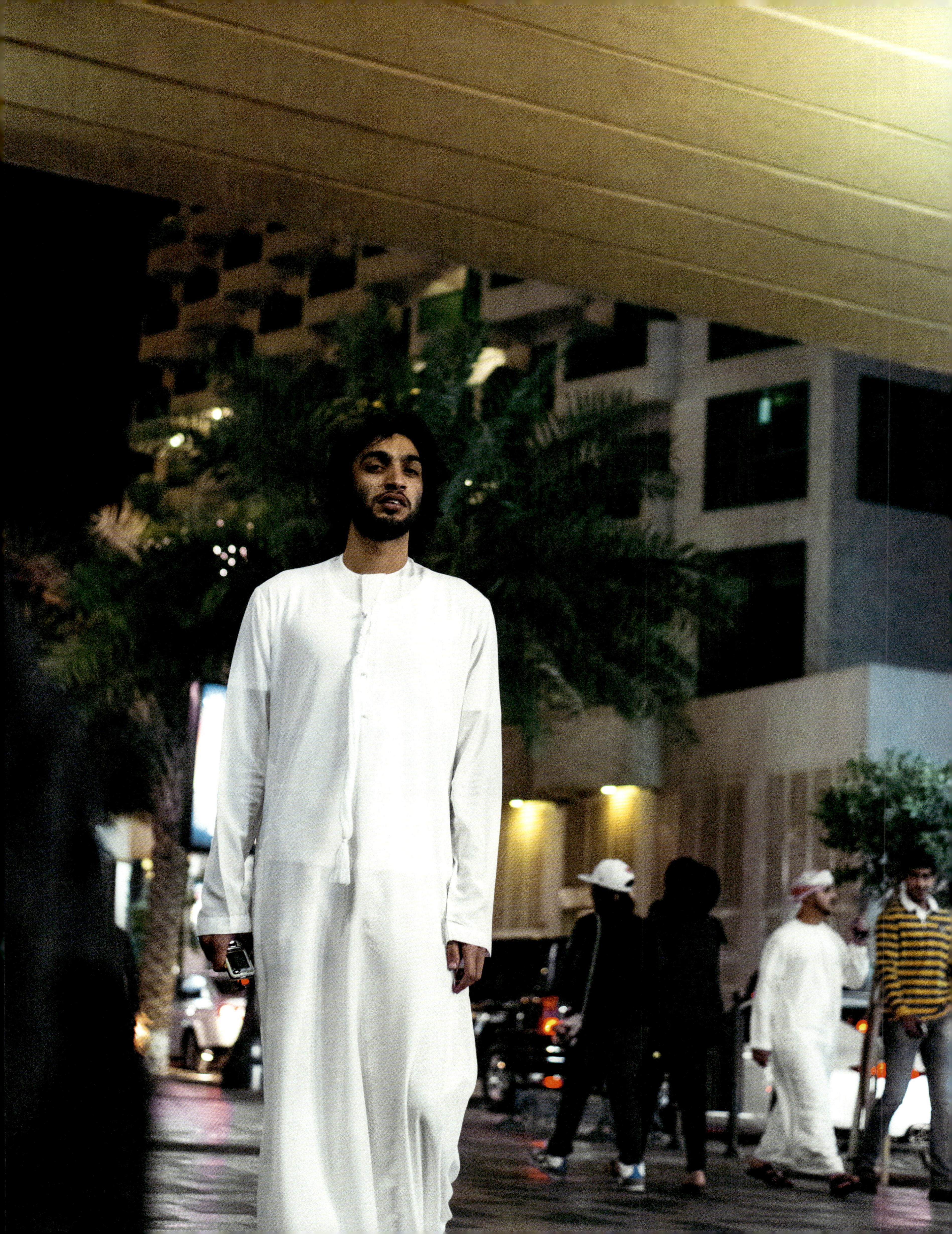

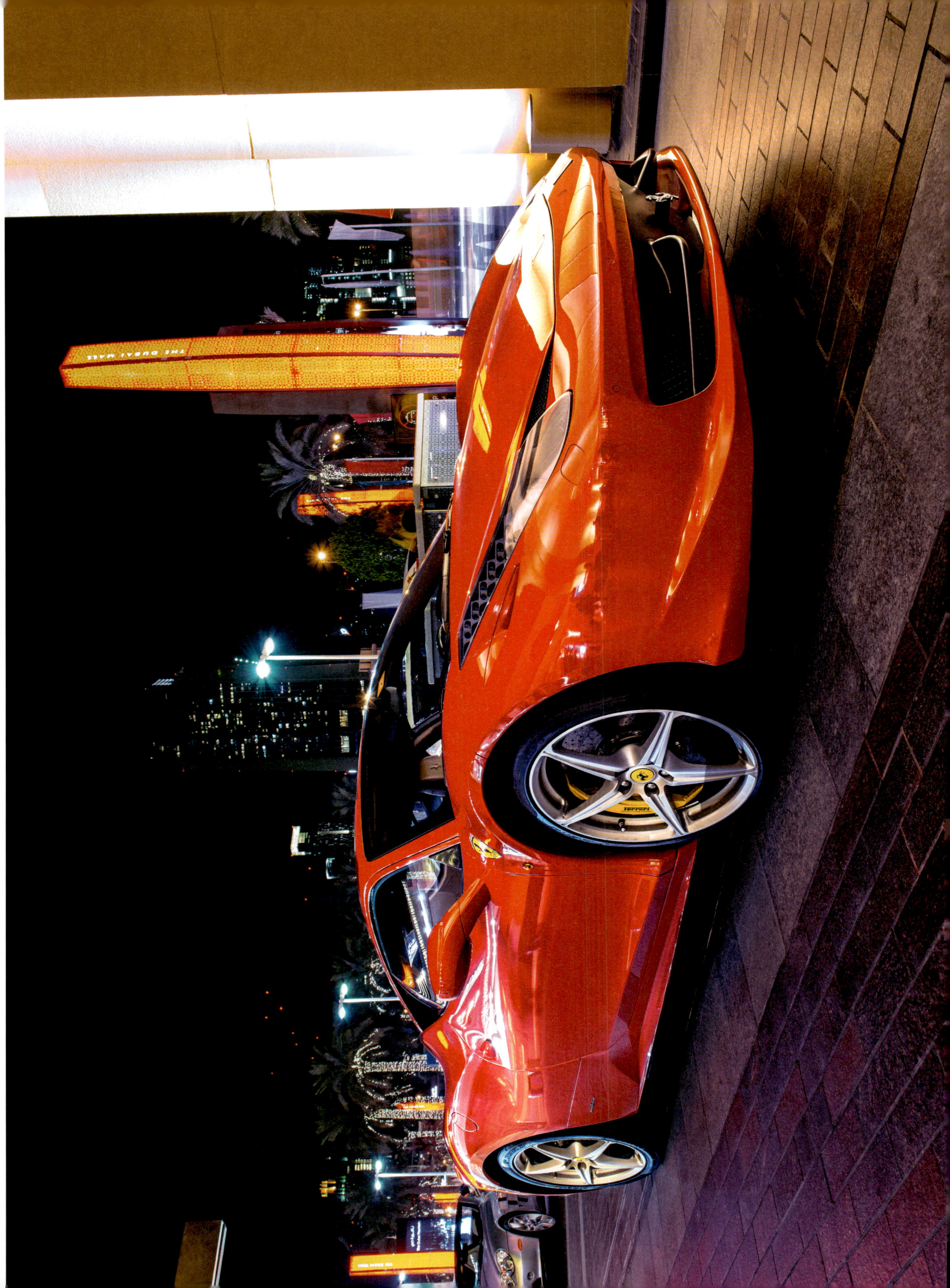
THE DUBAI MALL

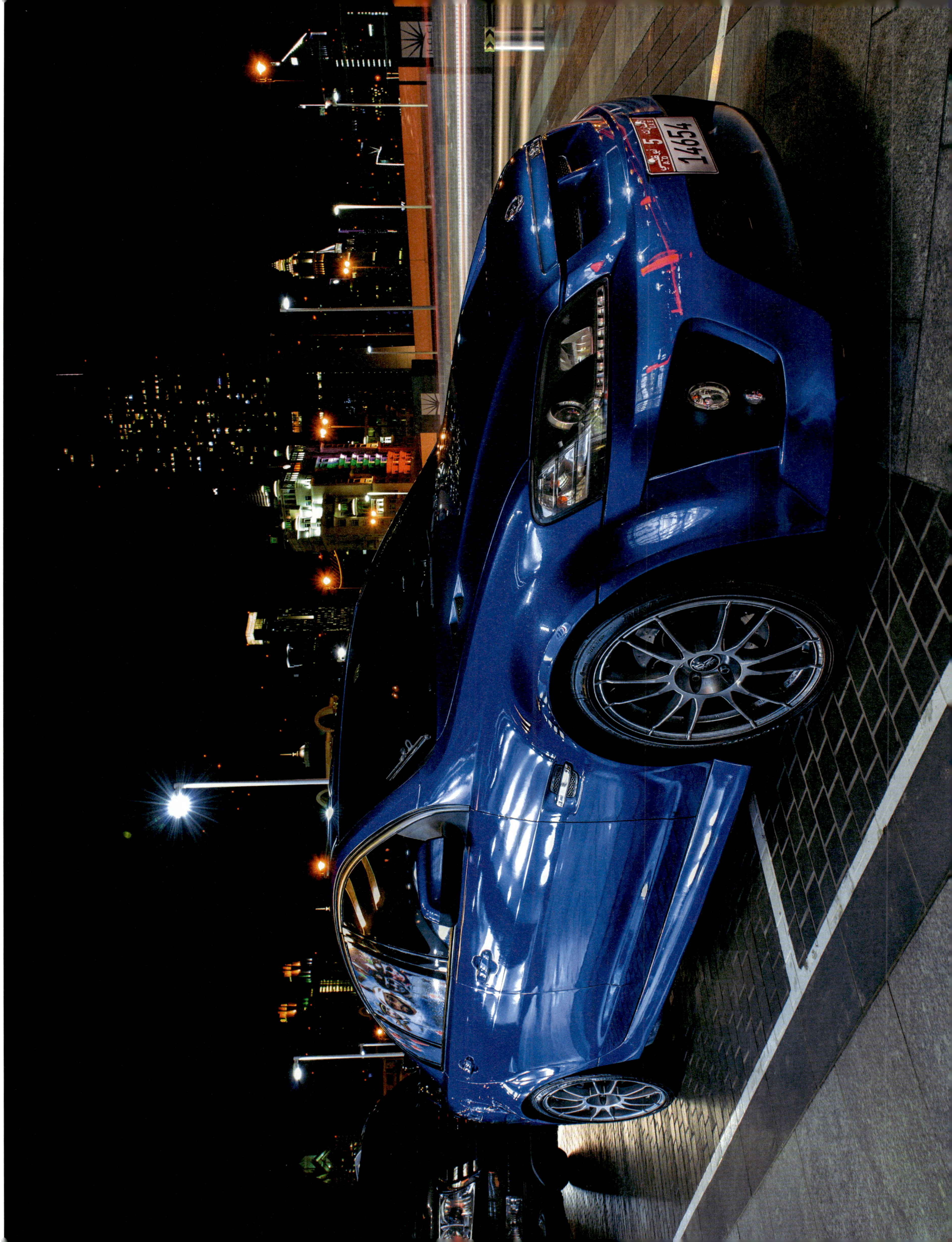
14654

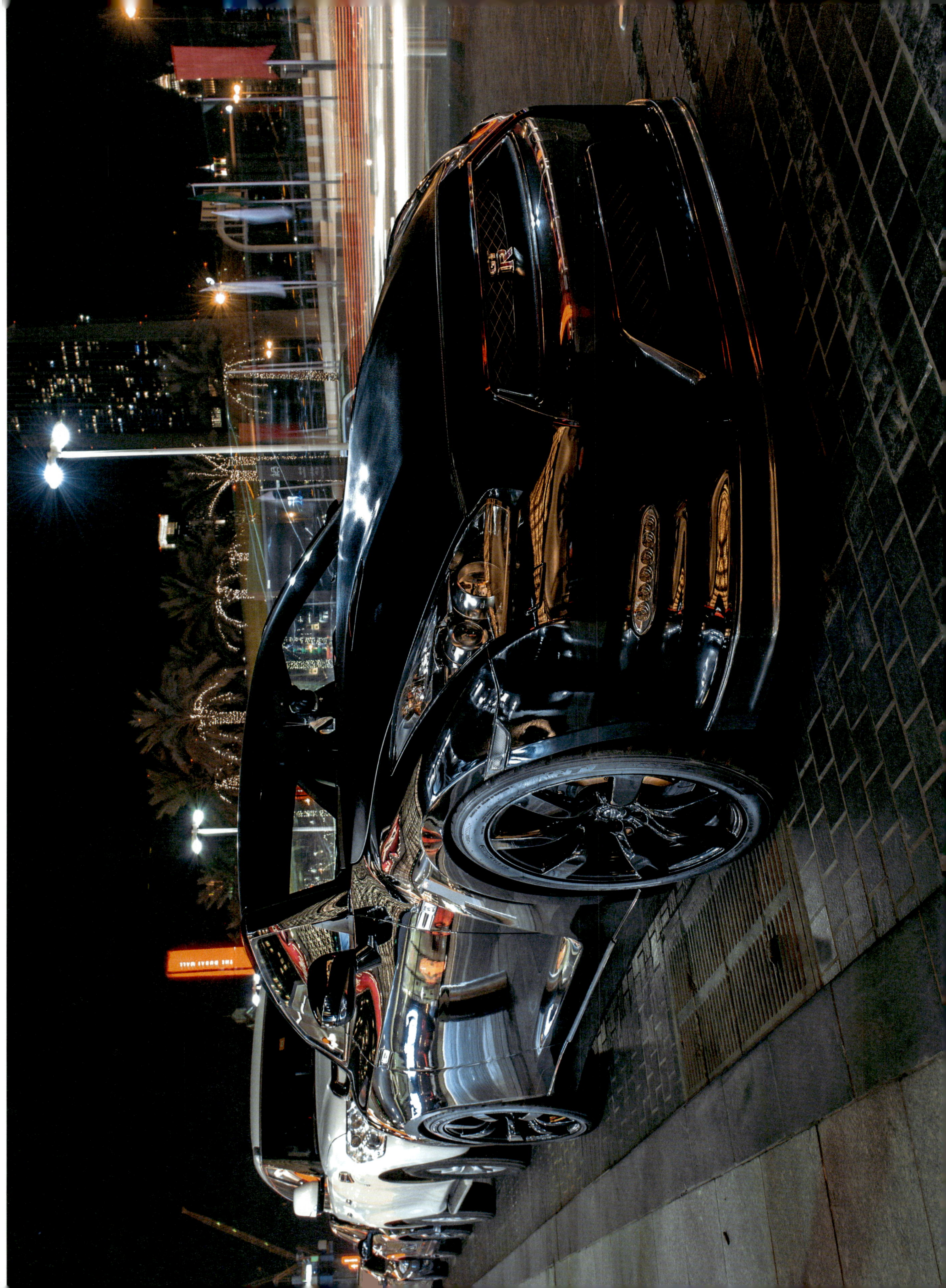

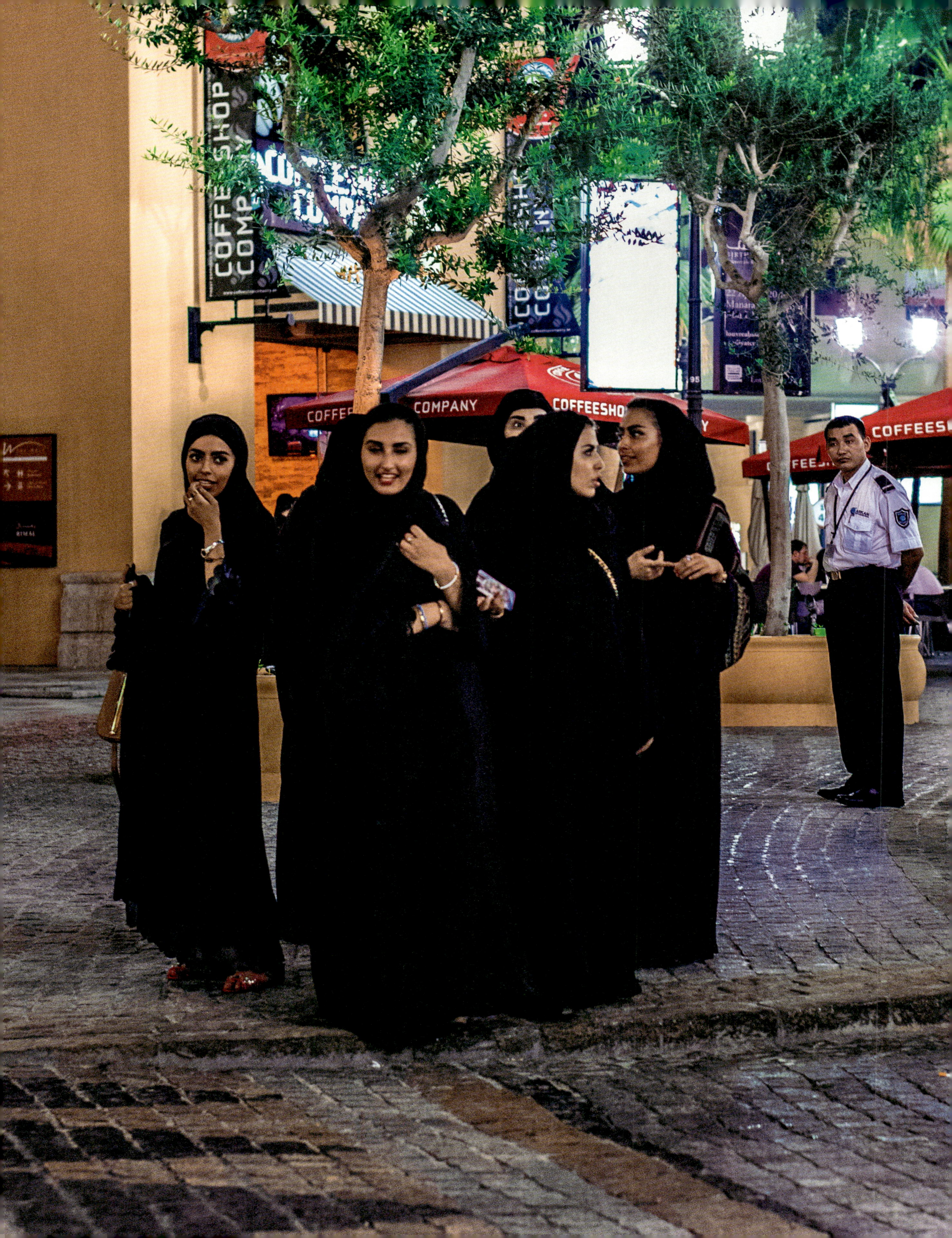

COFFEESHOP COMPANY
COMPANY
COFFEESHOP
COFFEESH

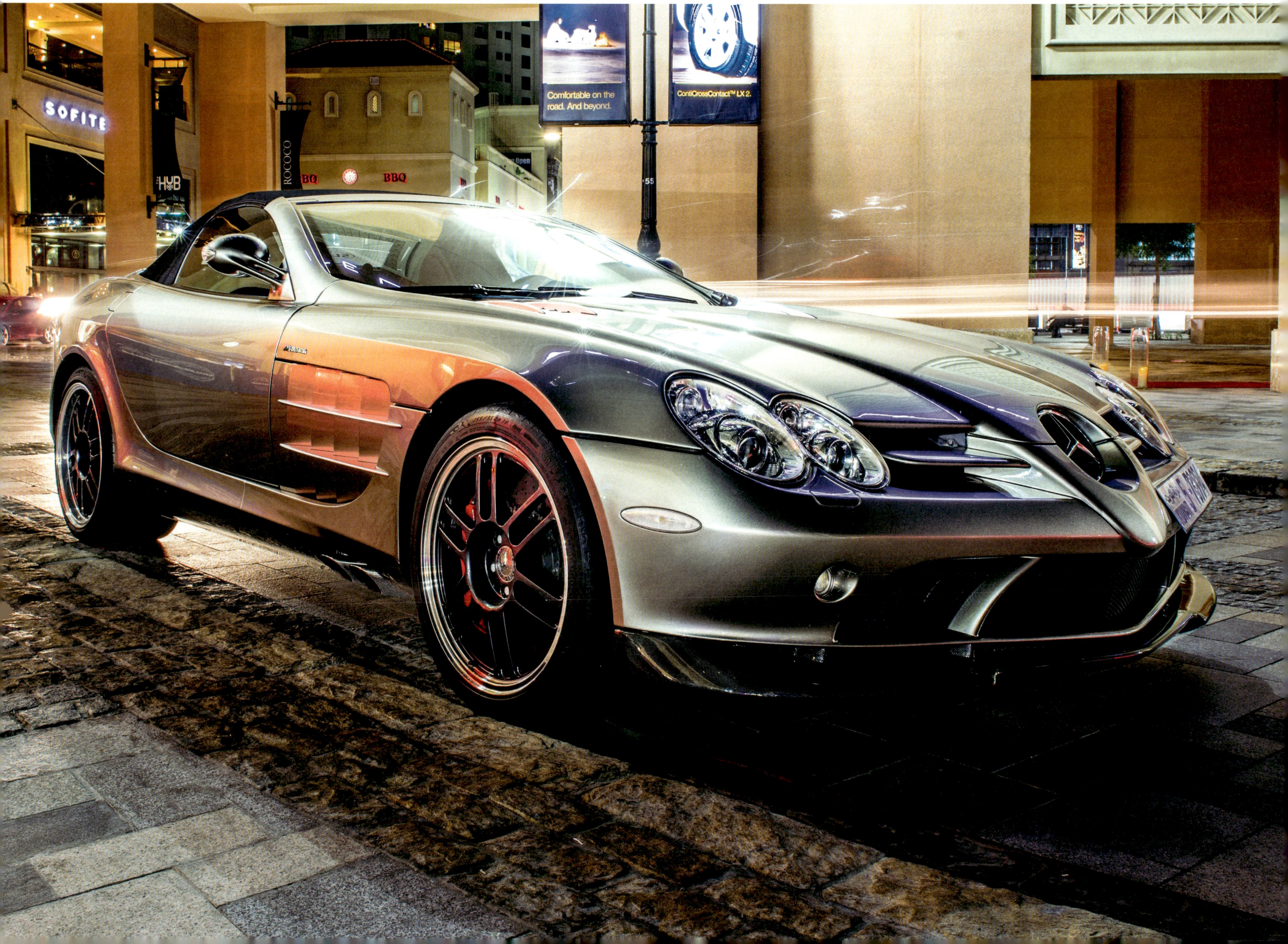
SOFITE
HUB
ROCOCO
BBQ
BBQ
Comfortable on the road. And beyond.
ContiCrossContact™ LX 2.

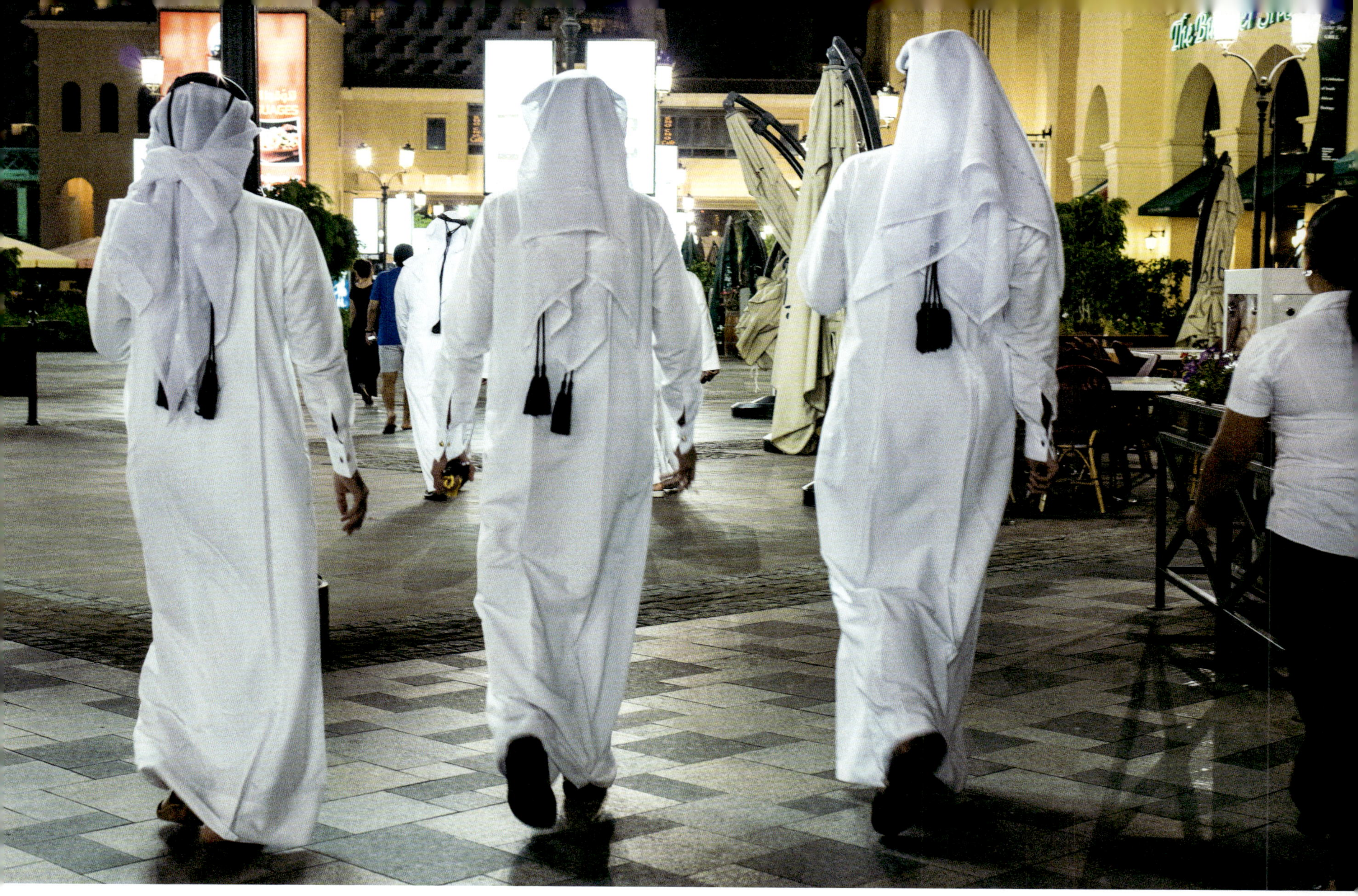

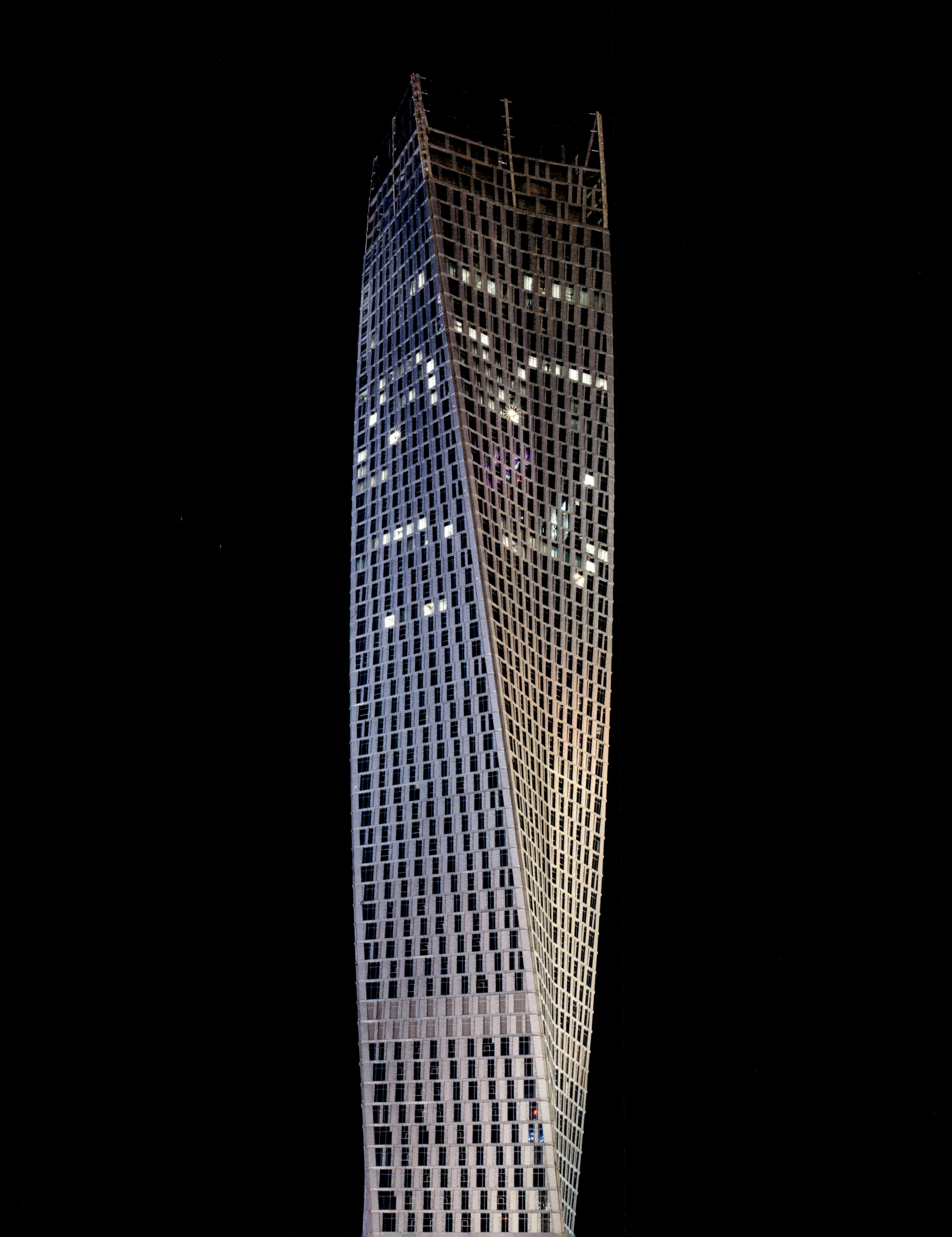

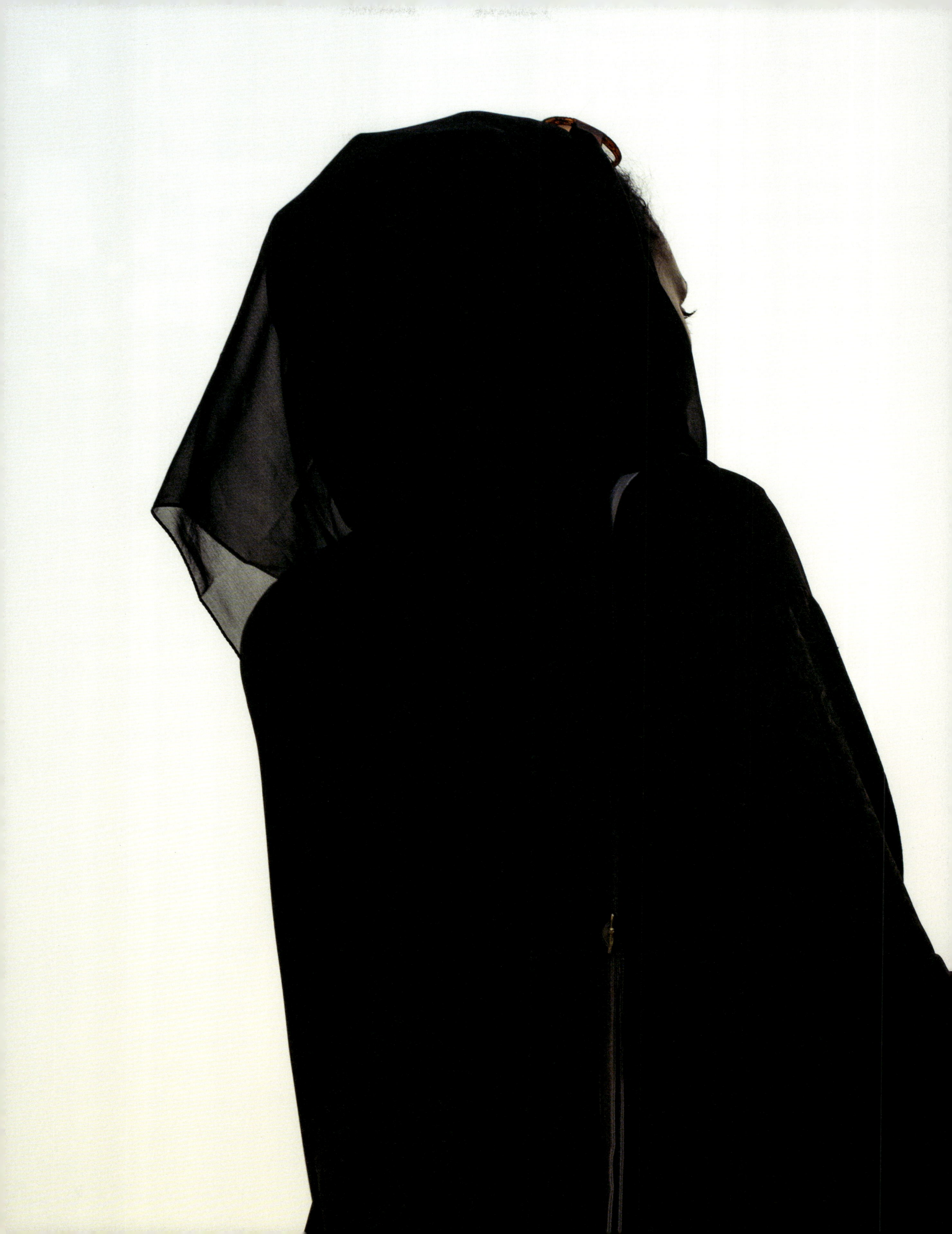

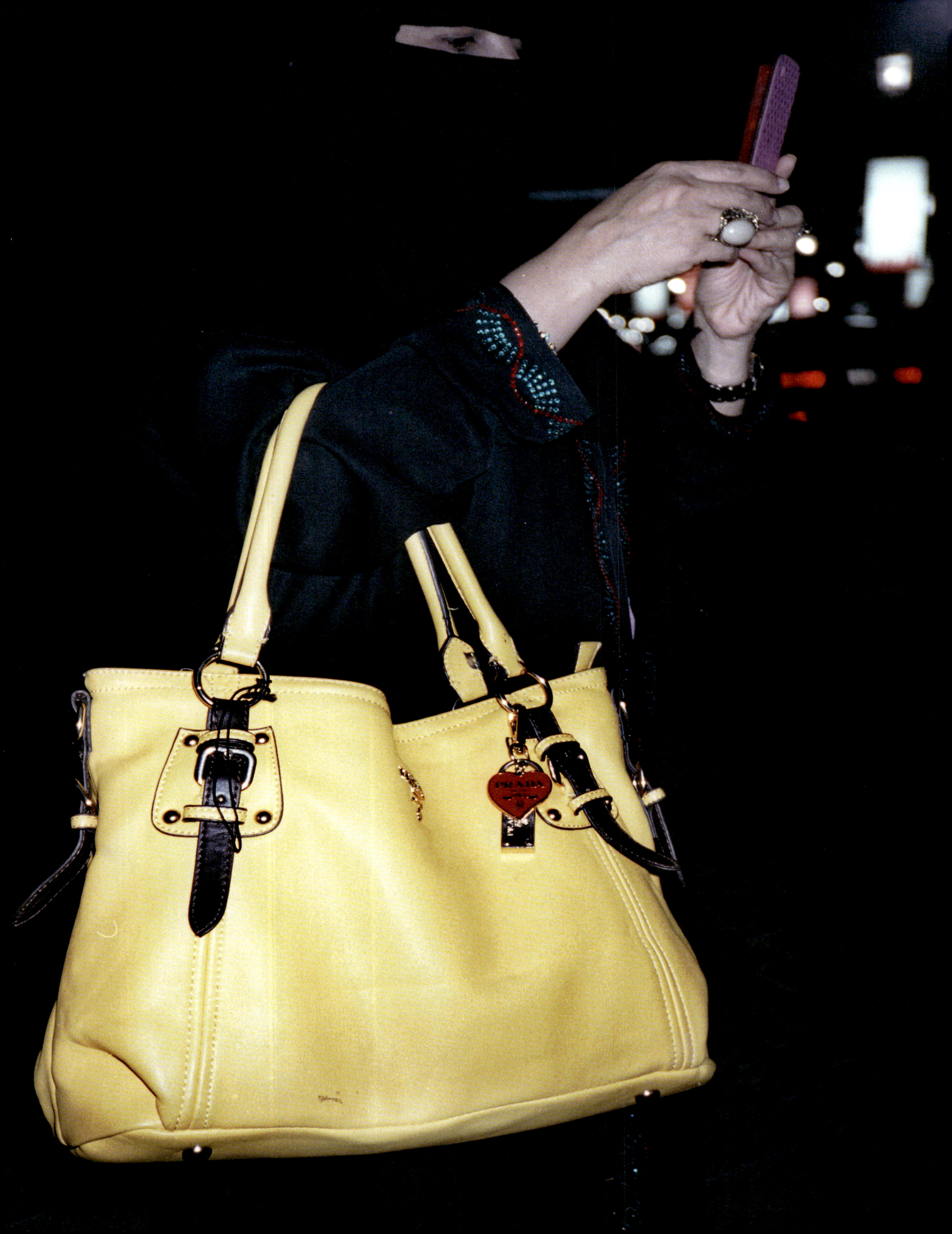
PRADA

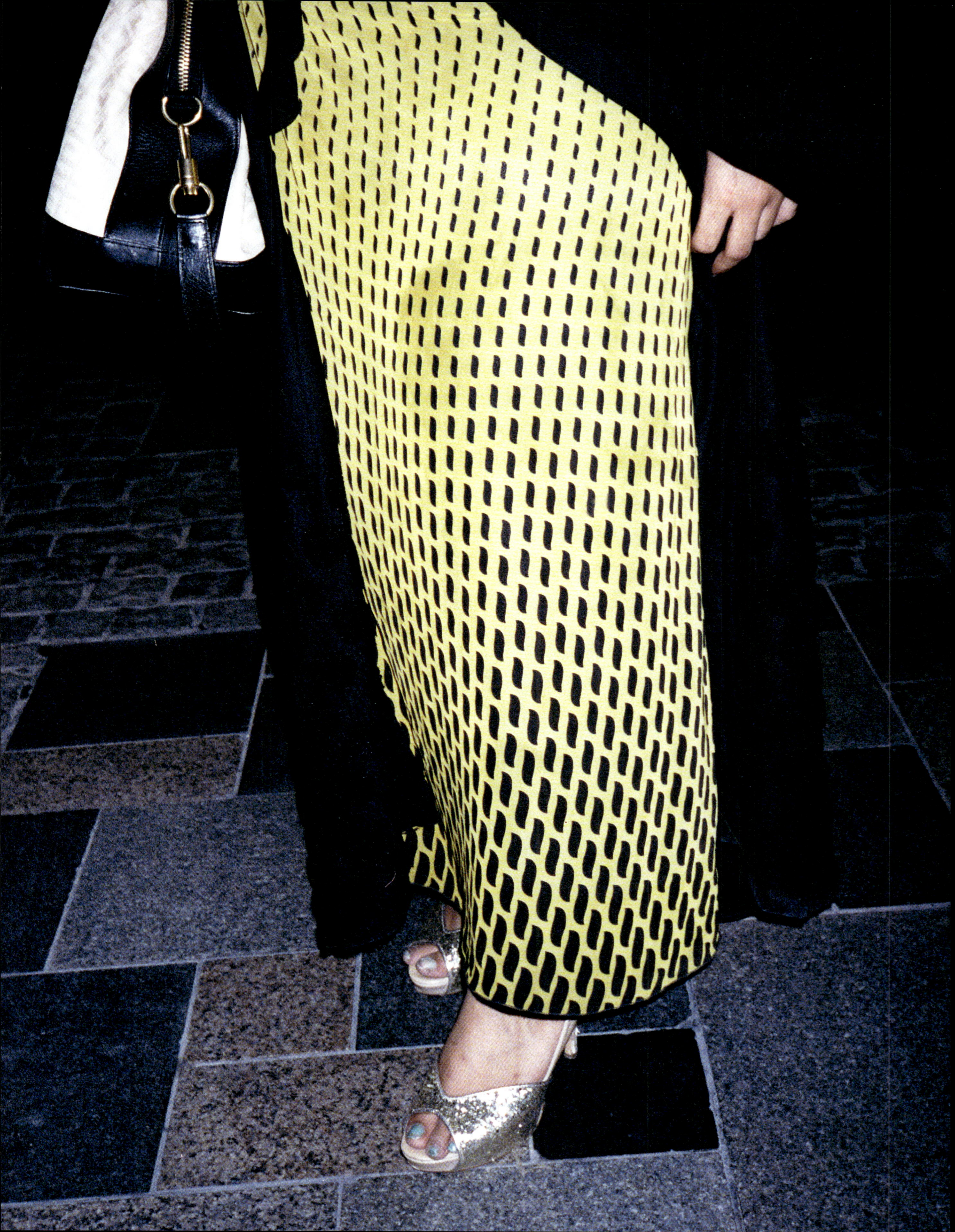

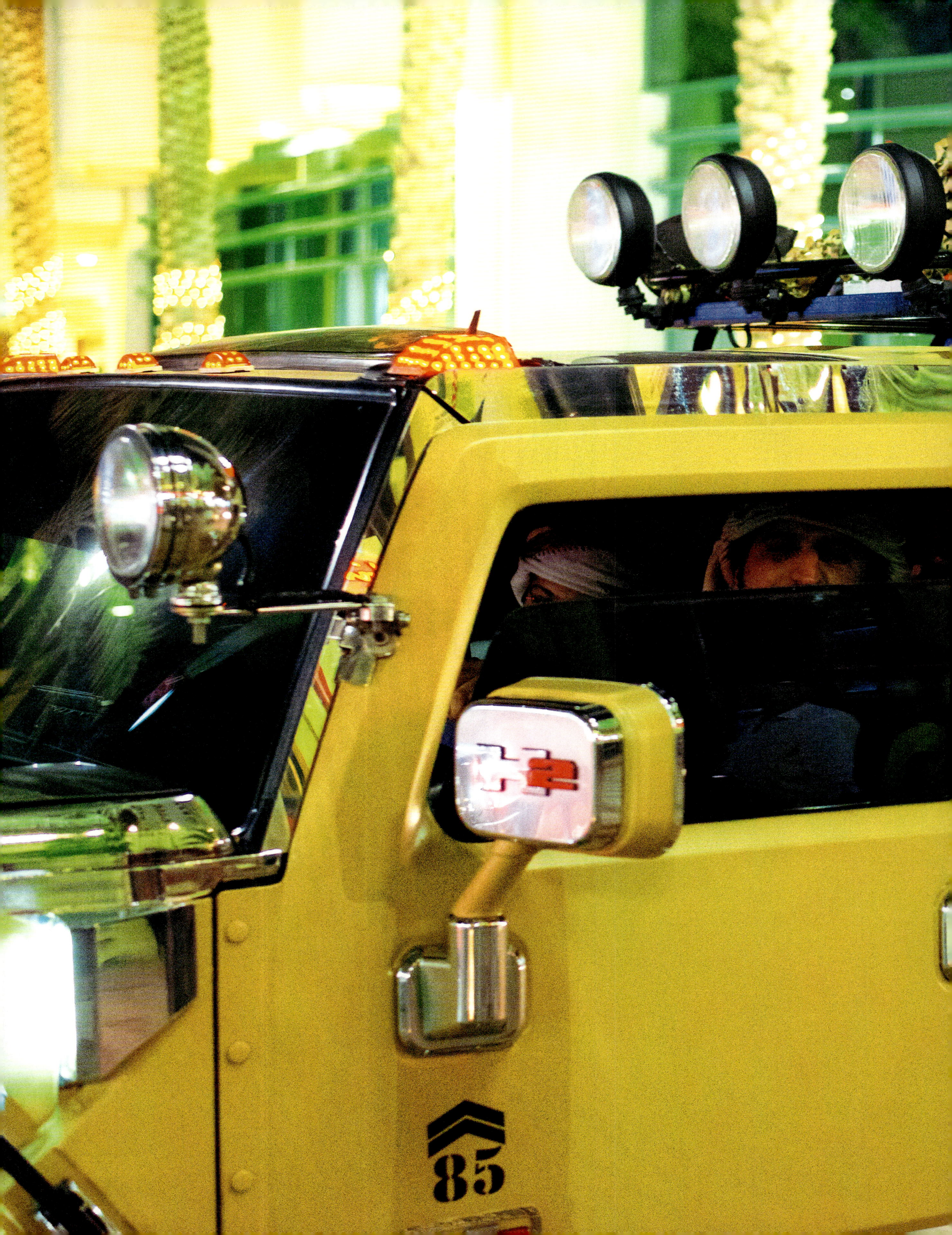
85

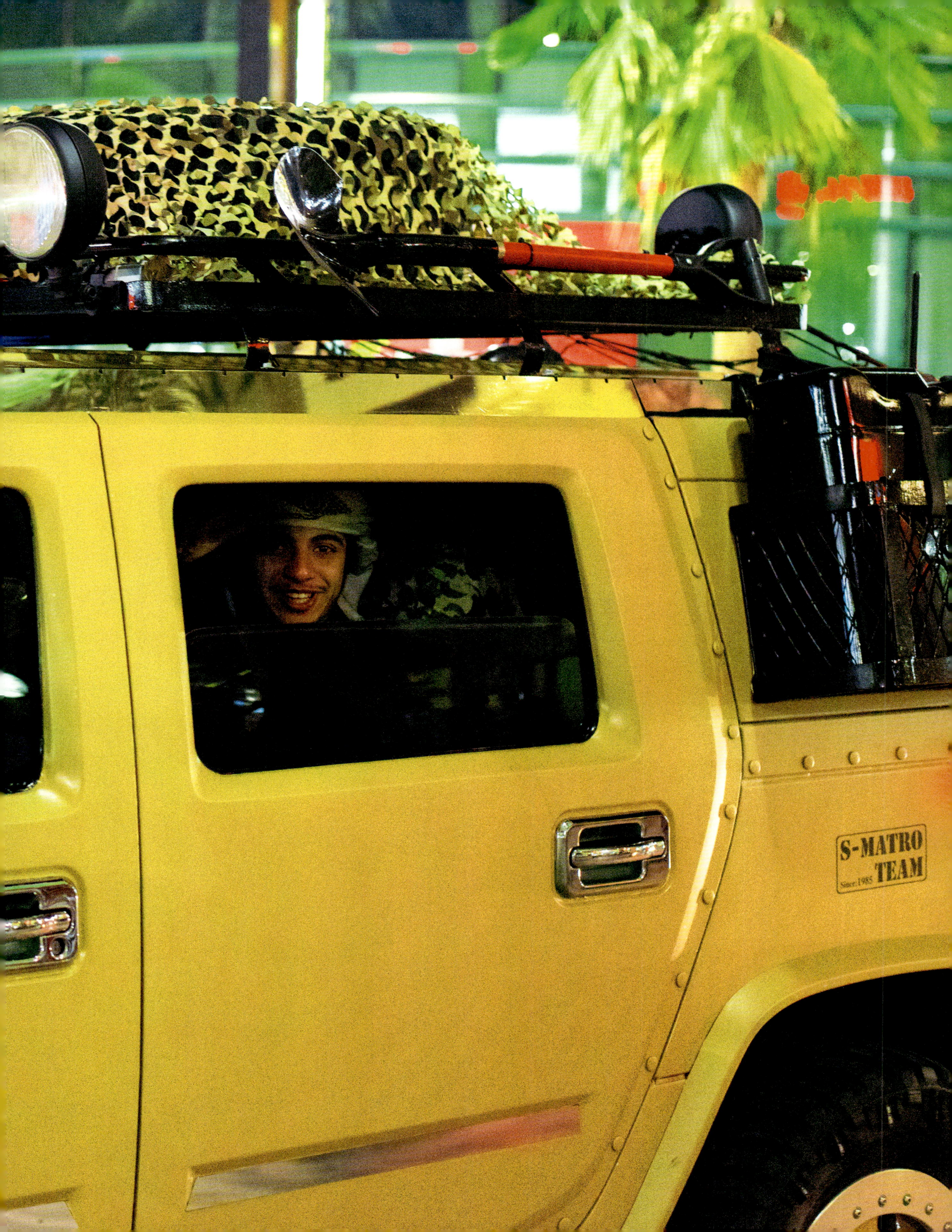
S-MATRO
TEAM
Since 1985

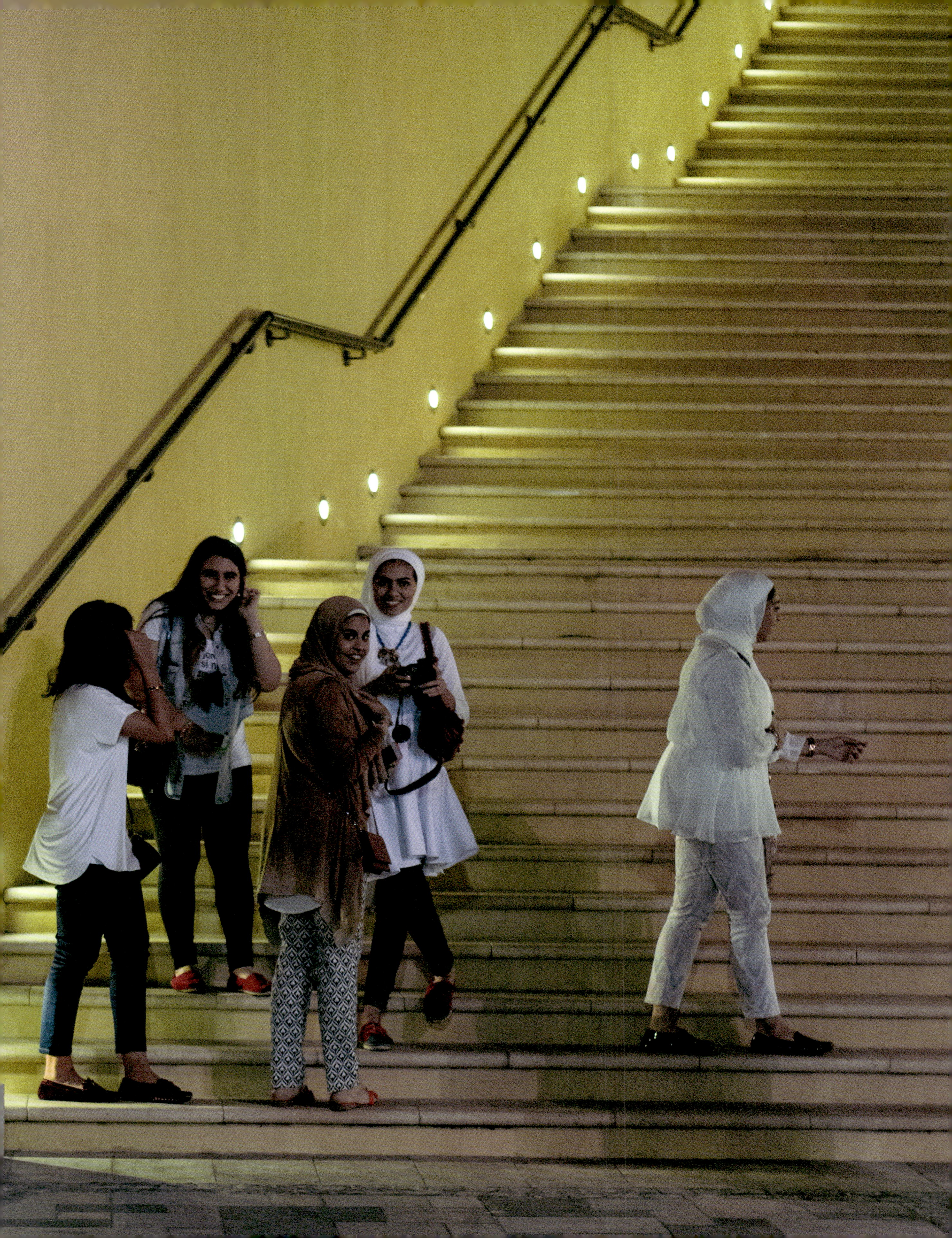

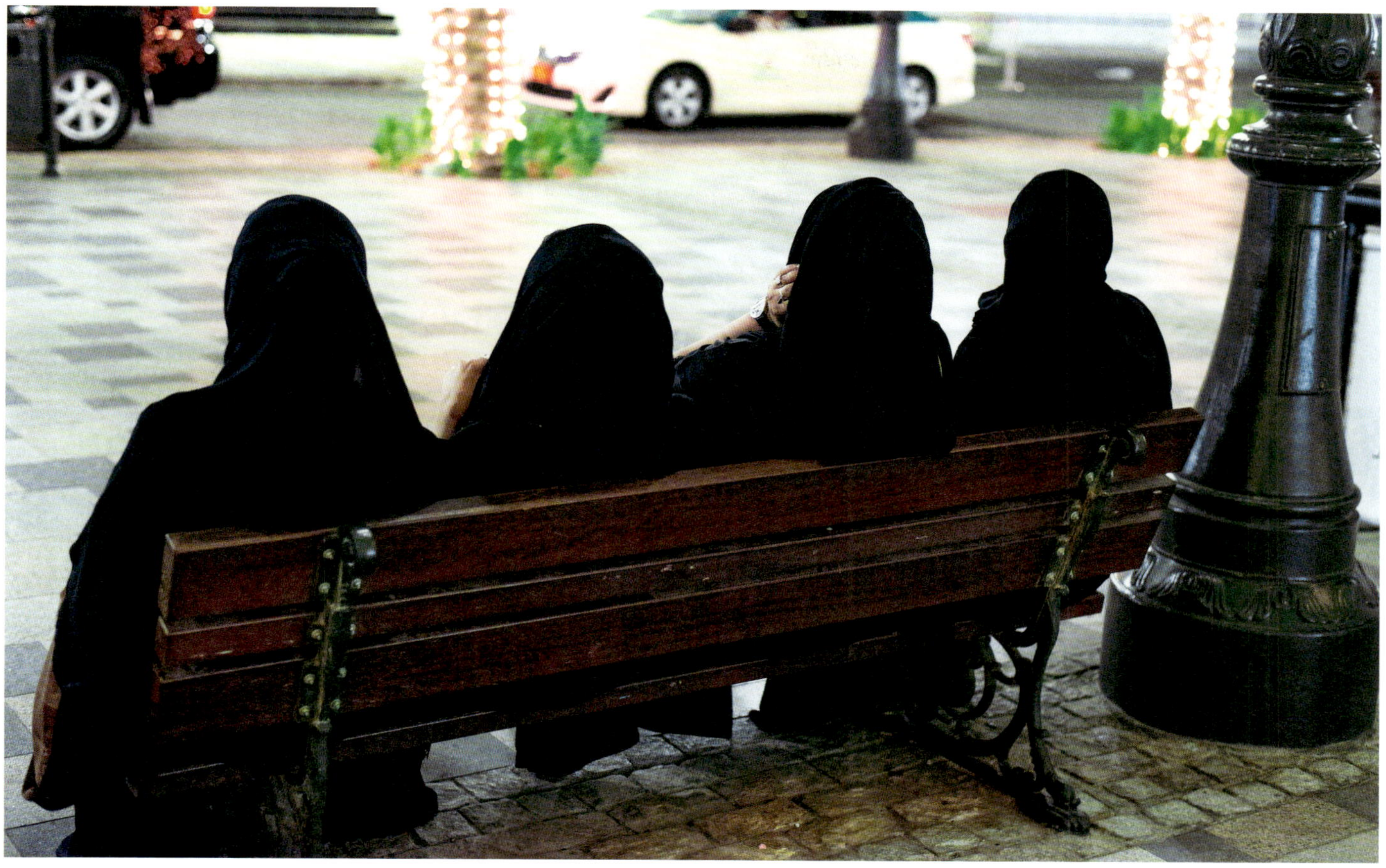

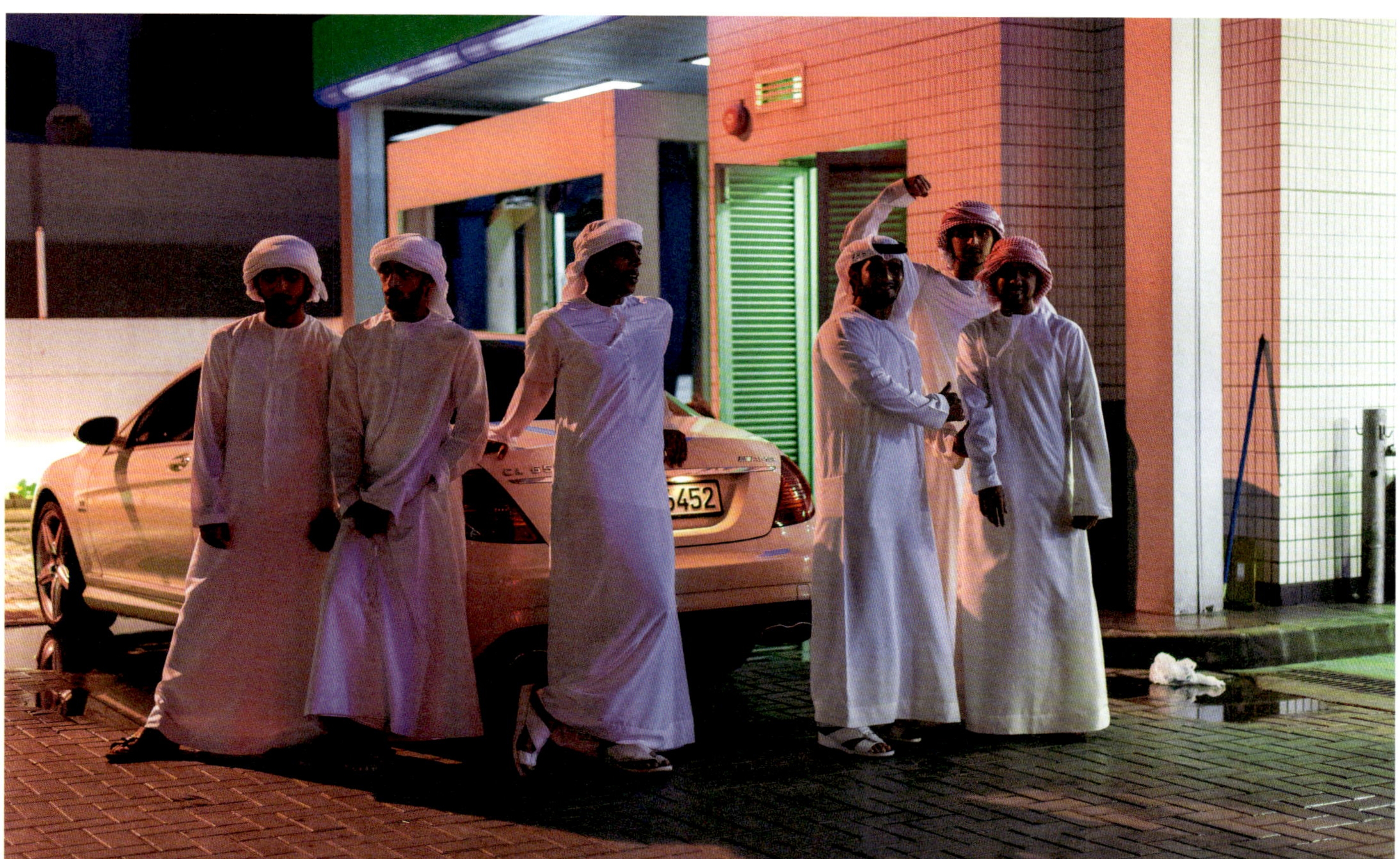

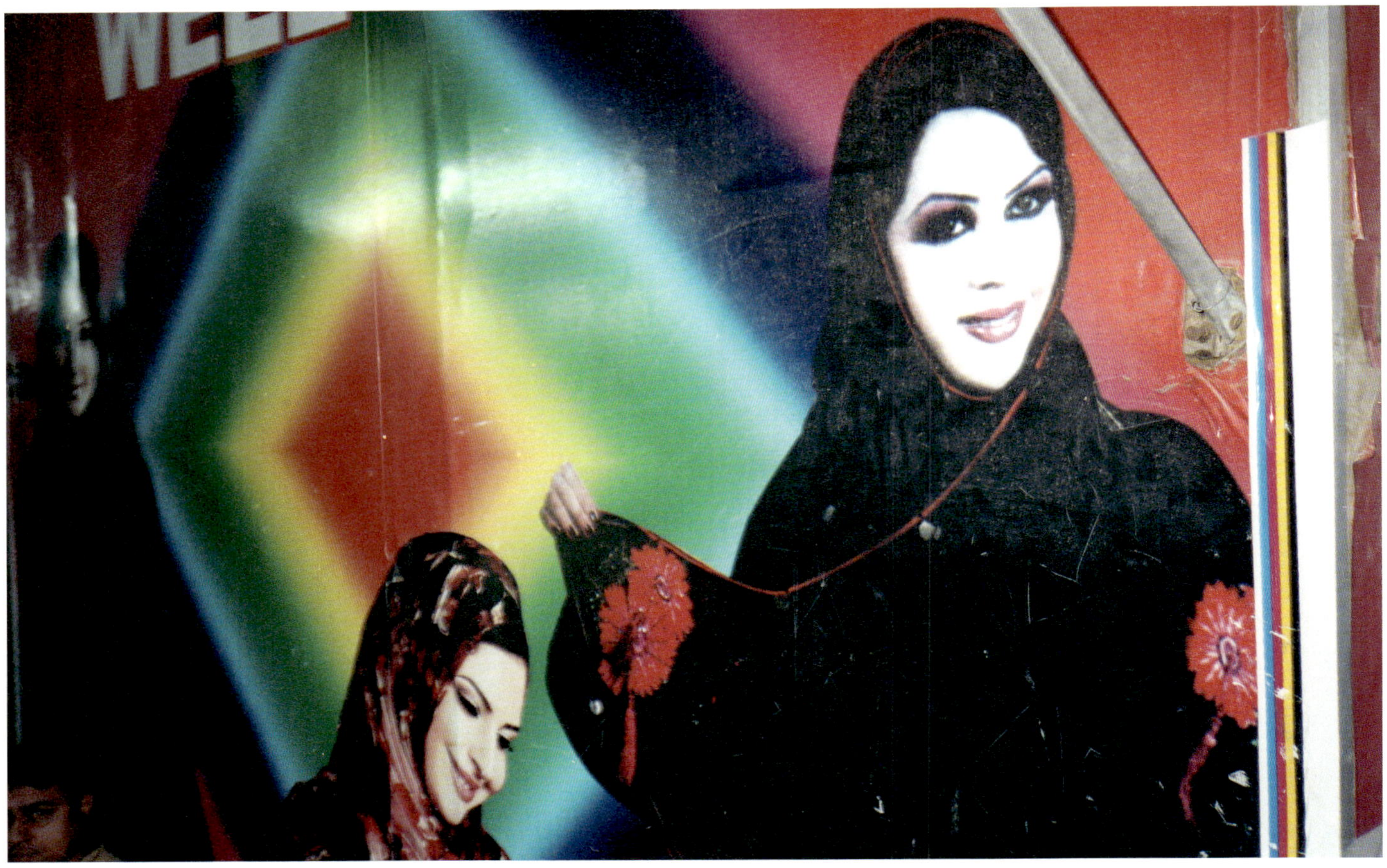

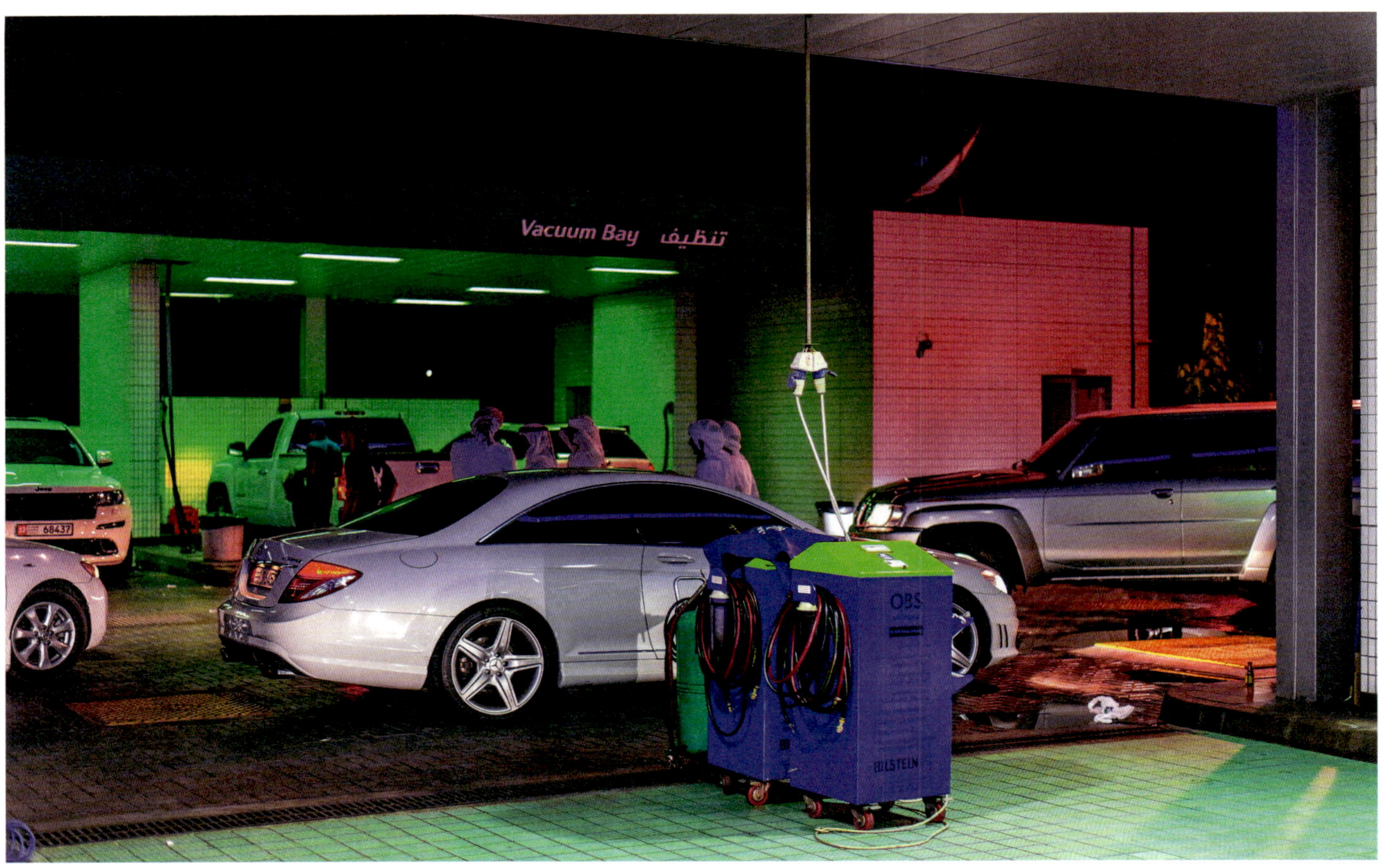
Vacuum Bay تنظيف

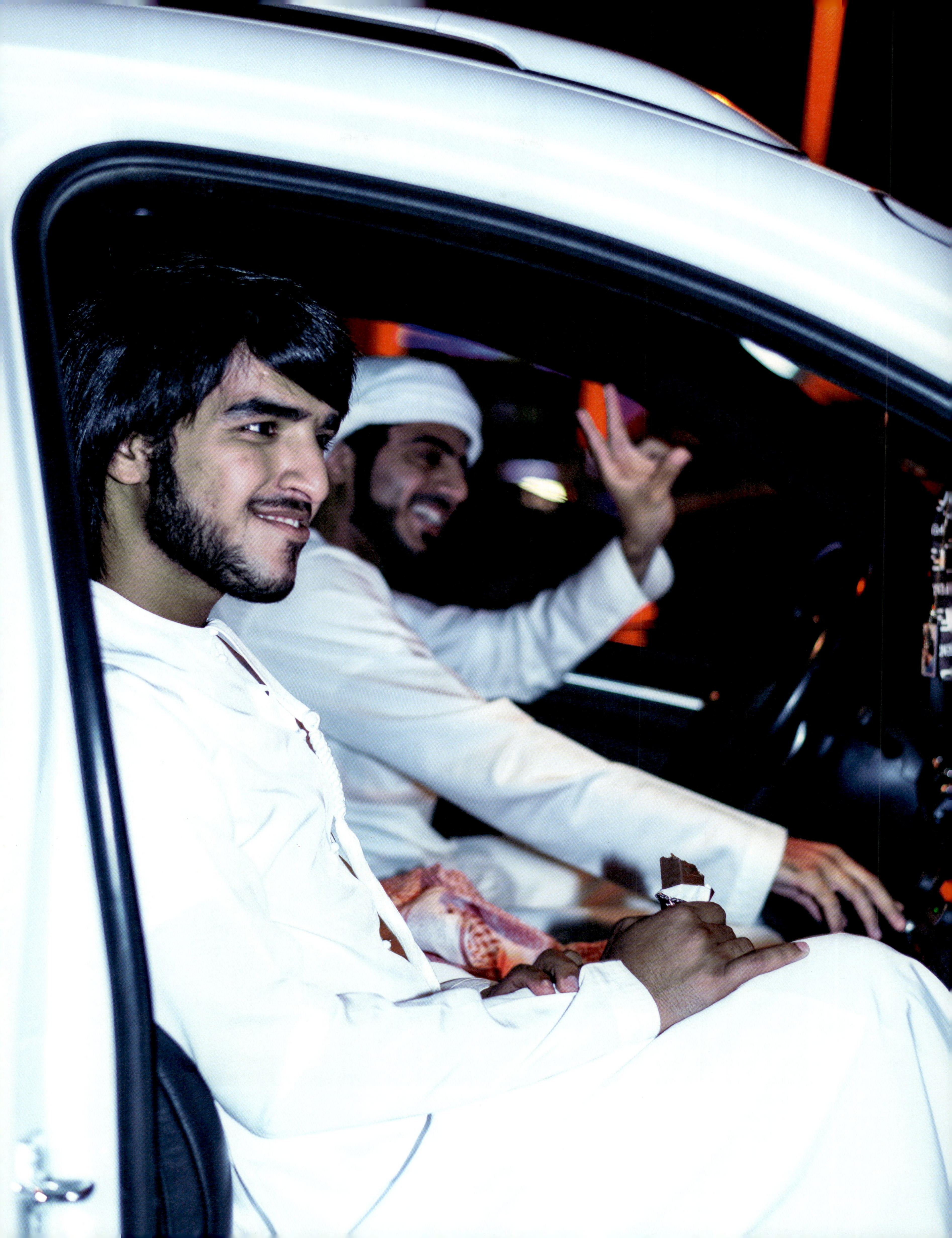

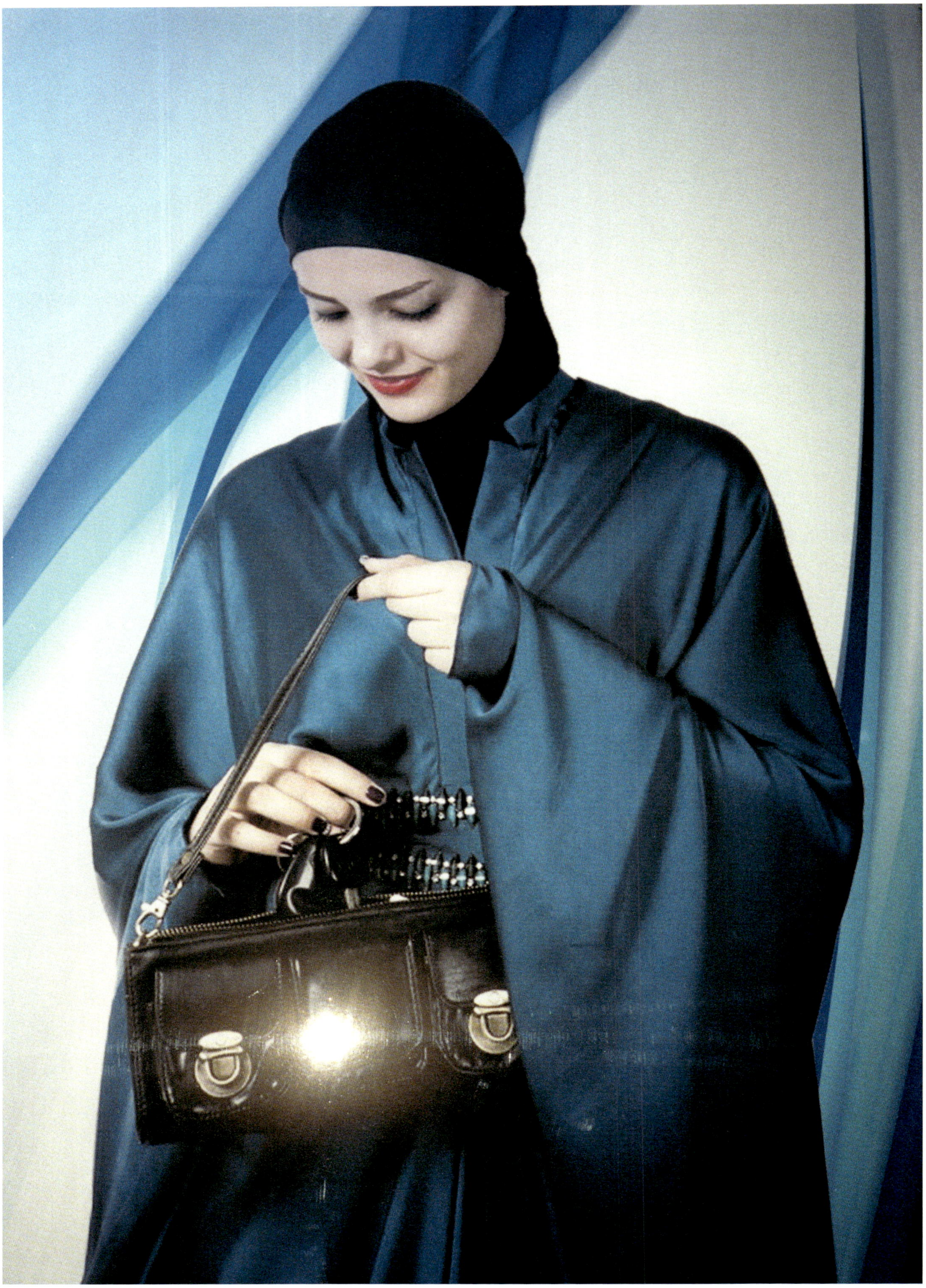

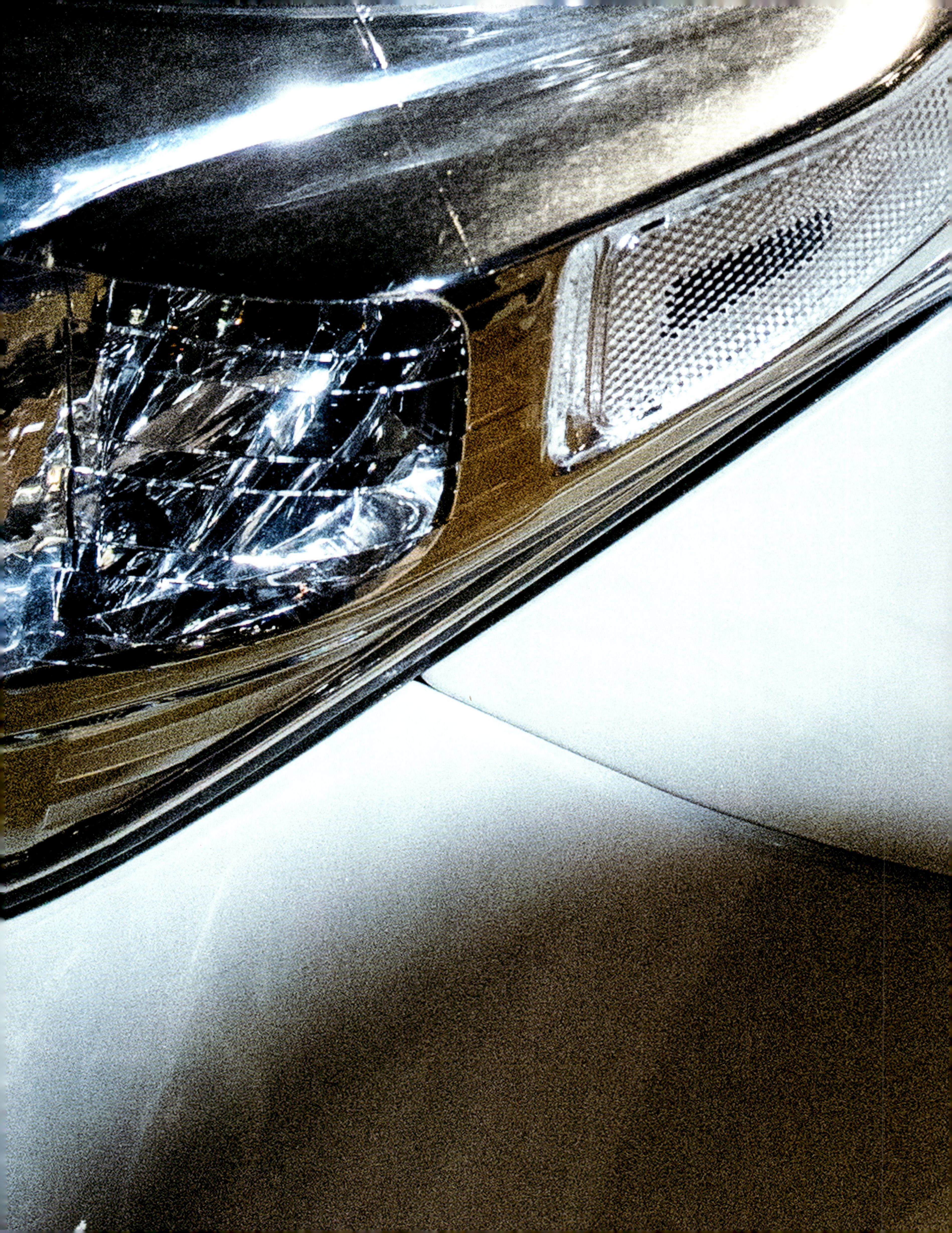

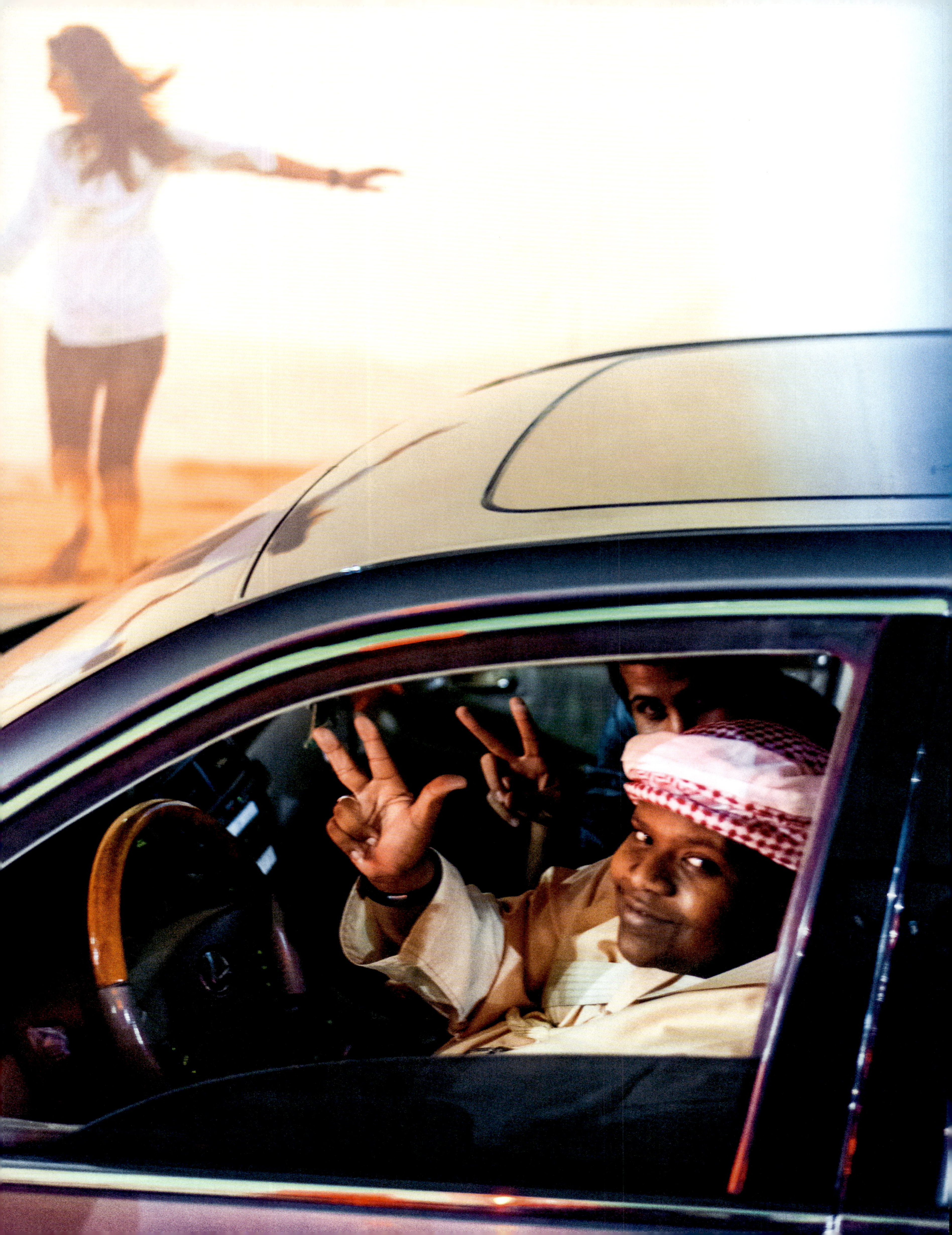

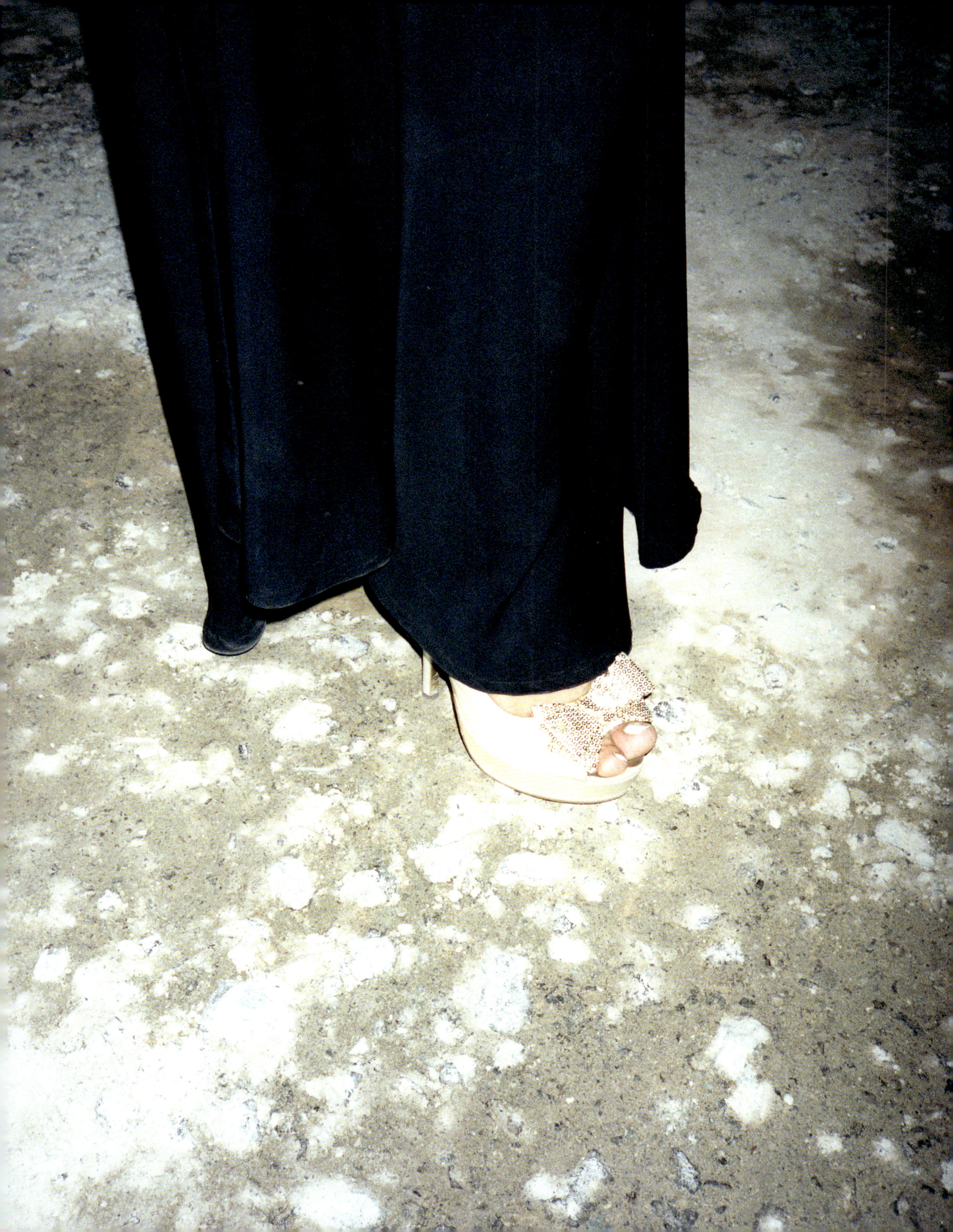

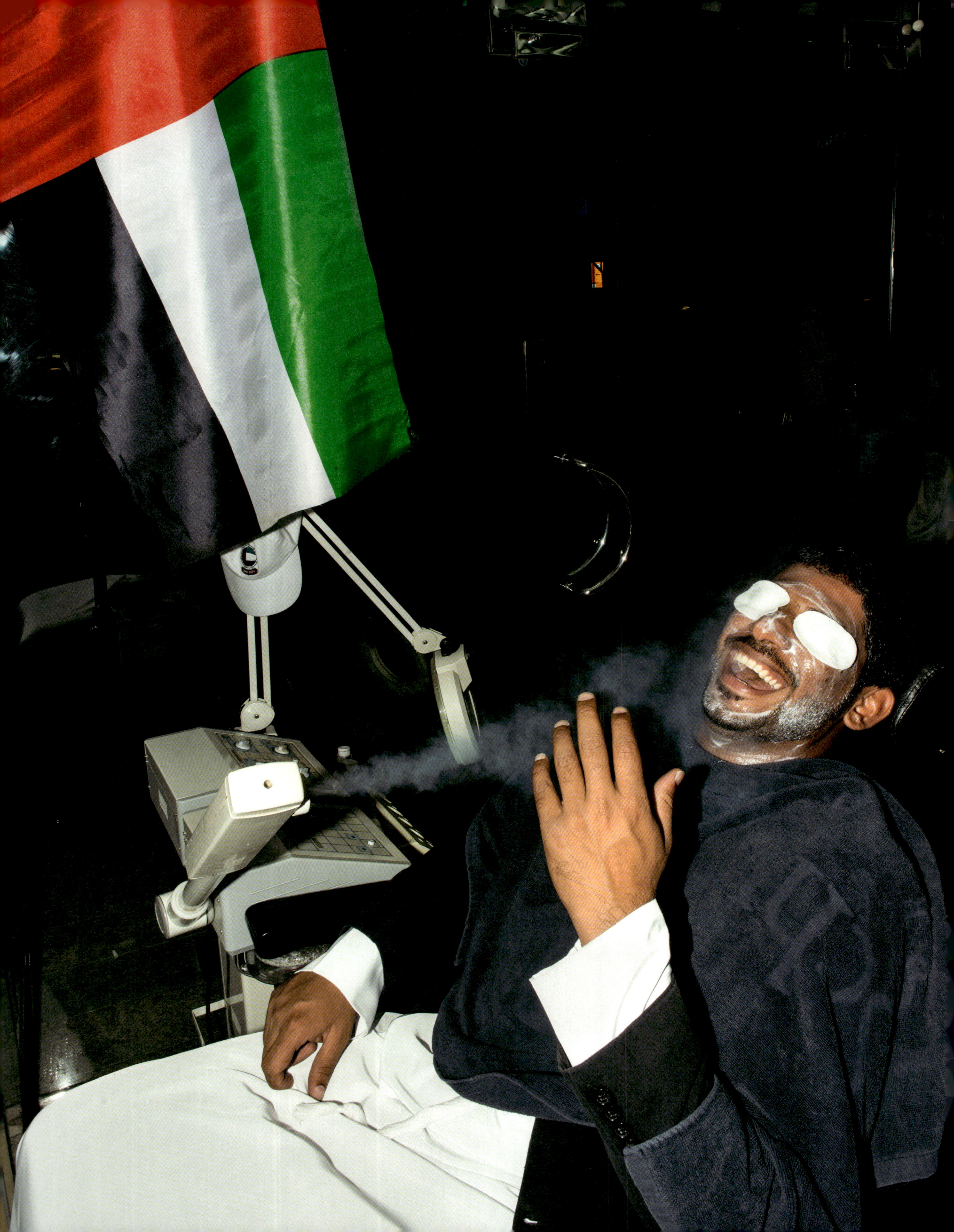

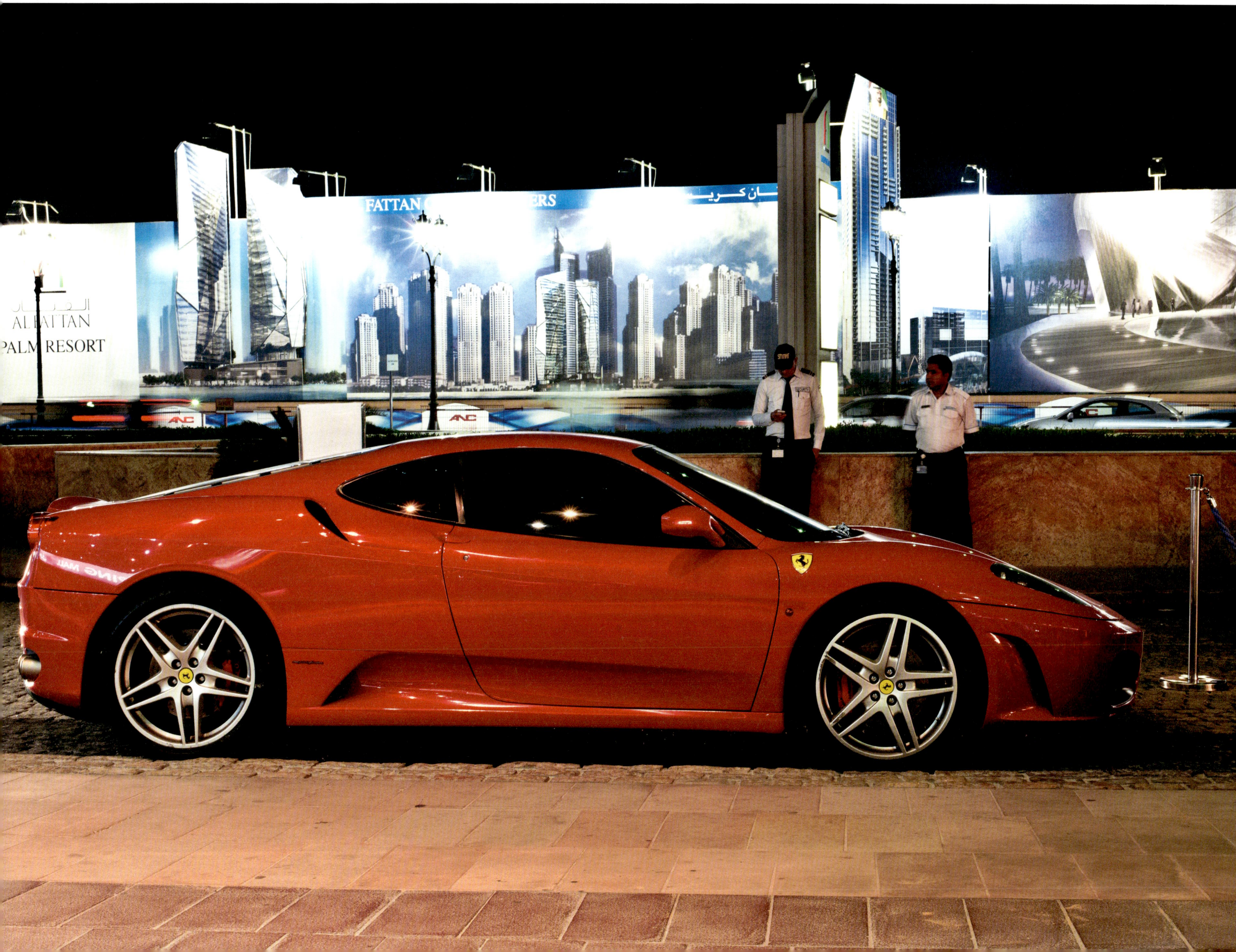
AL FATTAN
PALM RESORT
FATTAN
ERS
ANC
ANC

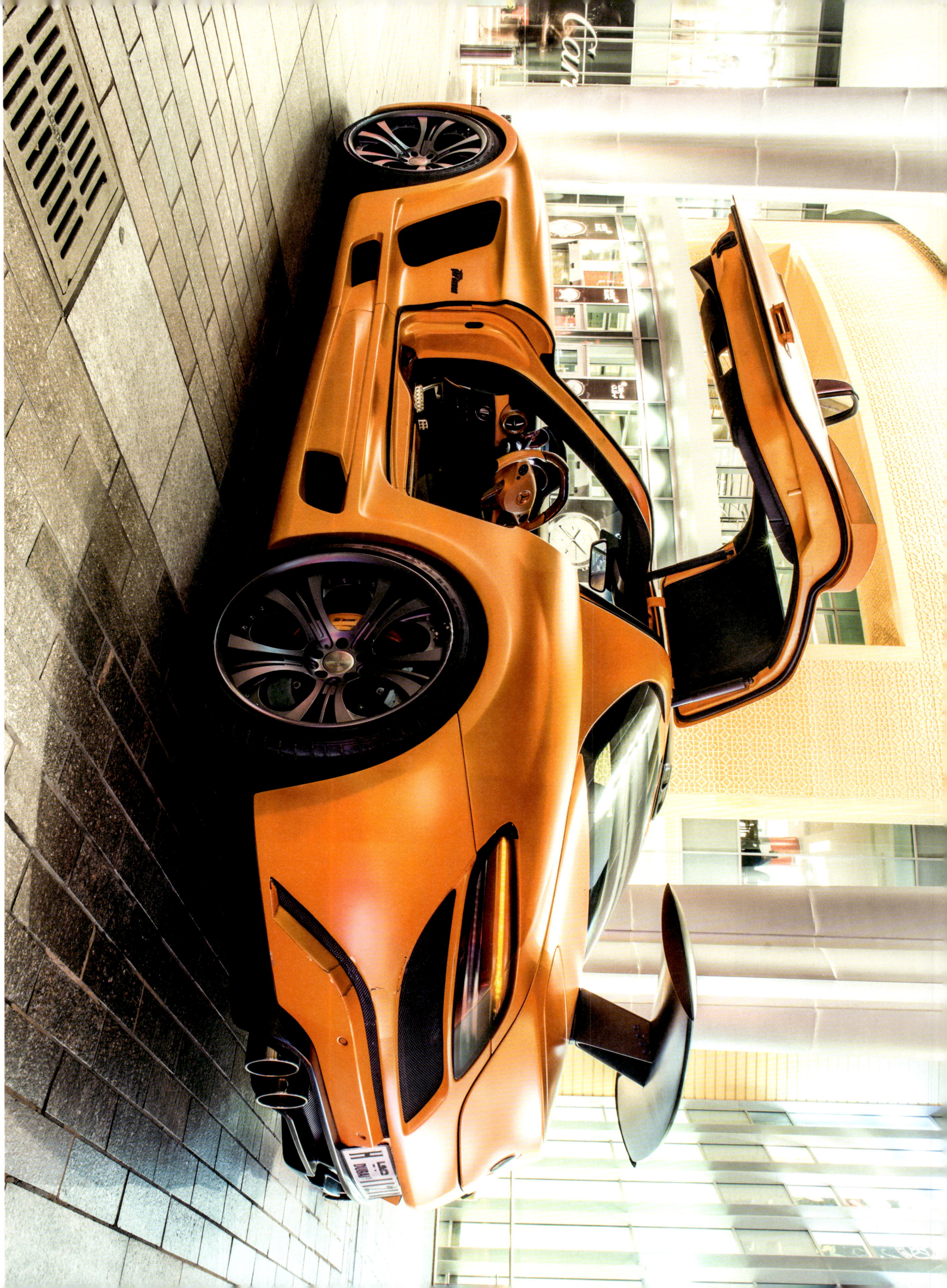

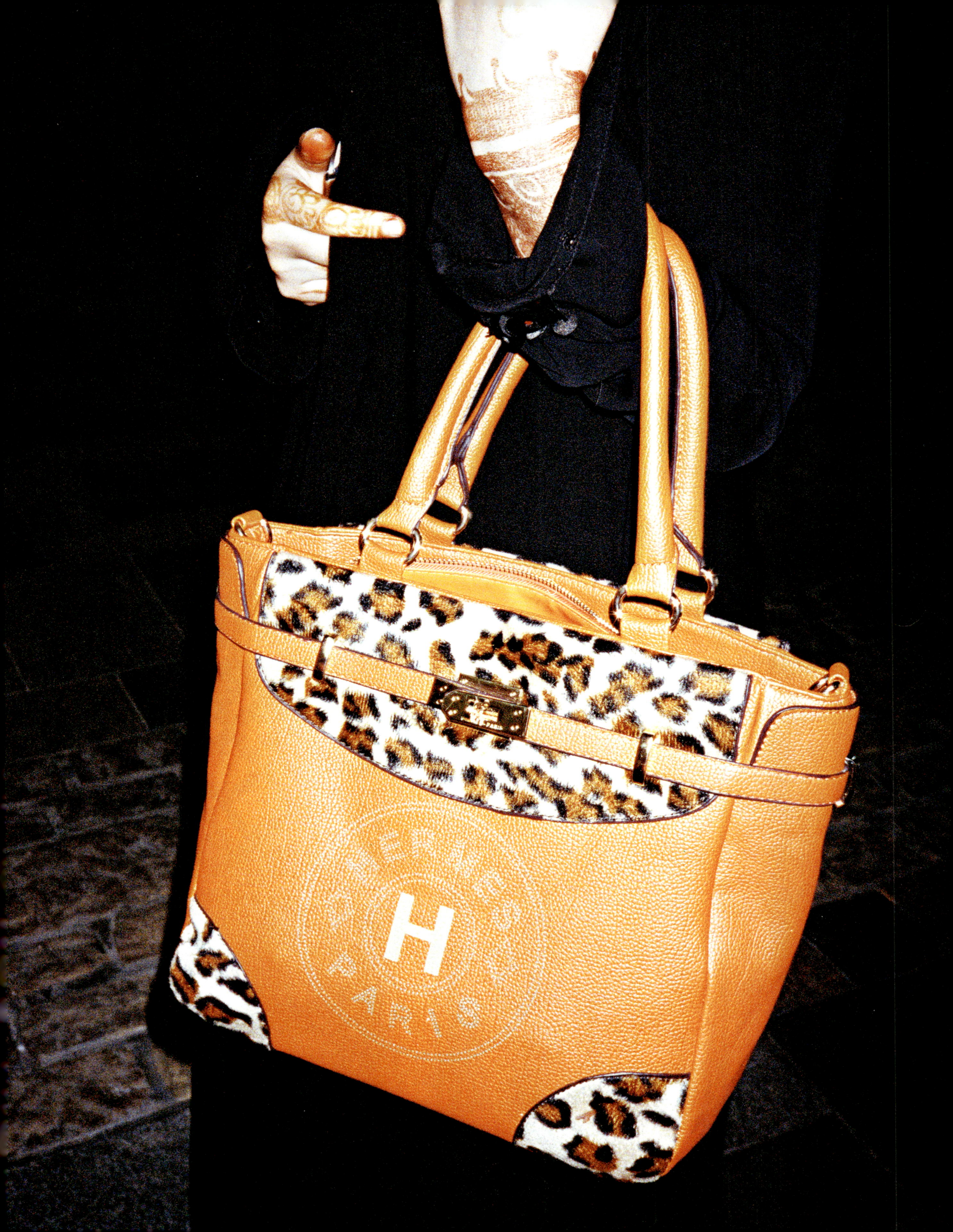
H
PARIS

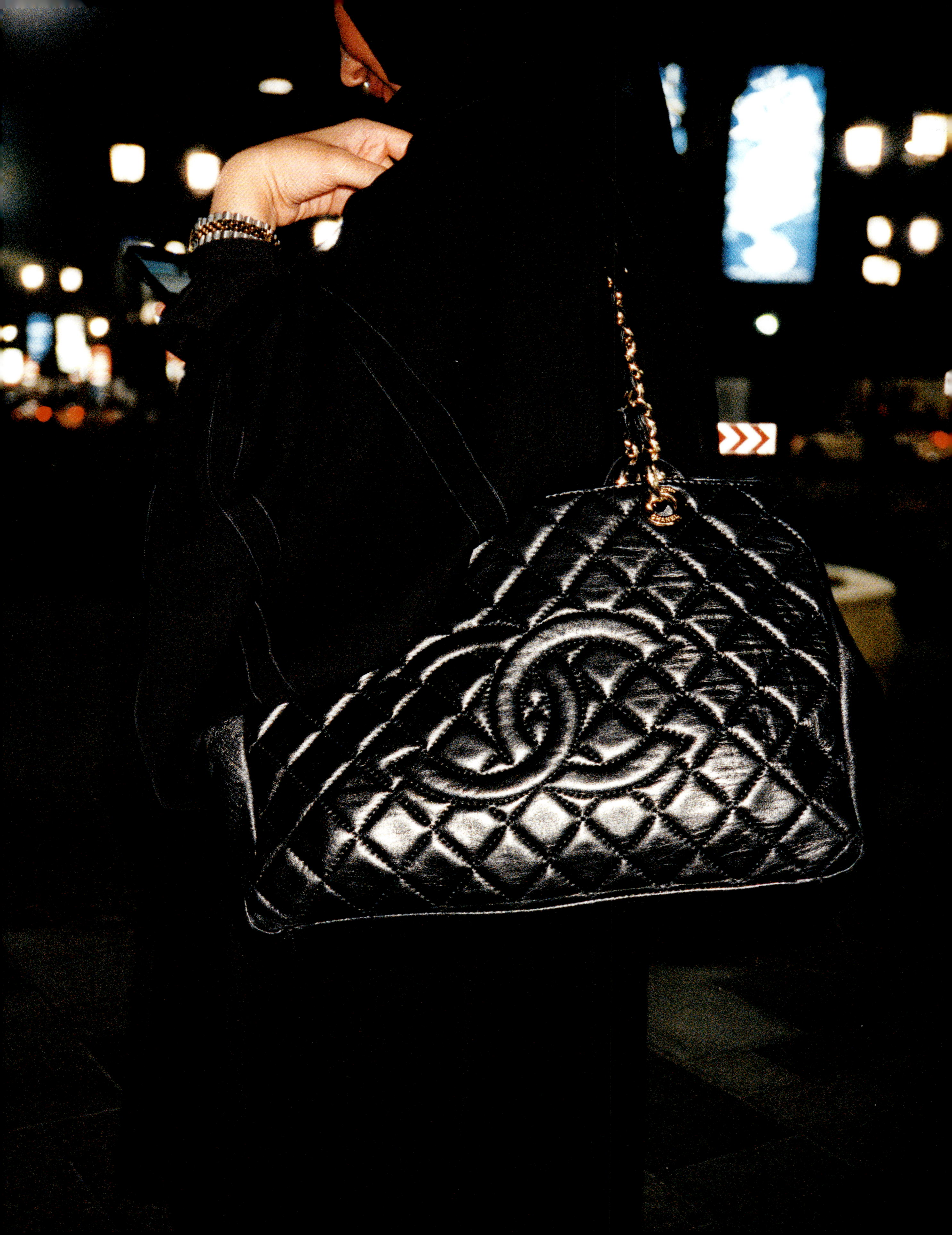

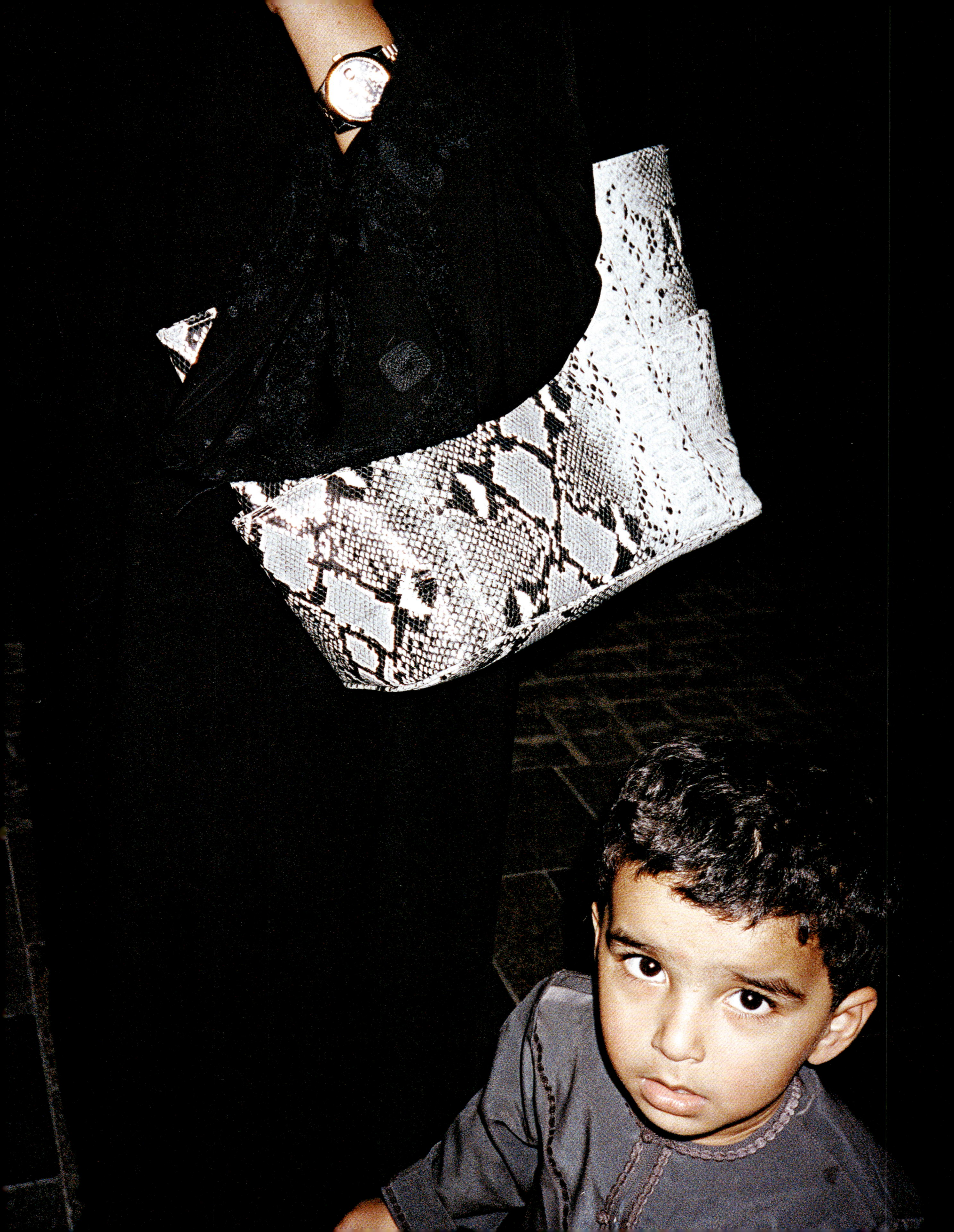

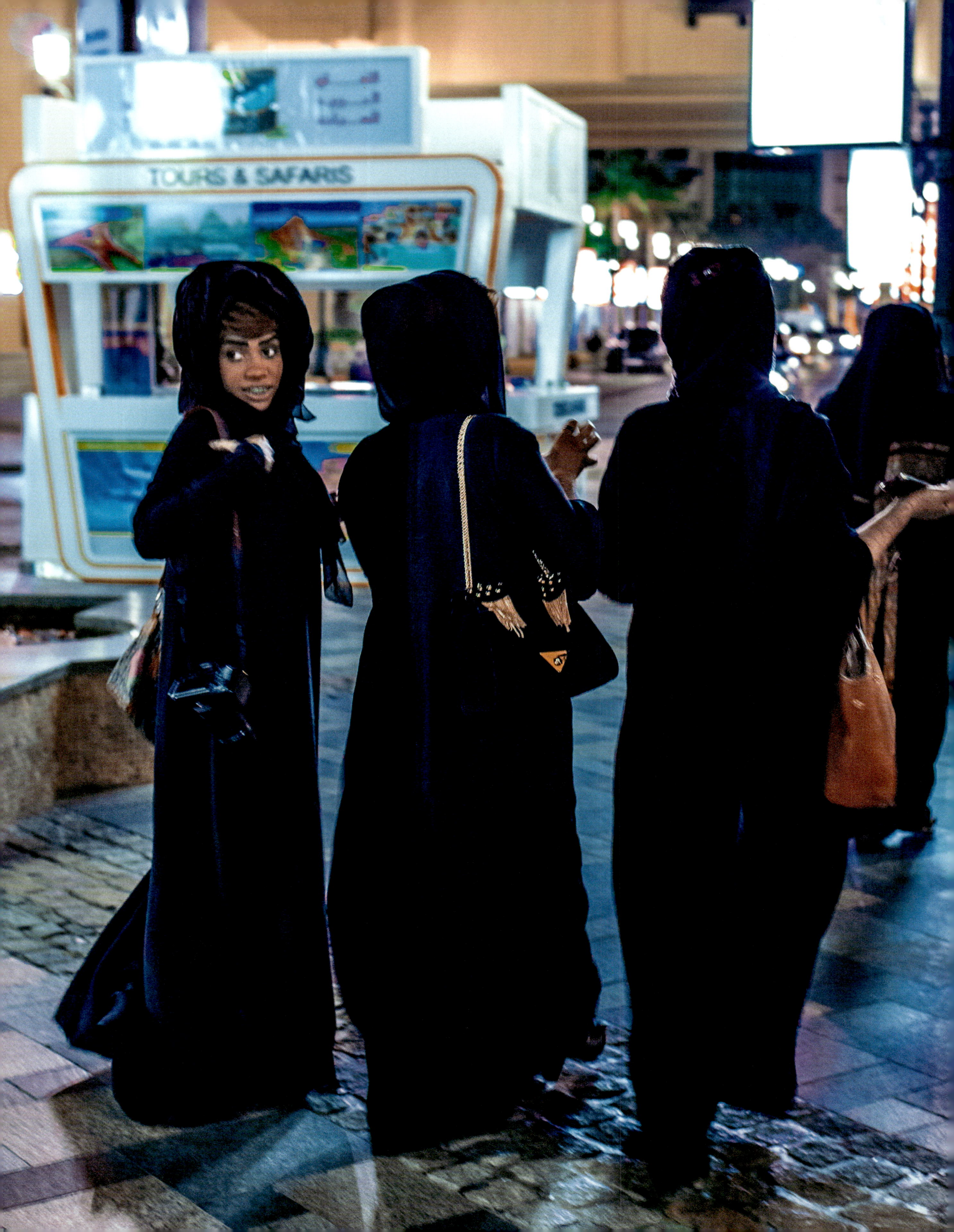
TOURS & SAFARIS

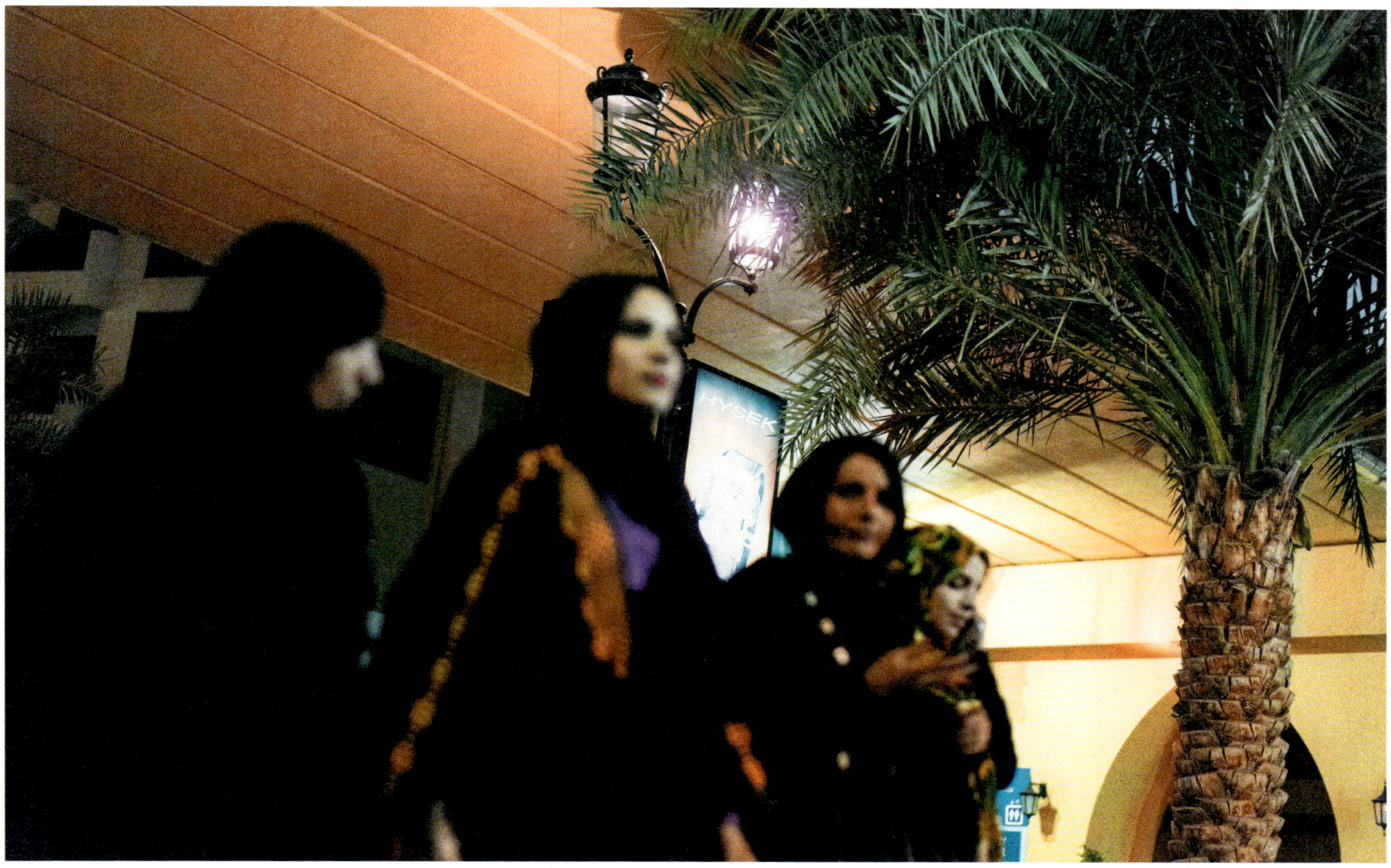
HYSEK

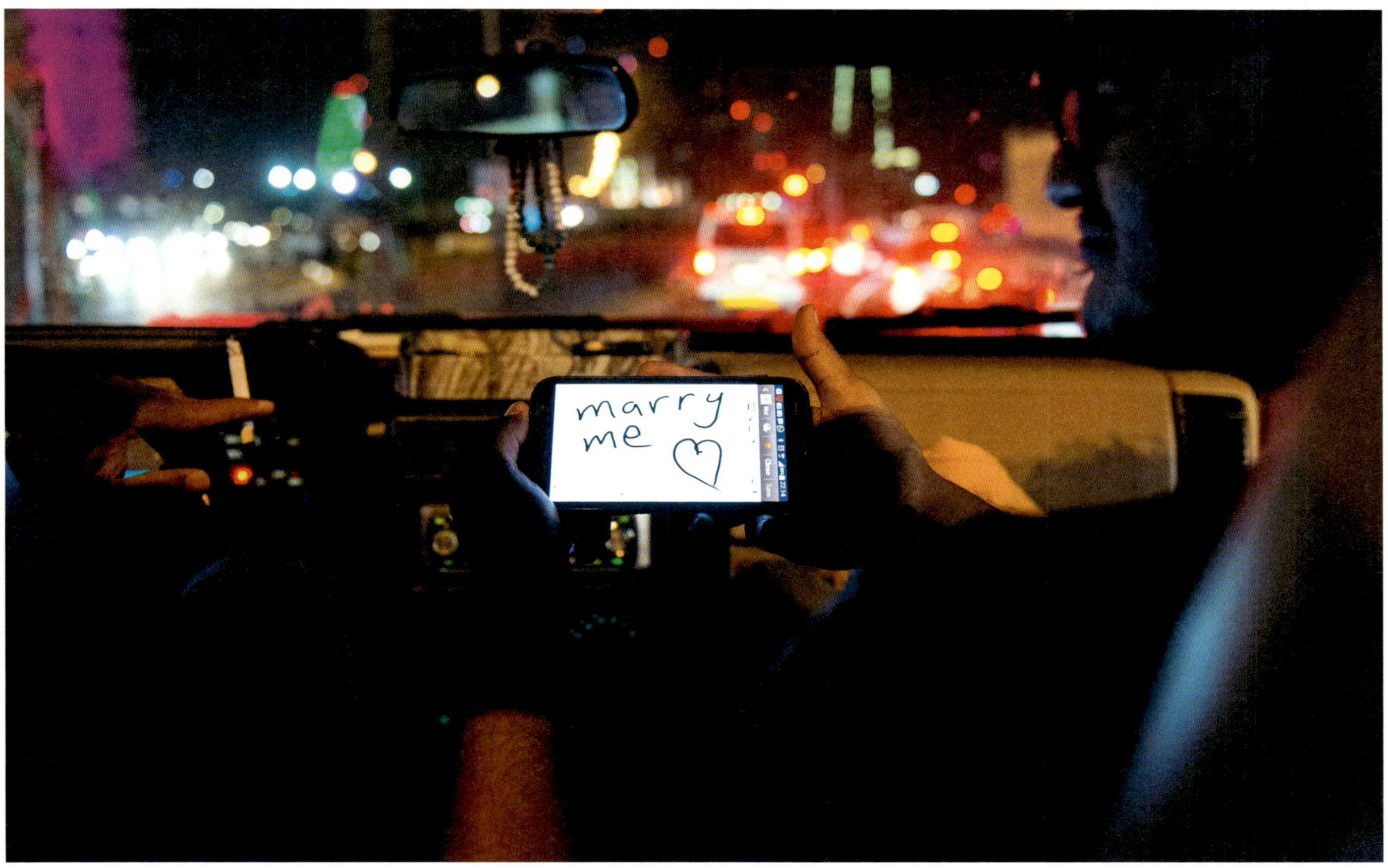
marry
me

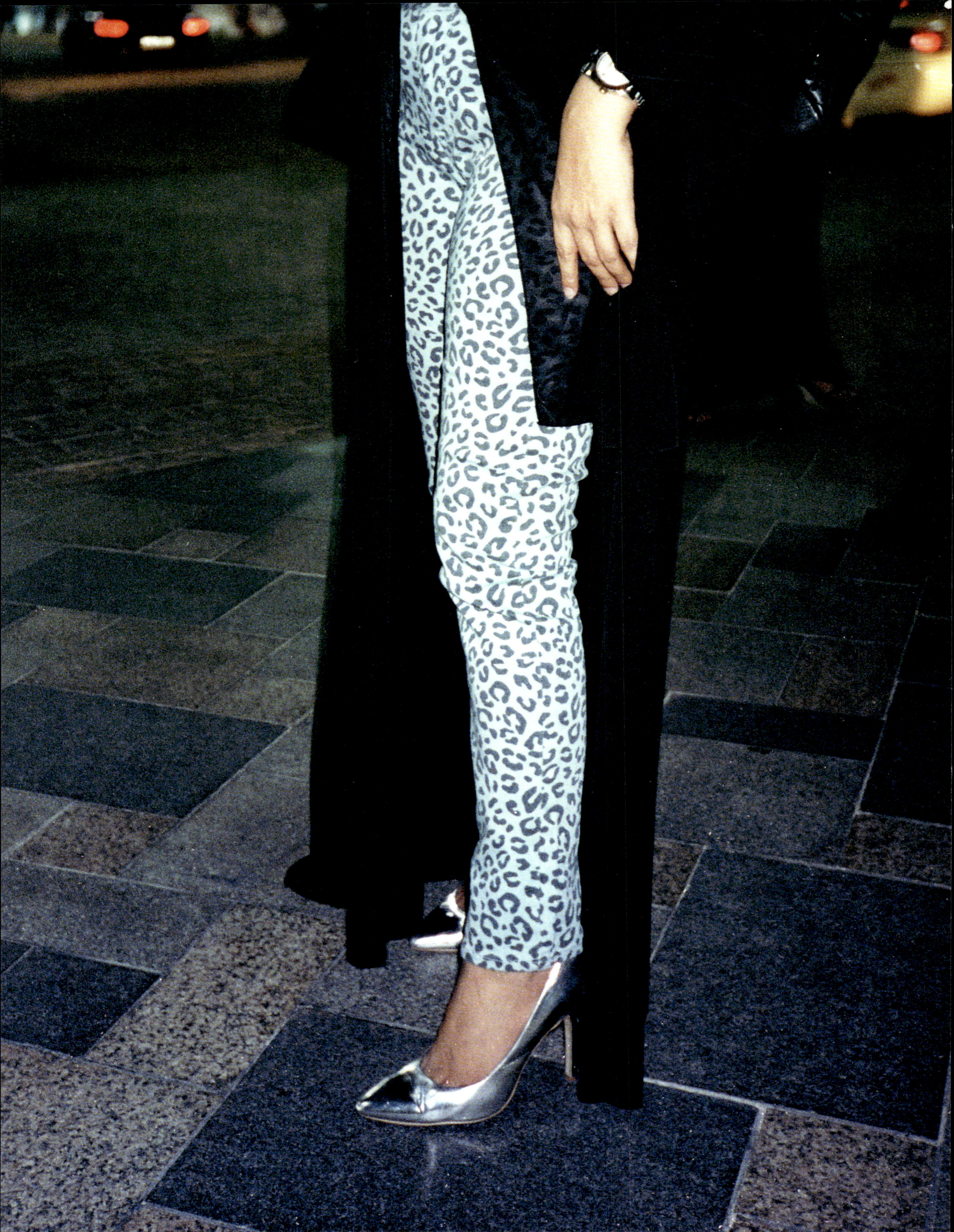

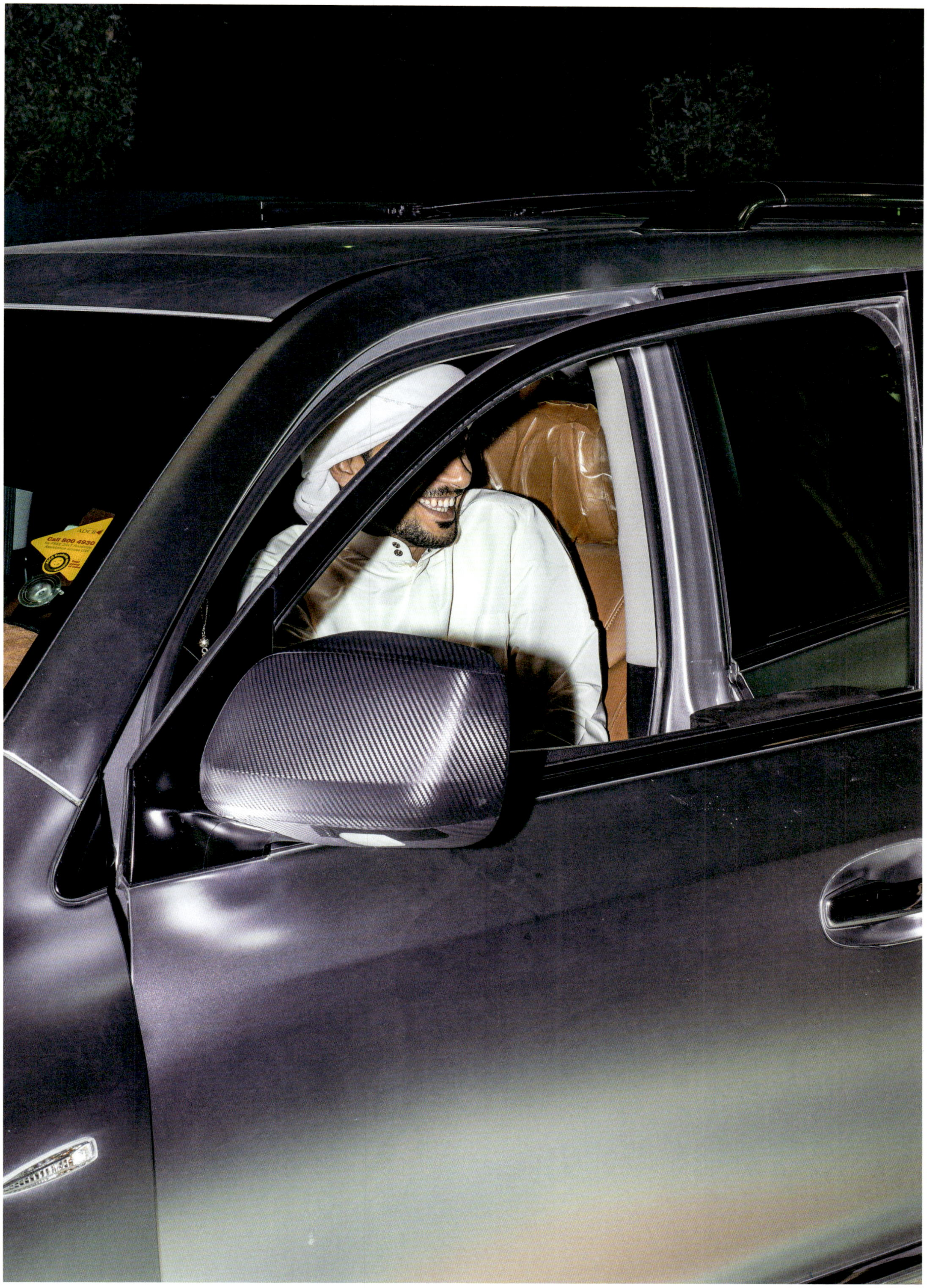
ADCB
Call 800 4930

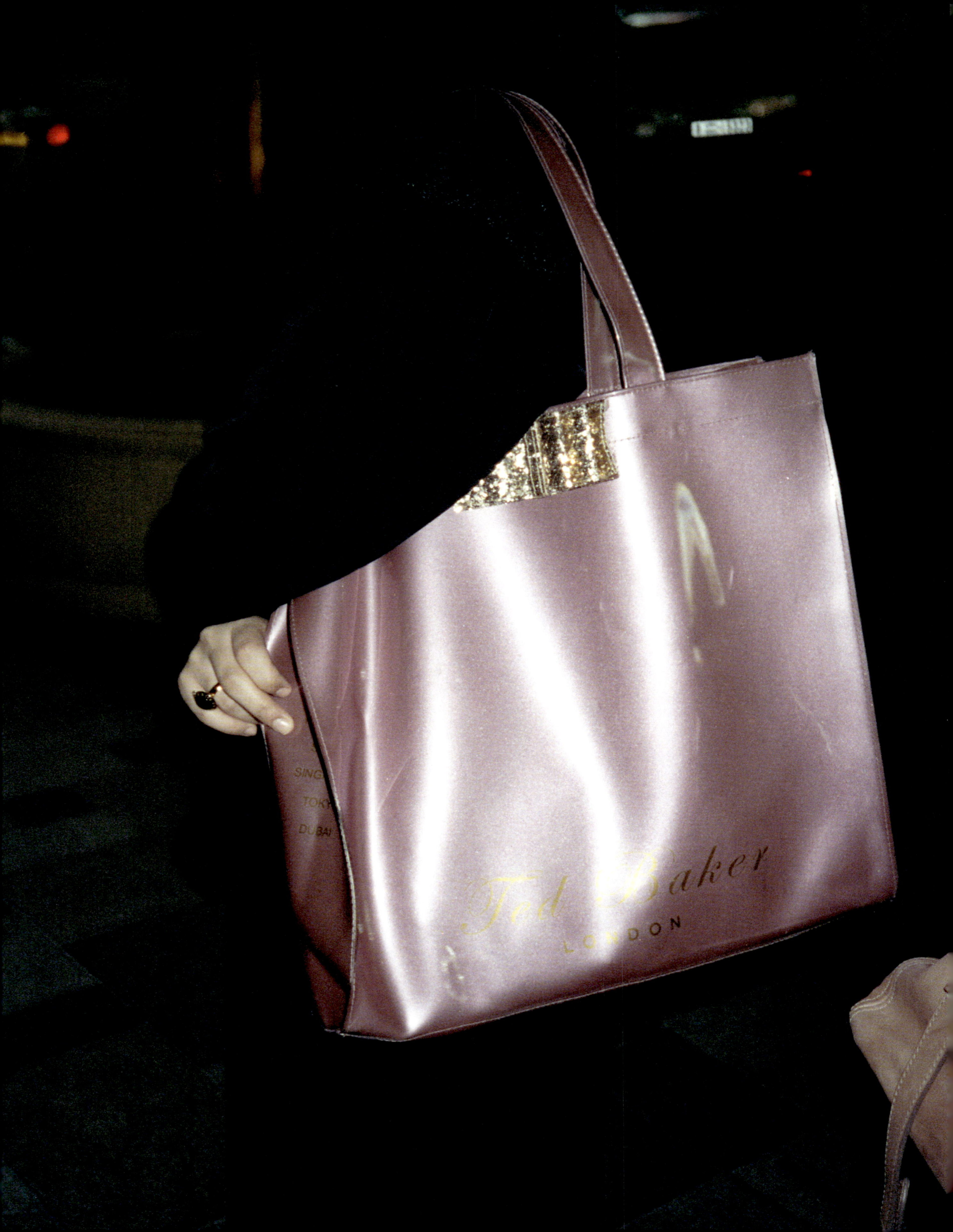
Ted Baker
LONDON
DUBAI

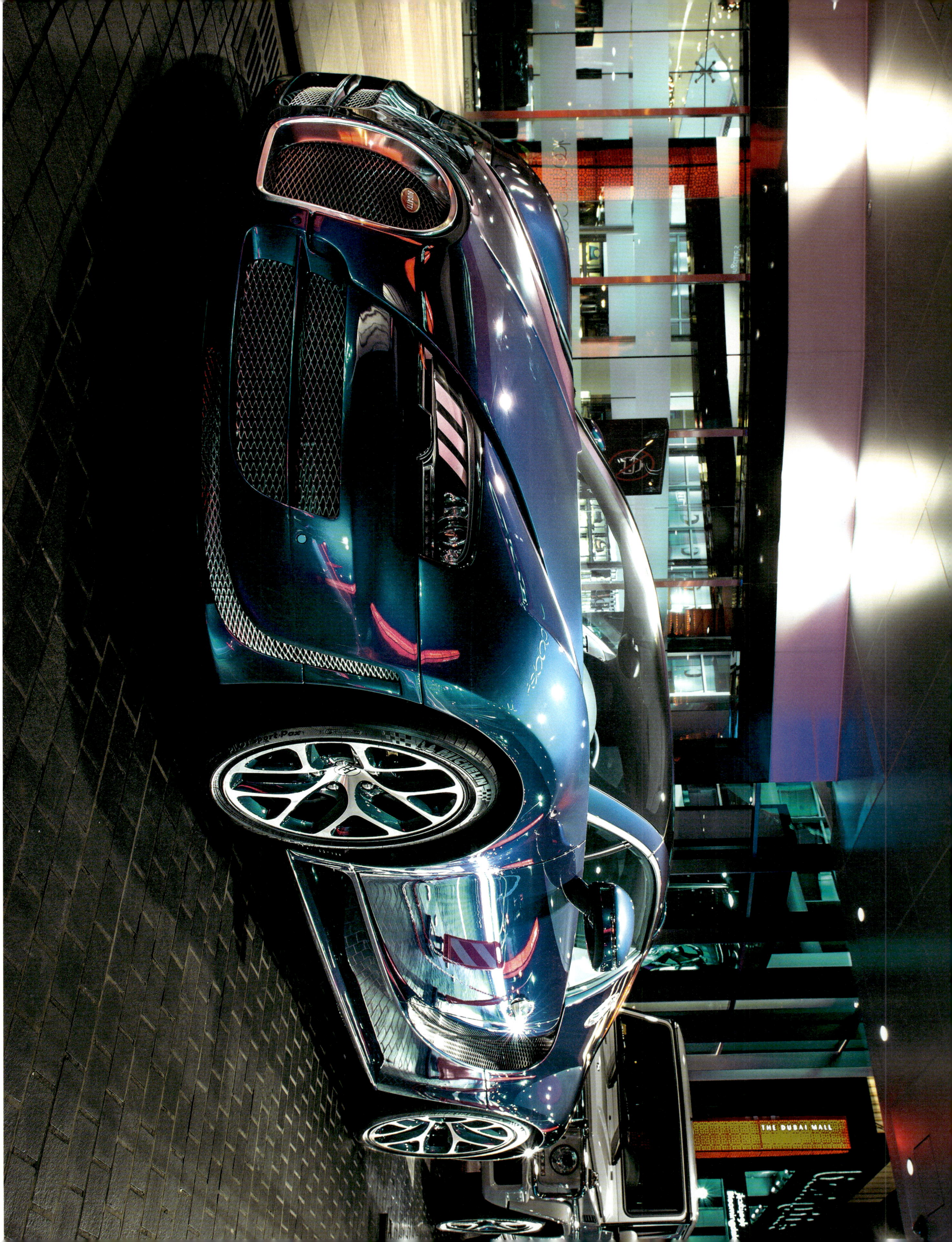
THE DUBAI MALL

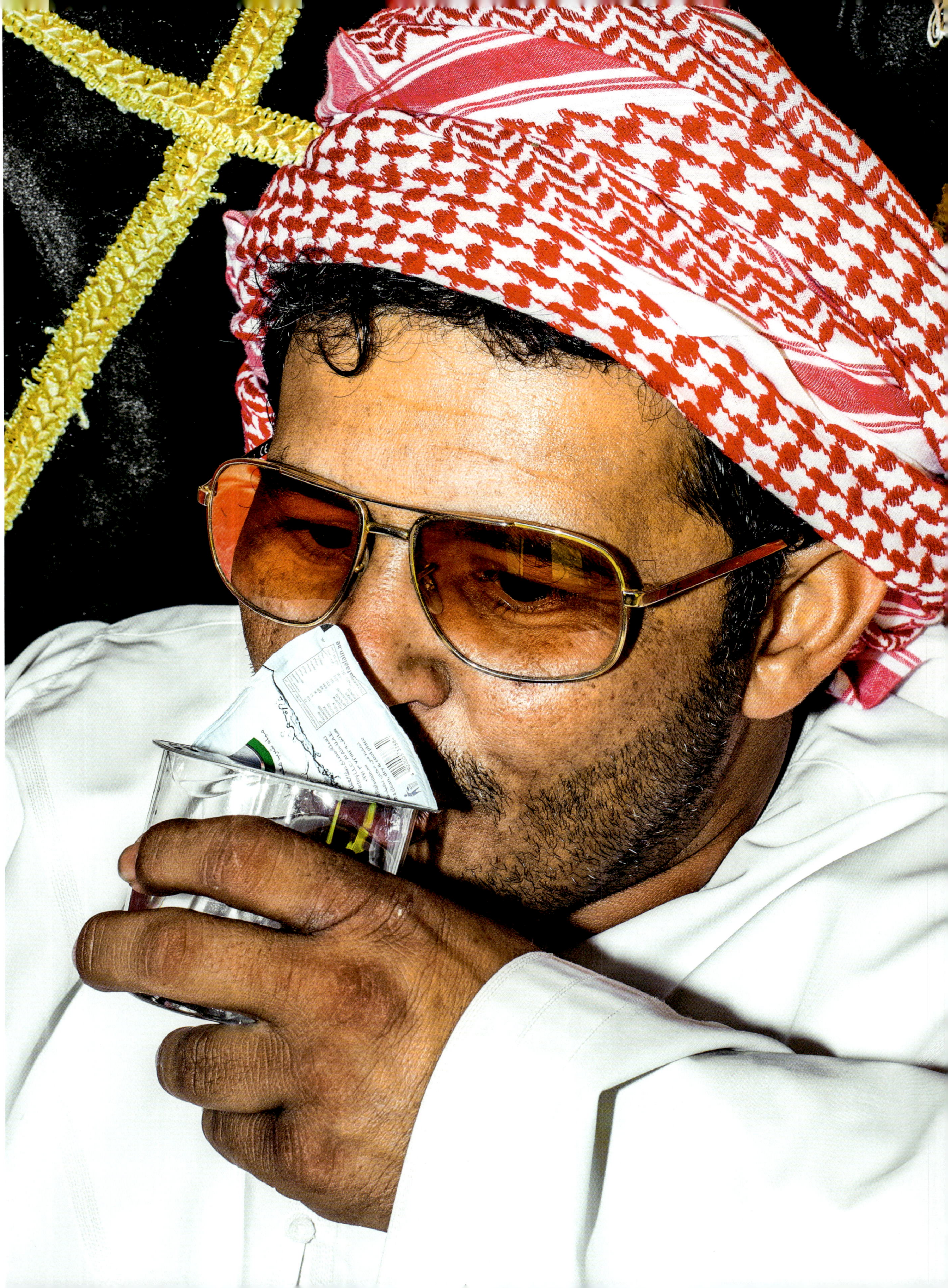

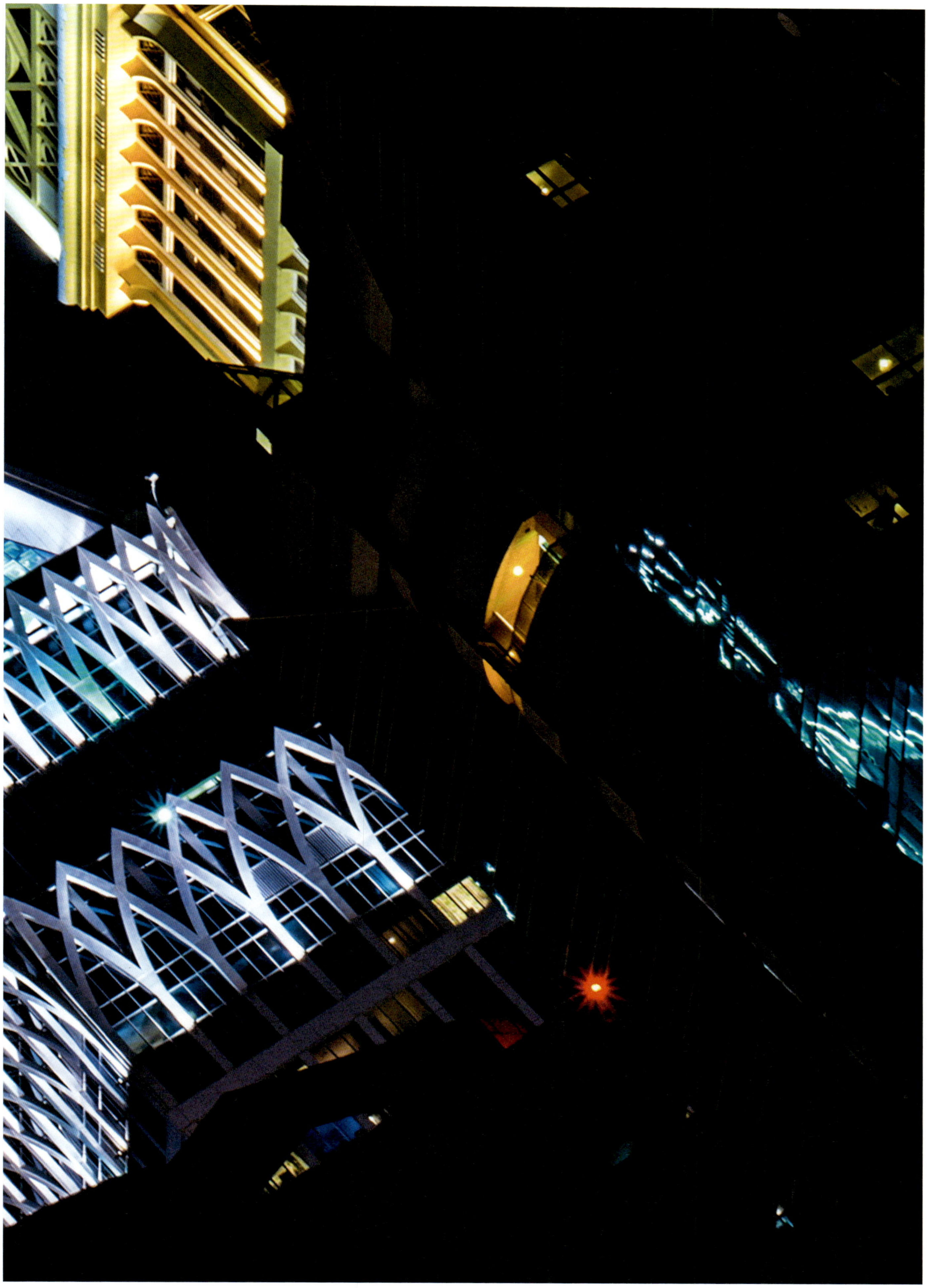

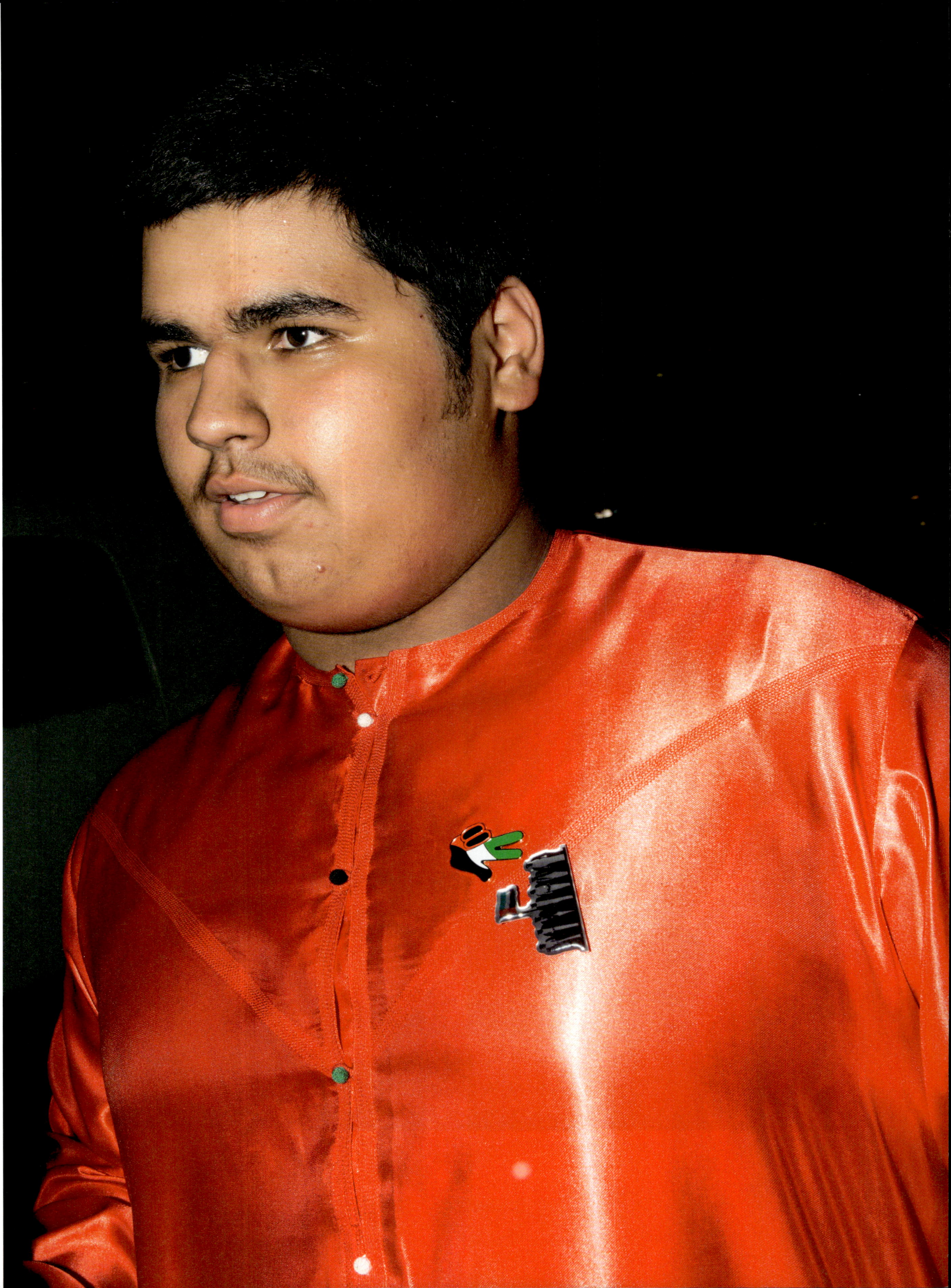

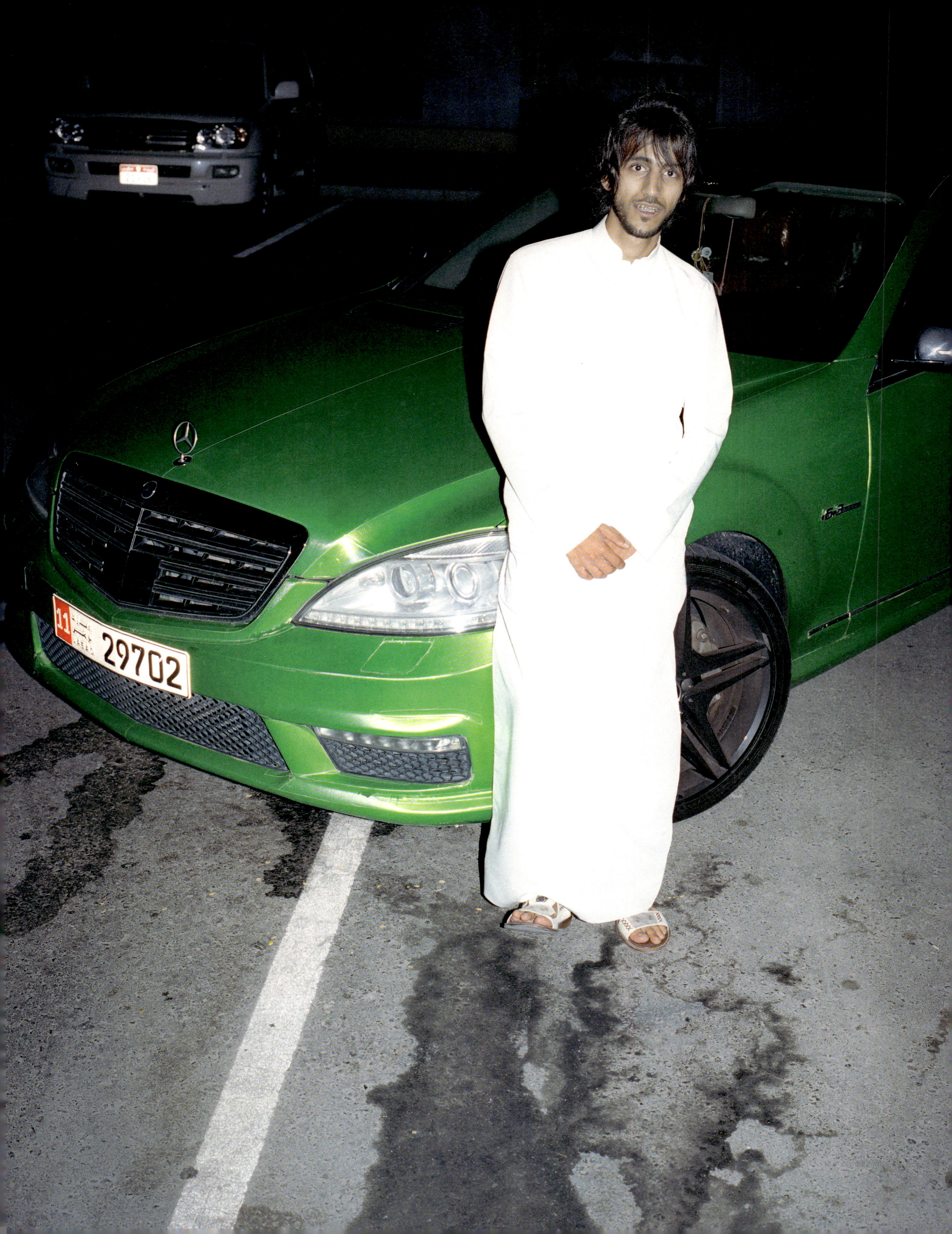
11
29702

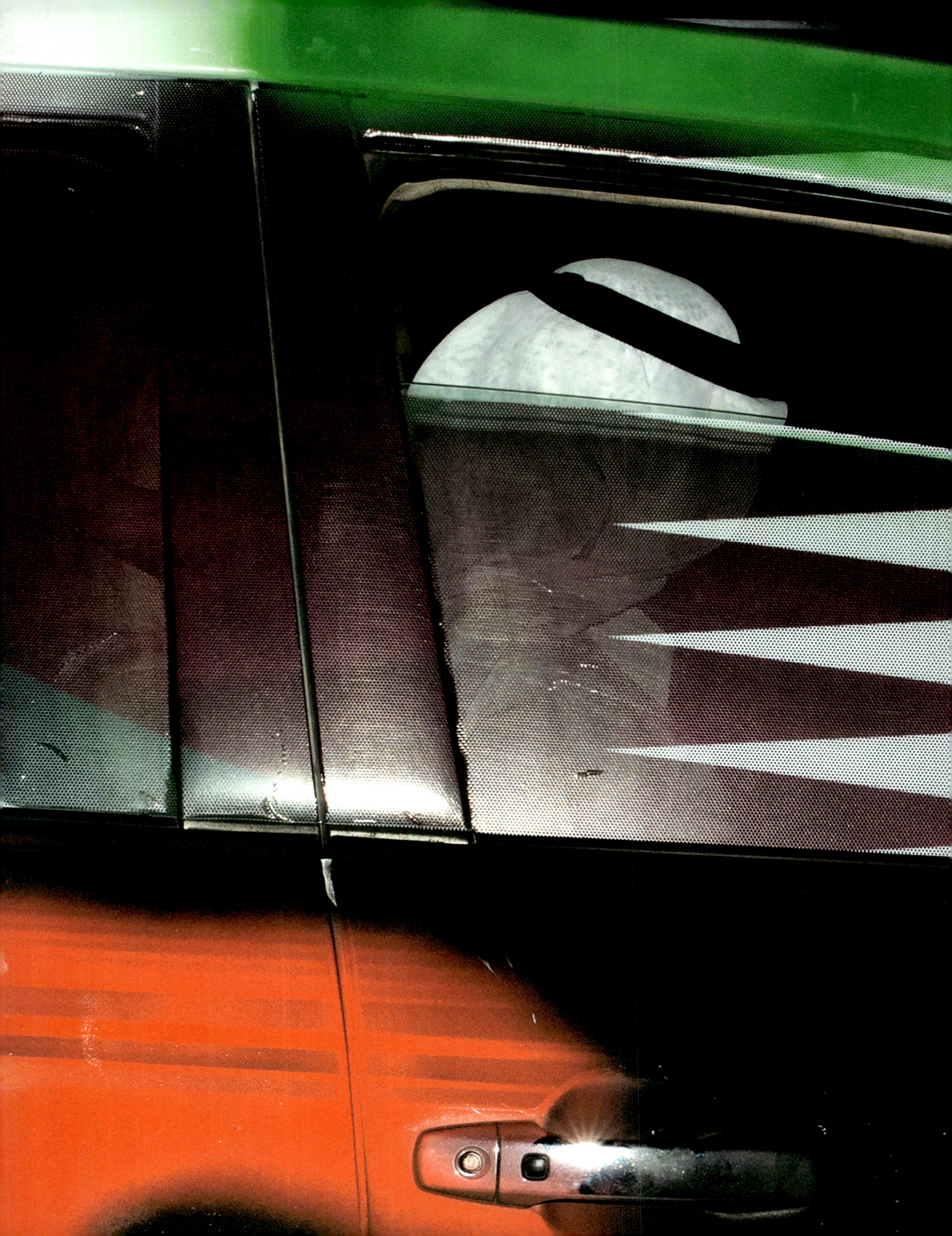

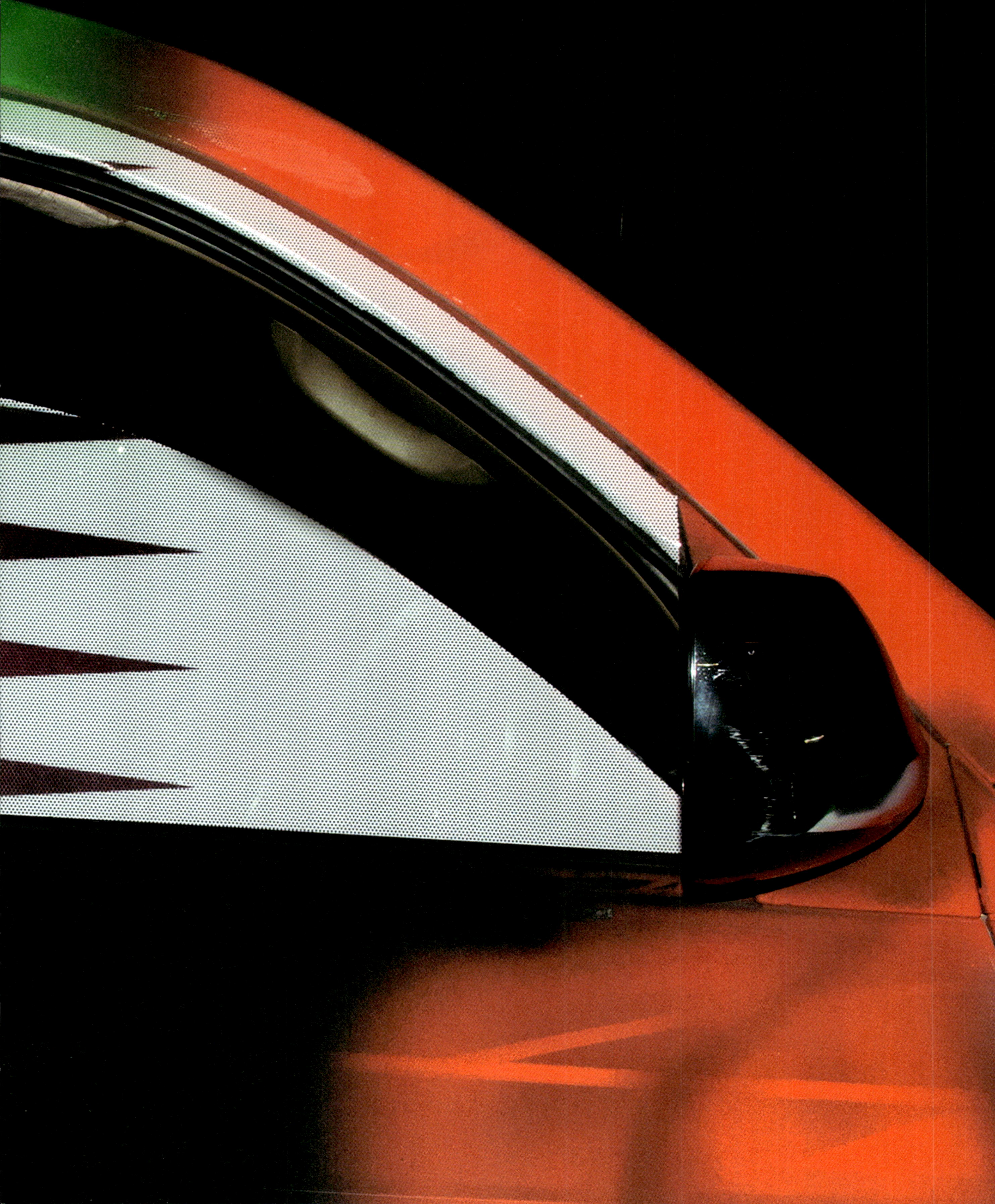

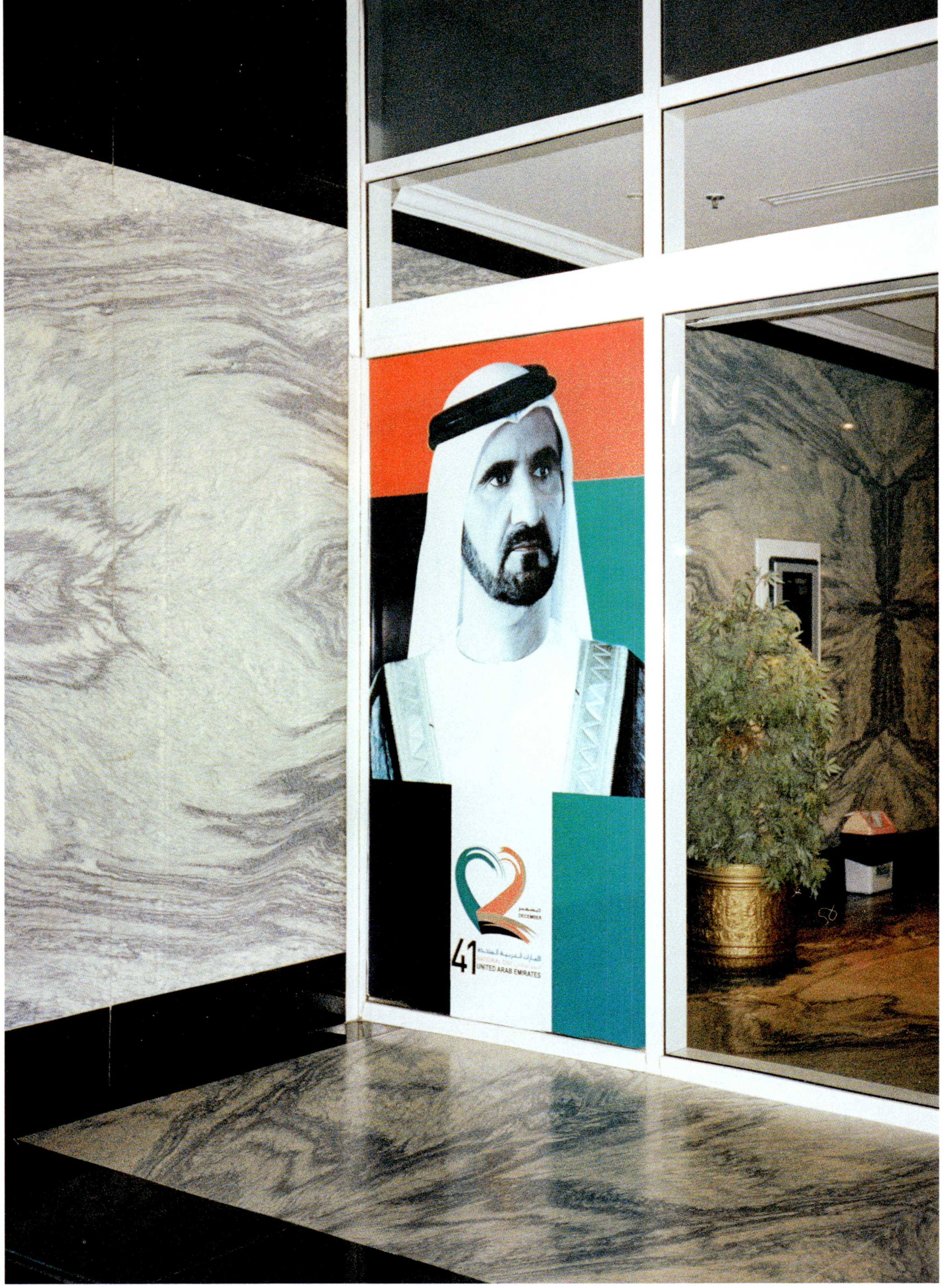
DECEMBER
41
UNITED ARAB EMIRATES

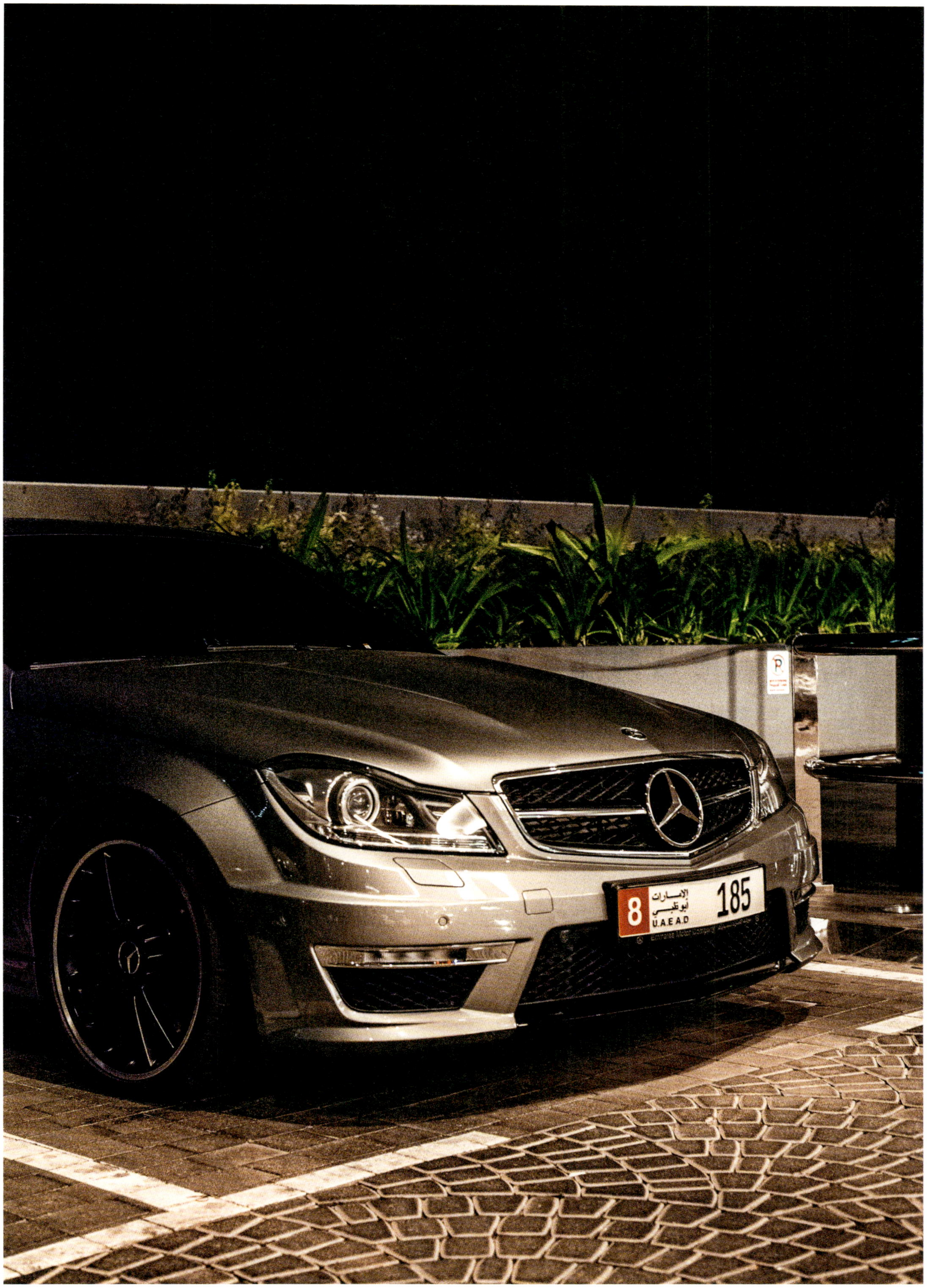
8
185
U.A.E A.D

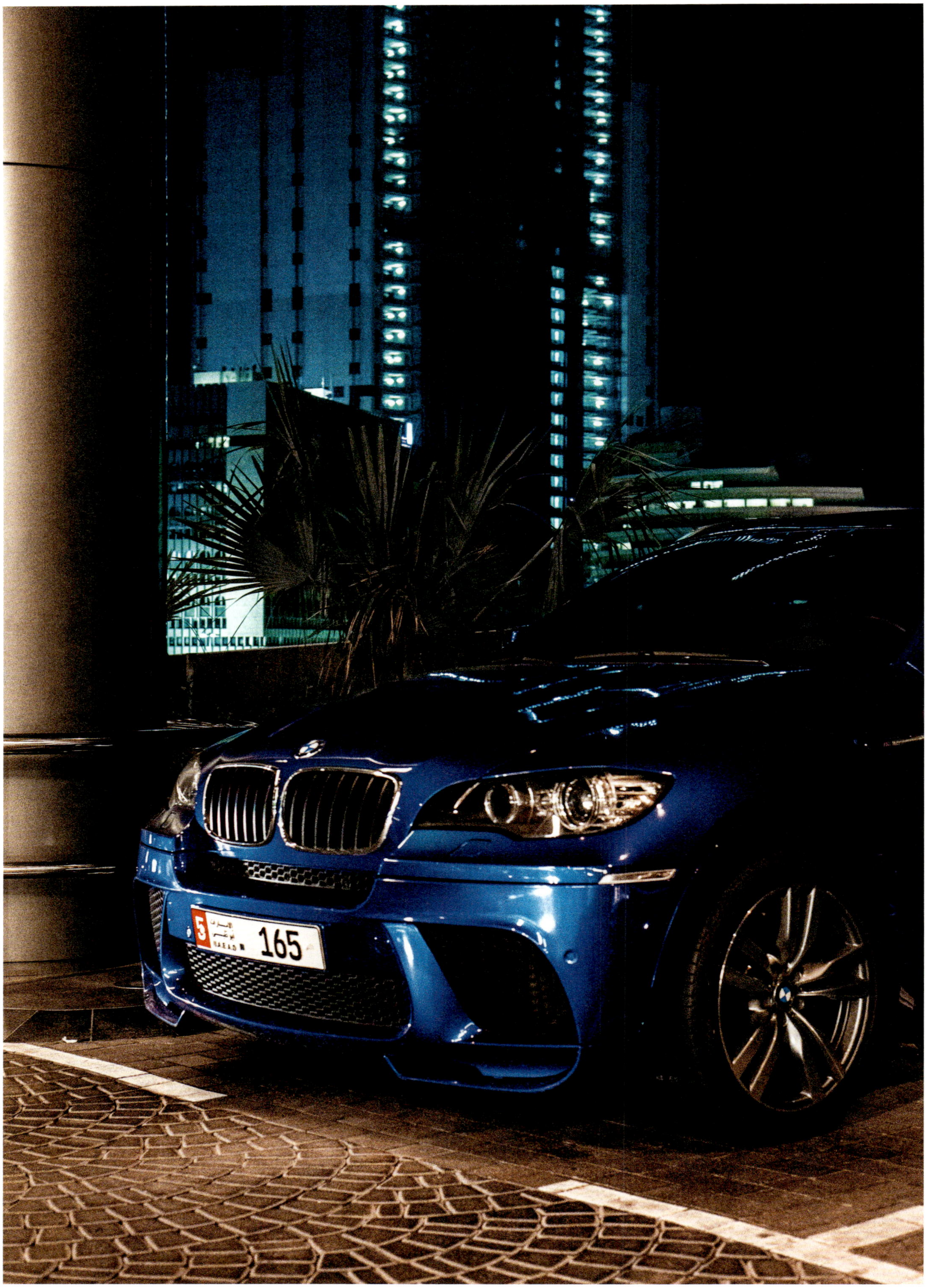
5
165

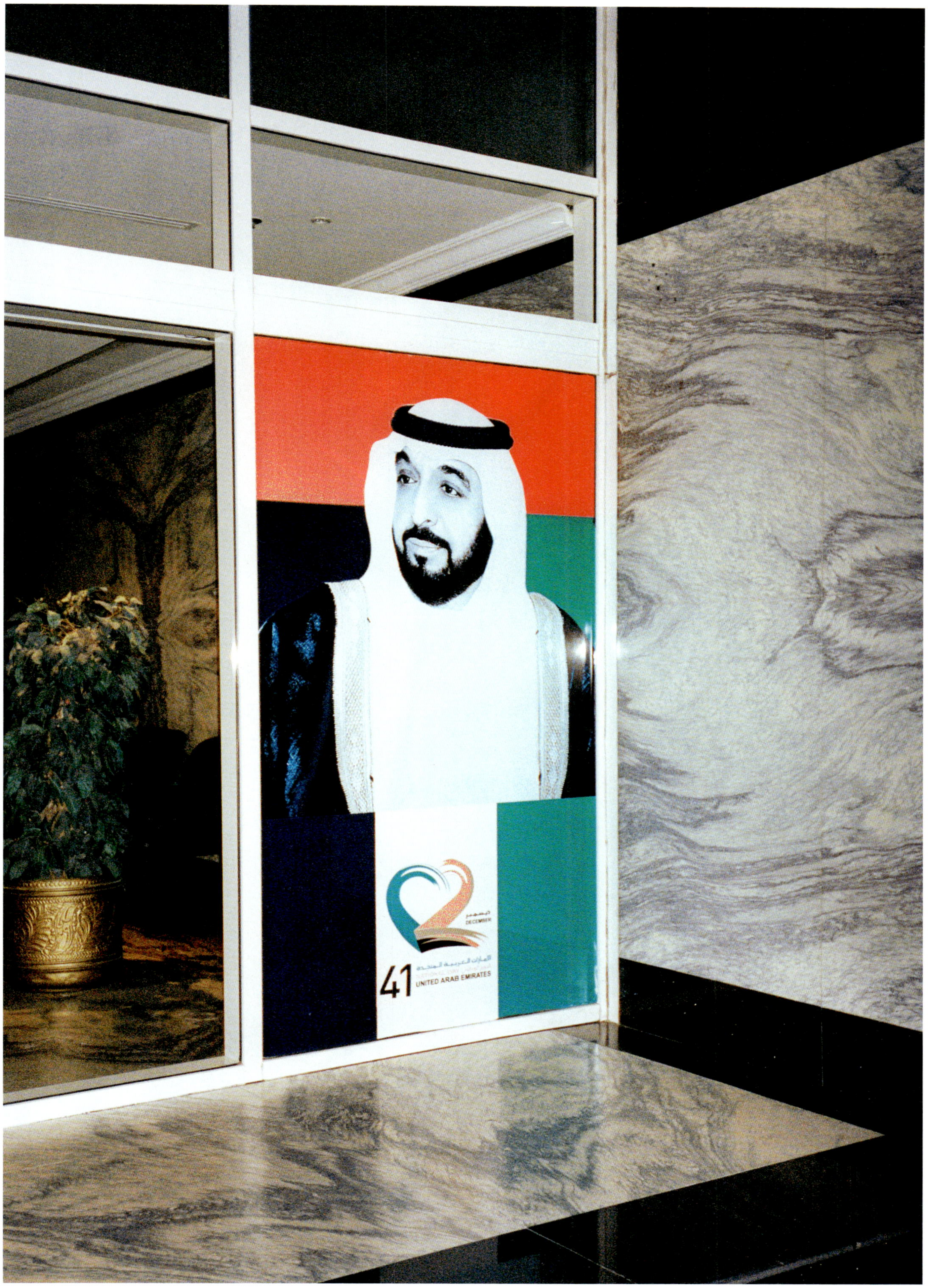
DECEMBER
41
UNITED ARAB EMIRATES

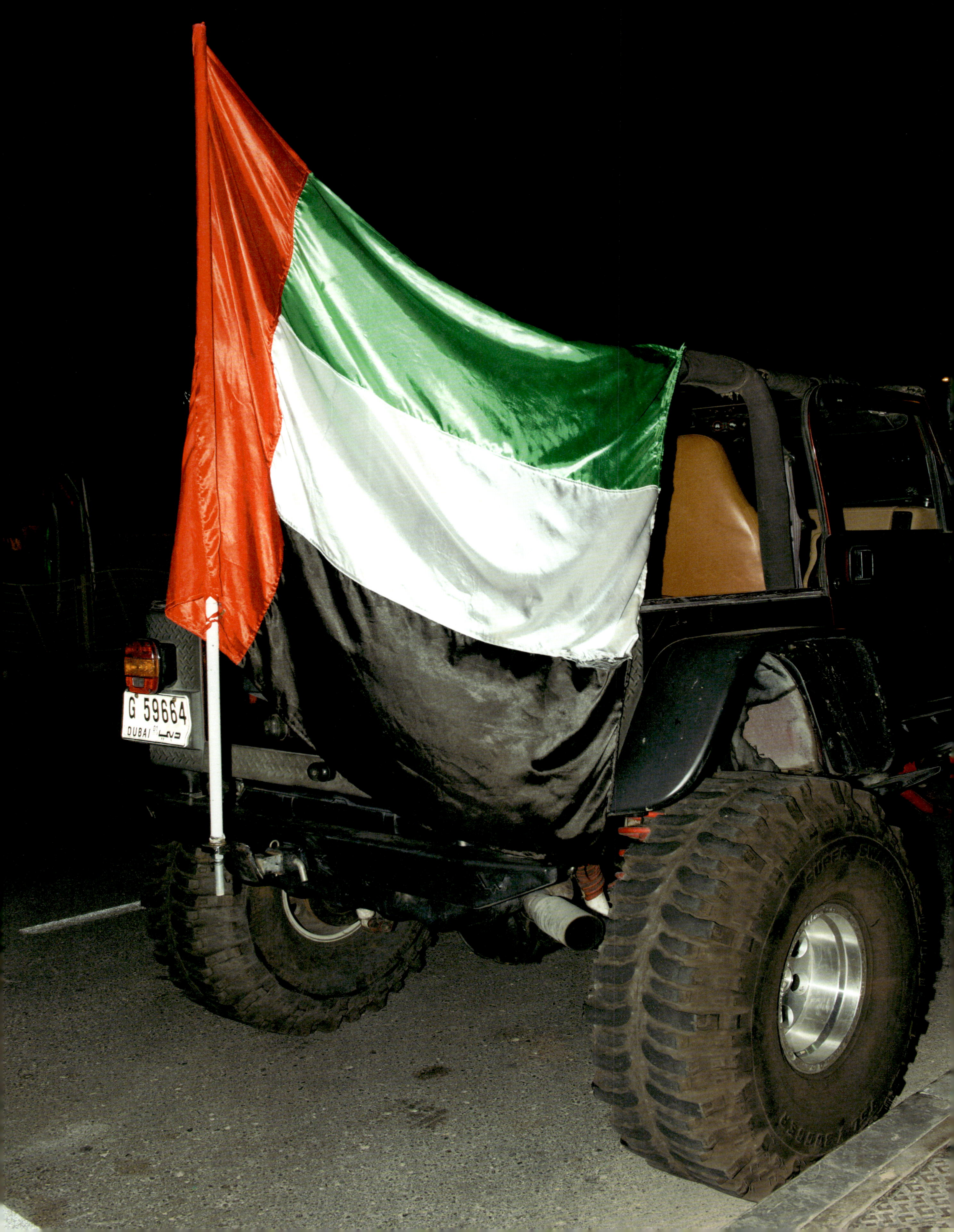
G 59664
DUBAI

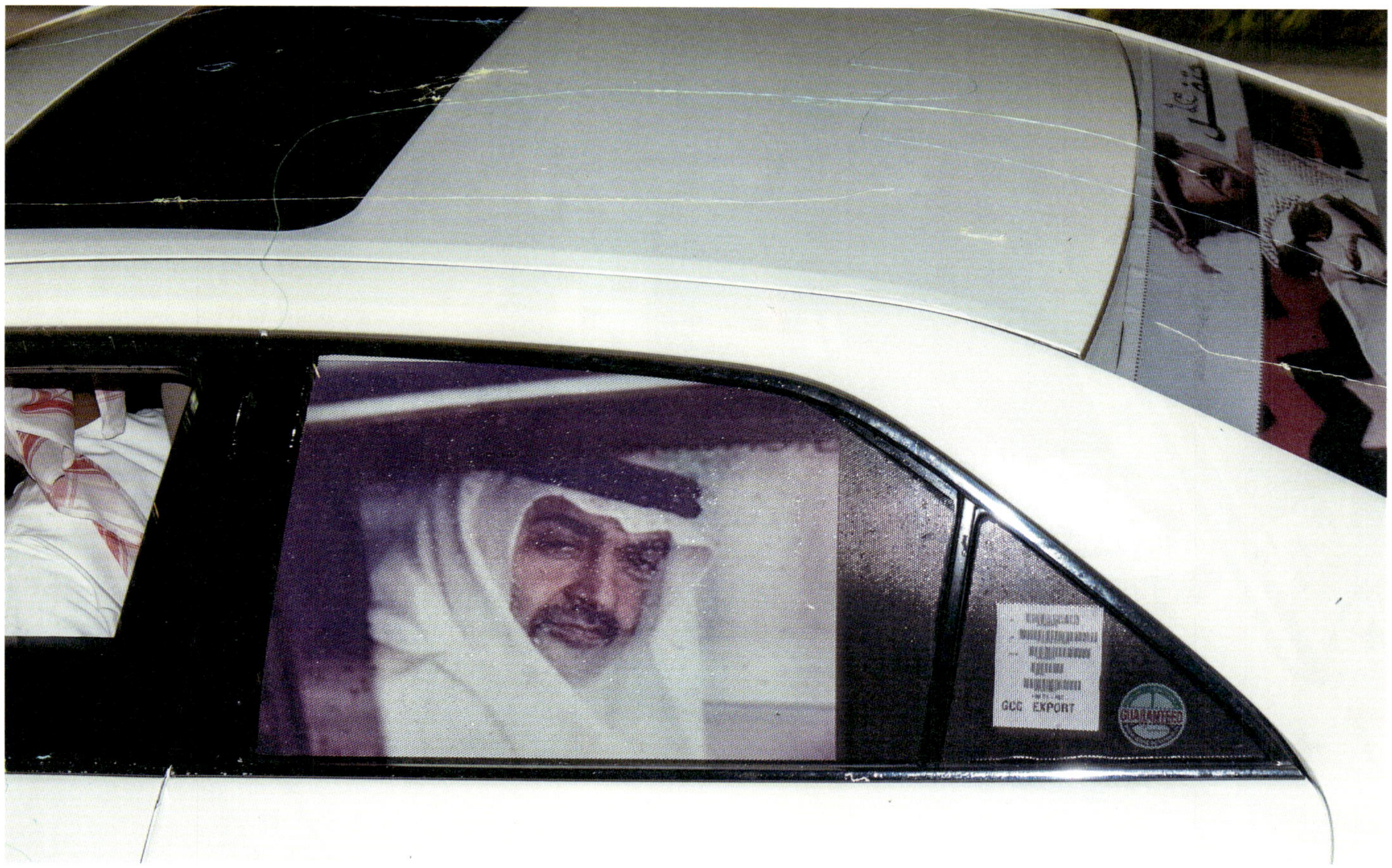
GCC EXPORT

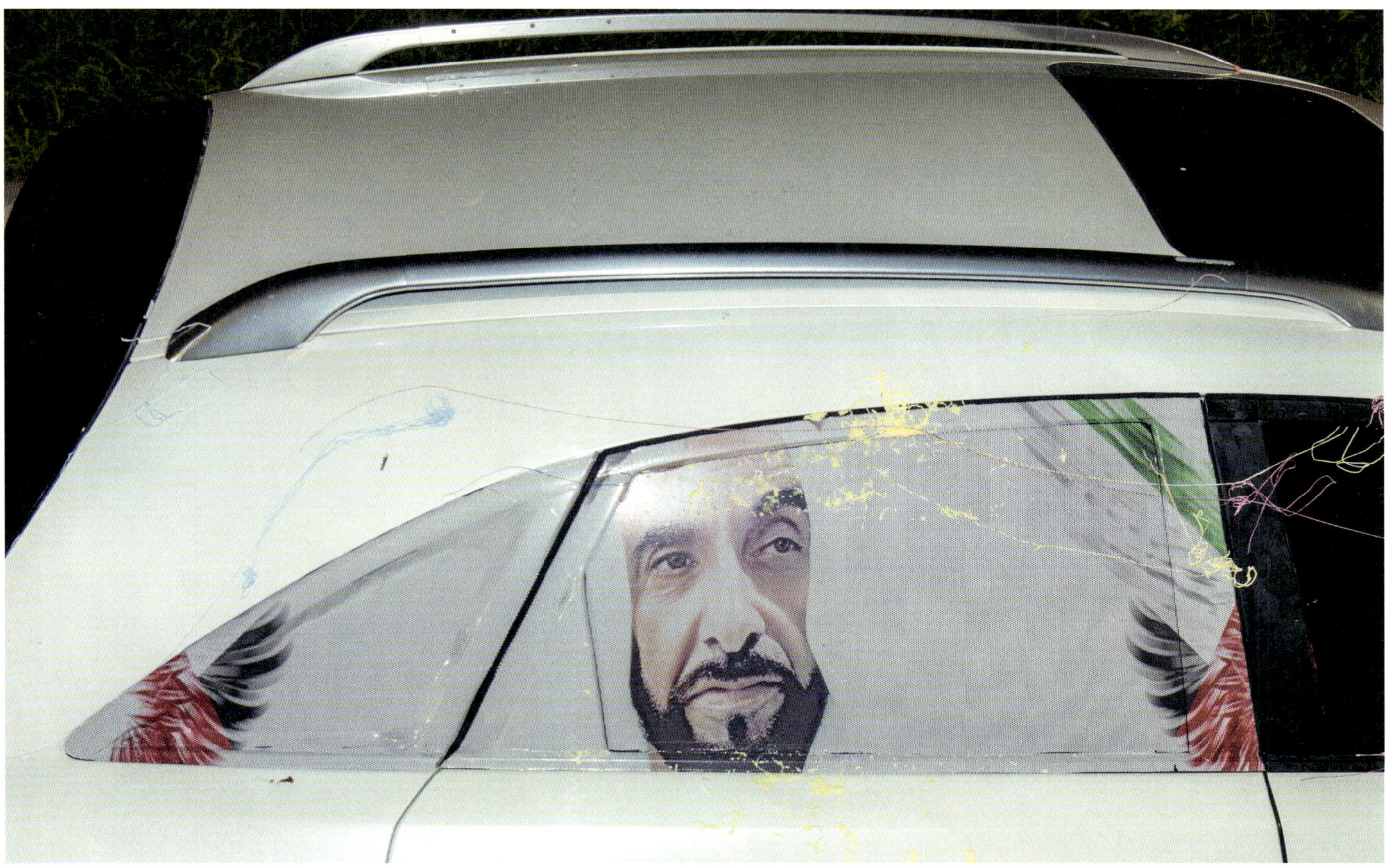

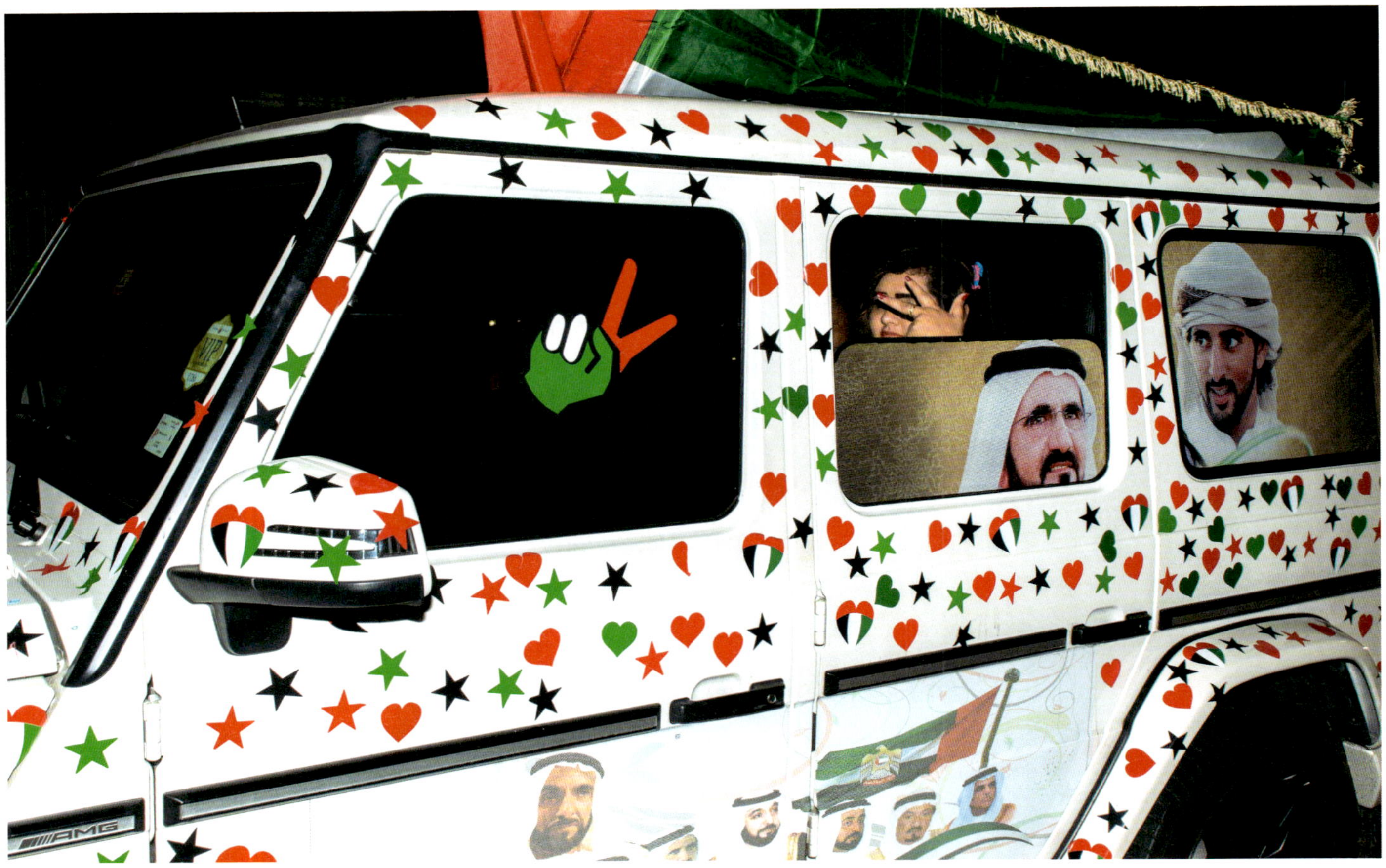

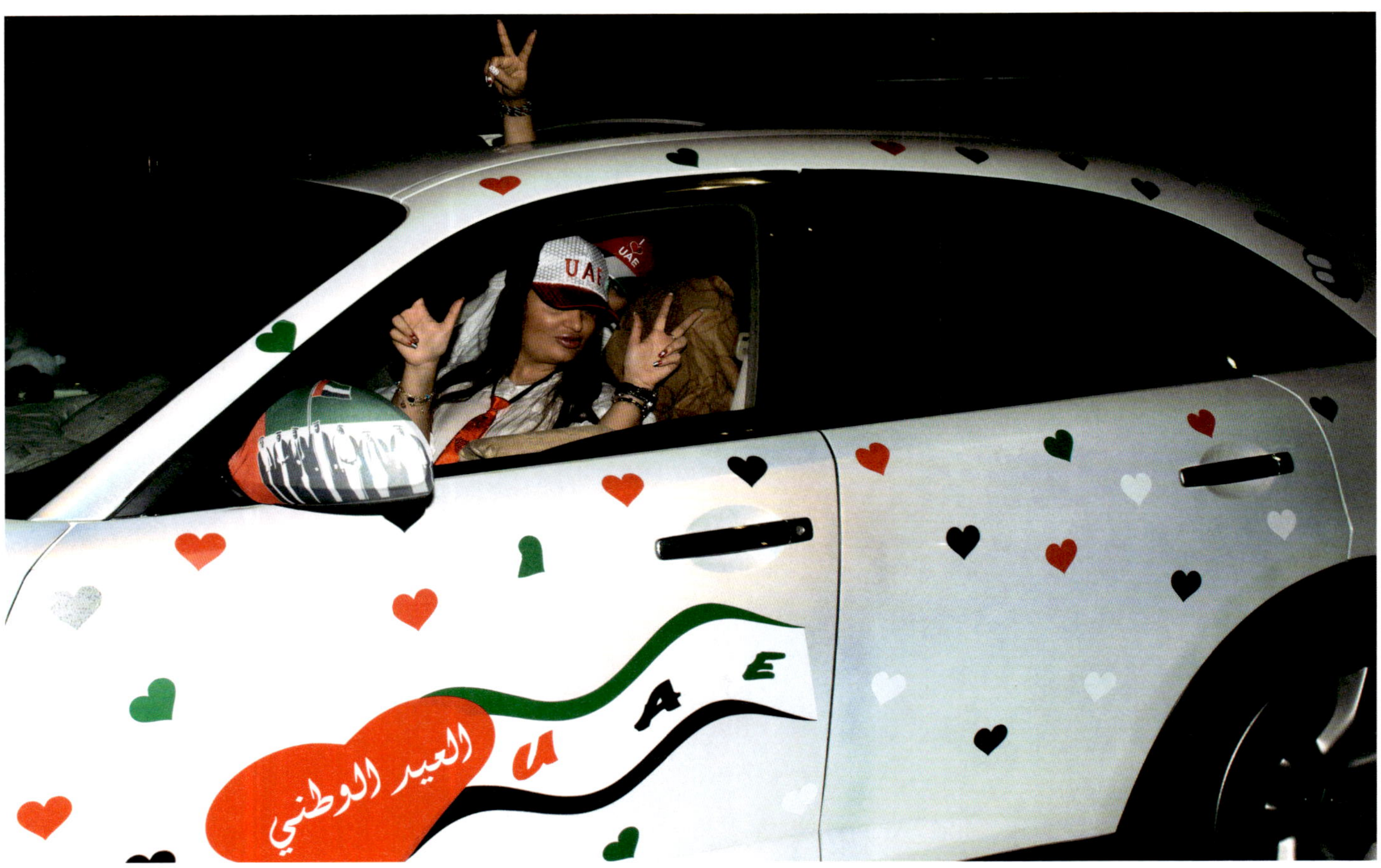
UAE
العيد الوطني
U A E

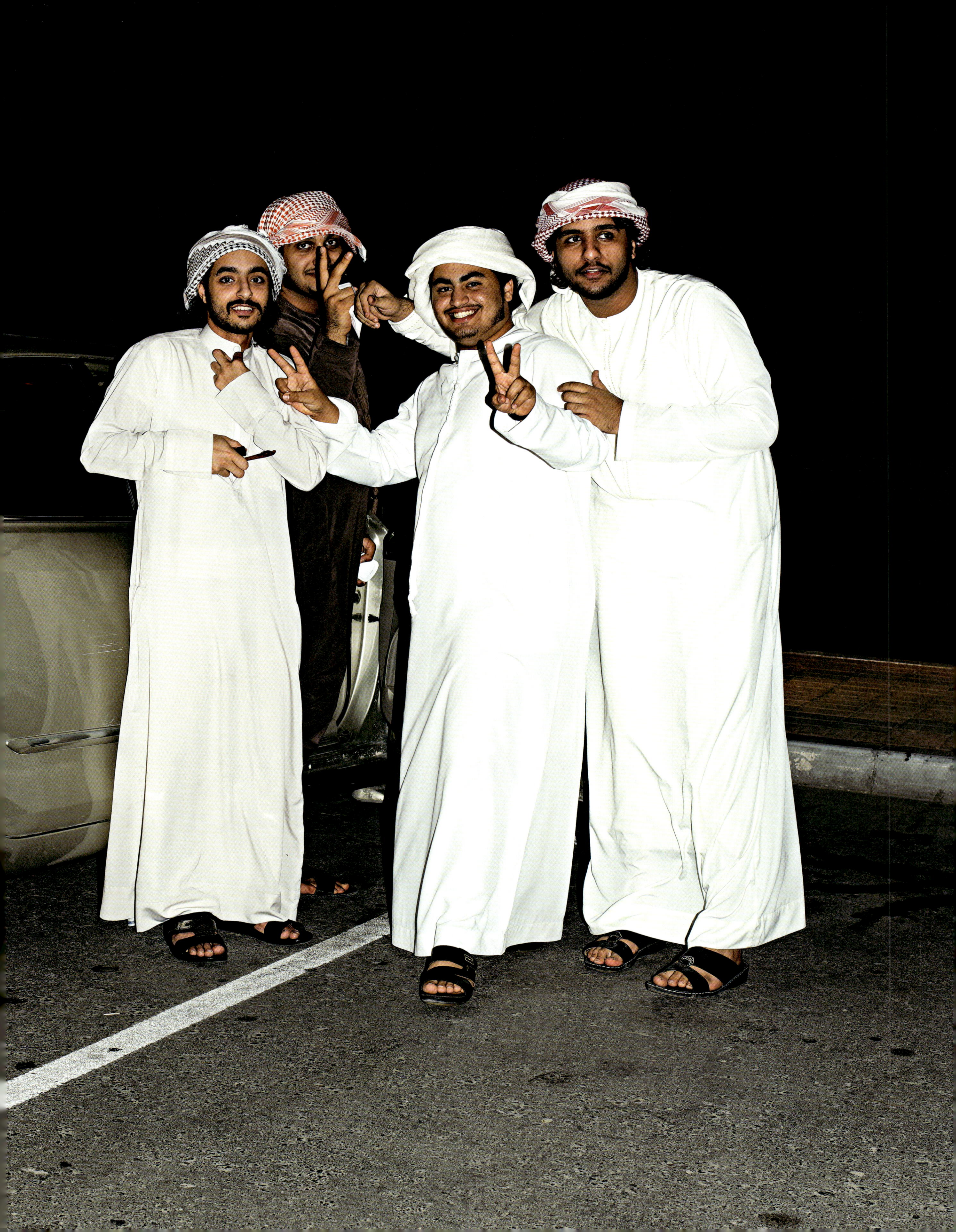

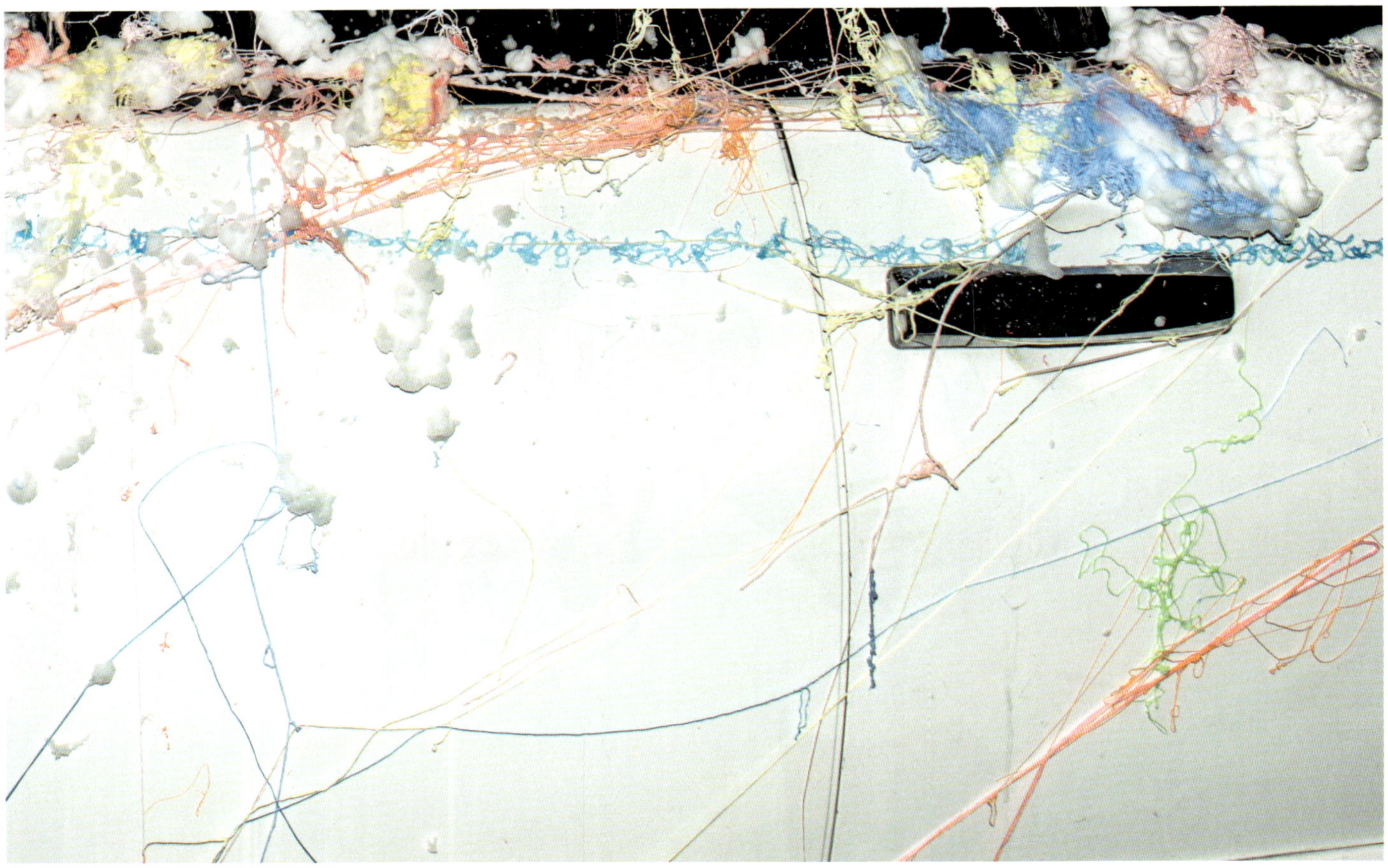

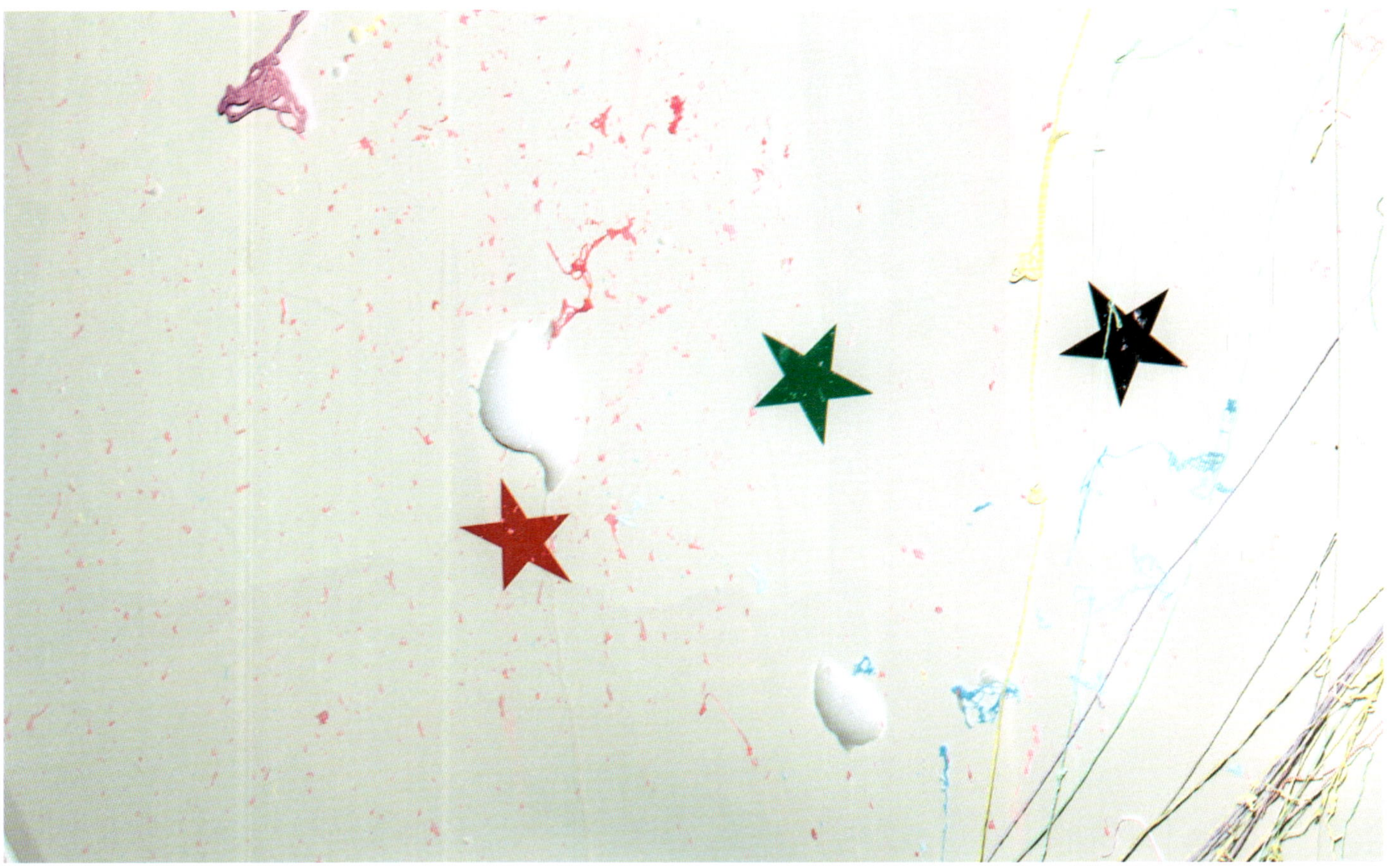

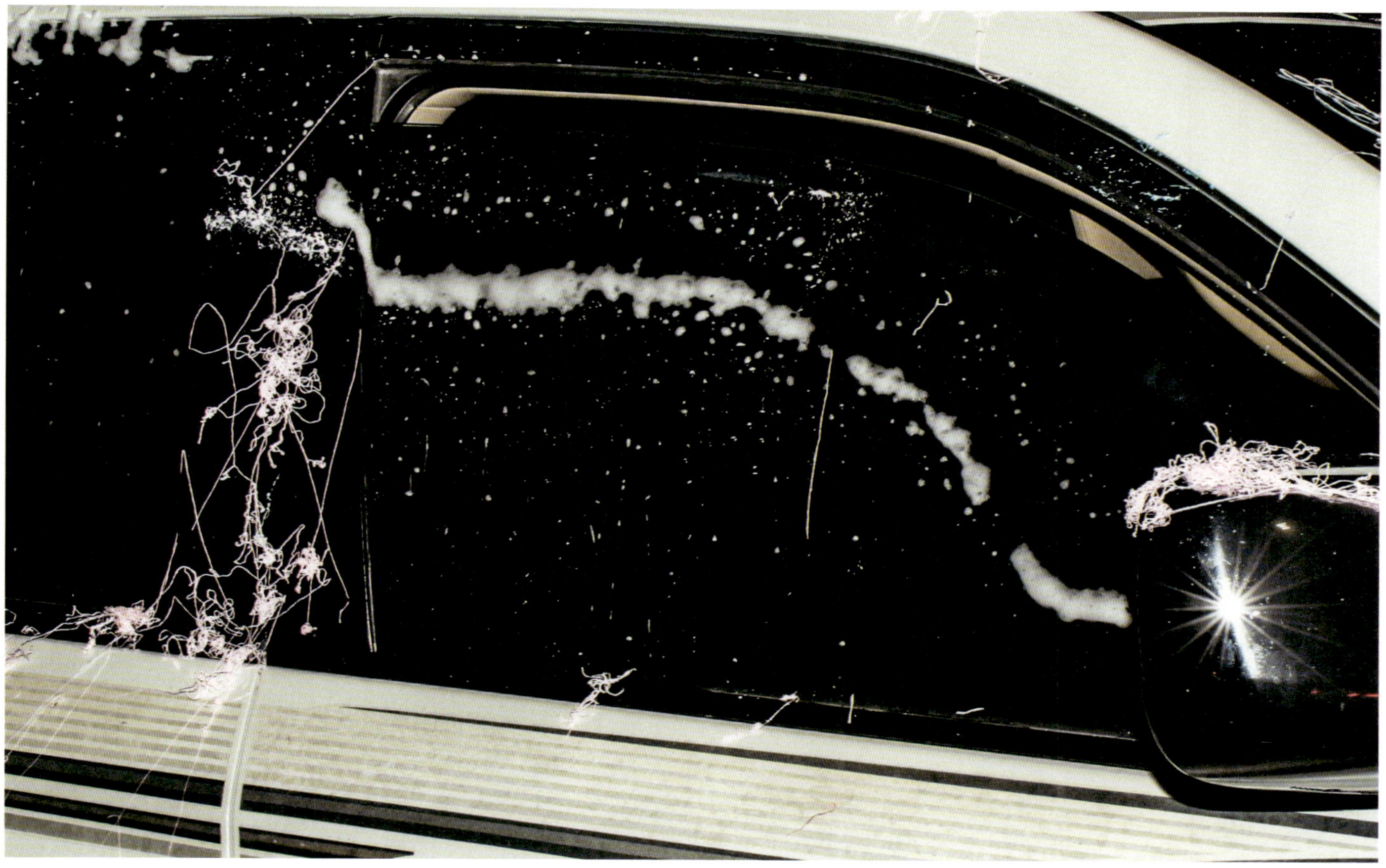

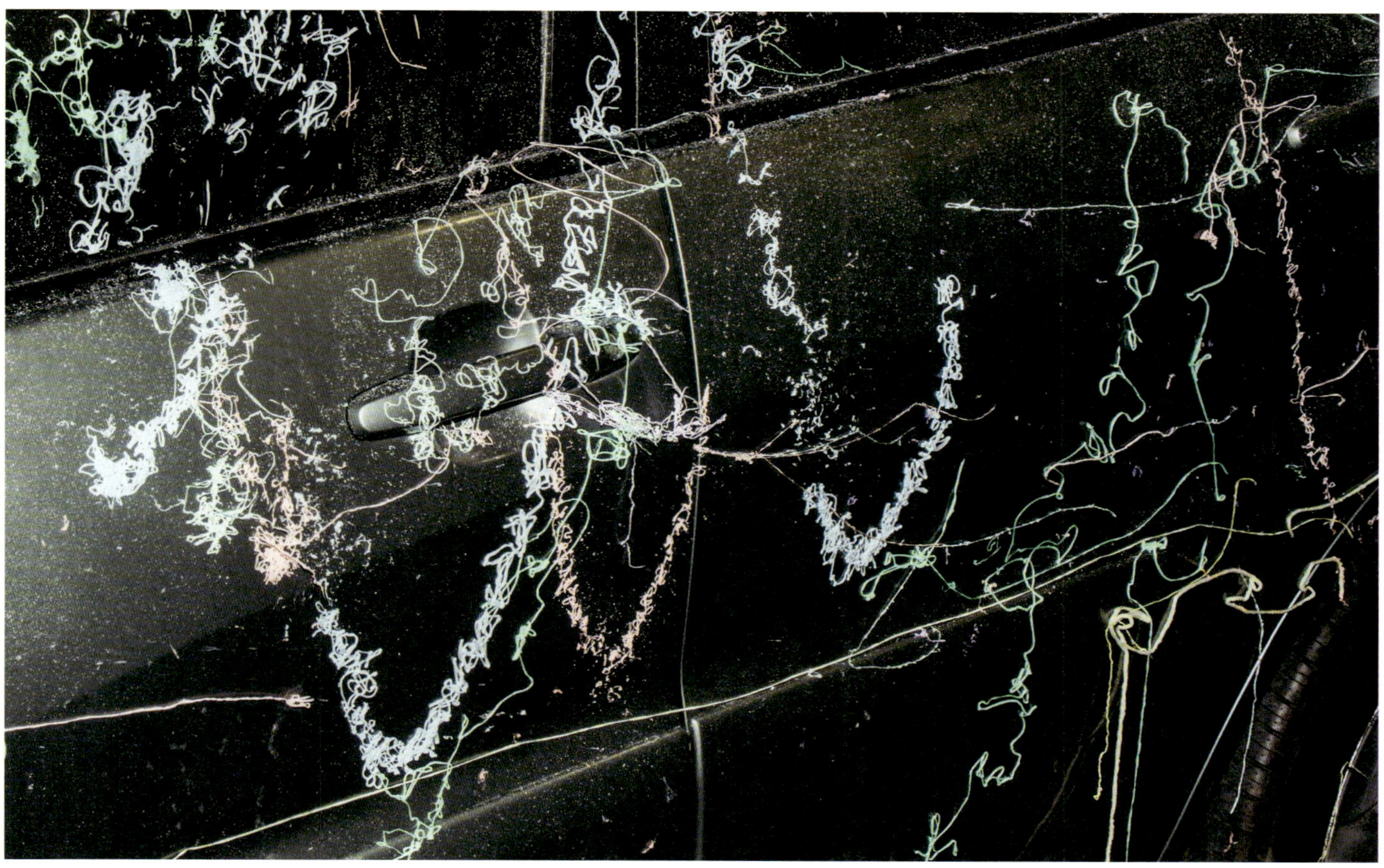

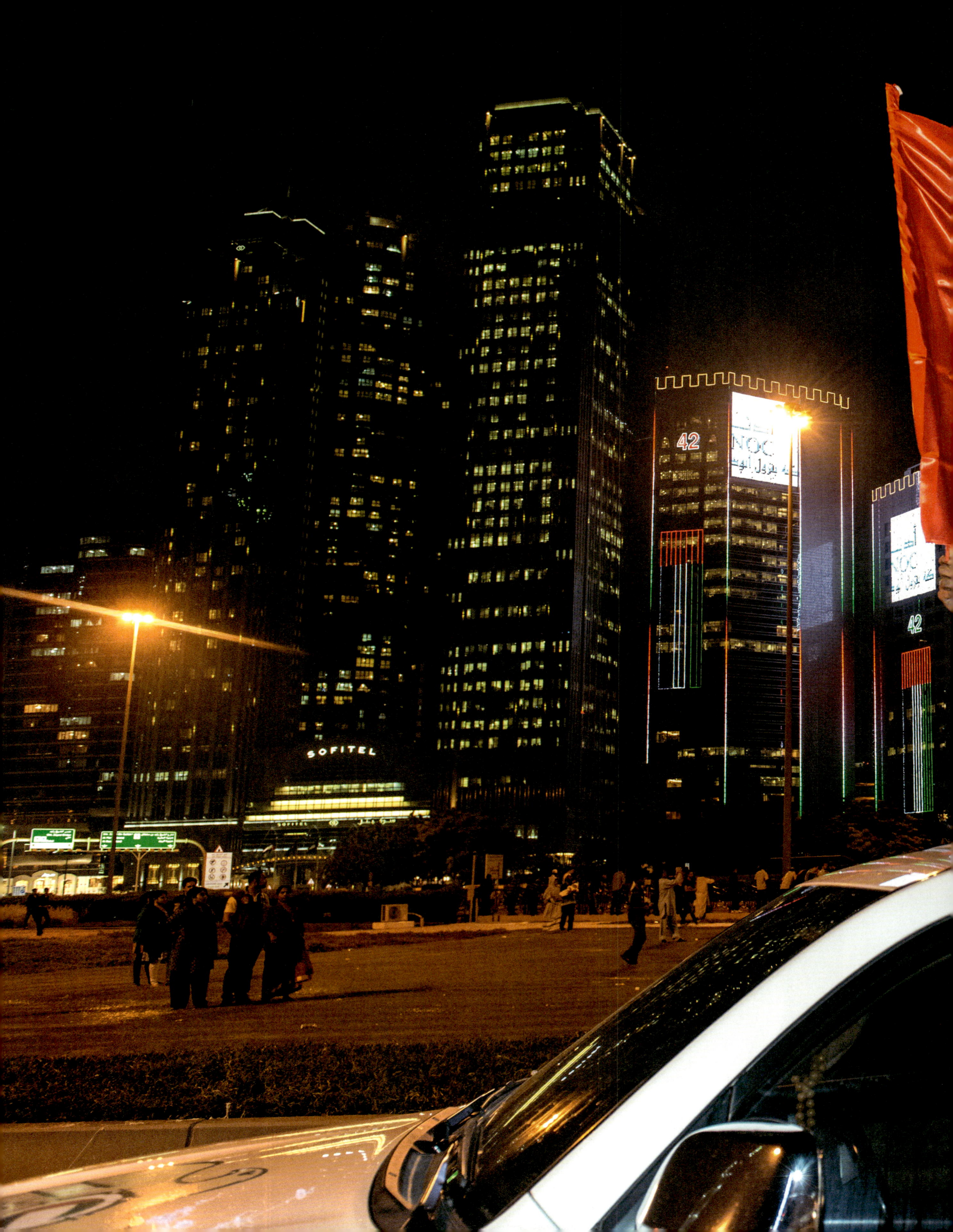
SOFITEL
42
NOC
42
NOC

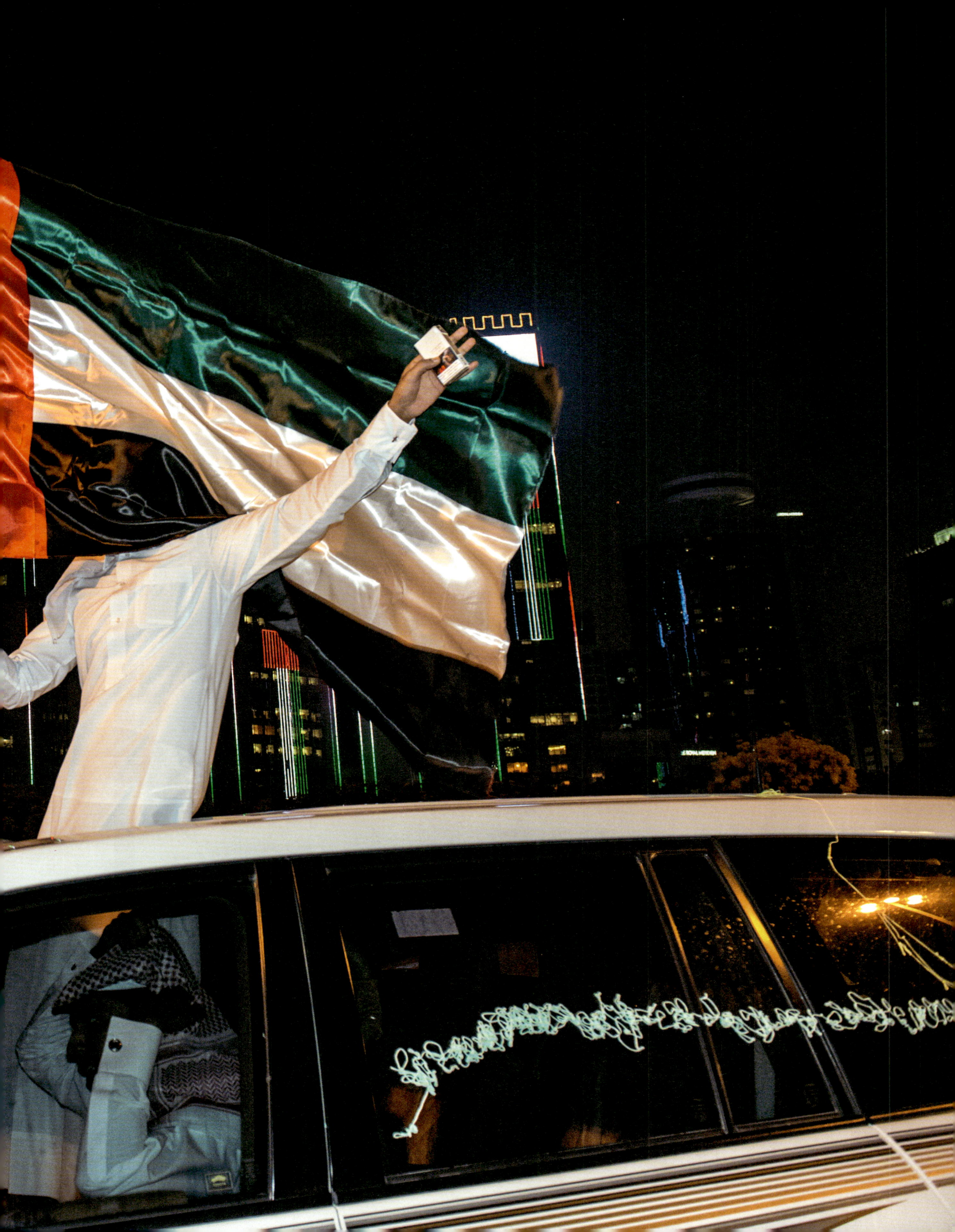

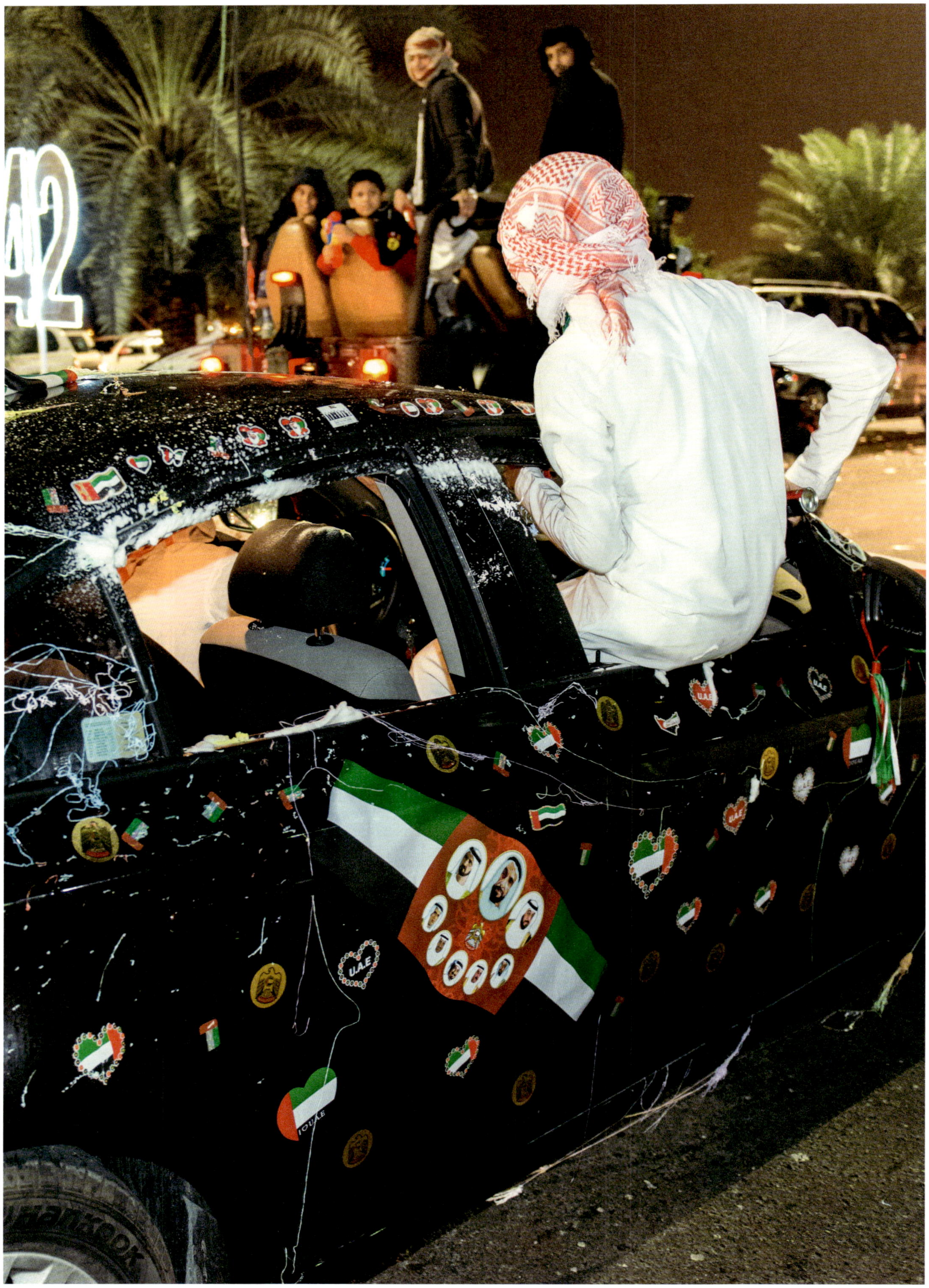

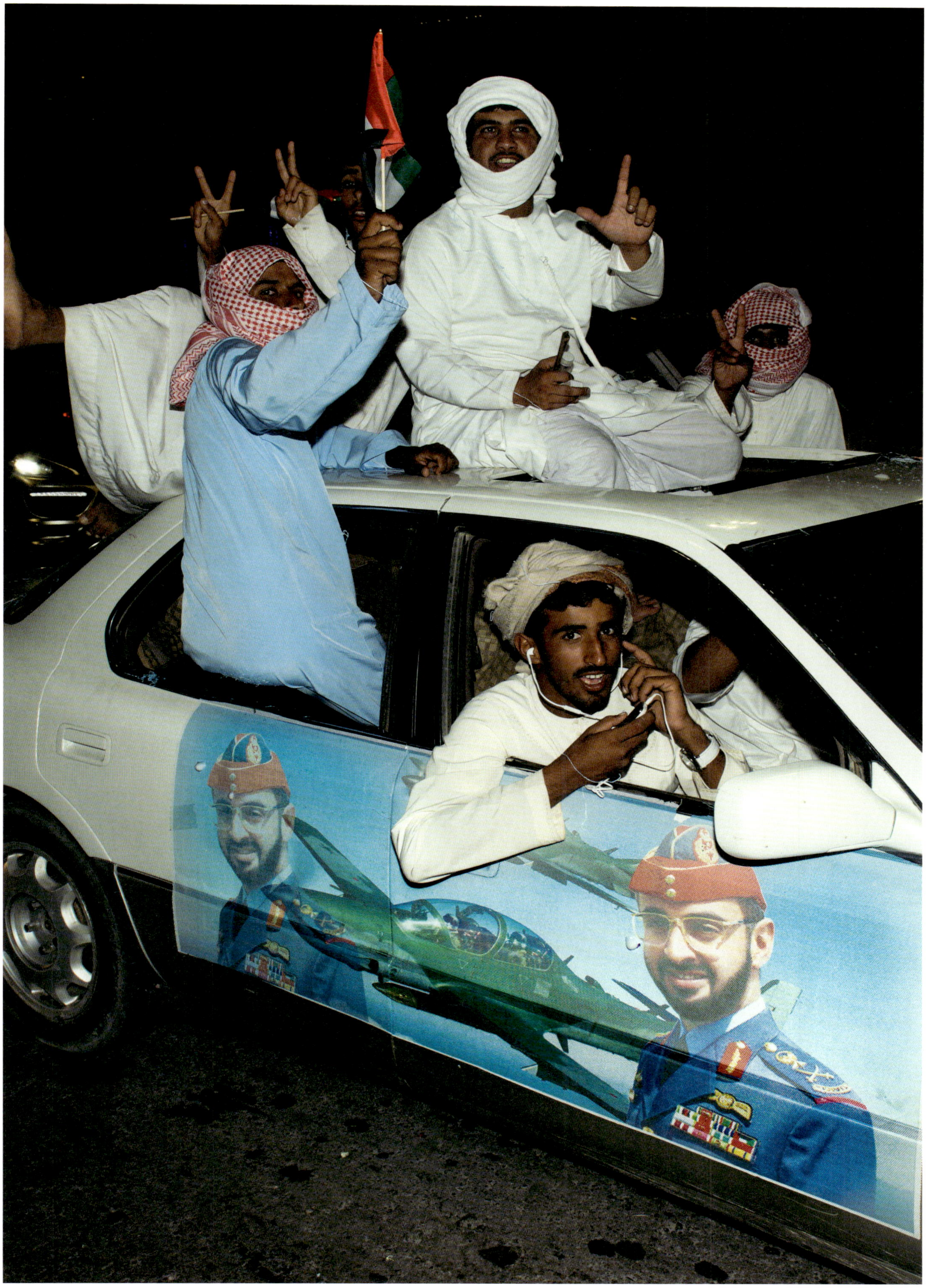

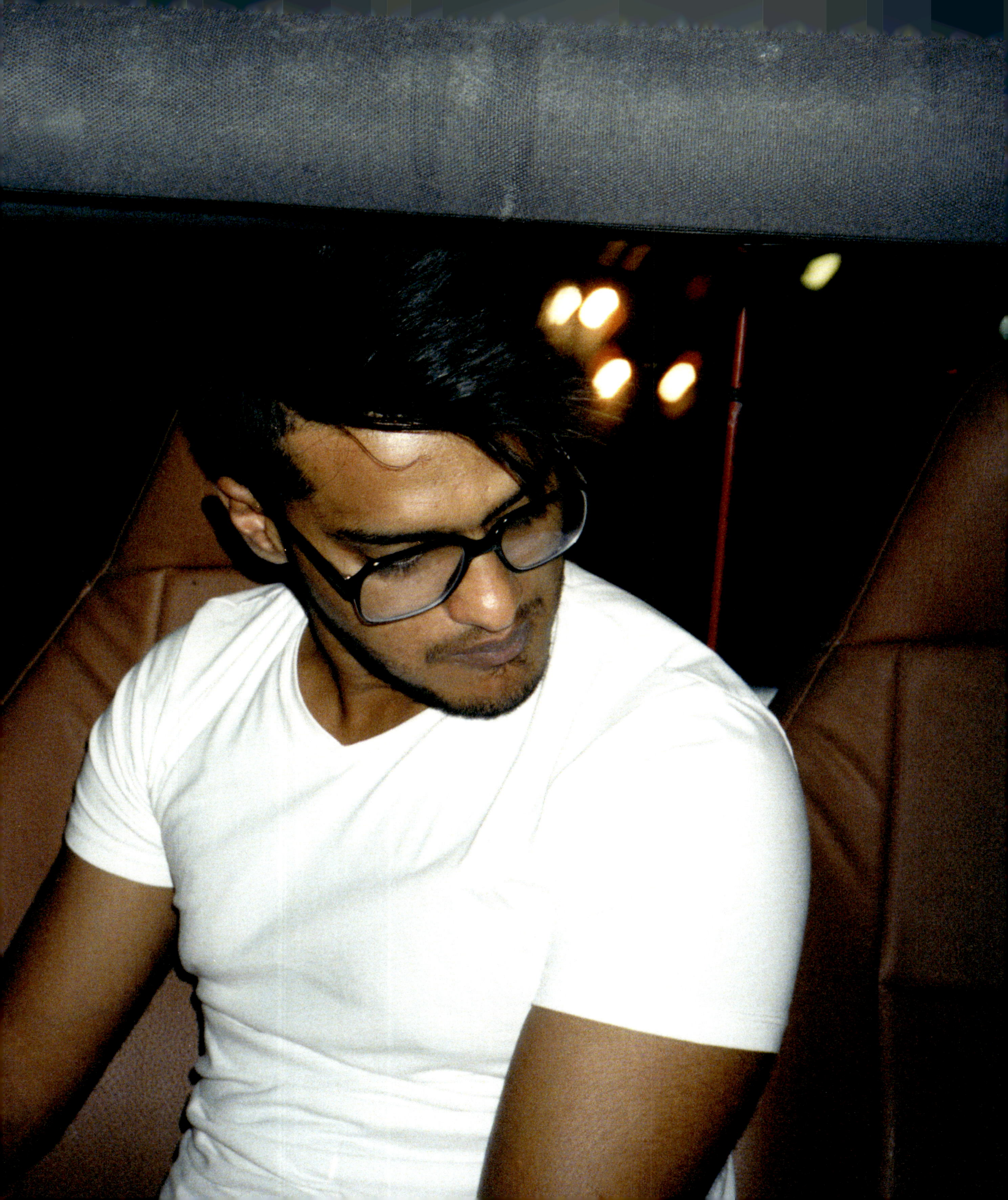

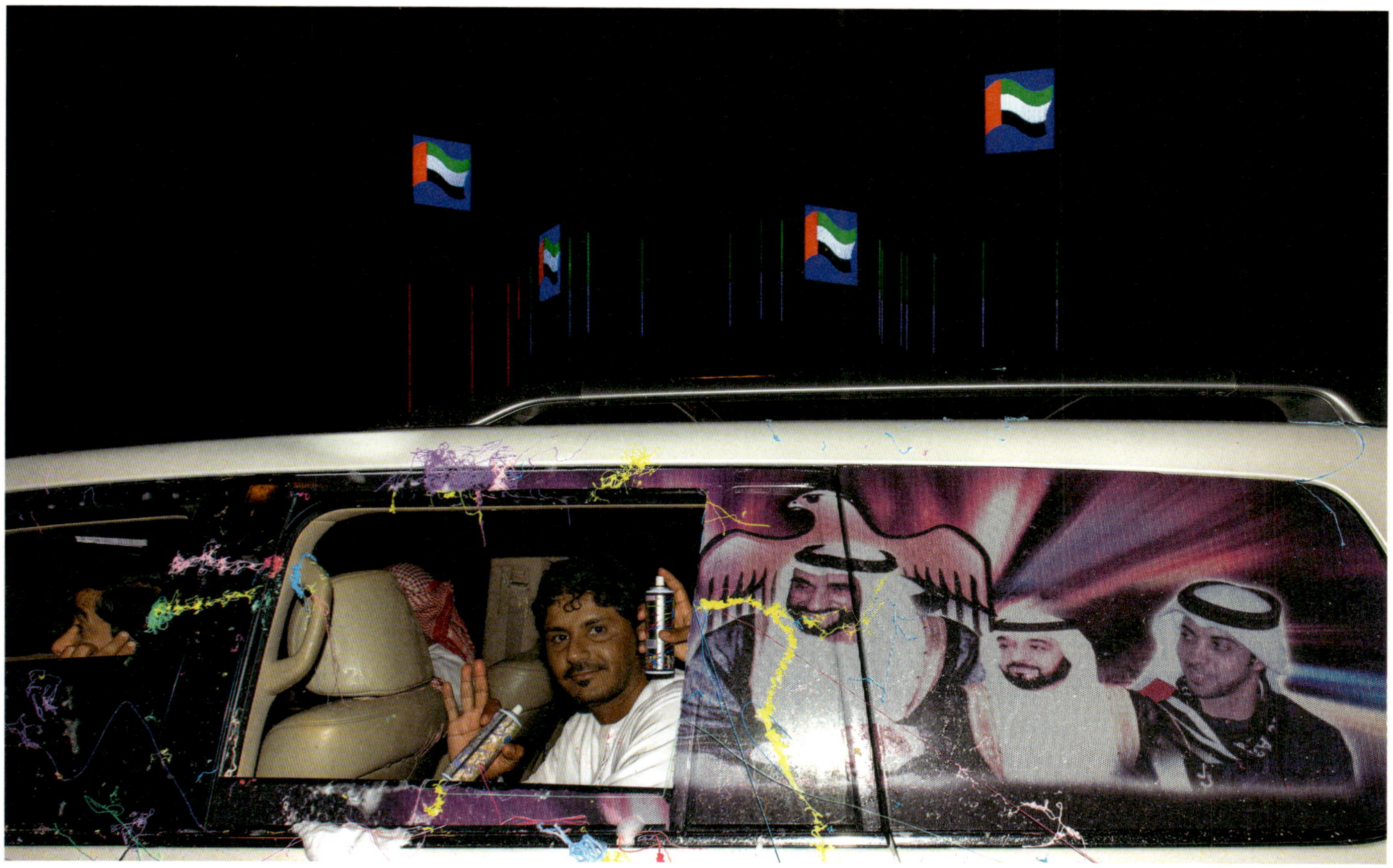

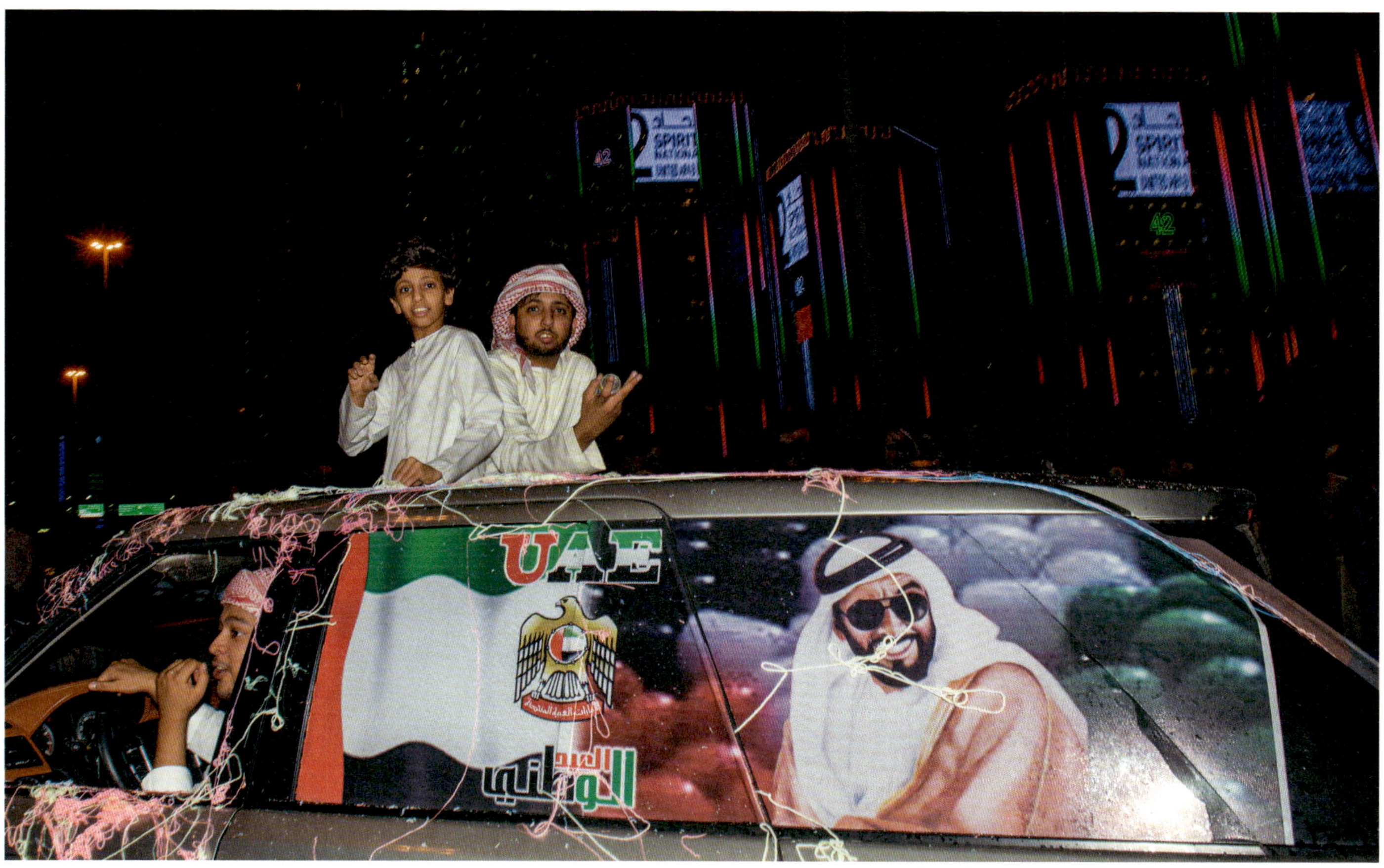
UAE
العيد الوطني

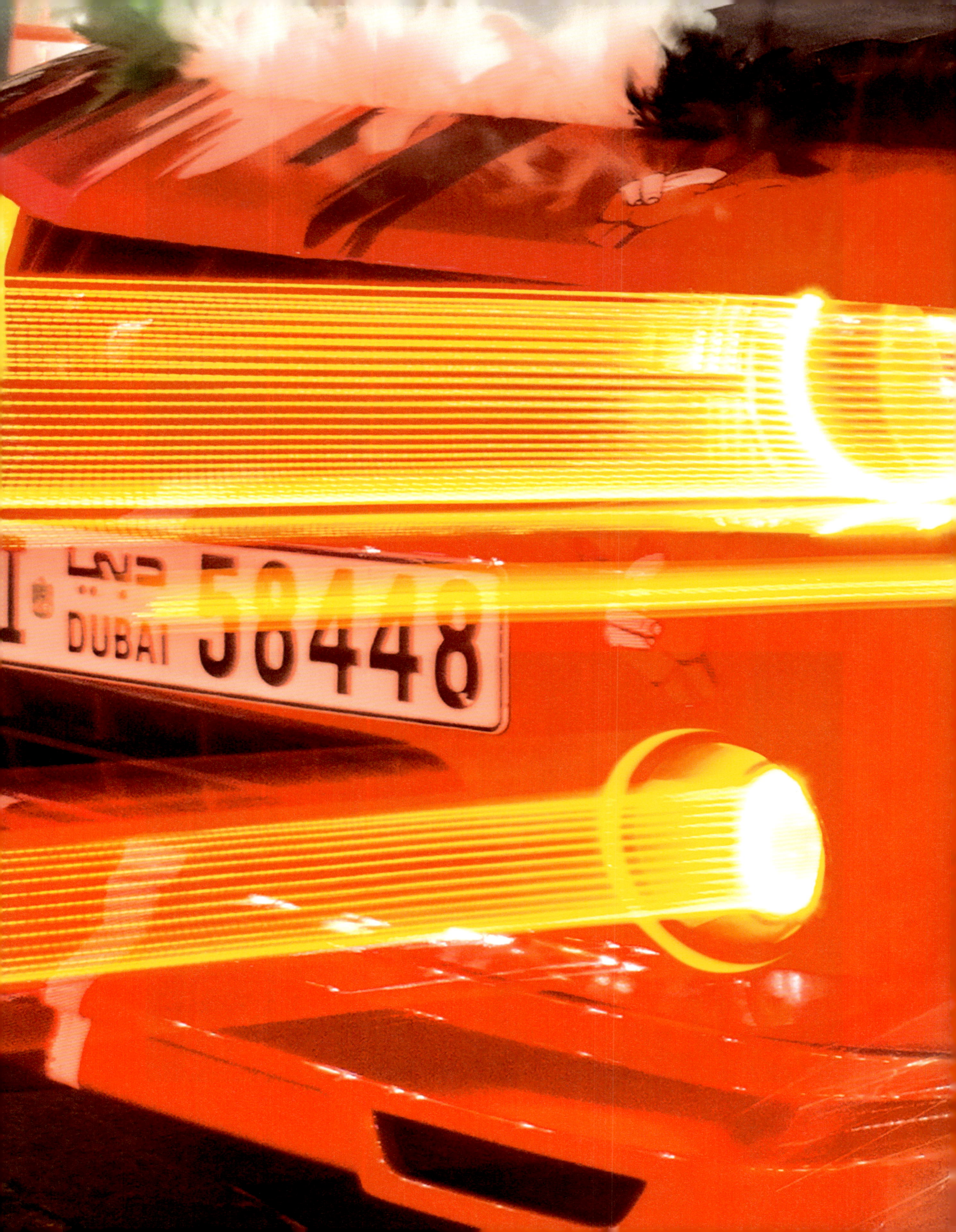
دبي
DUBAI 58448

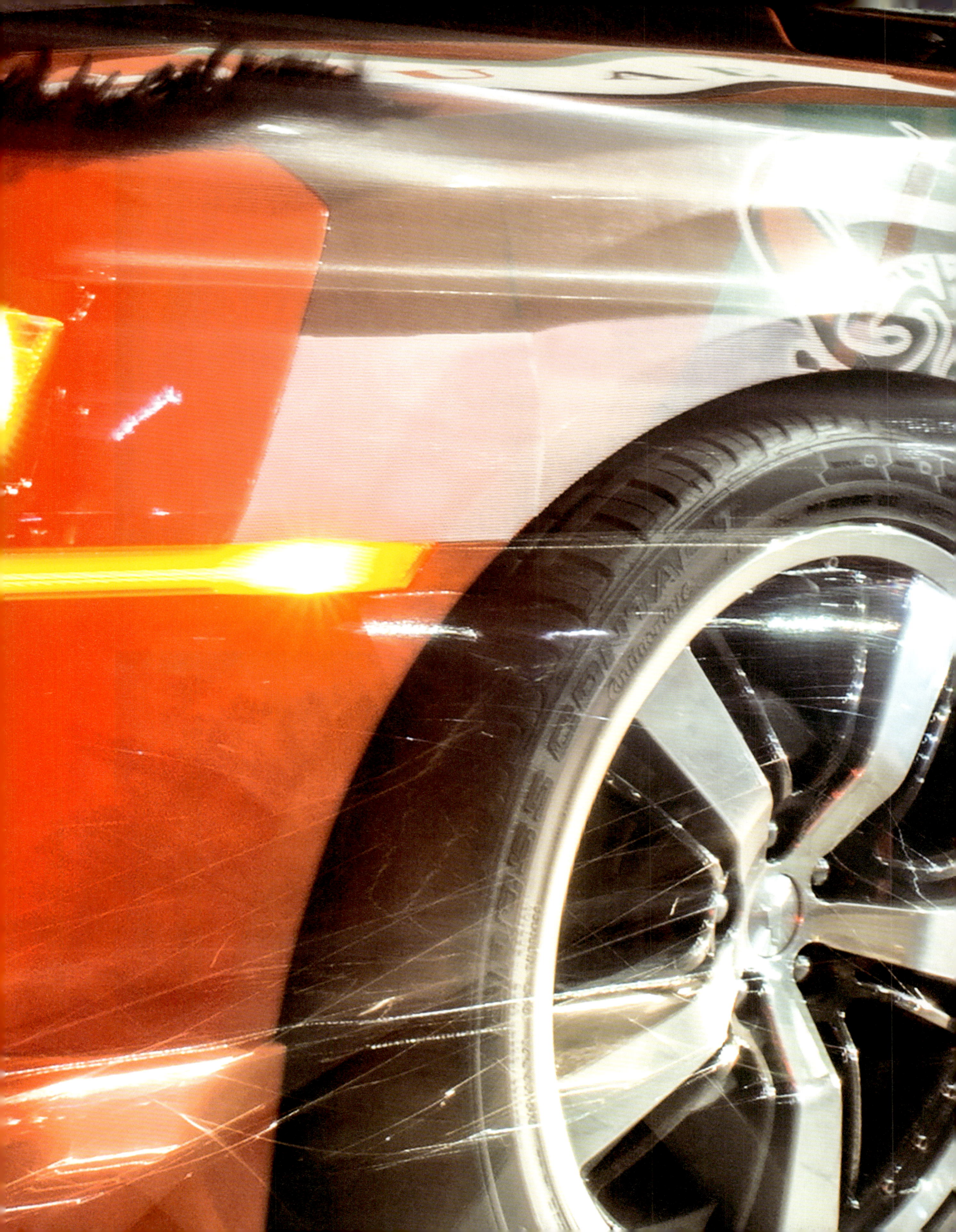

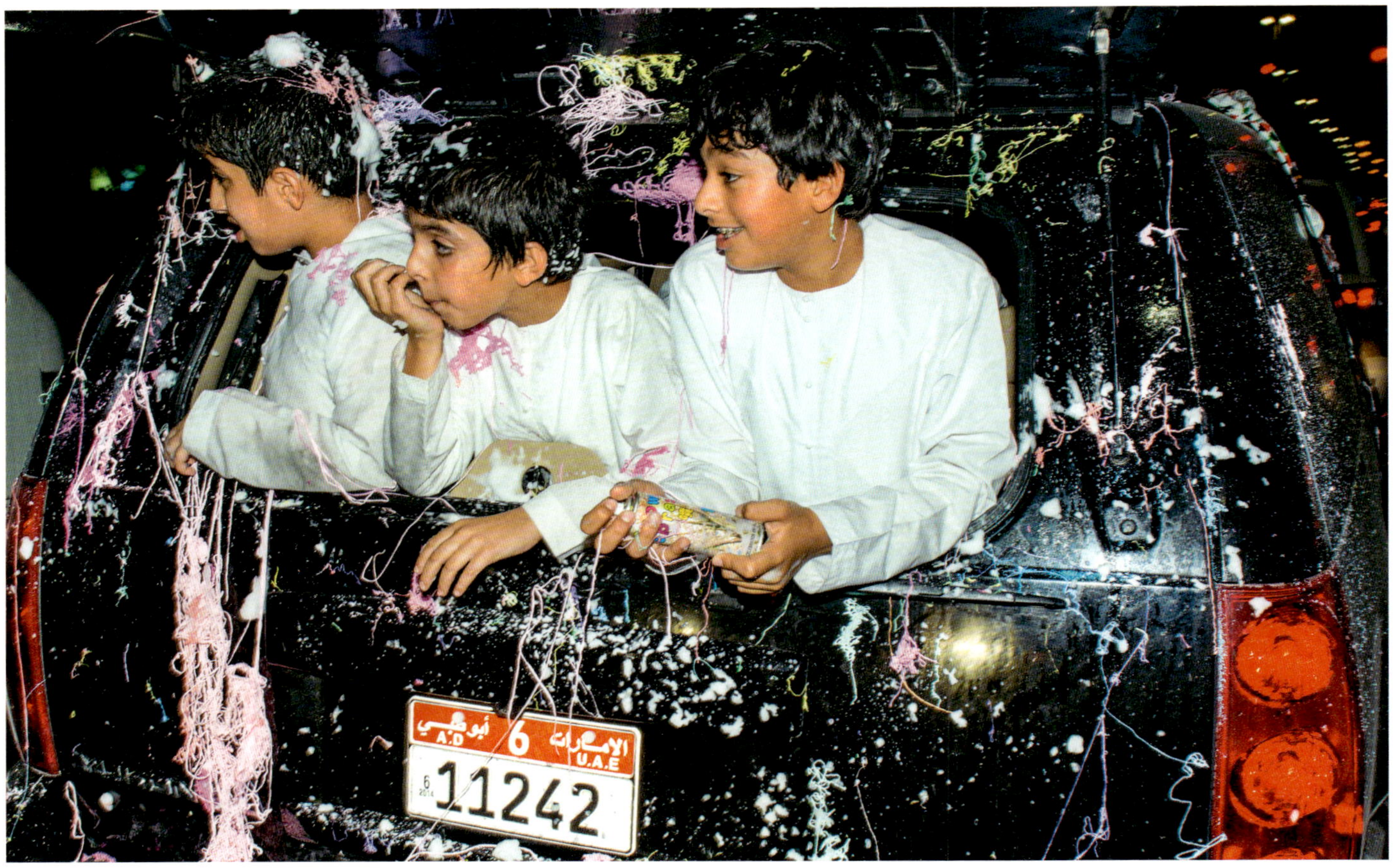
الامارات U.A.E
6
ابوظبي A.D
11242

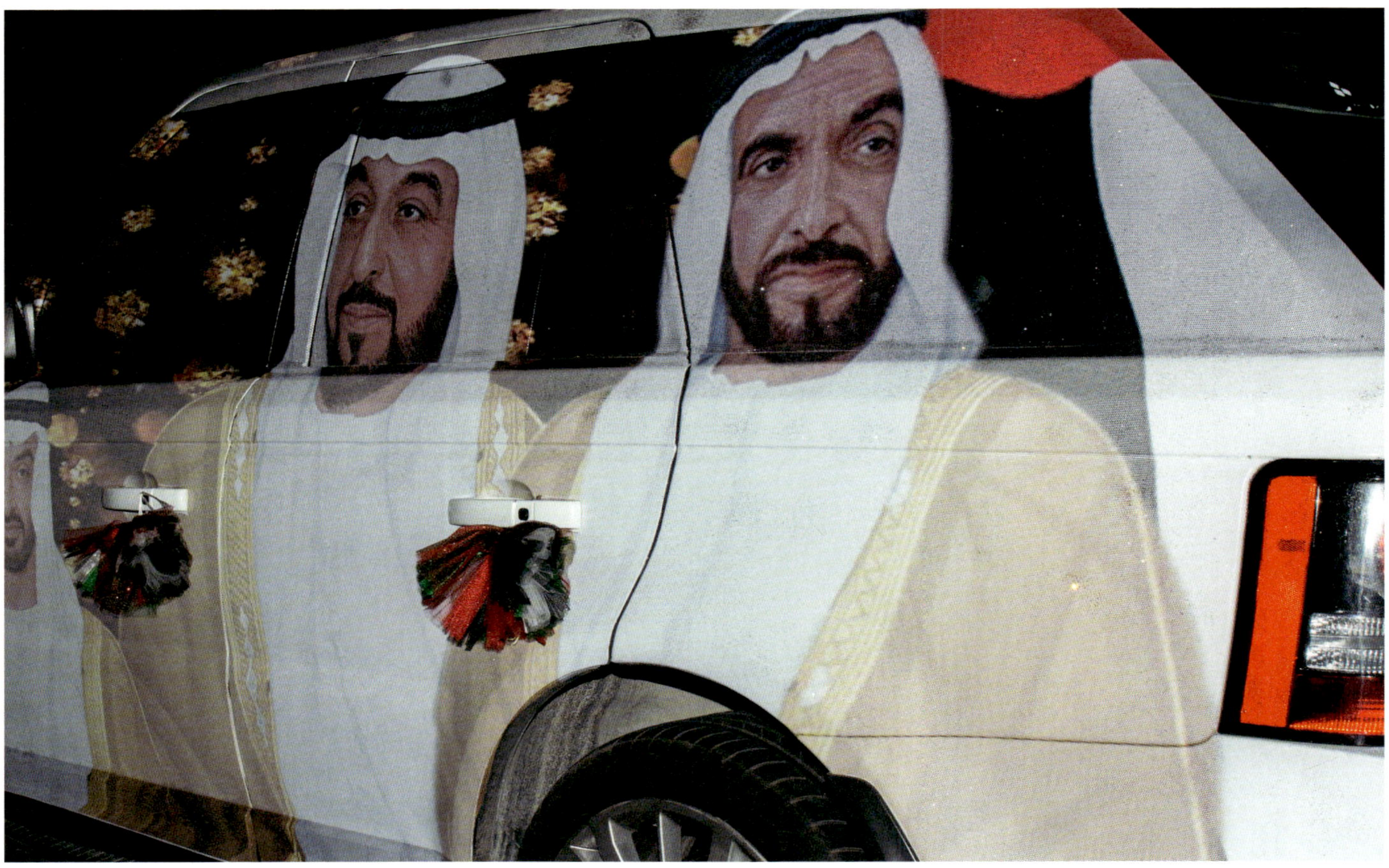

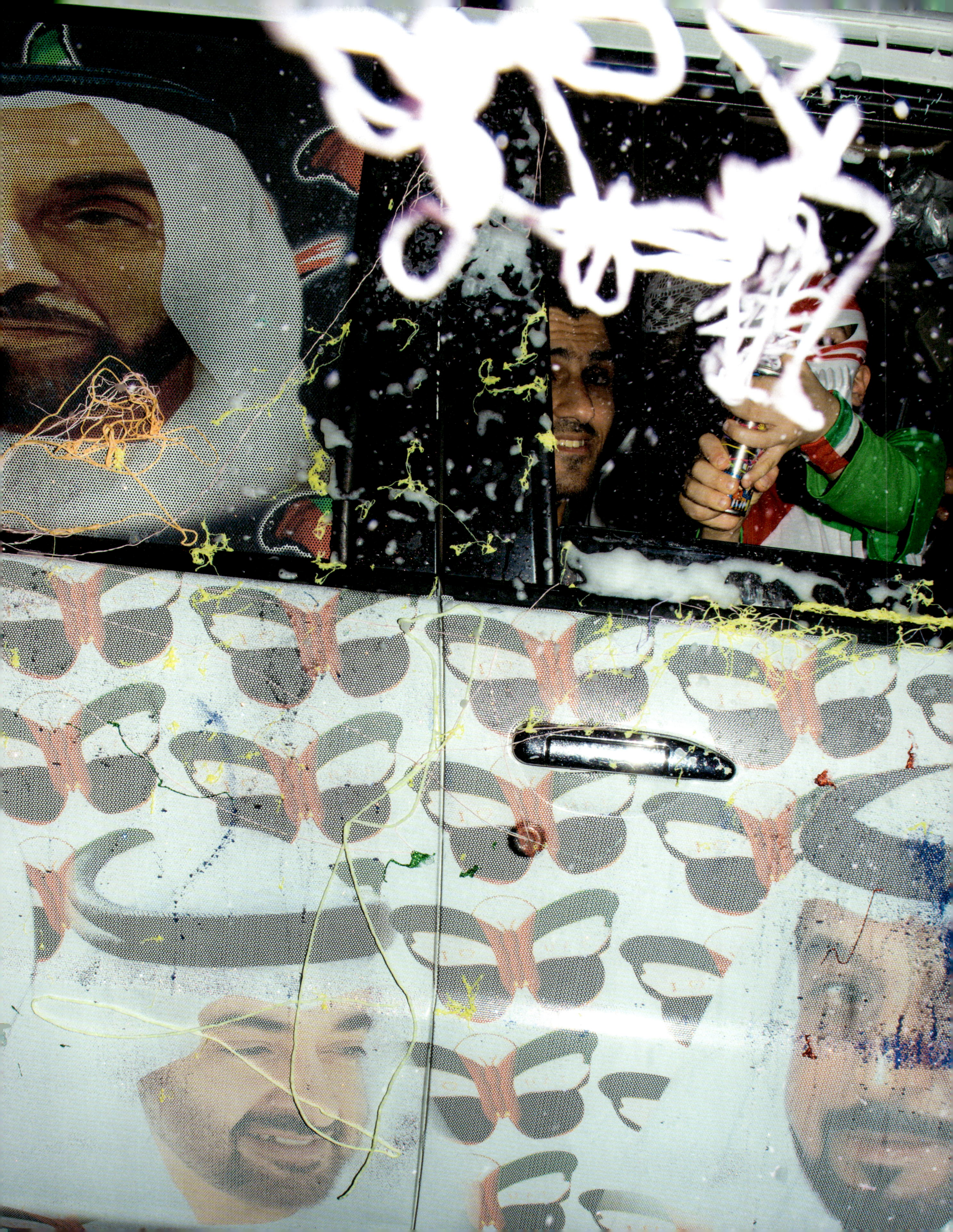

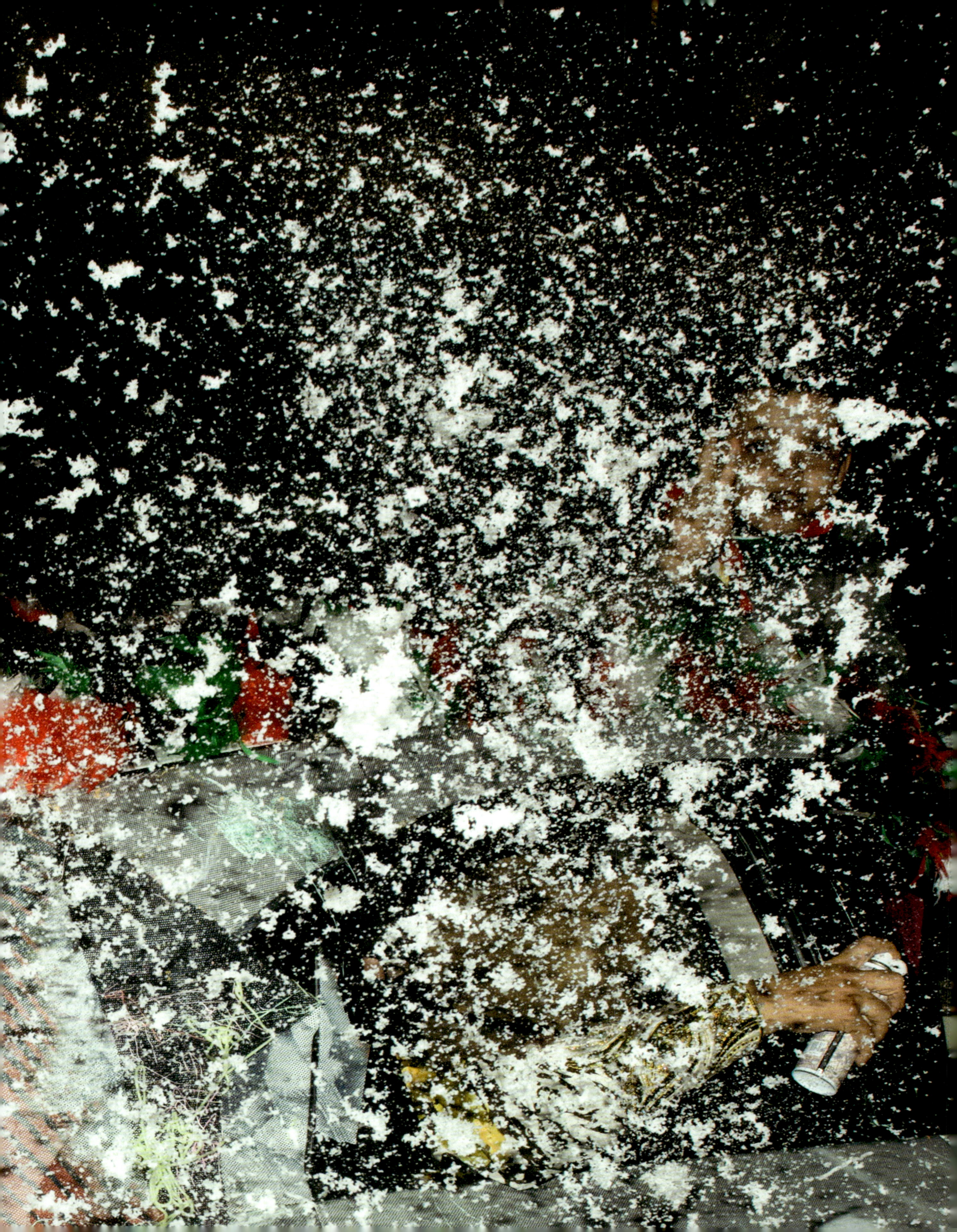

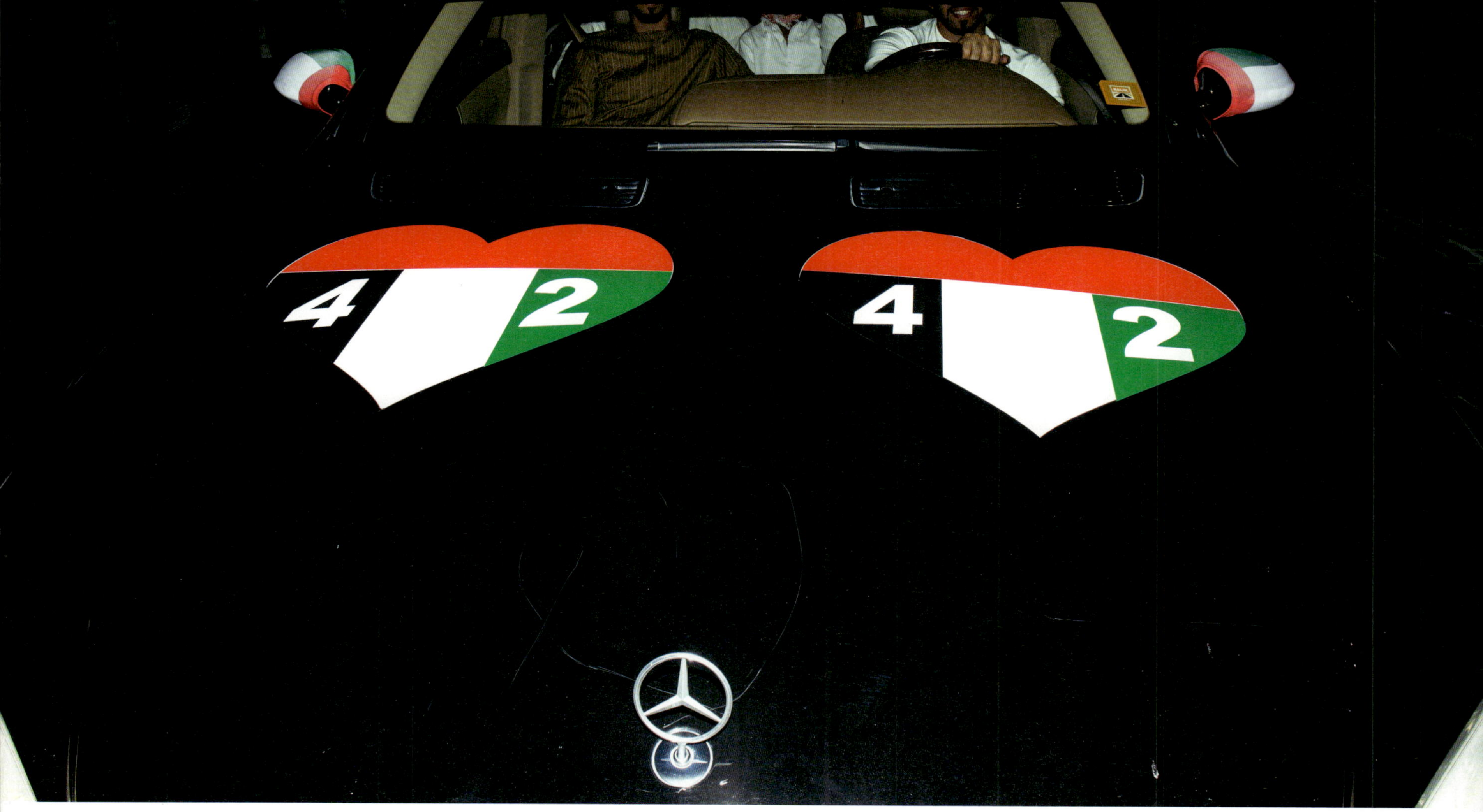
4 2
4 2

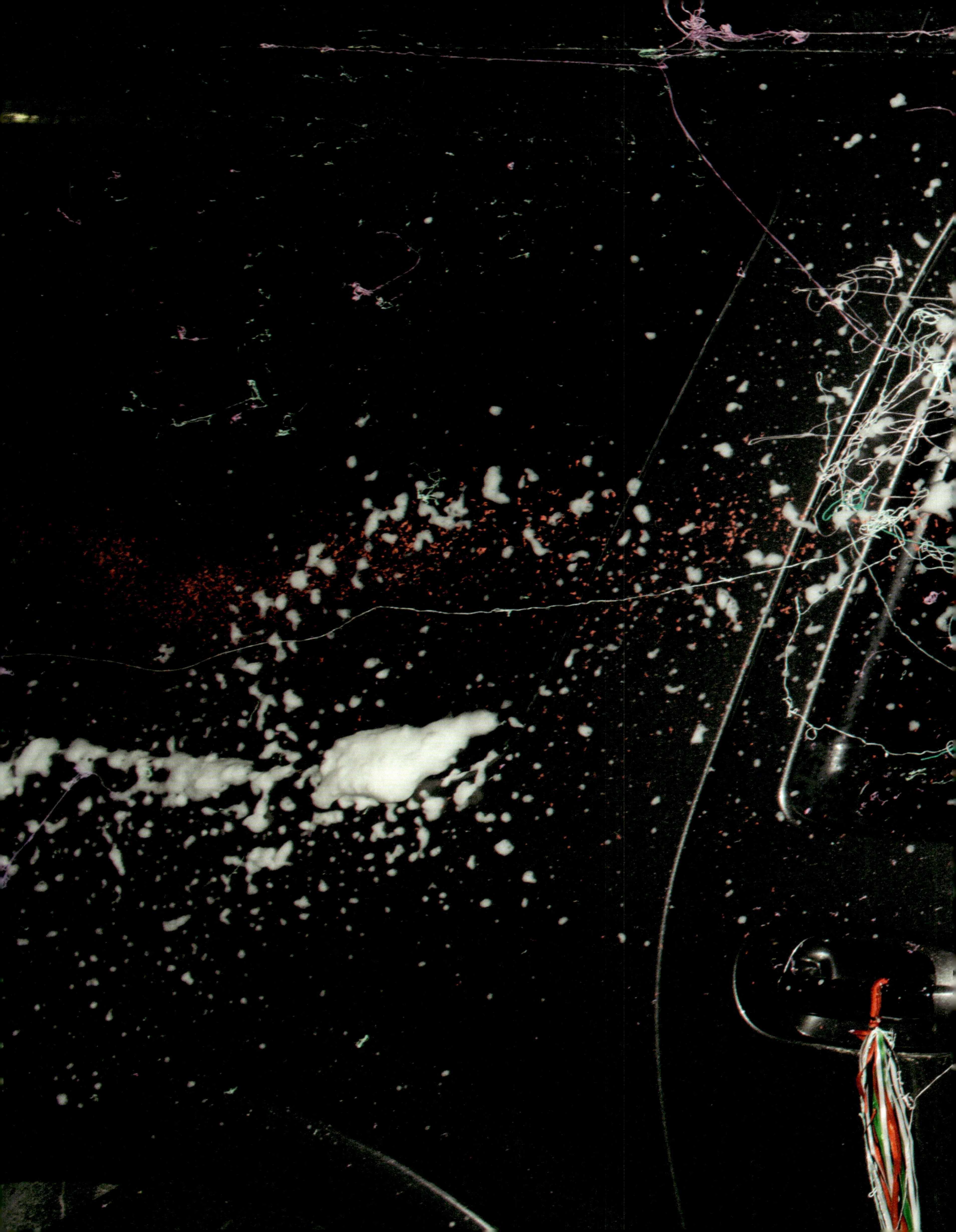

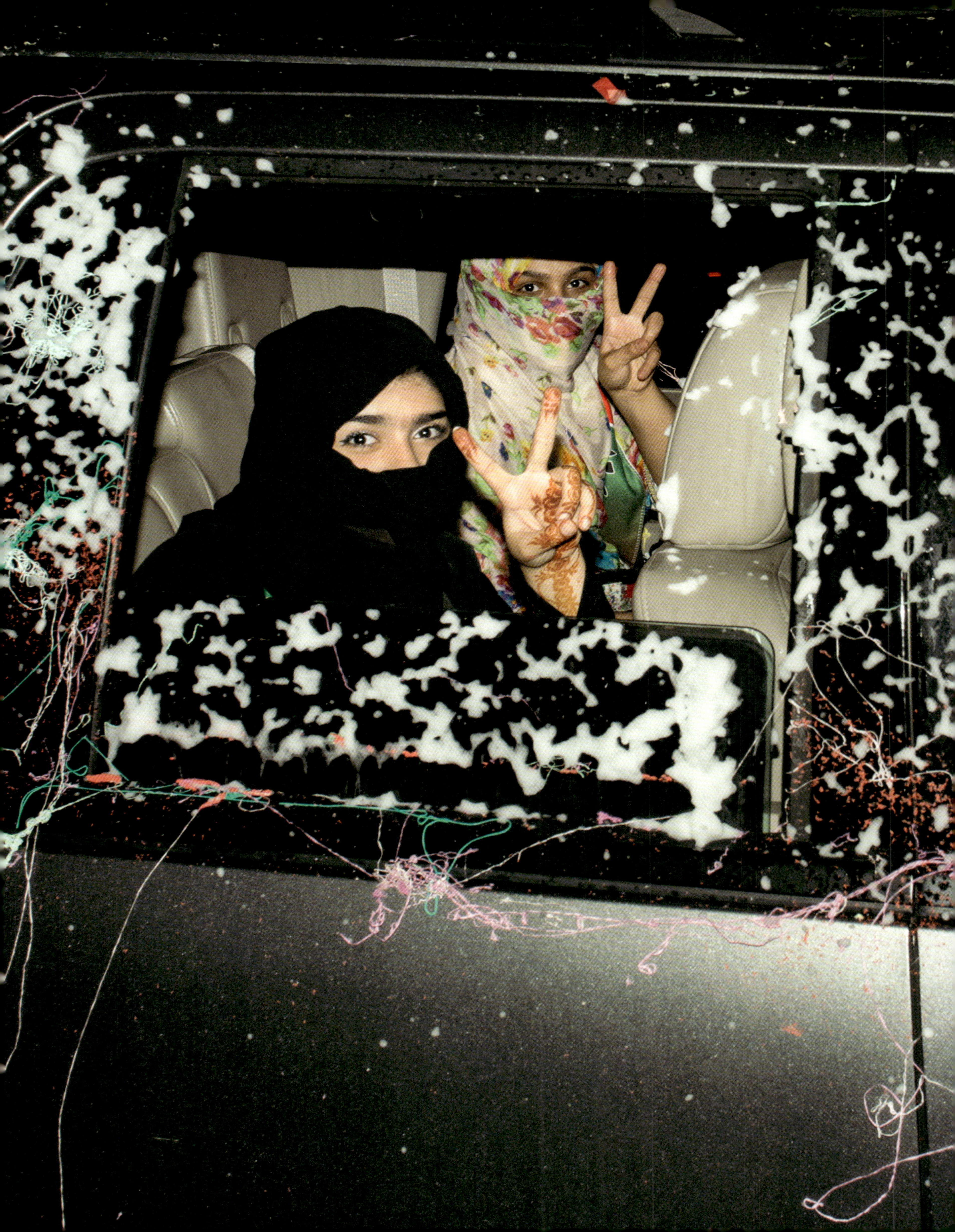

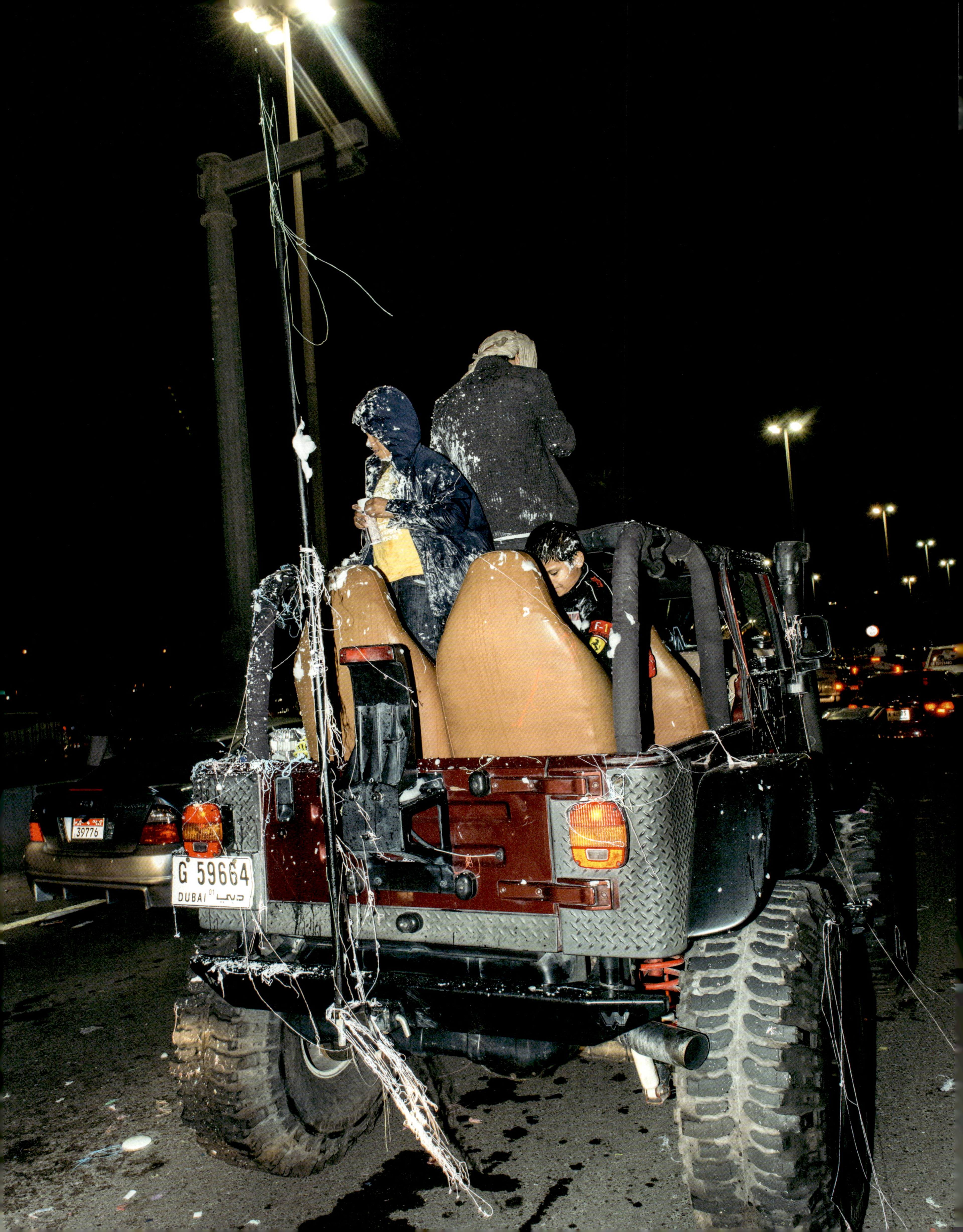
G 59664
DUBAI 01 دبي
39776

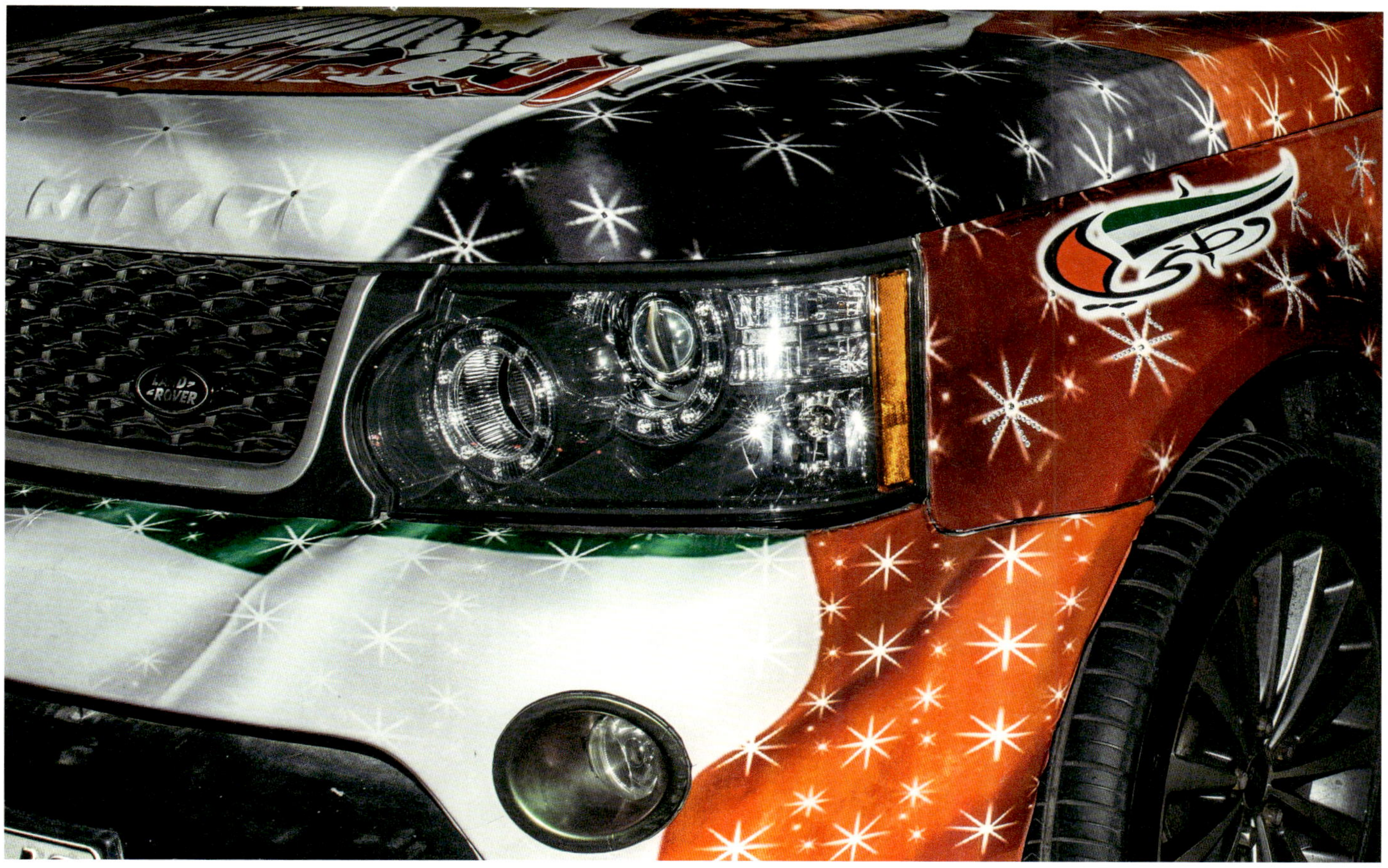

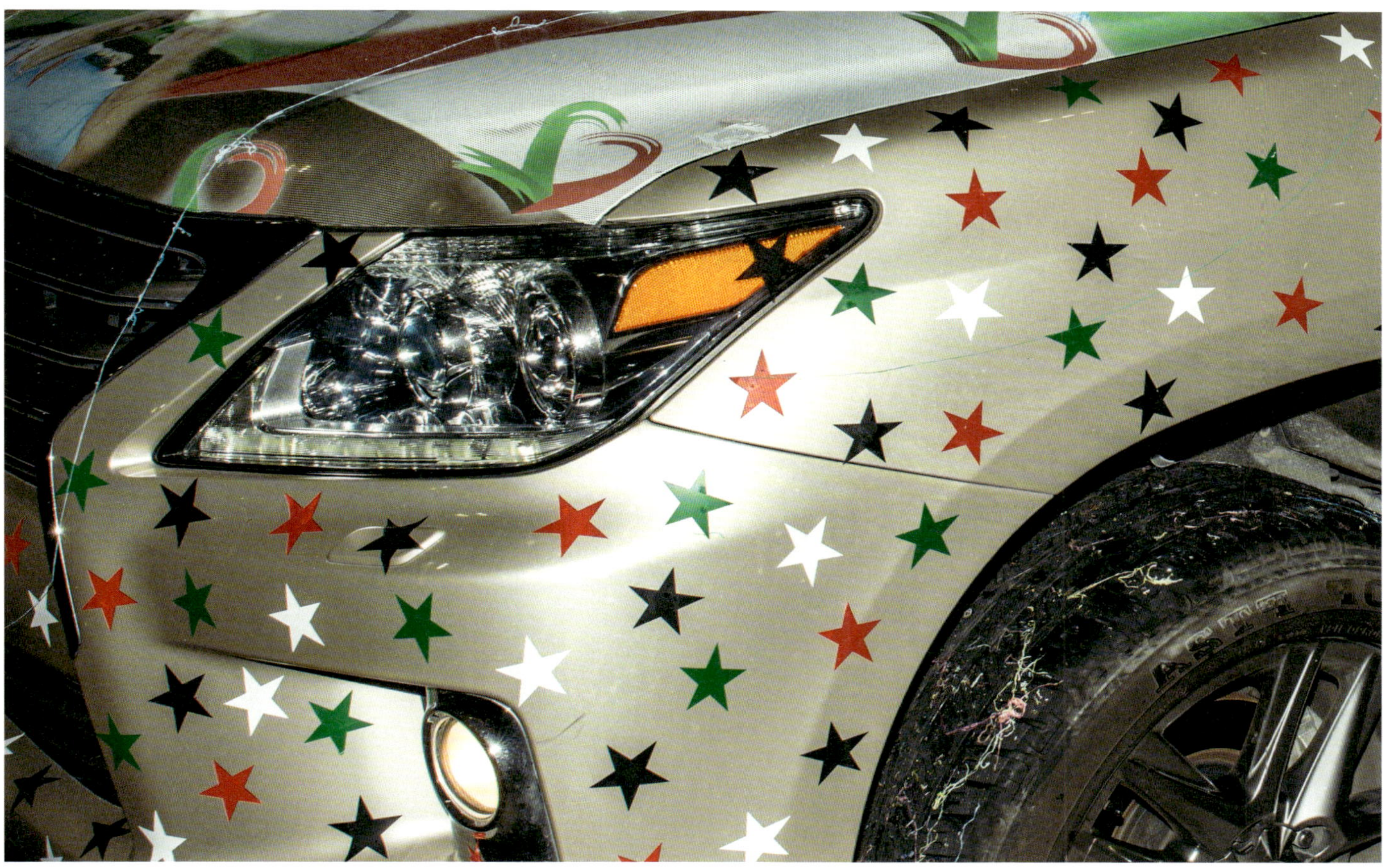

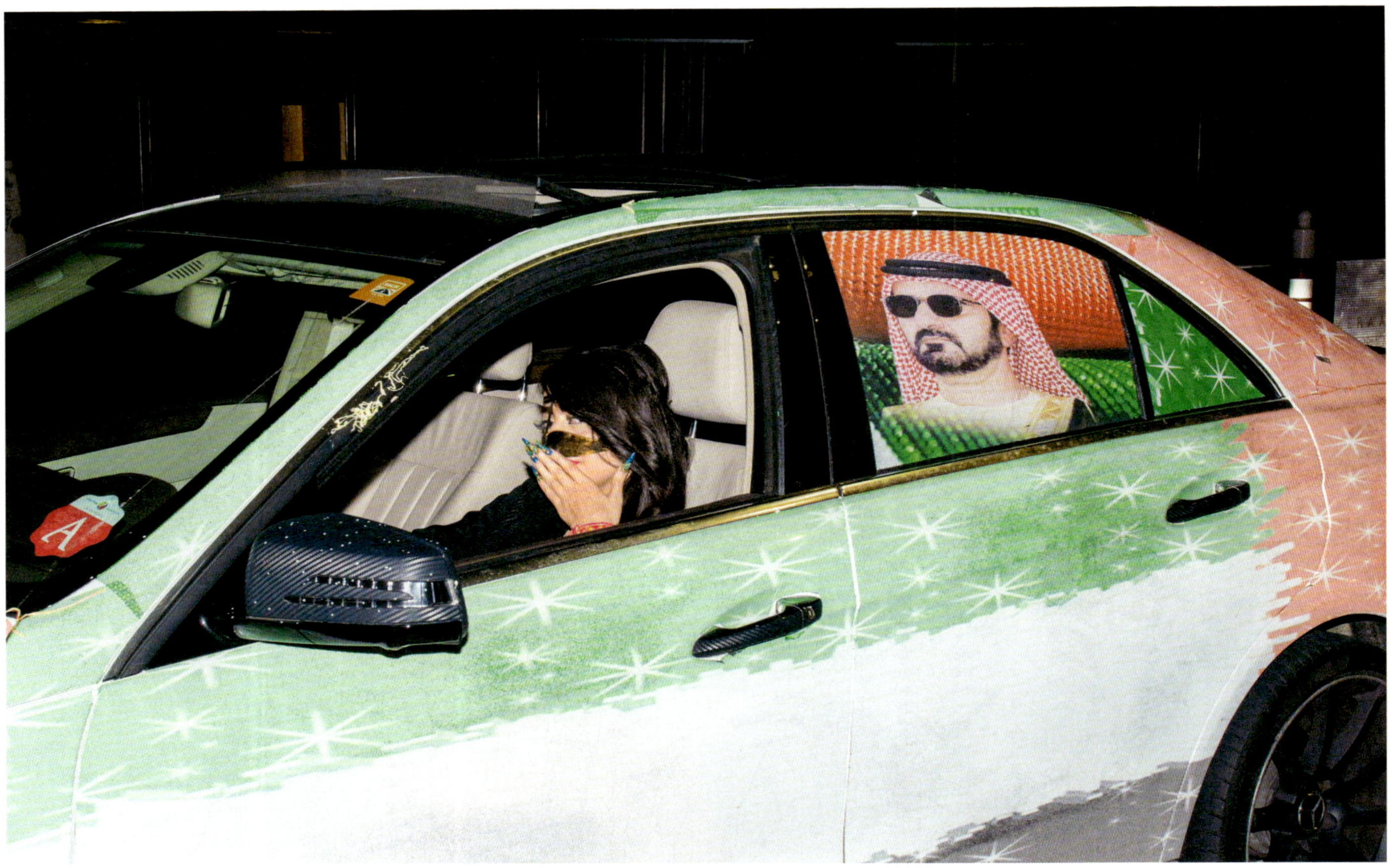

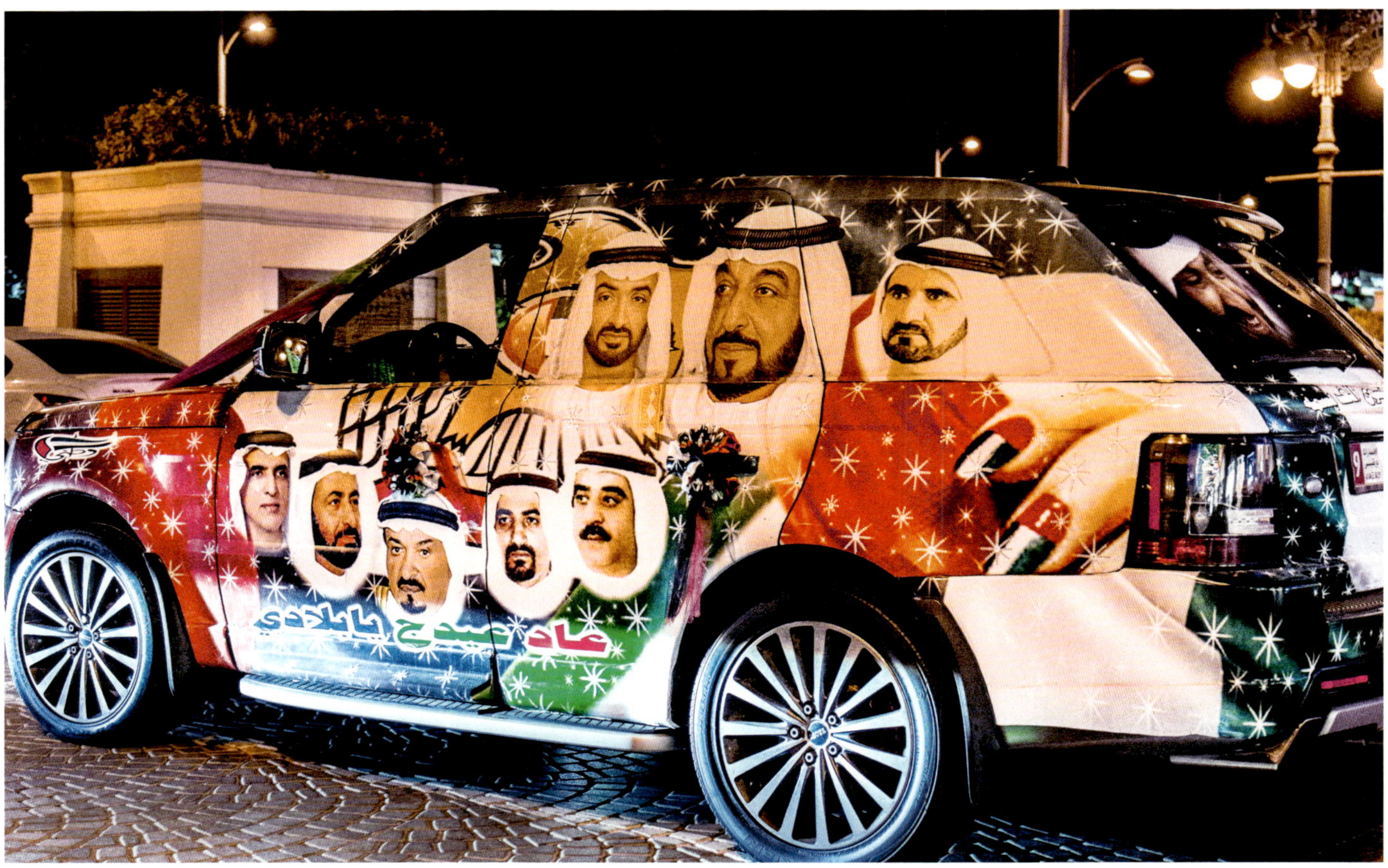

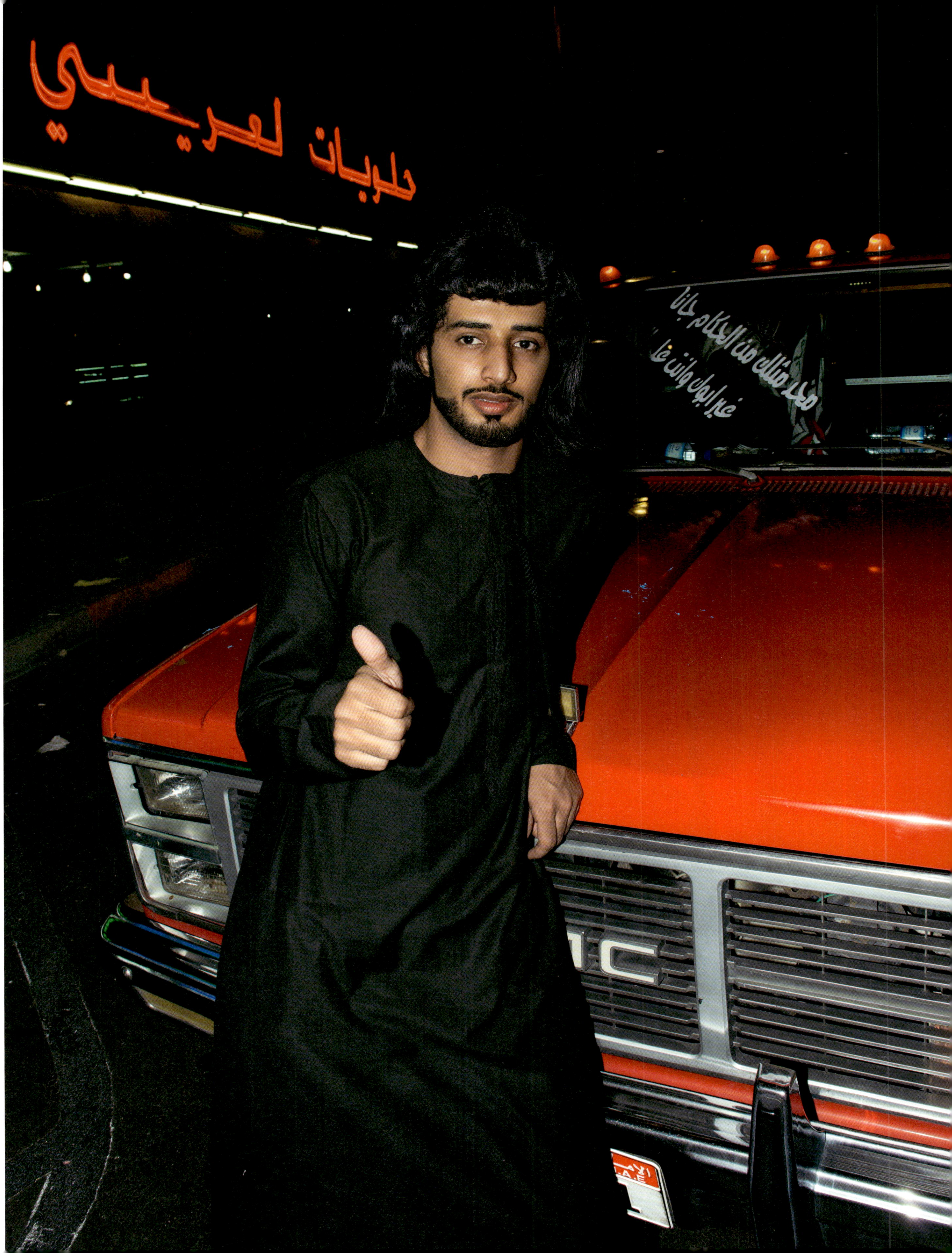

حلويات لعريبي

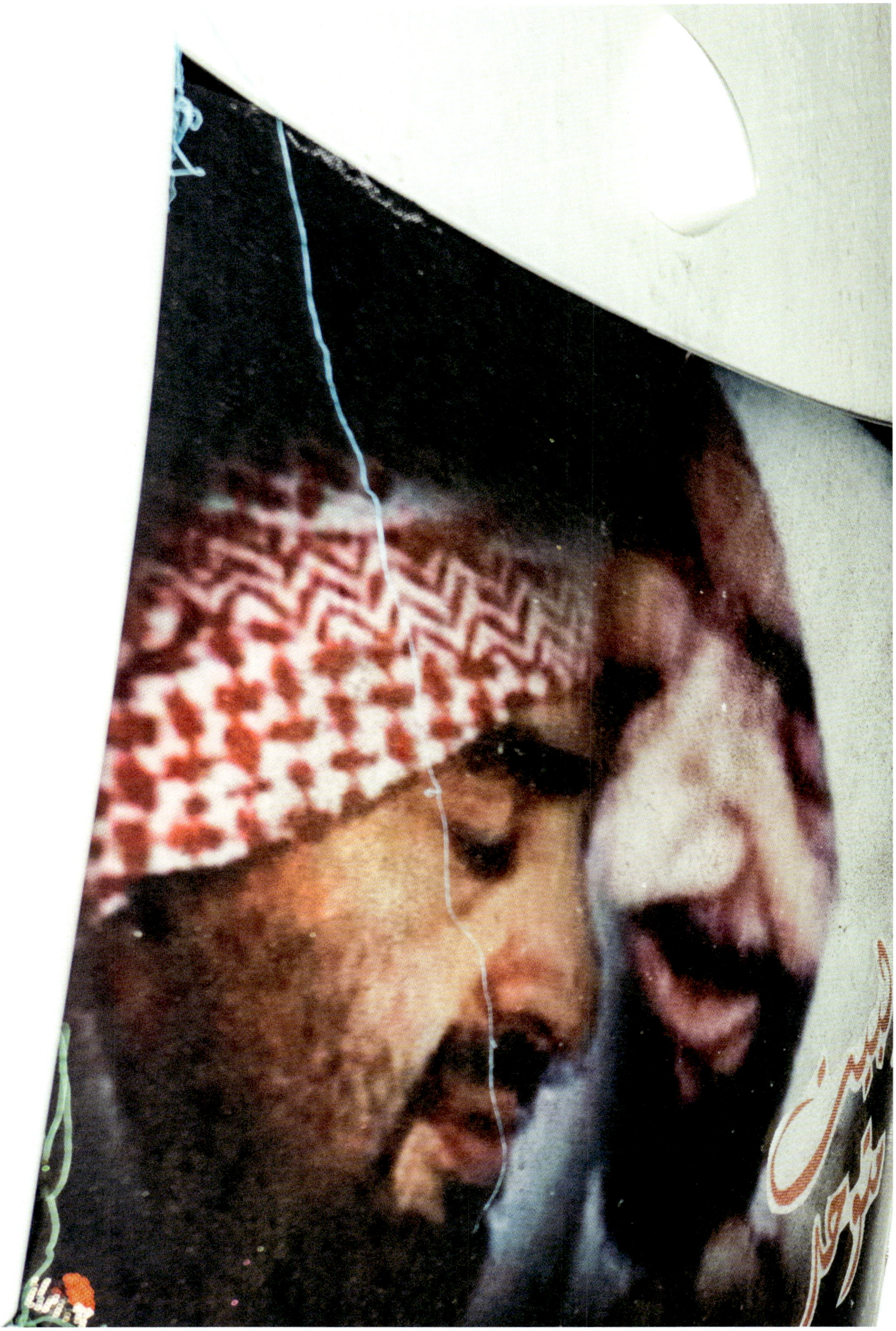

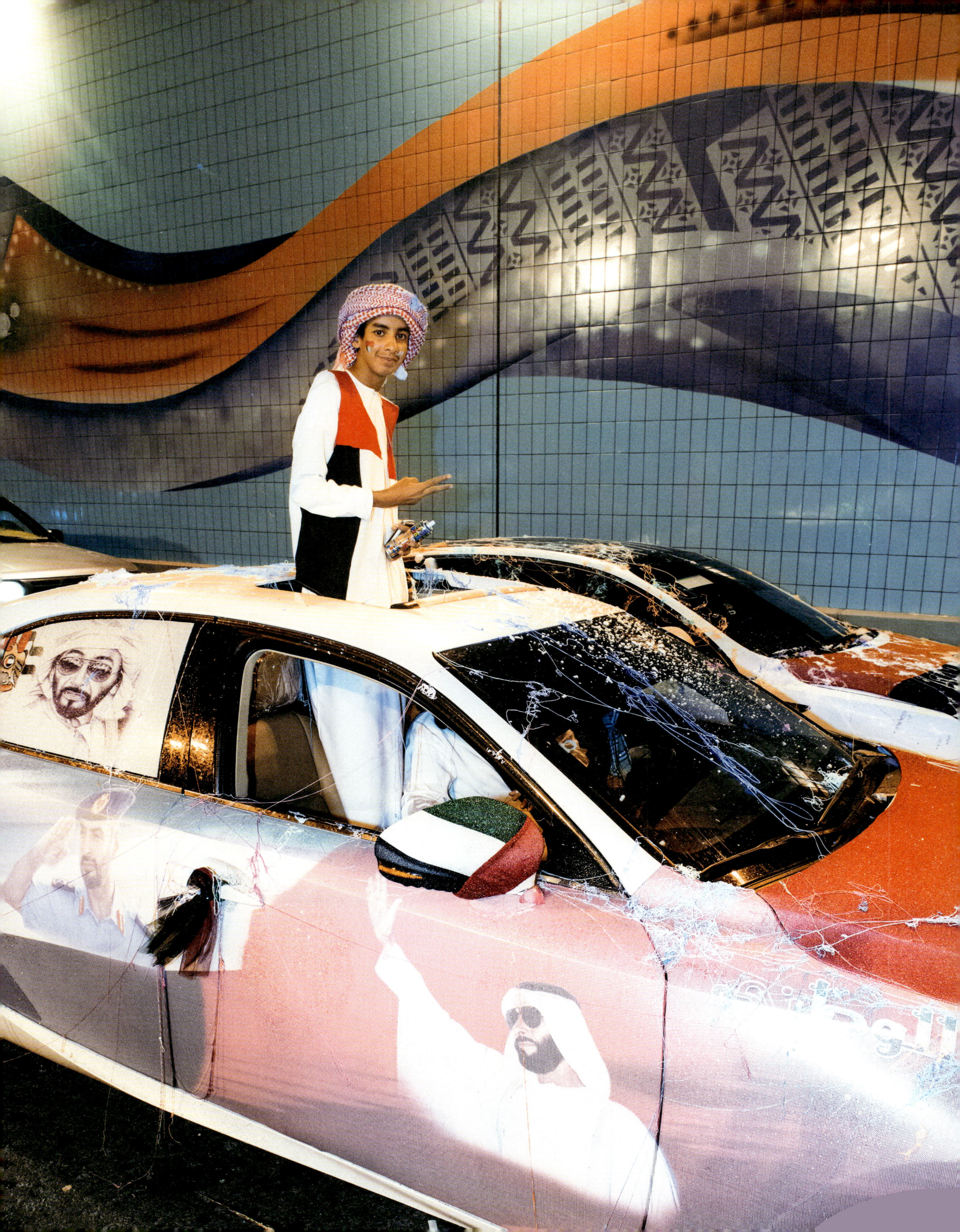

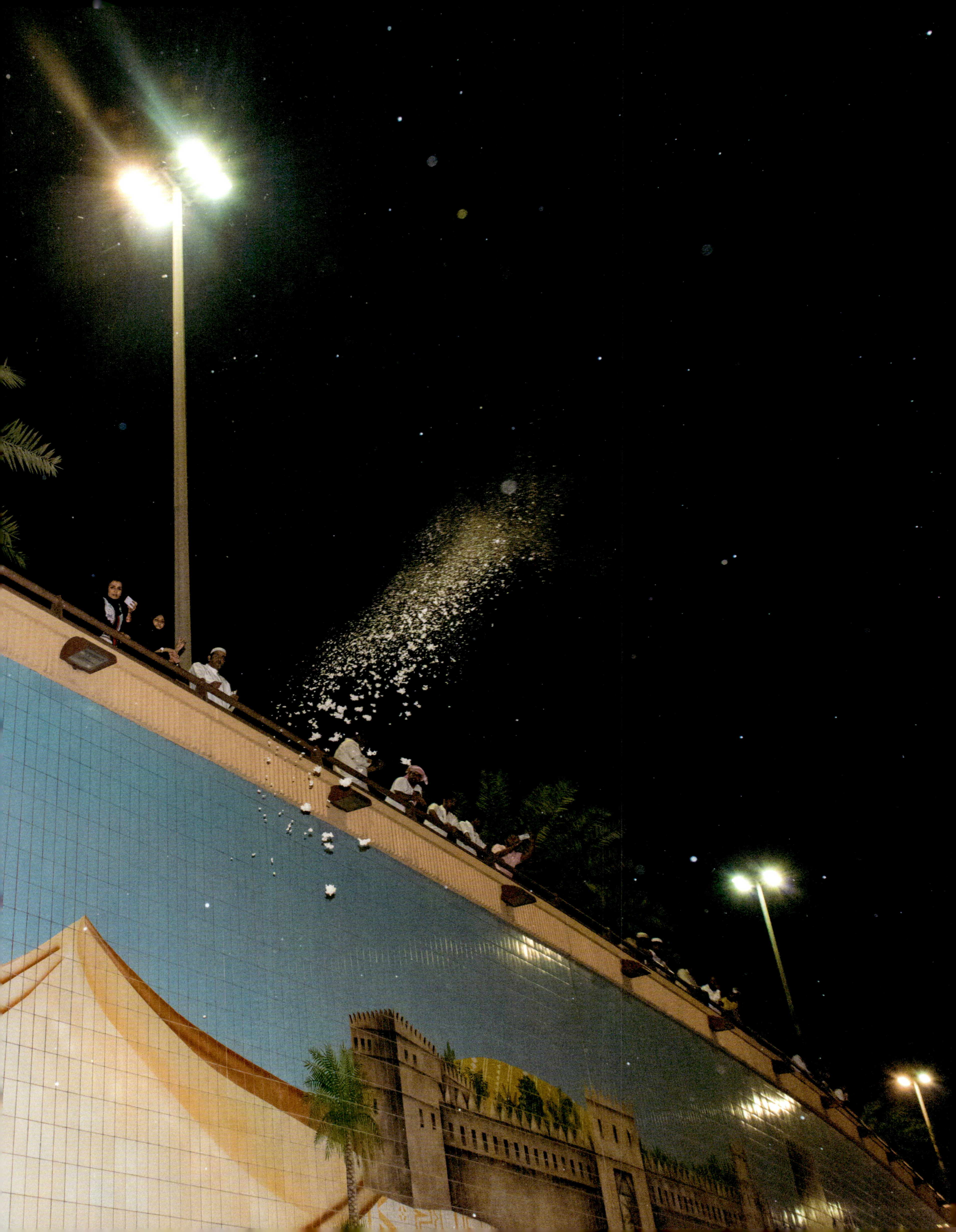

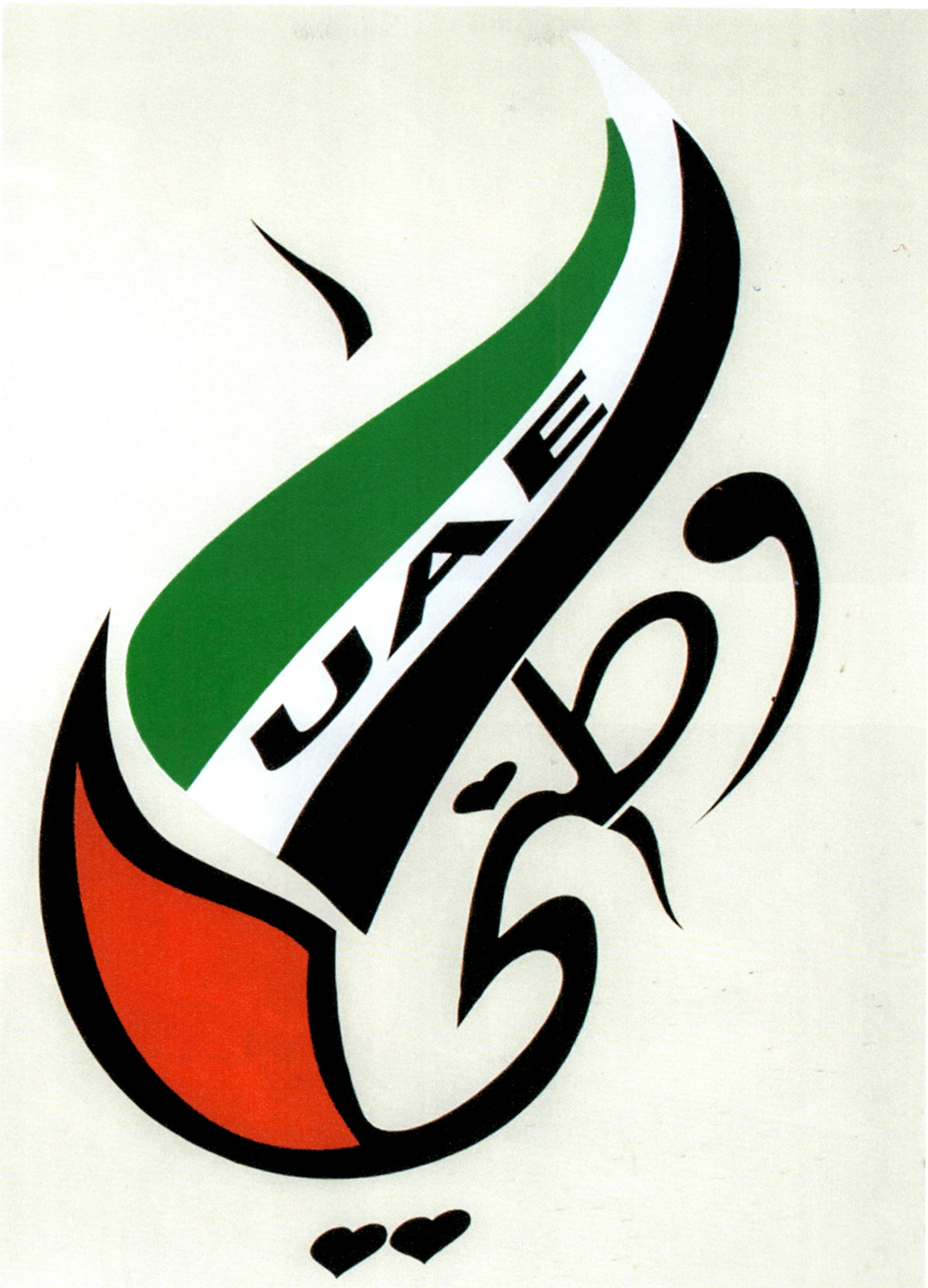
UAE
وطني

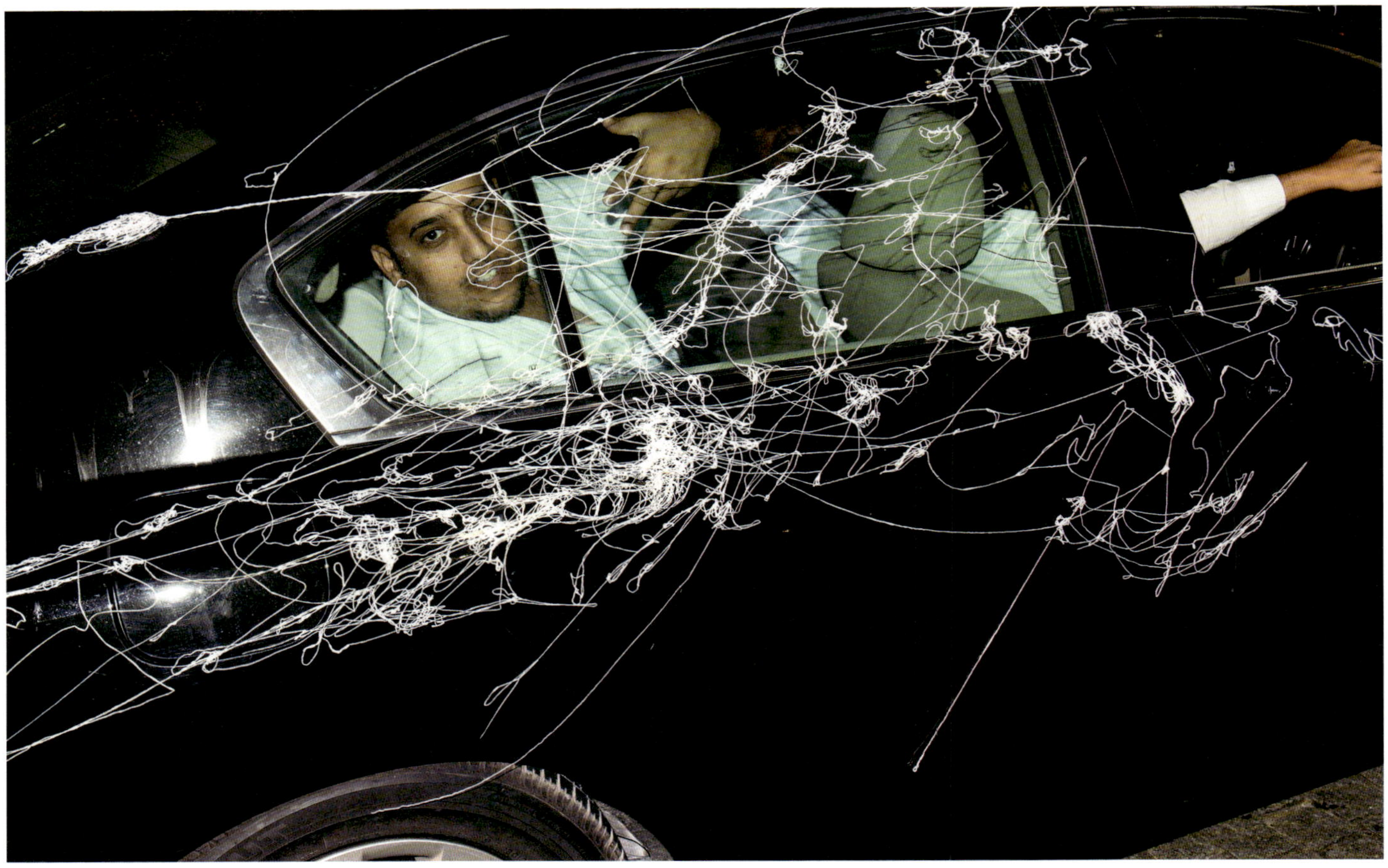

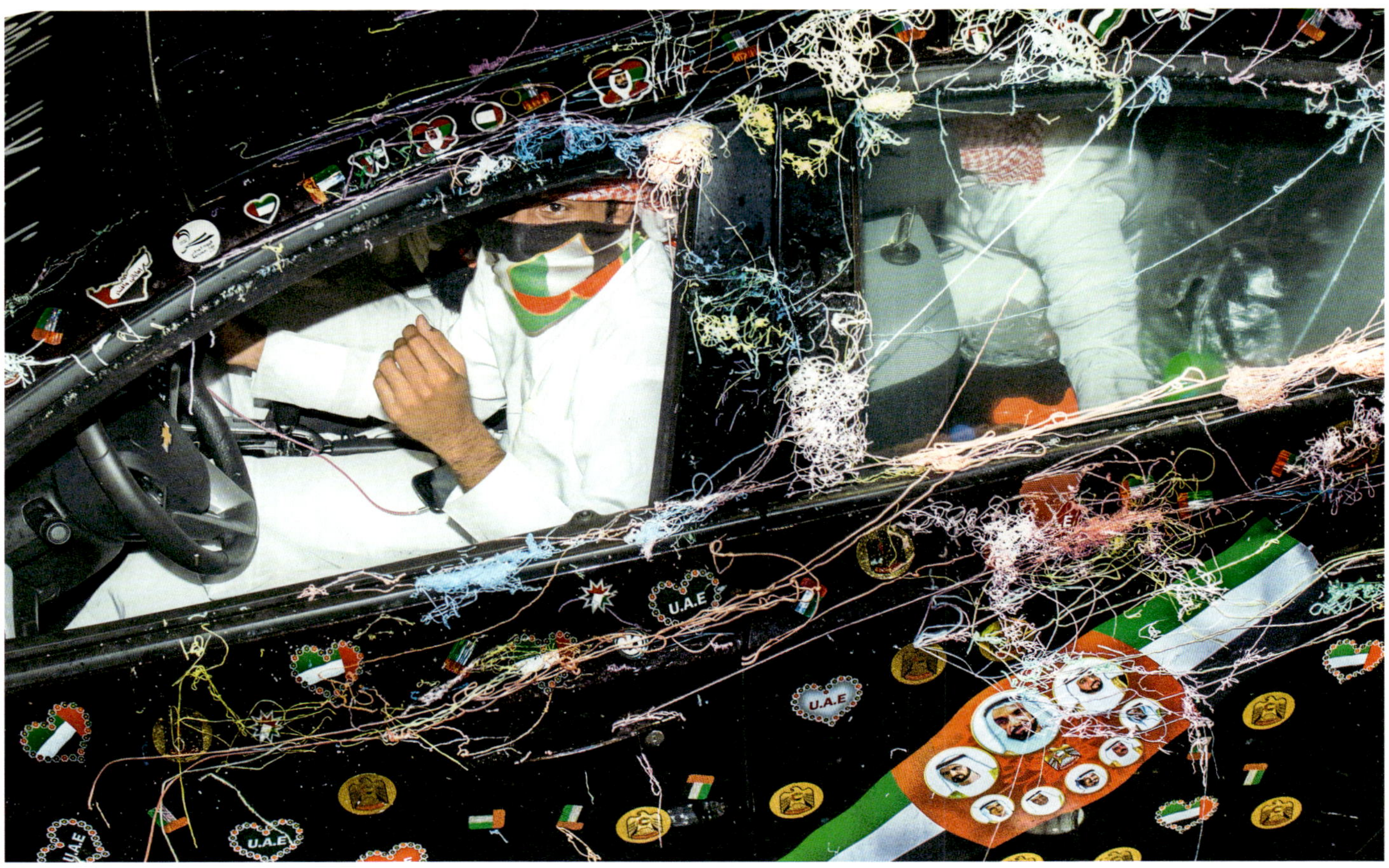
U.A.E
U.A.E
U.A.E
U.A.E

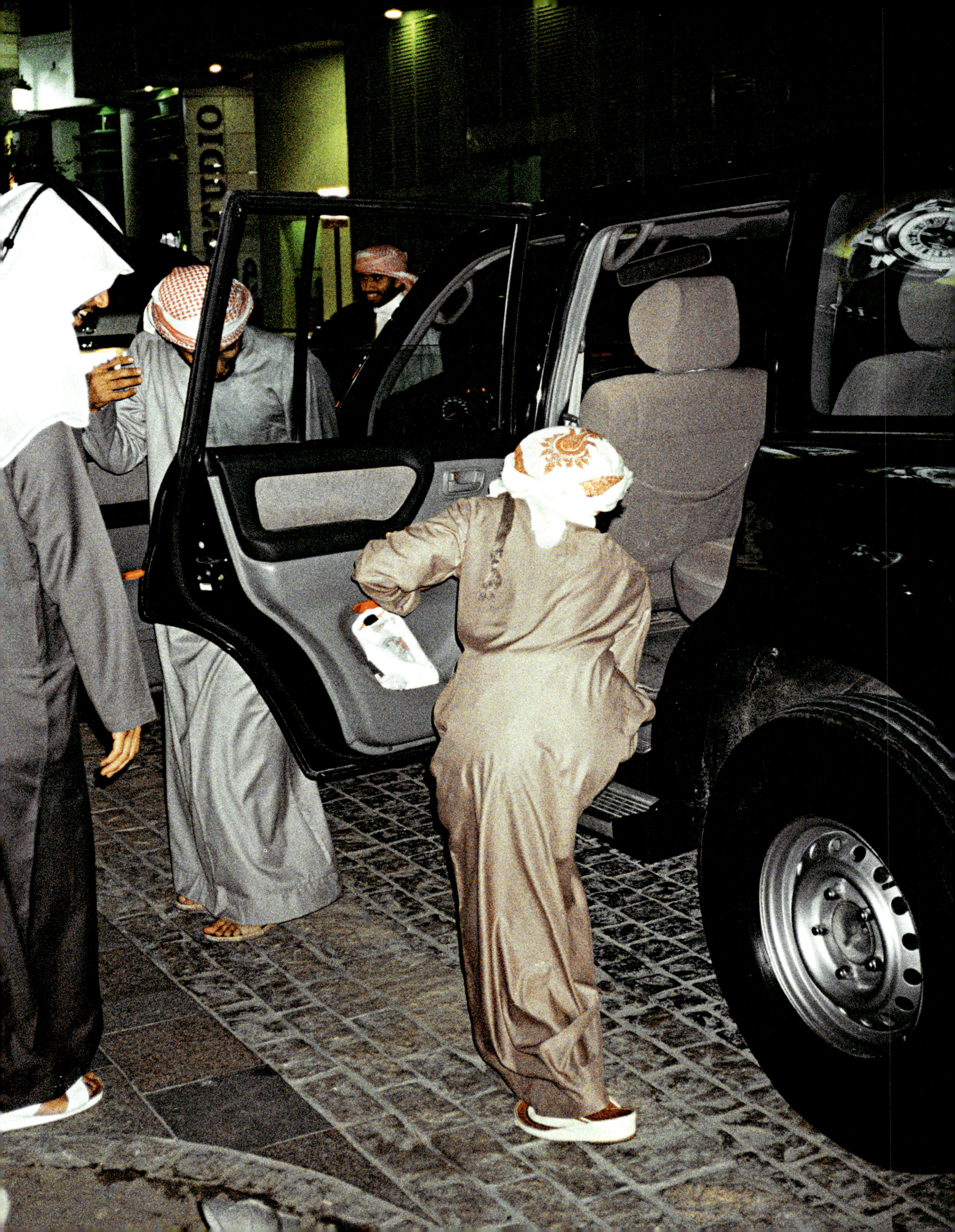

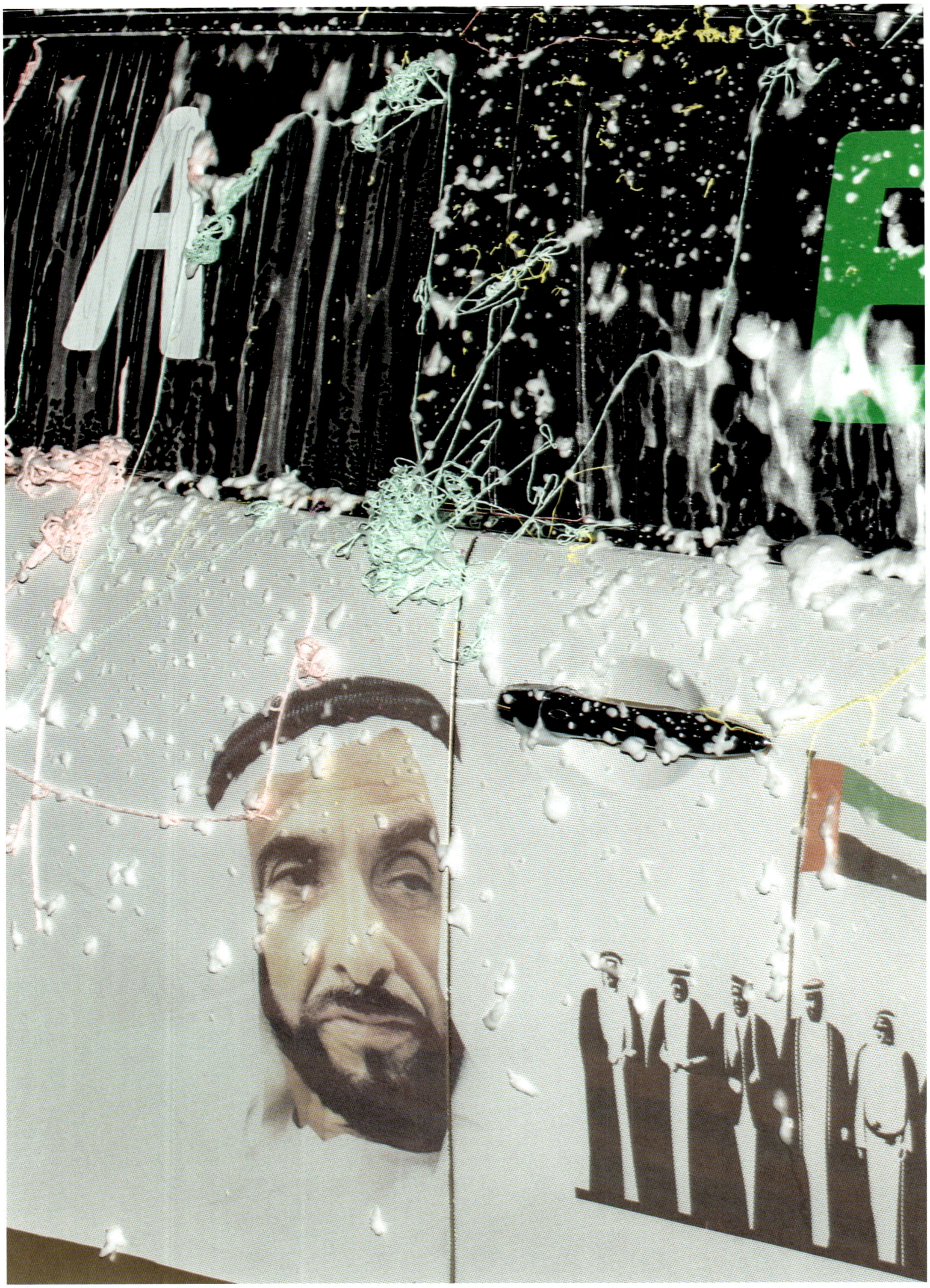

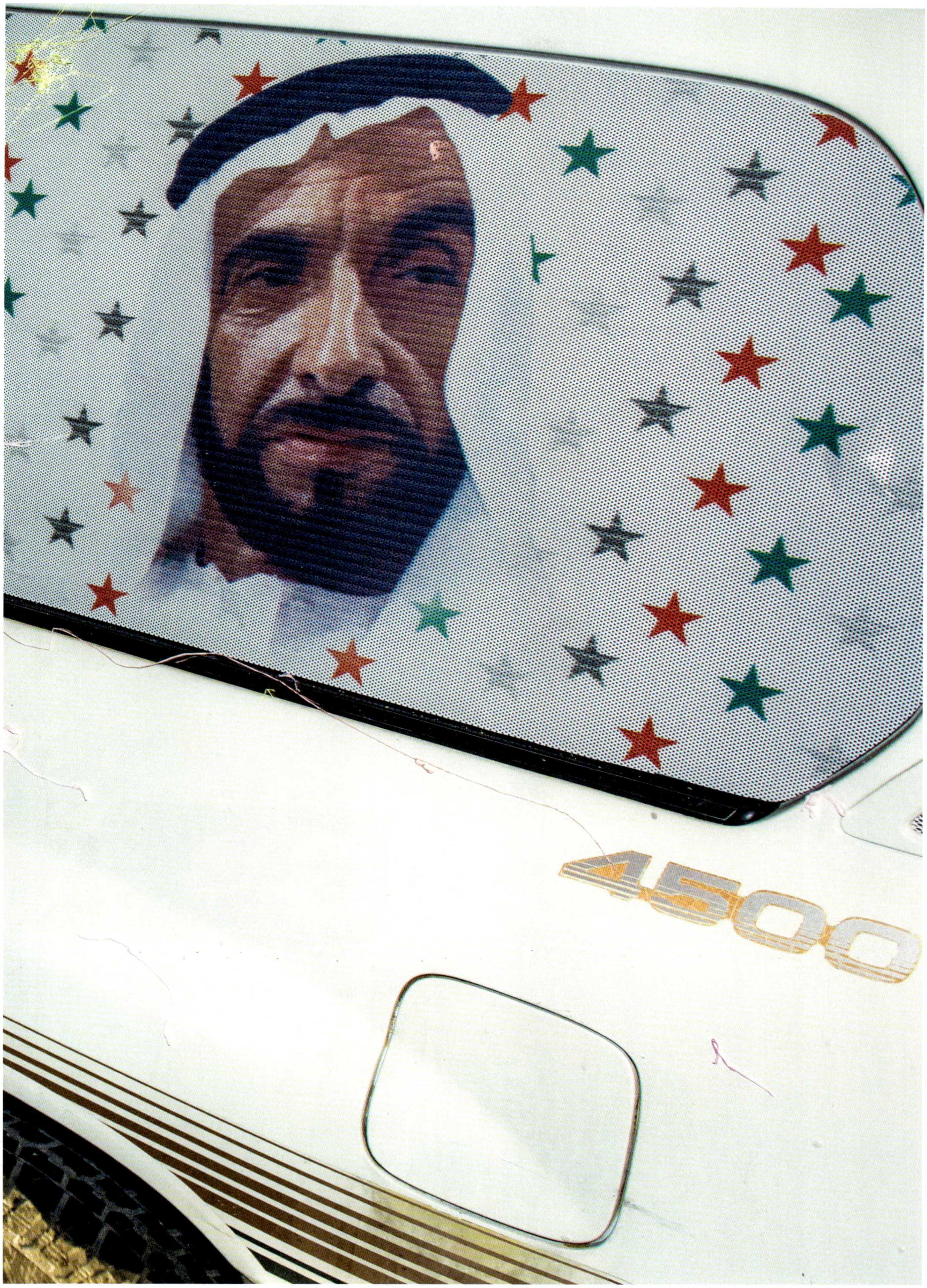
4500

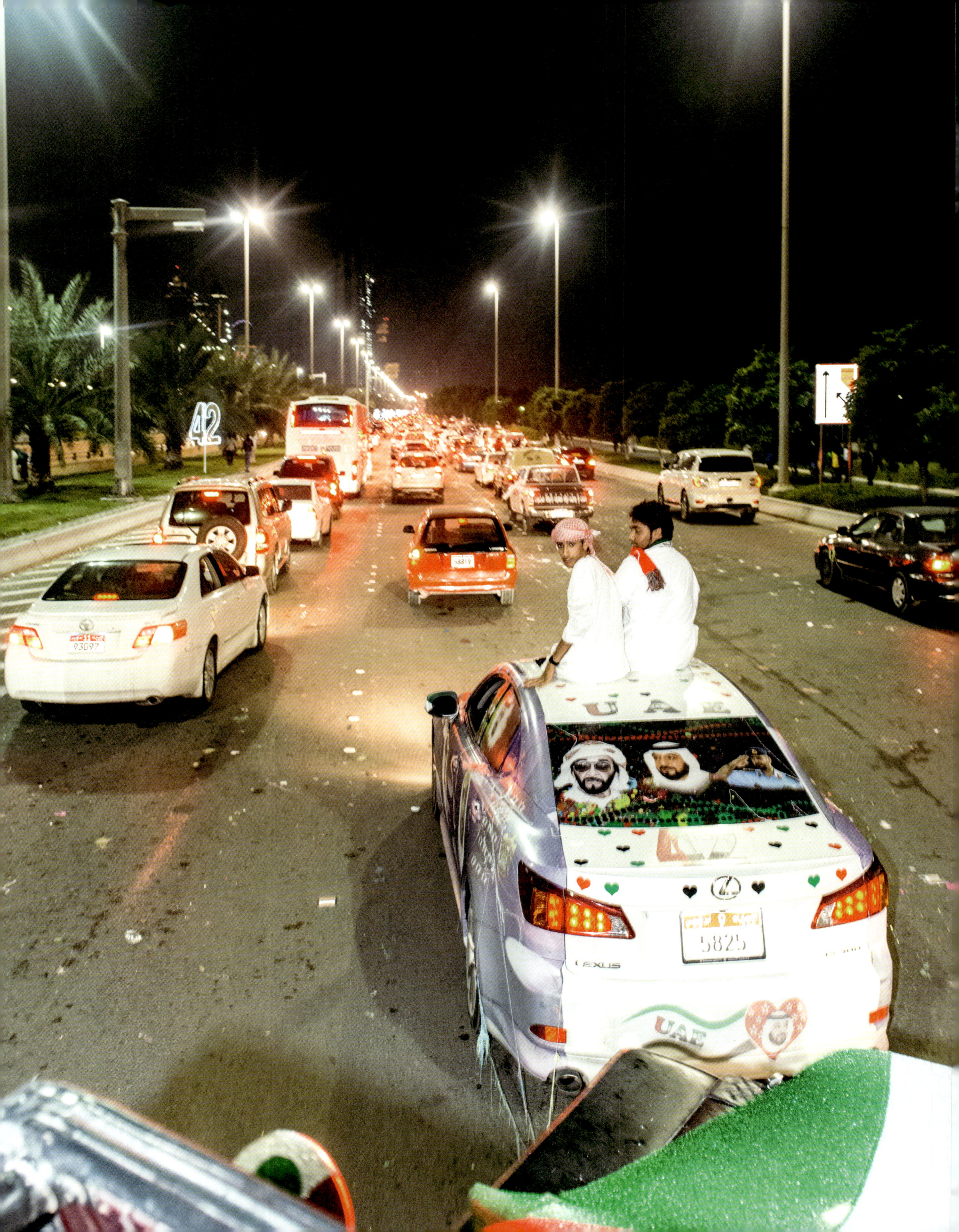
42
93097
U A E
LEXUS
5825
UAE

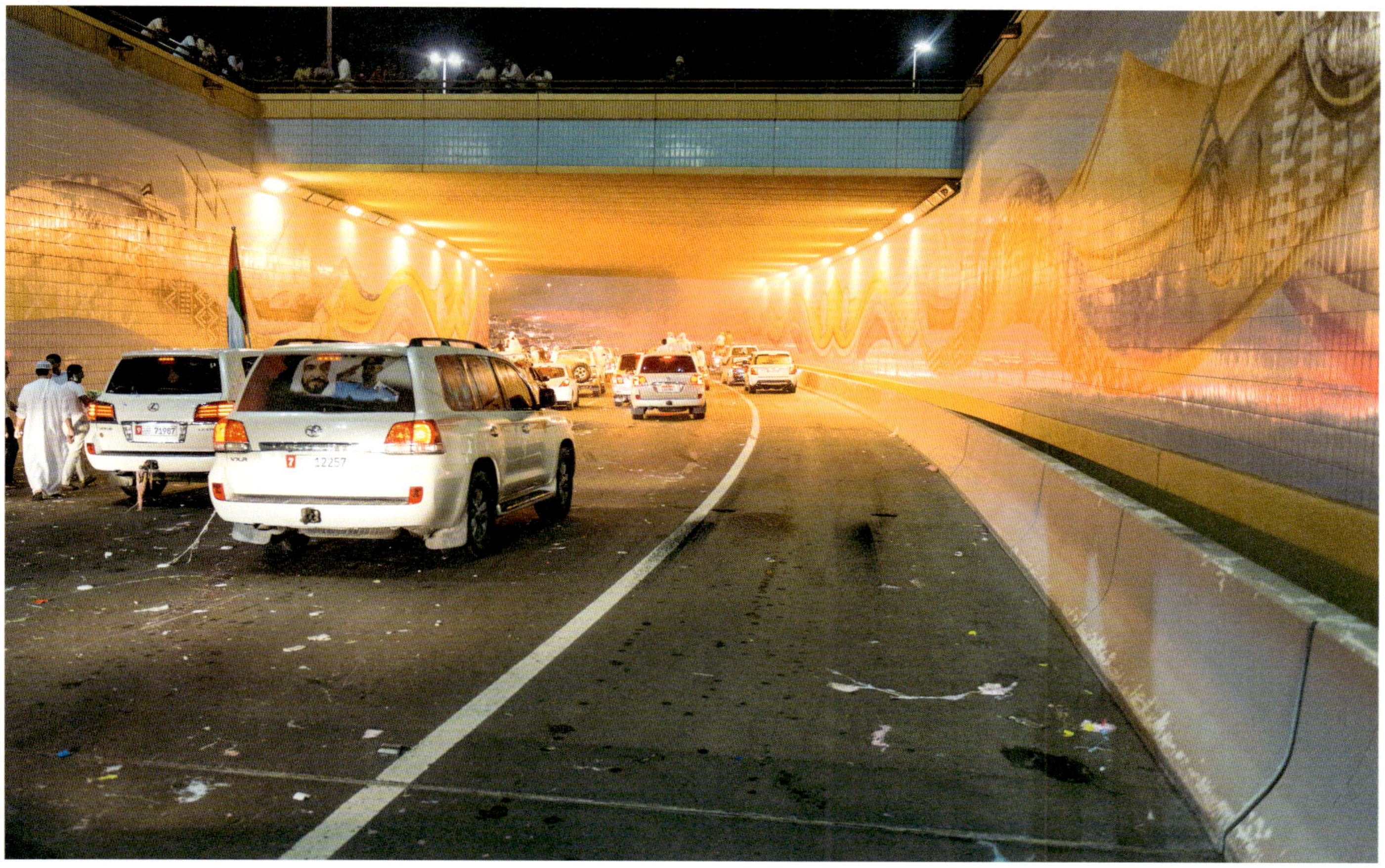

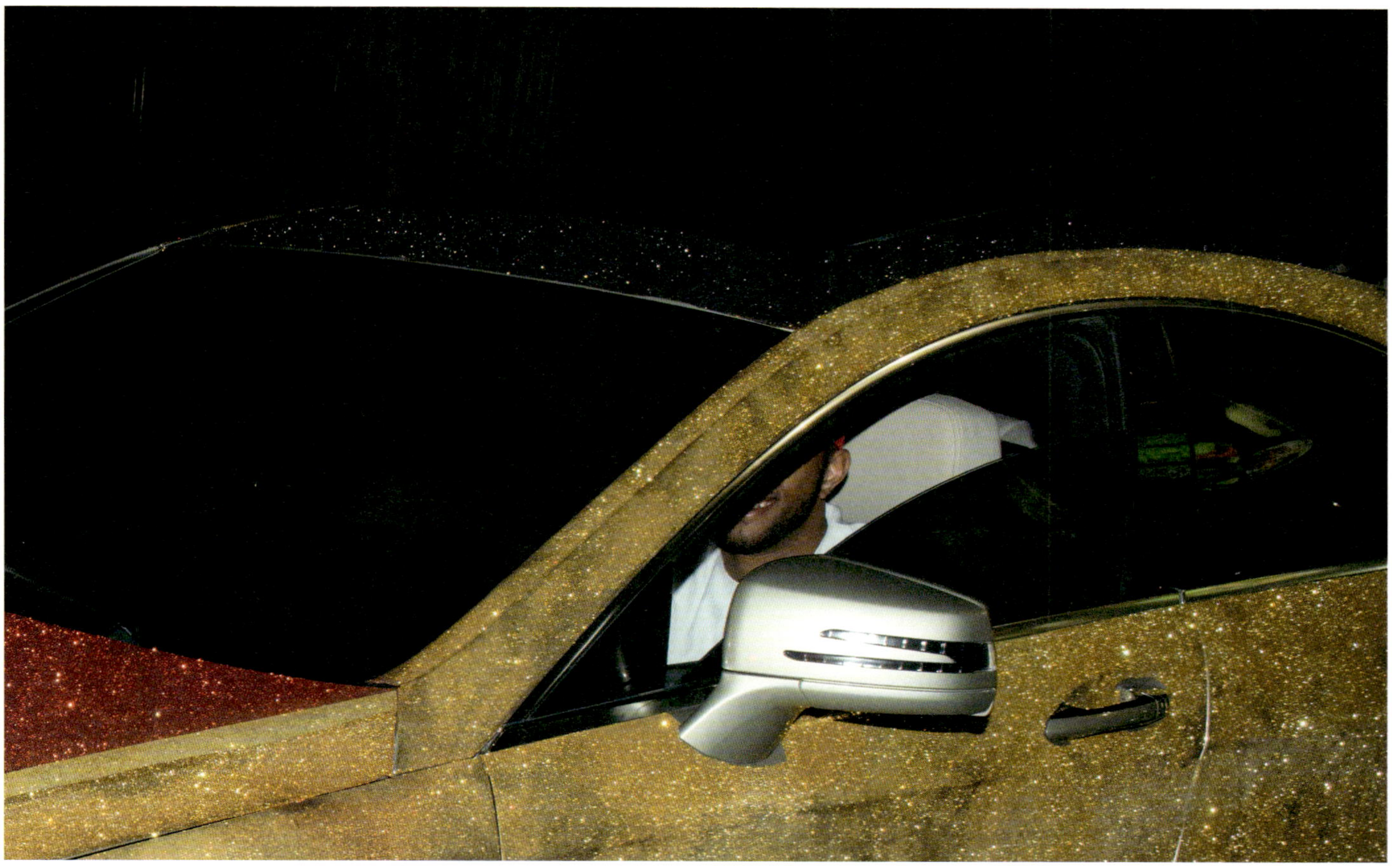

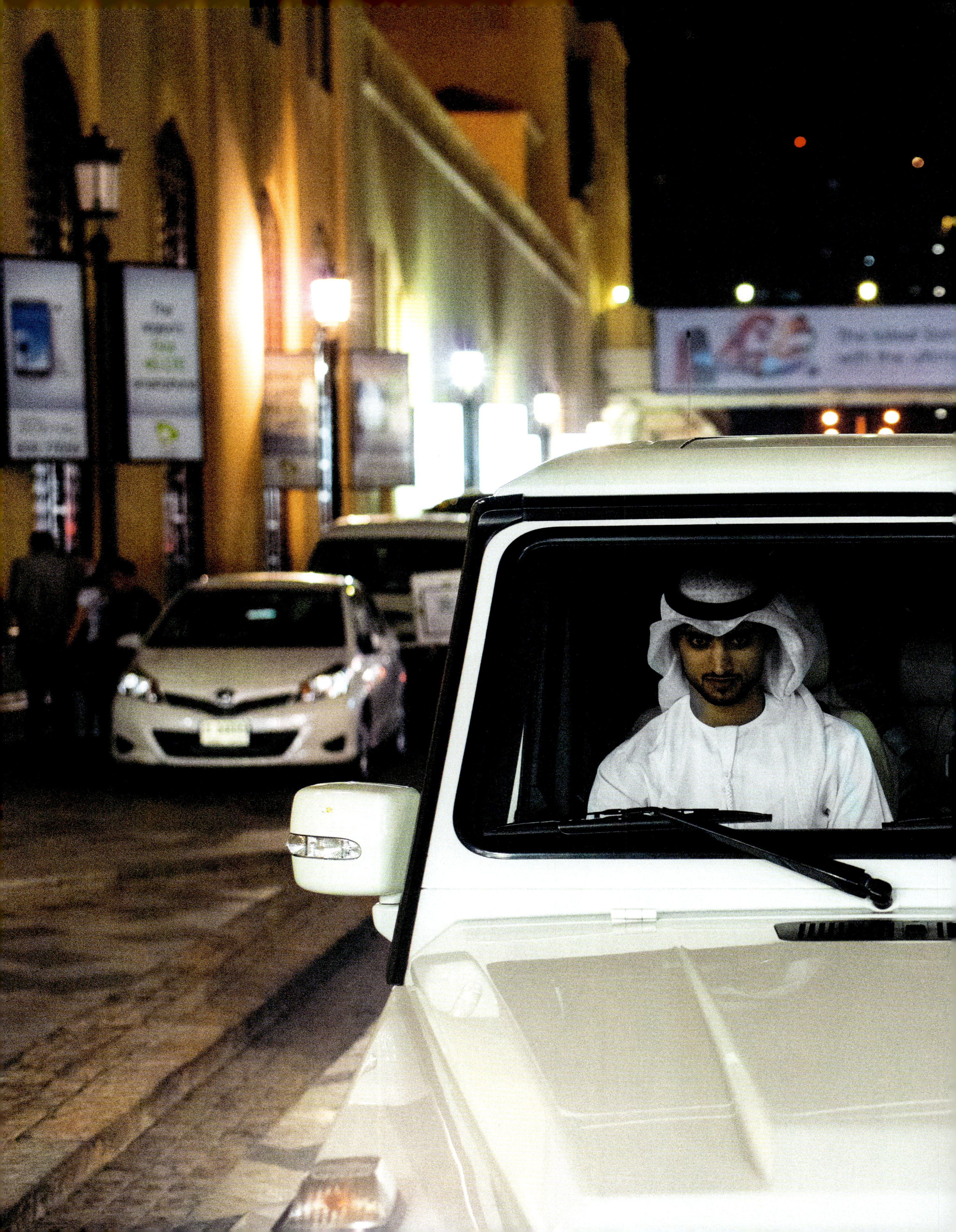

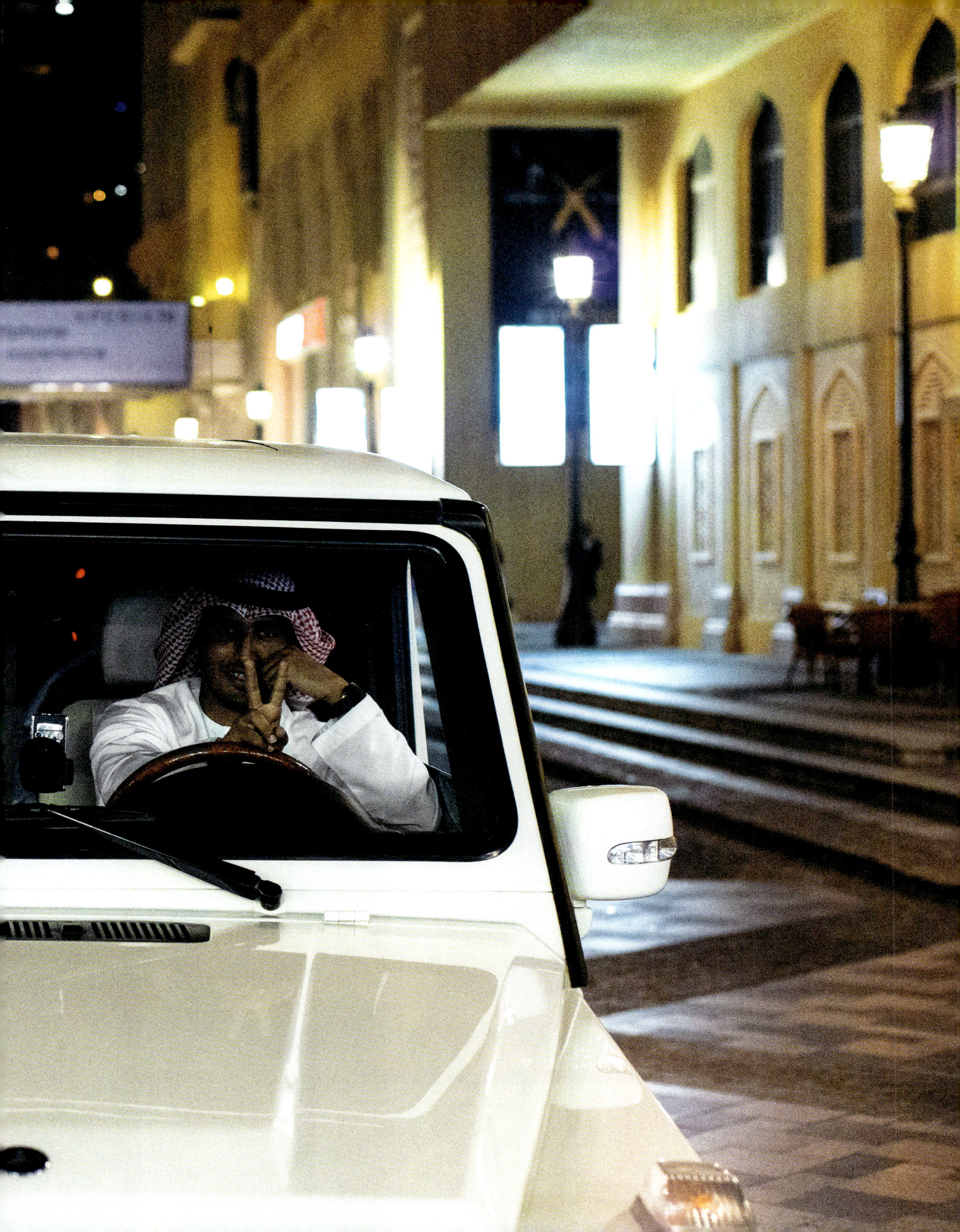

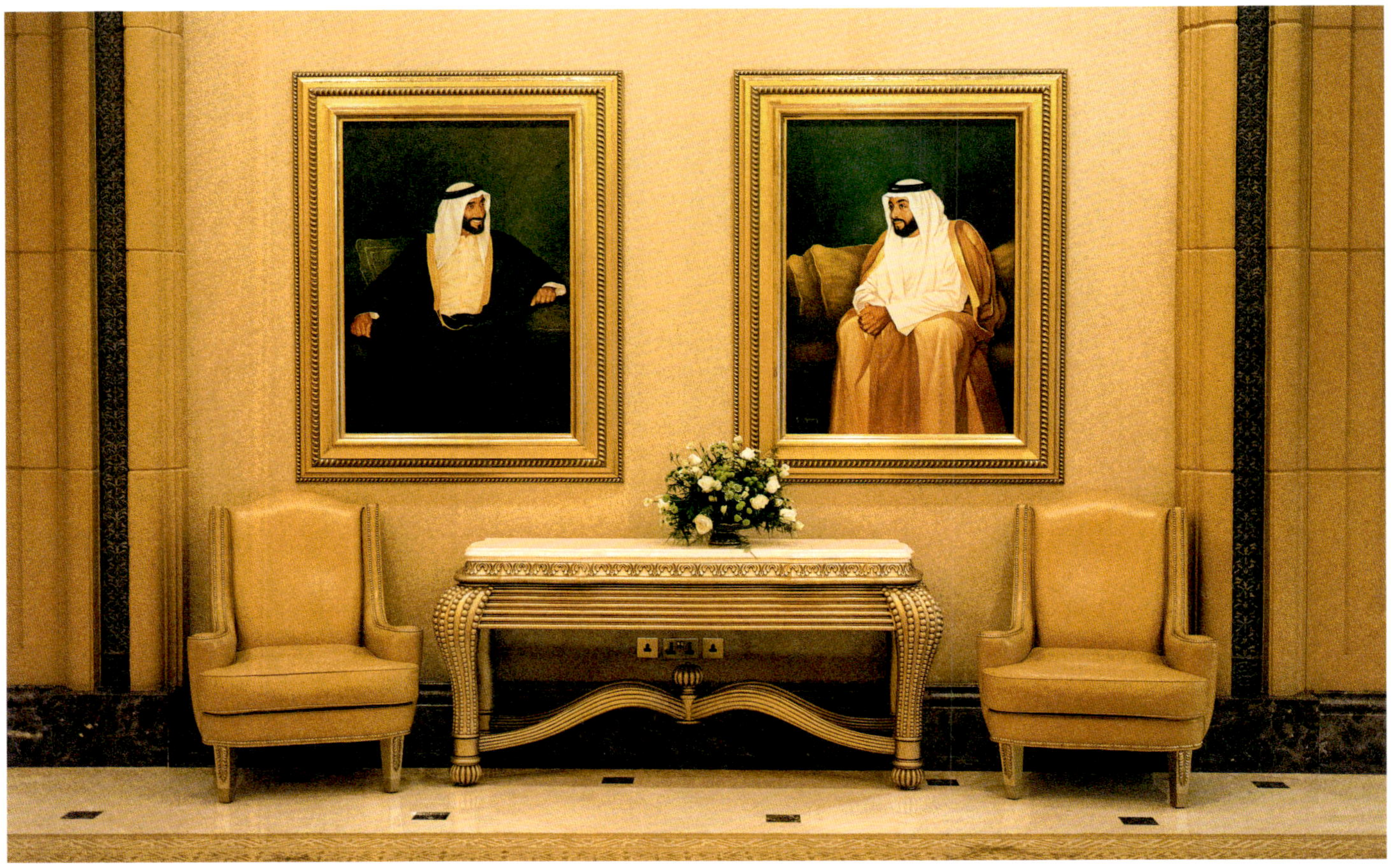

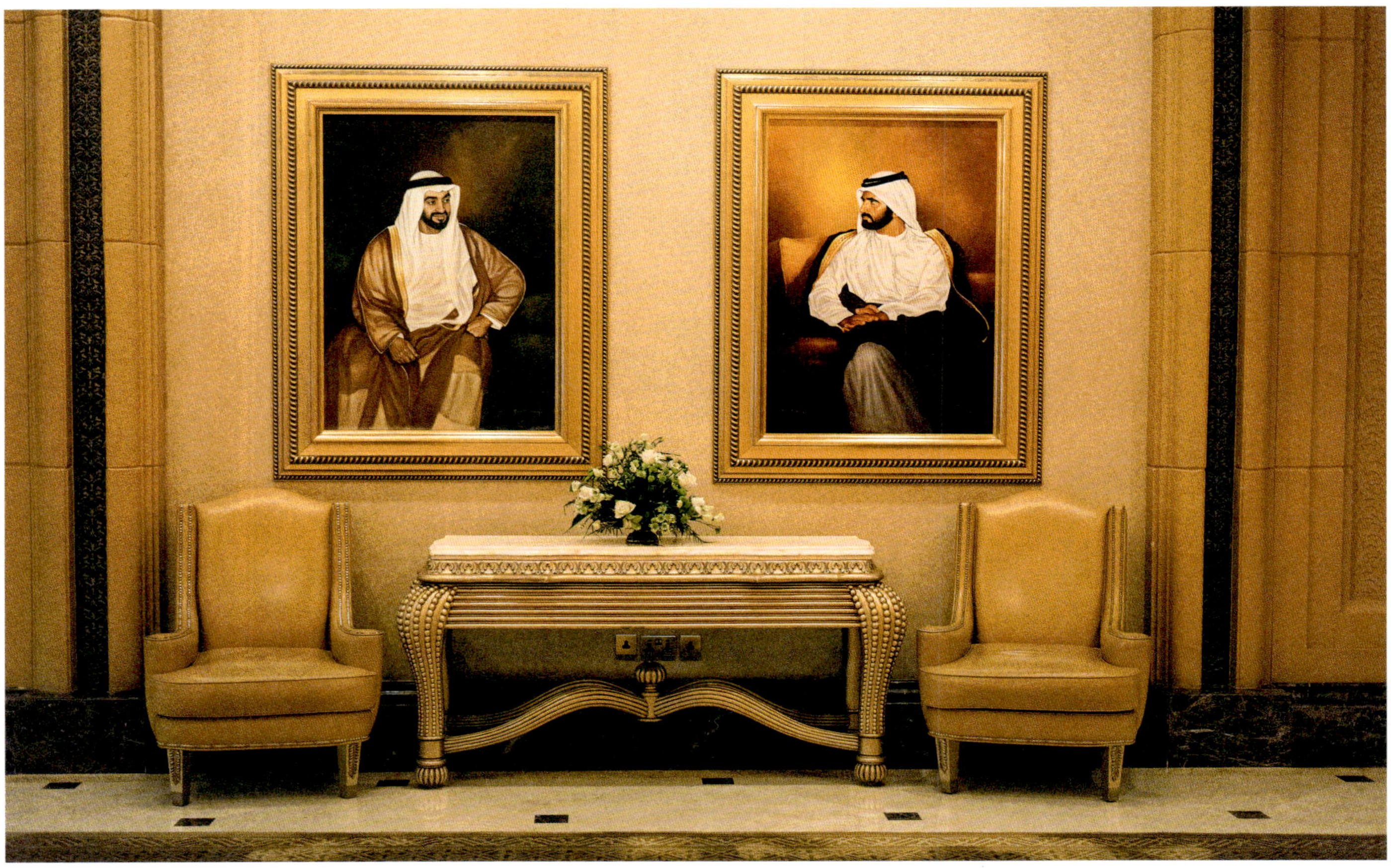

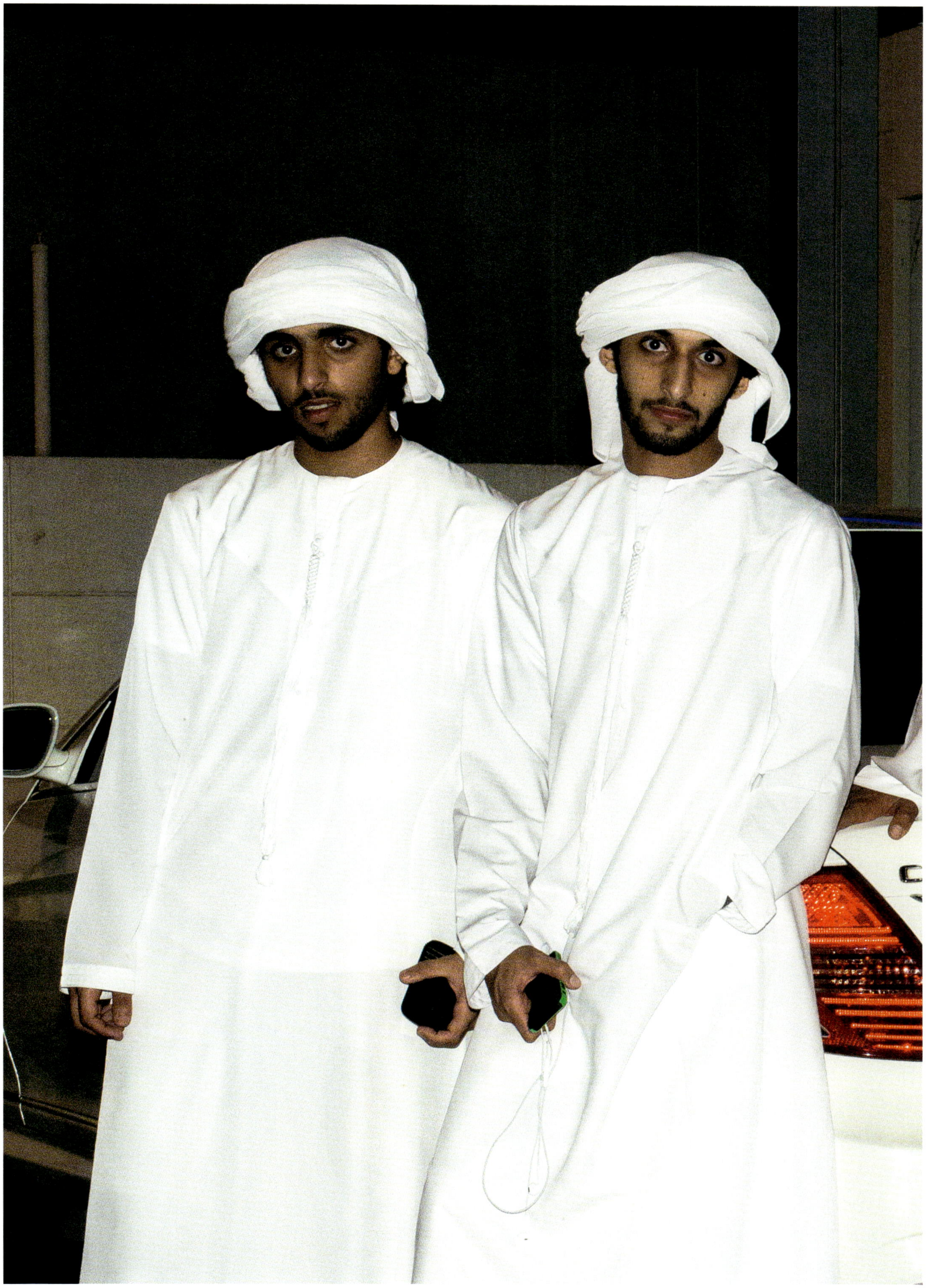

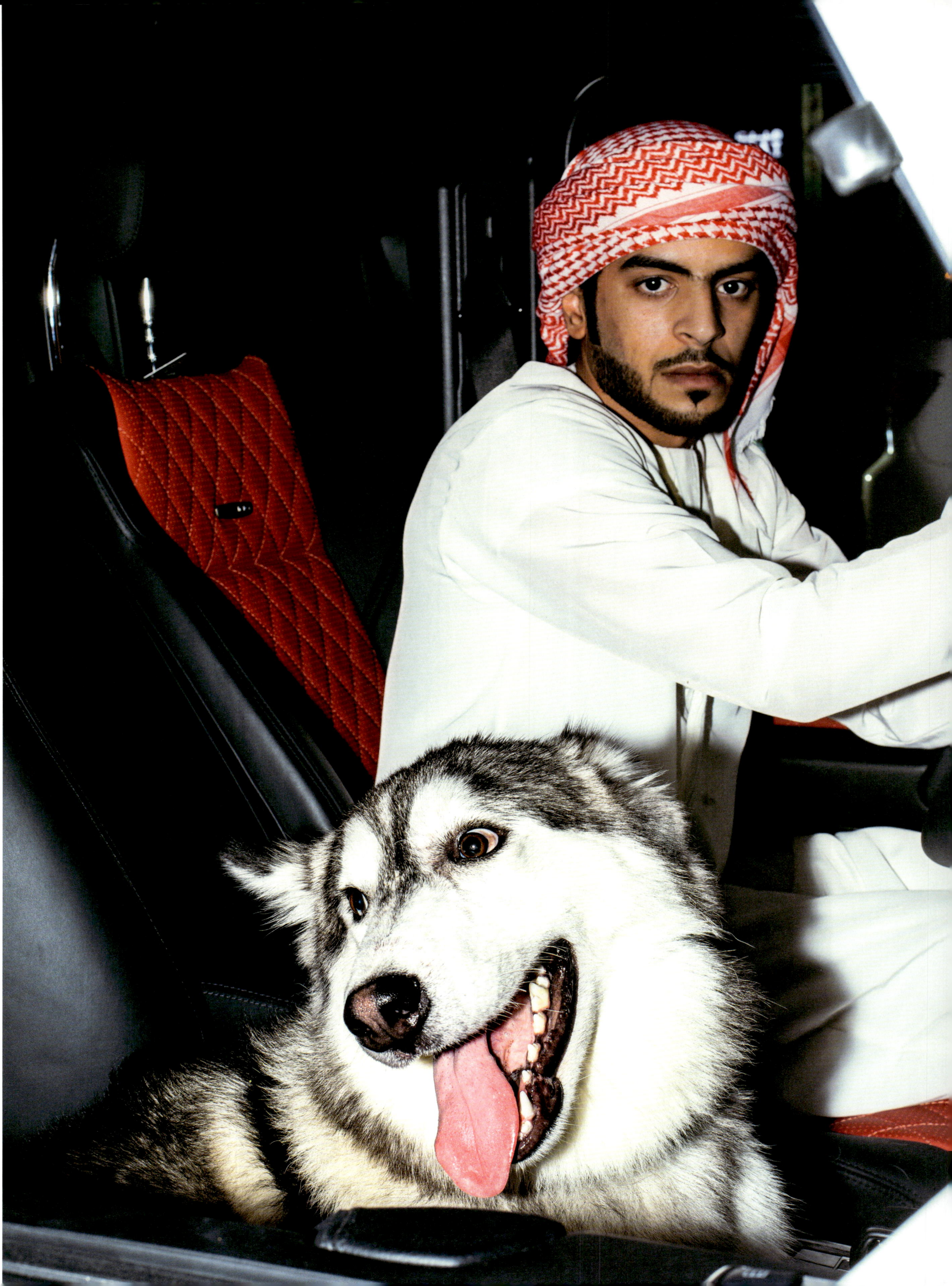

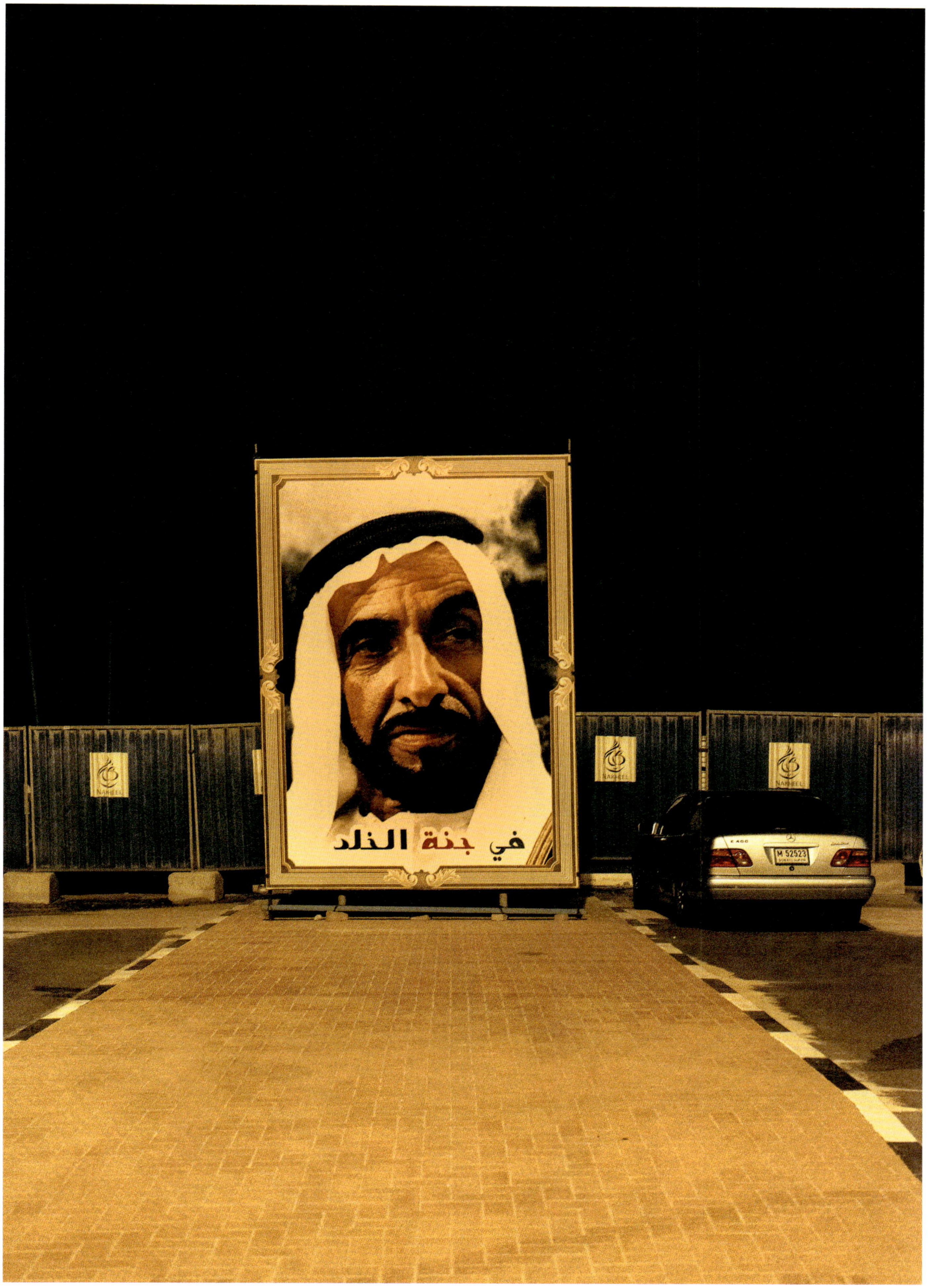
في جنة الخلد

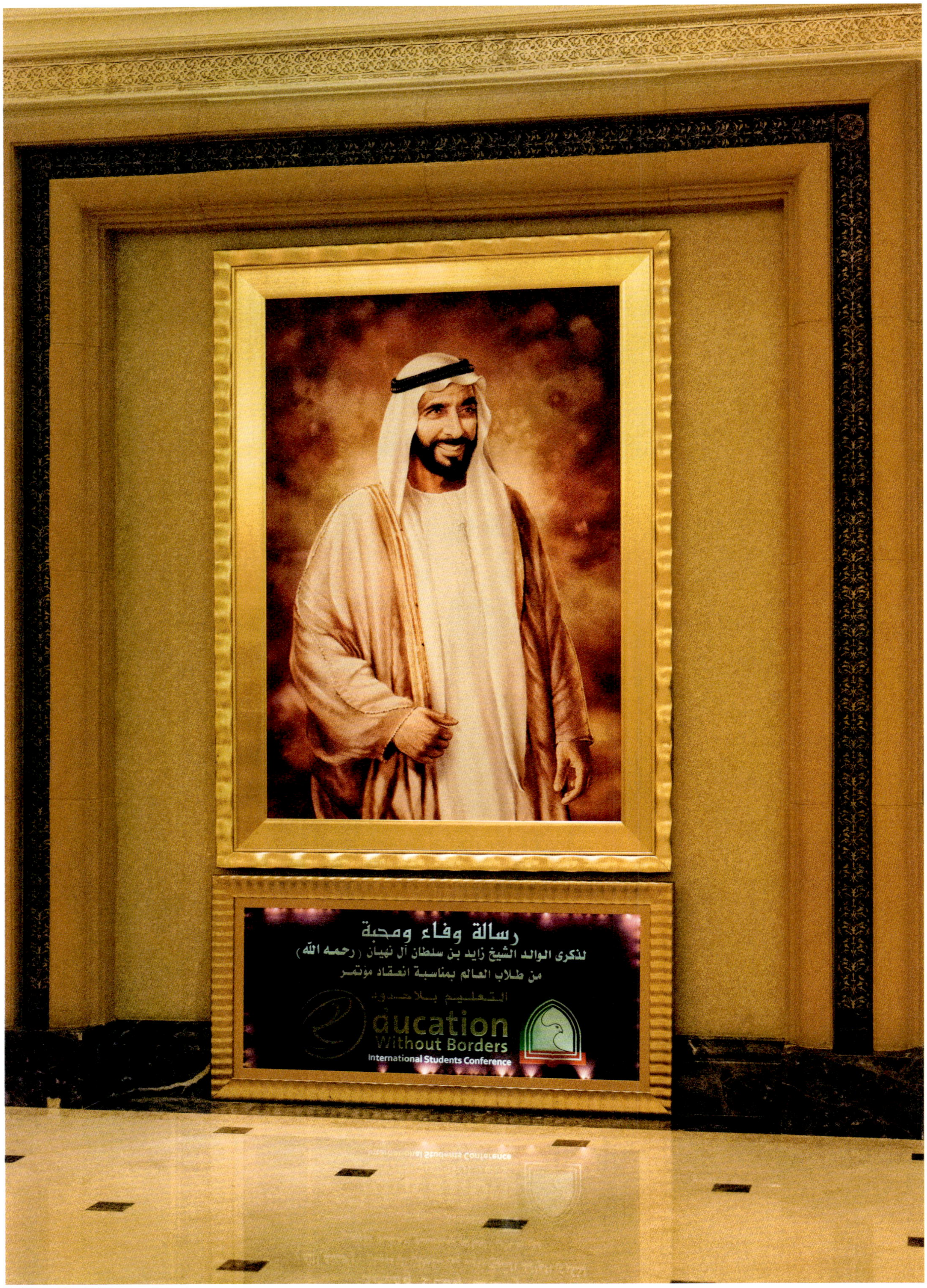

رسالة وفاء ومحبة
لذكرى الوالد الشيخ زايد بن سلطان آل نهيان (رحمه الله)
من طلاب العالم بمناسبة انعقاد مؤتمر
التعليم بلا حدود
Education Without Borders
International Students Conference

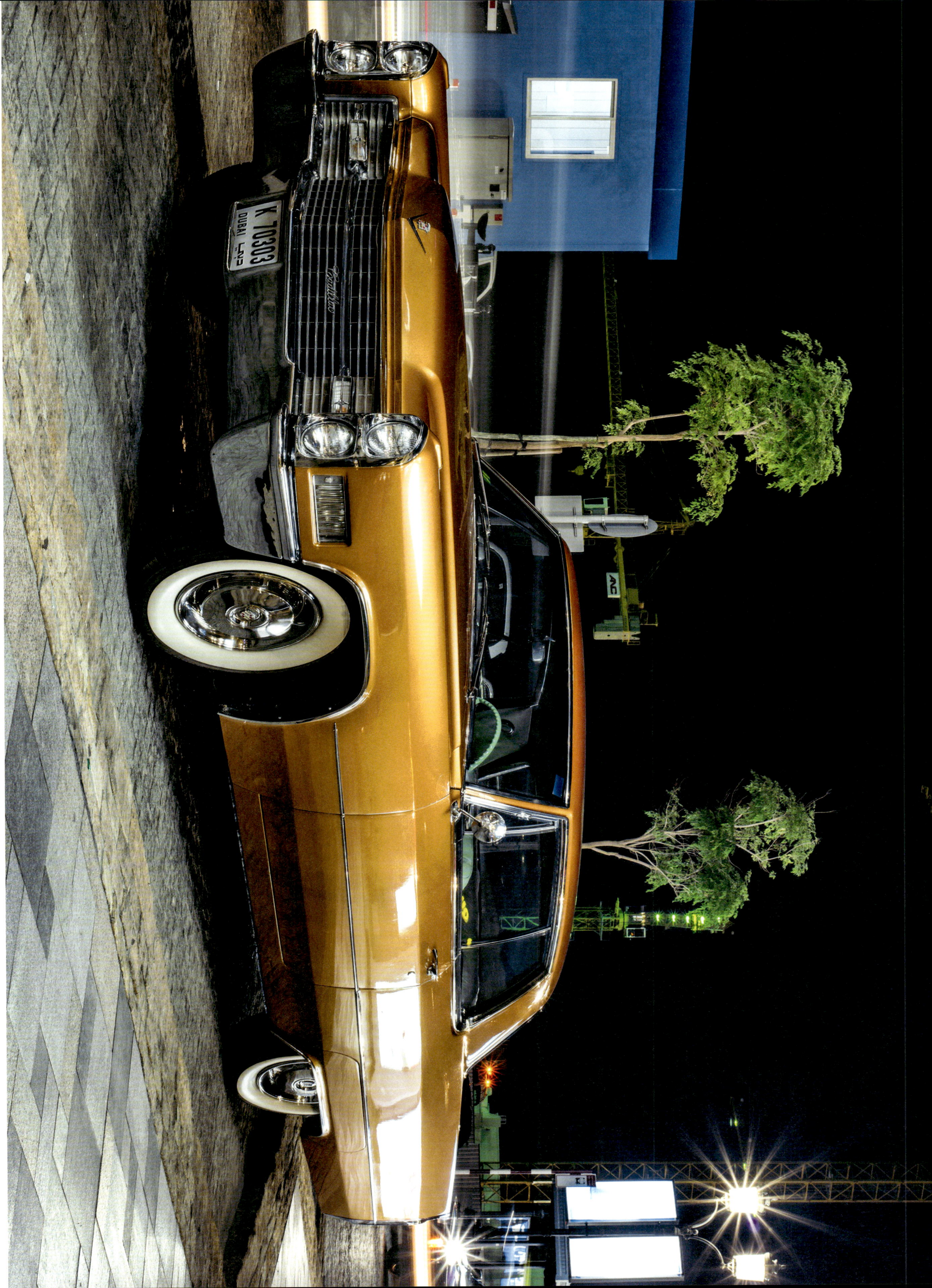
K 70303
DUBAI

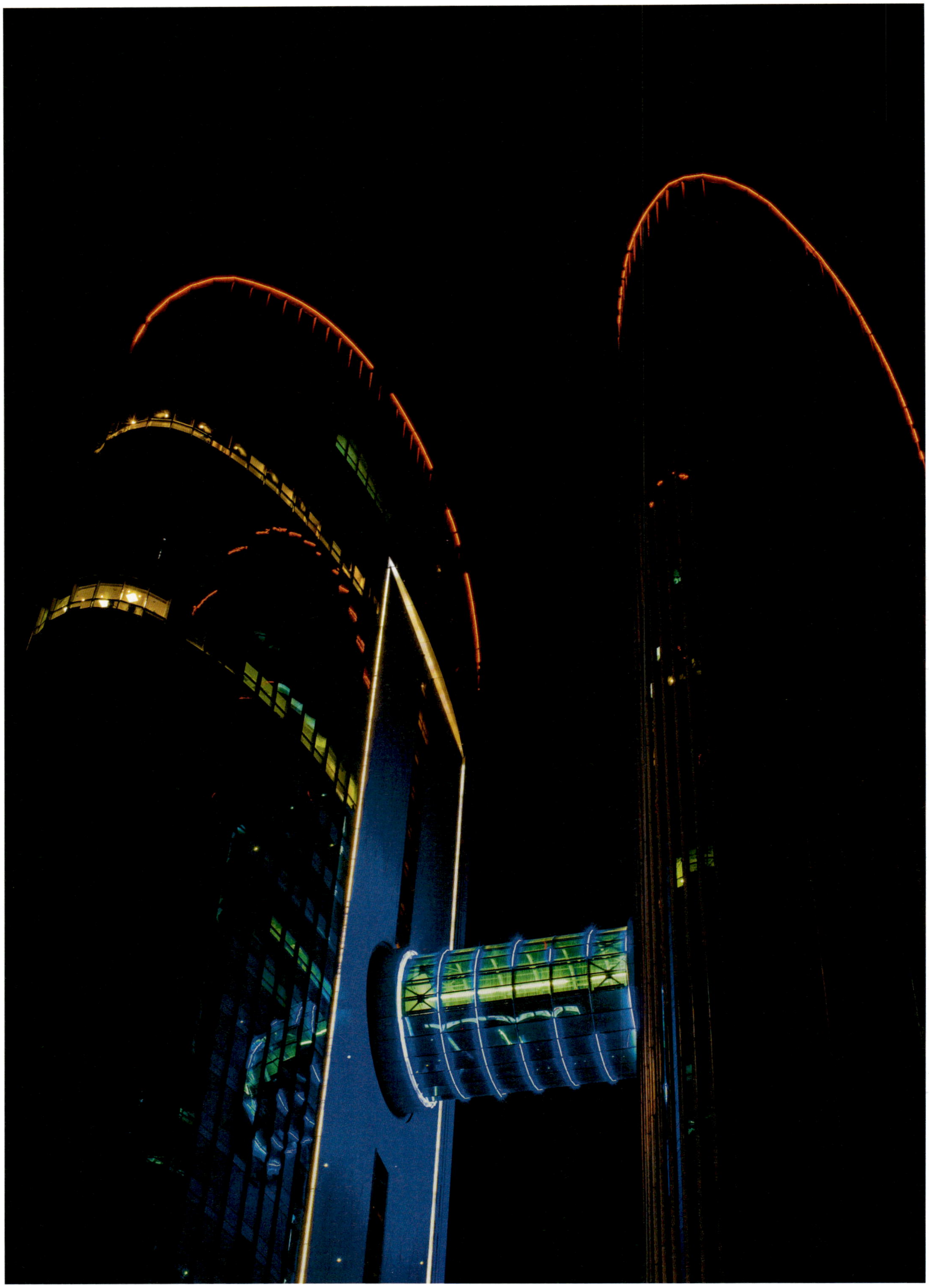

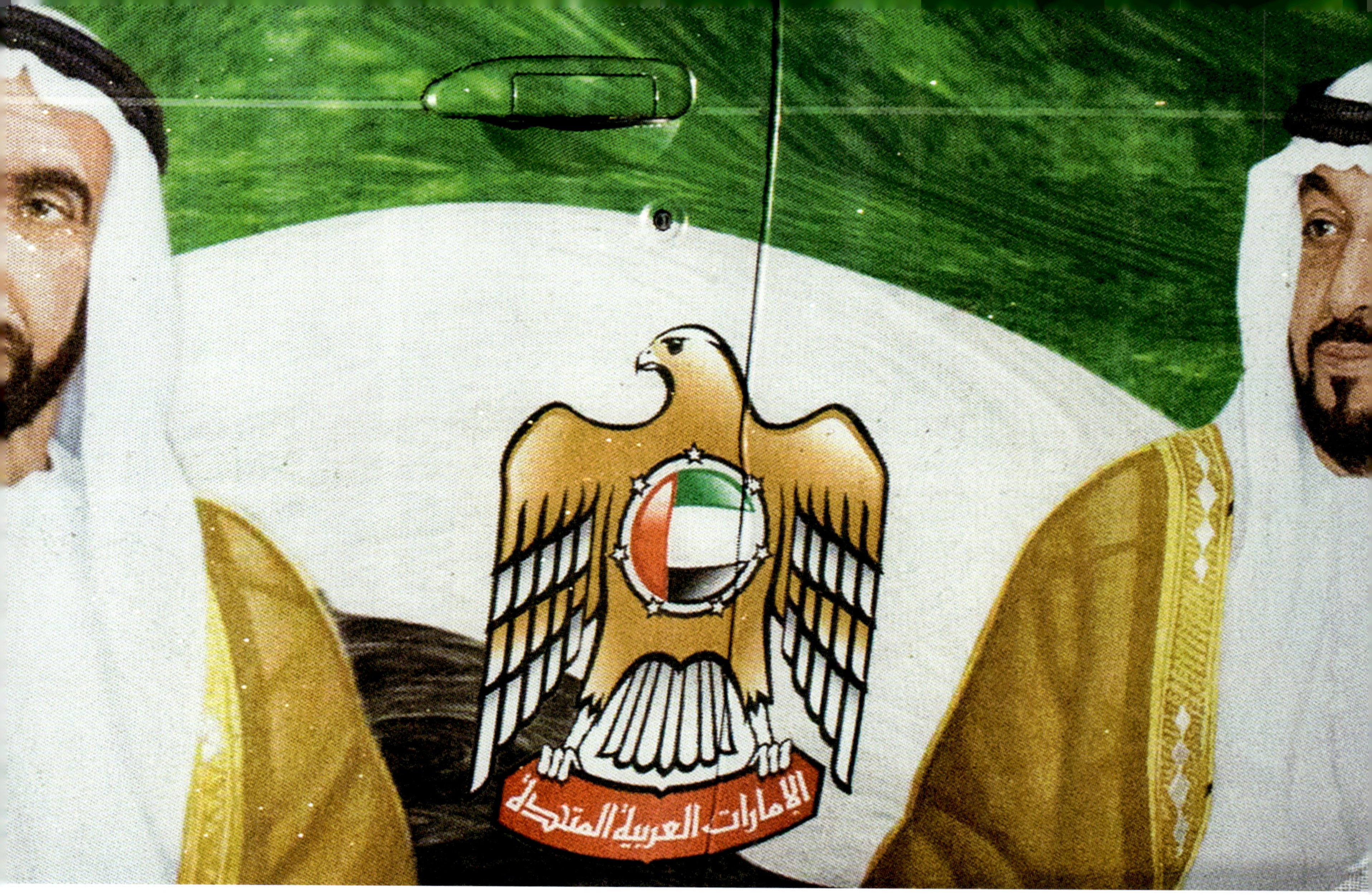
الإمارات العربية المتحدة

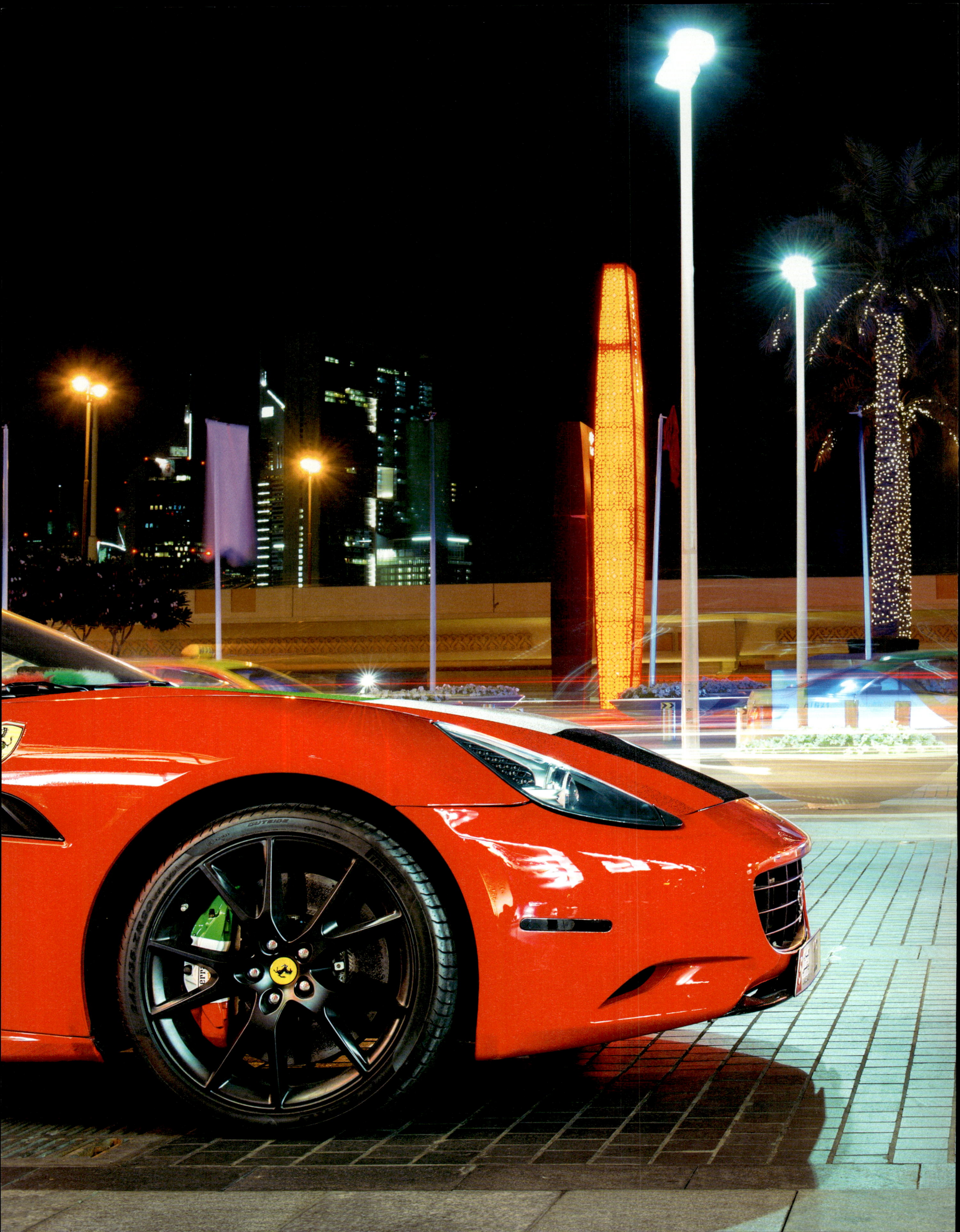

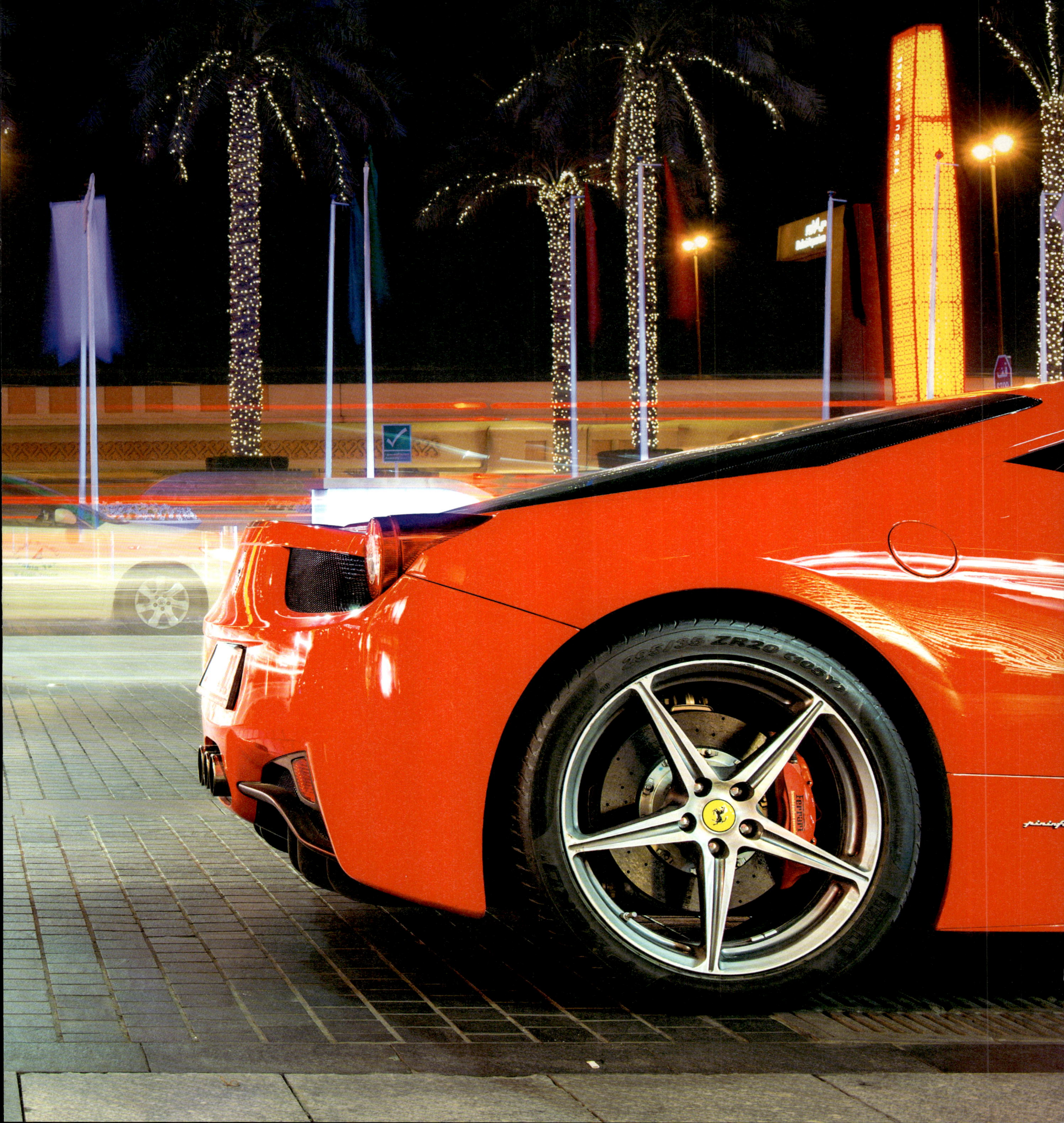

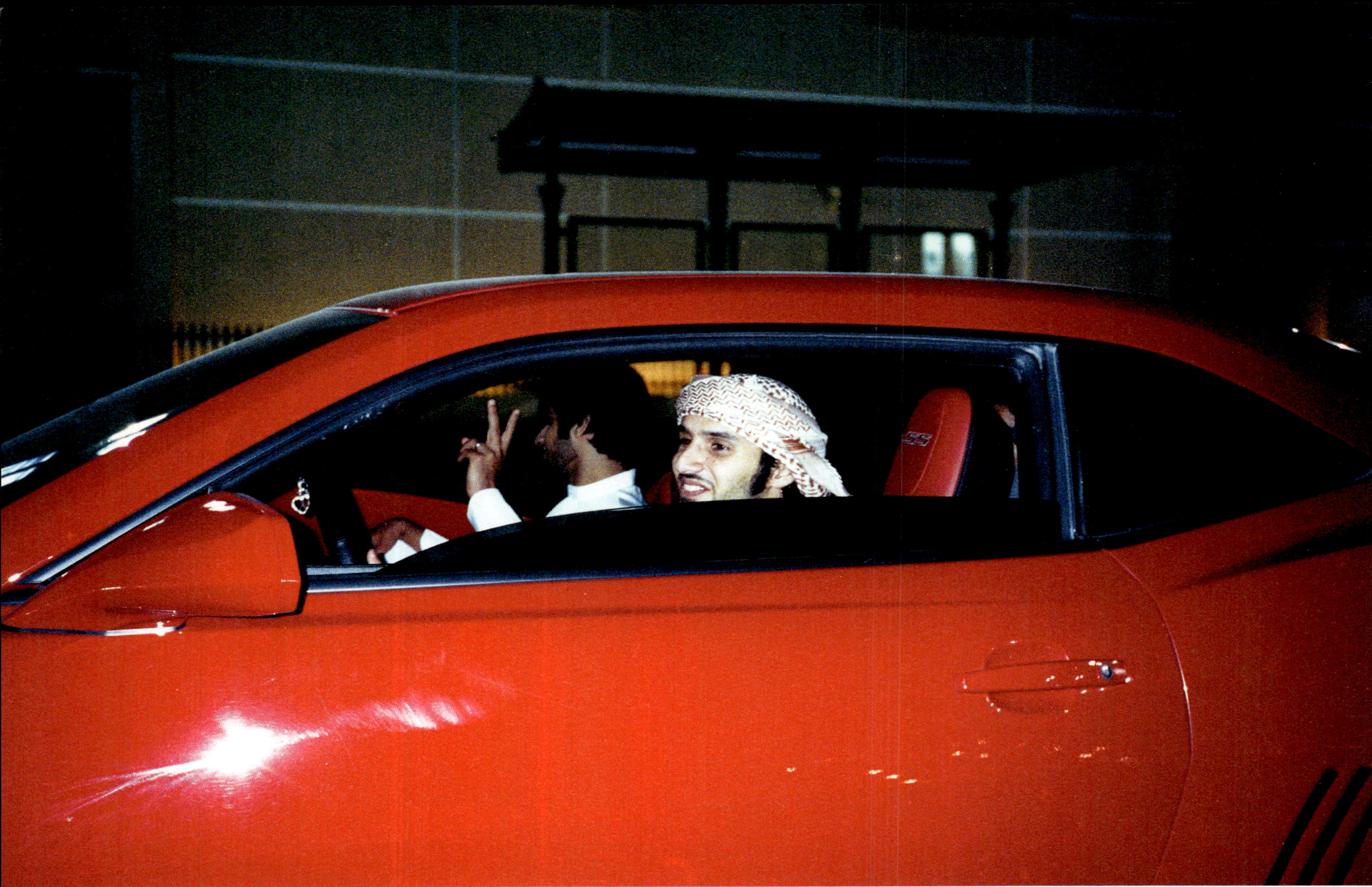

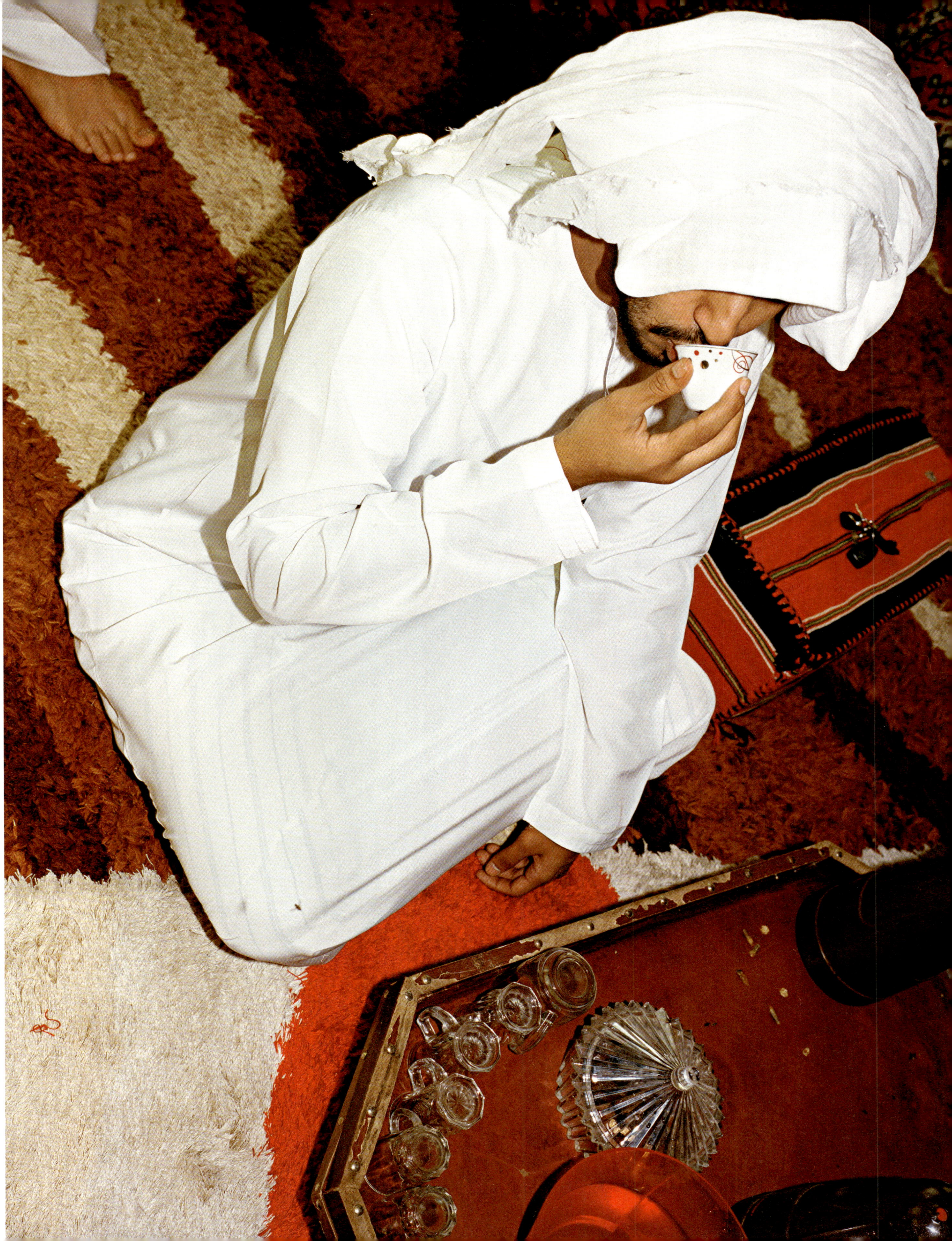

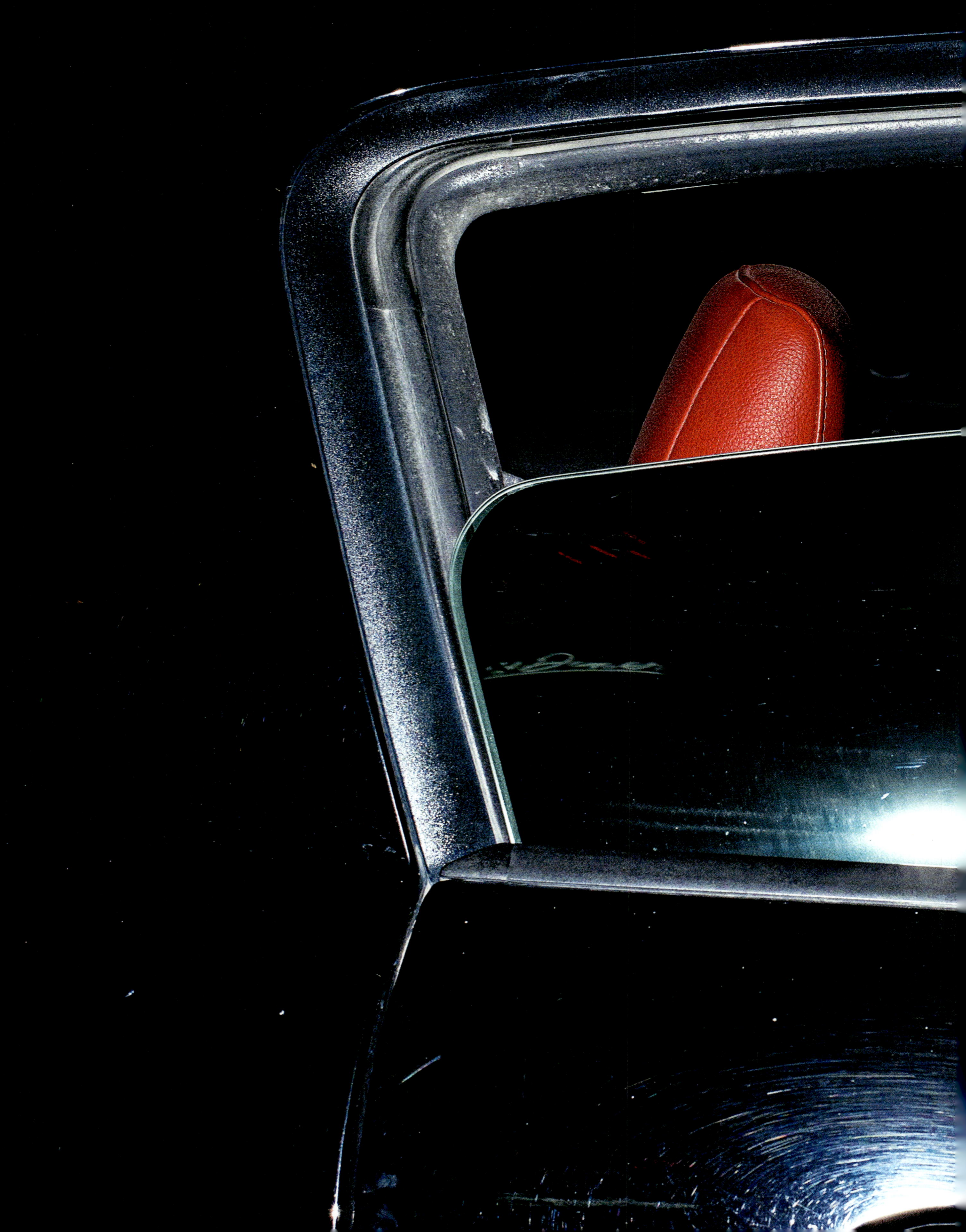

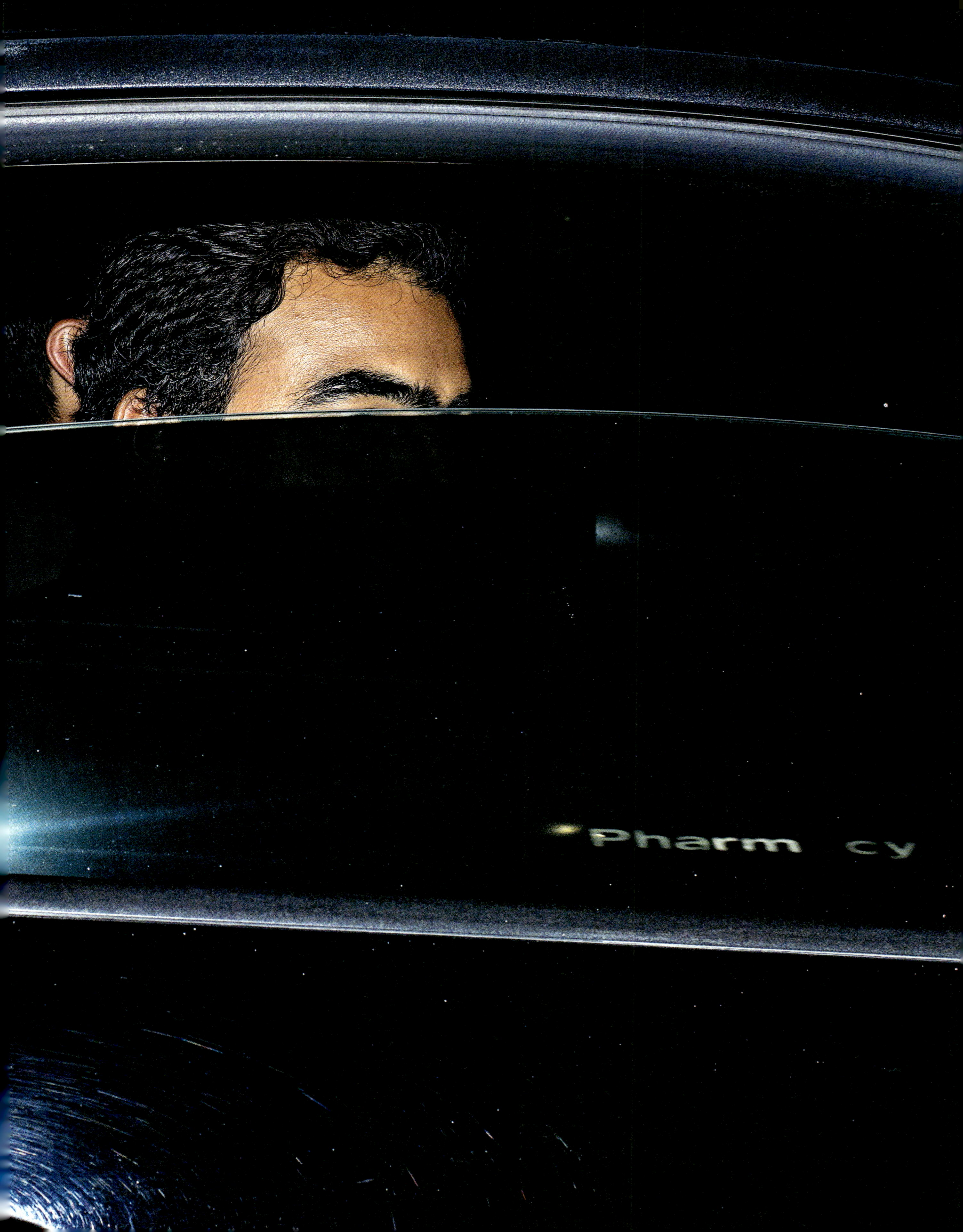
Pharm cy

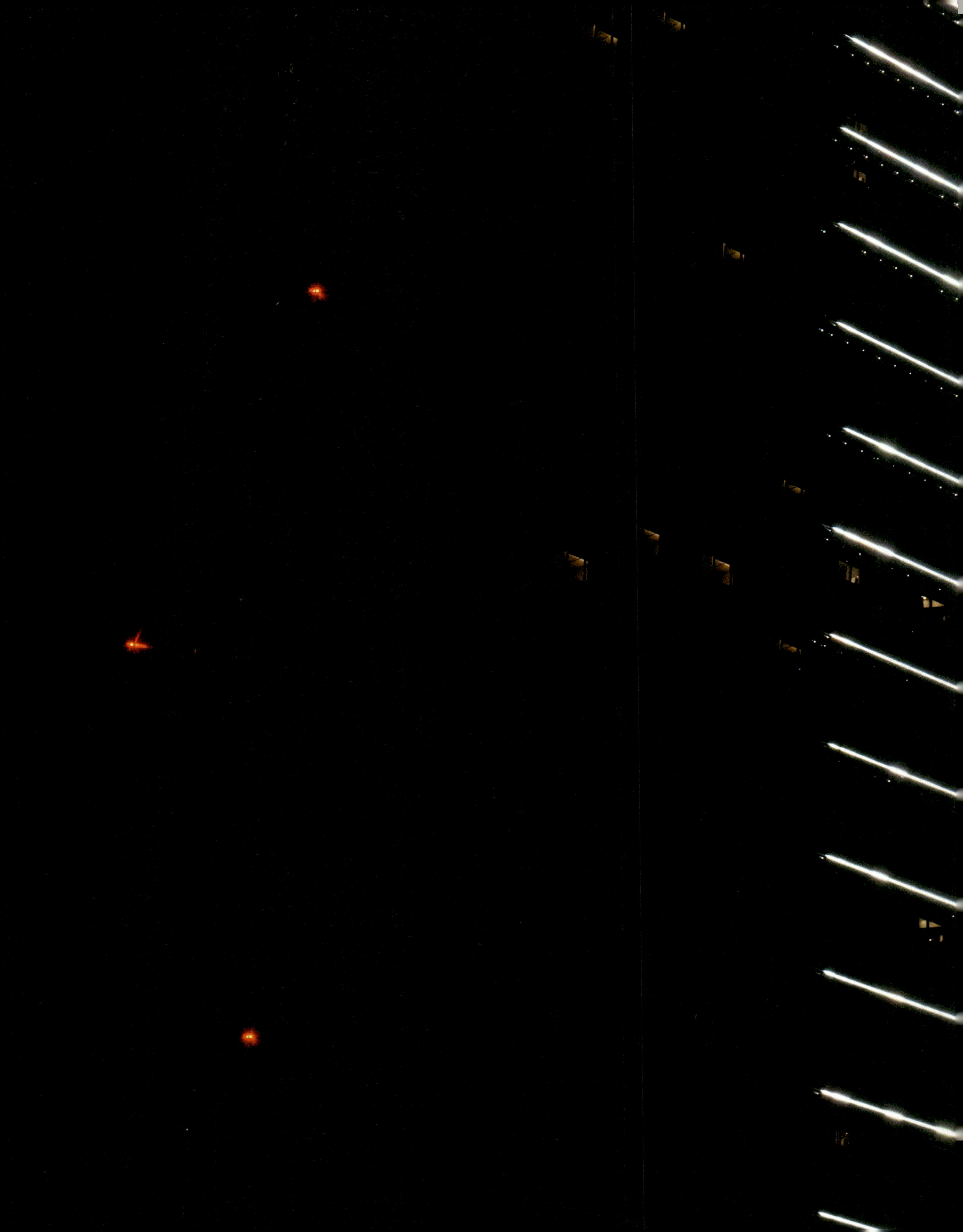

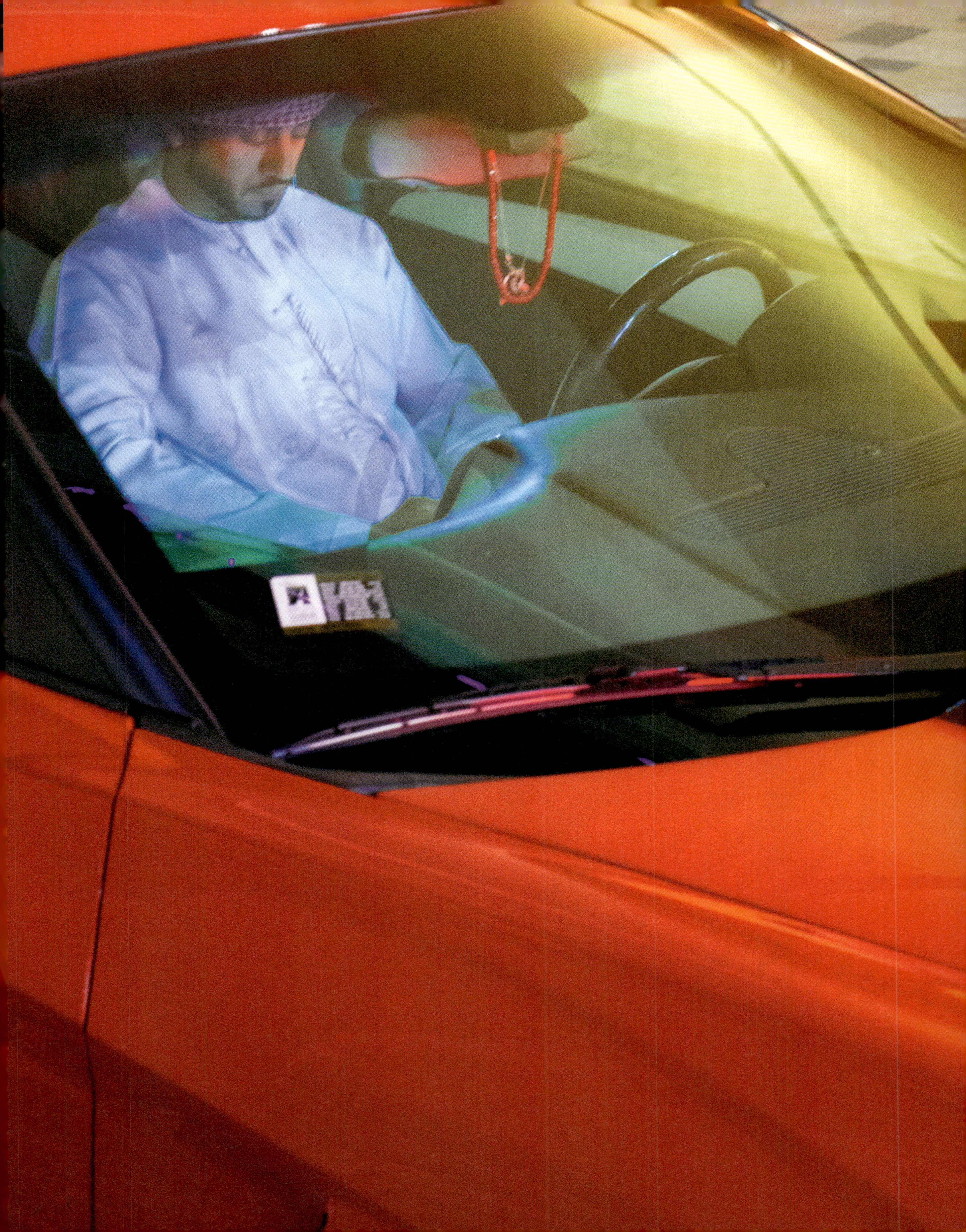

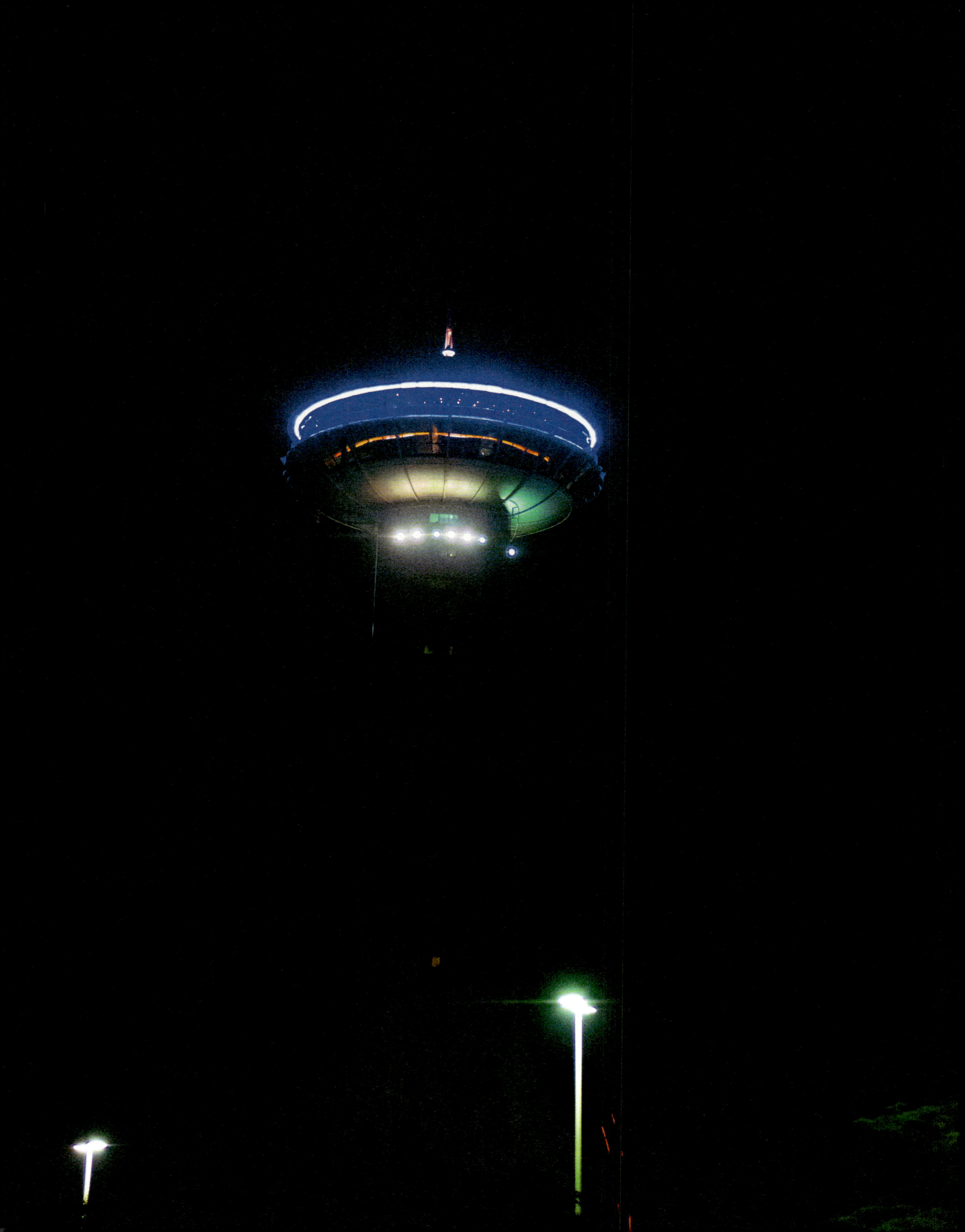

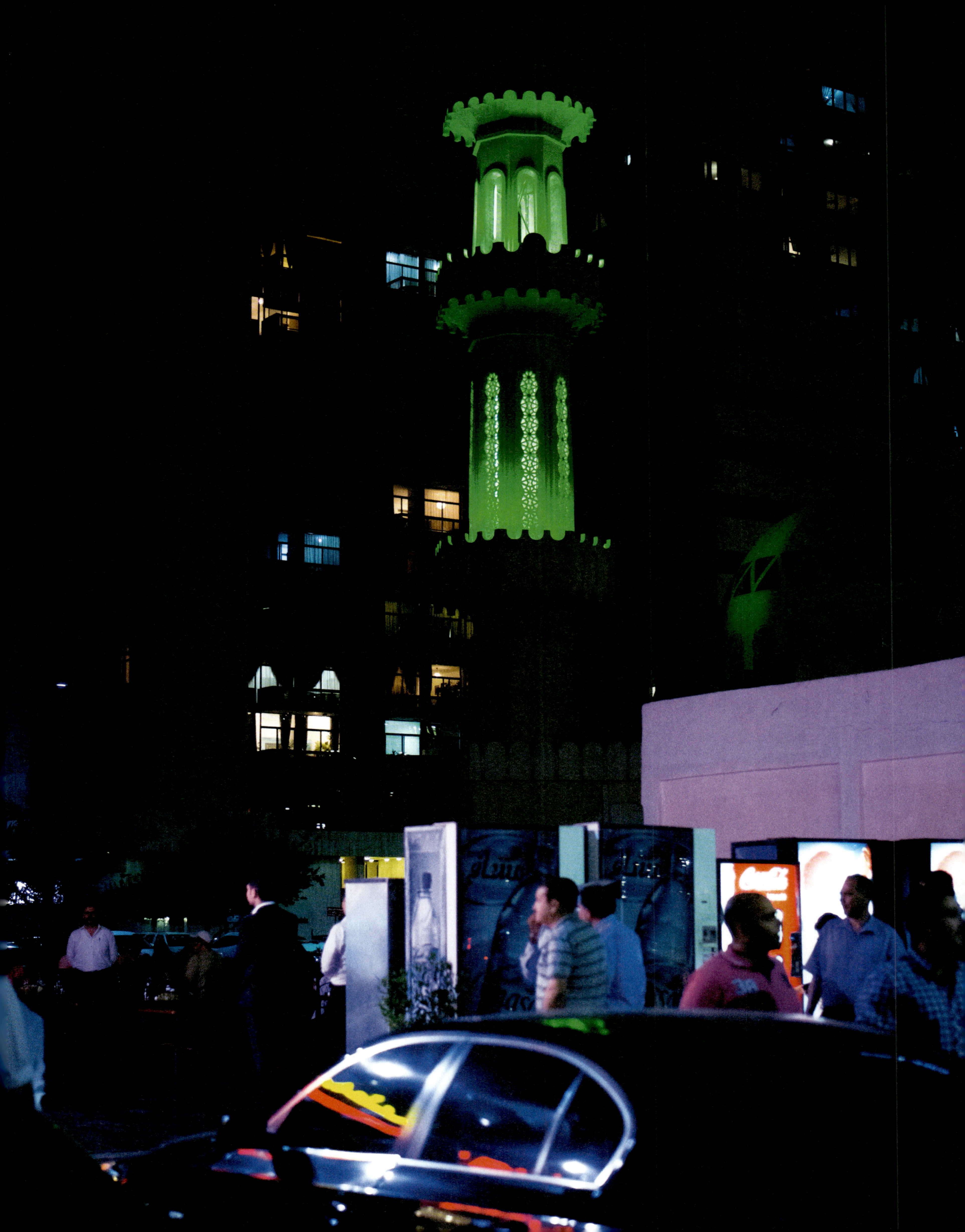

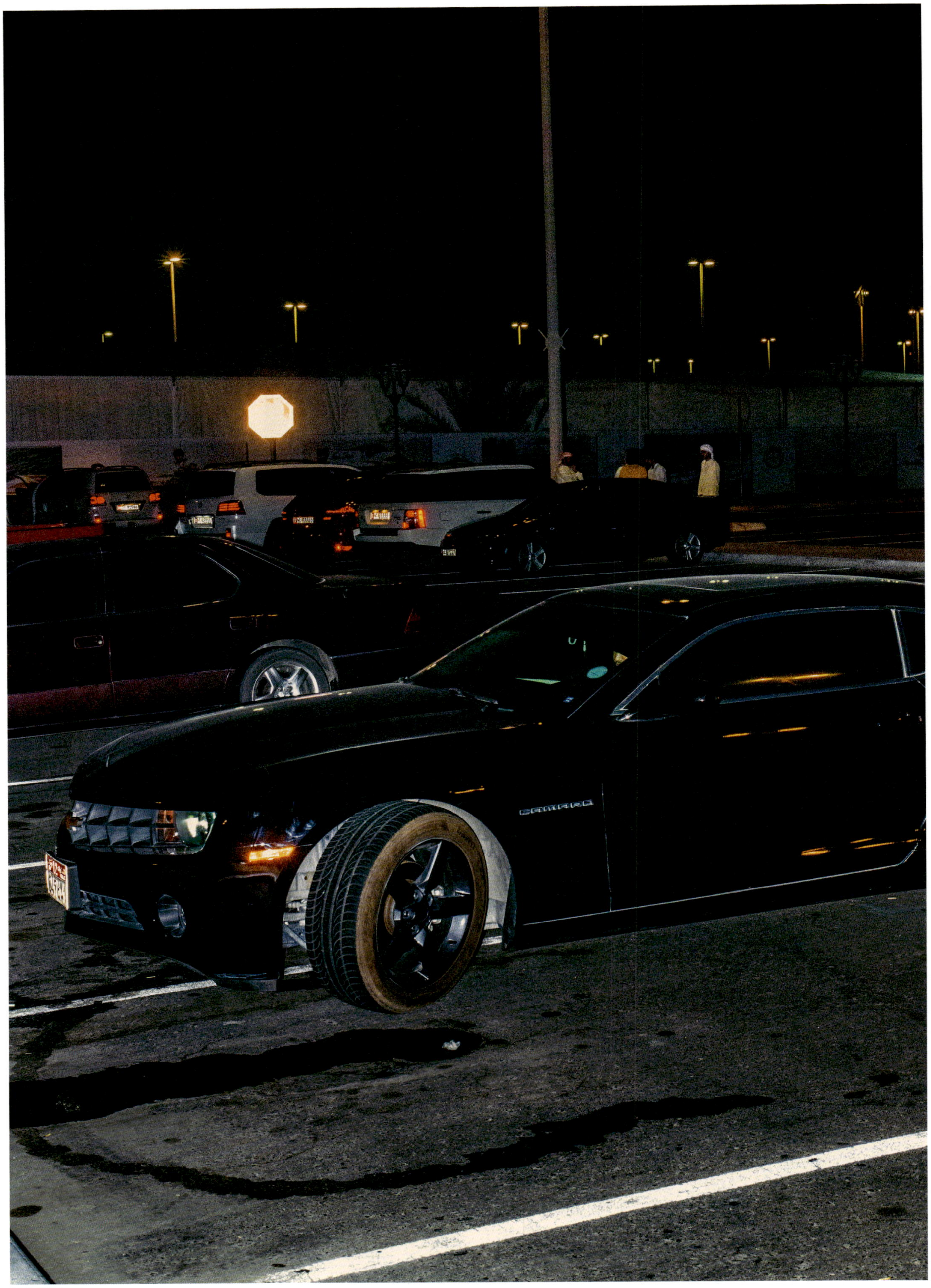

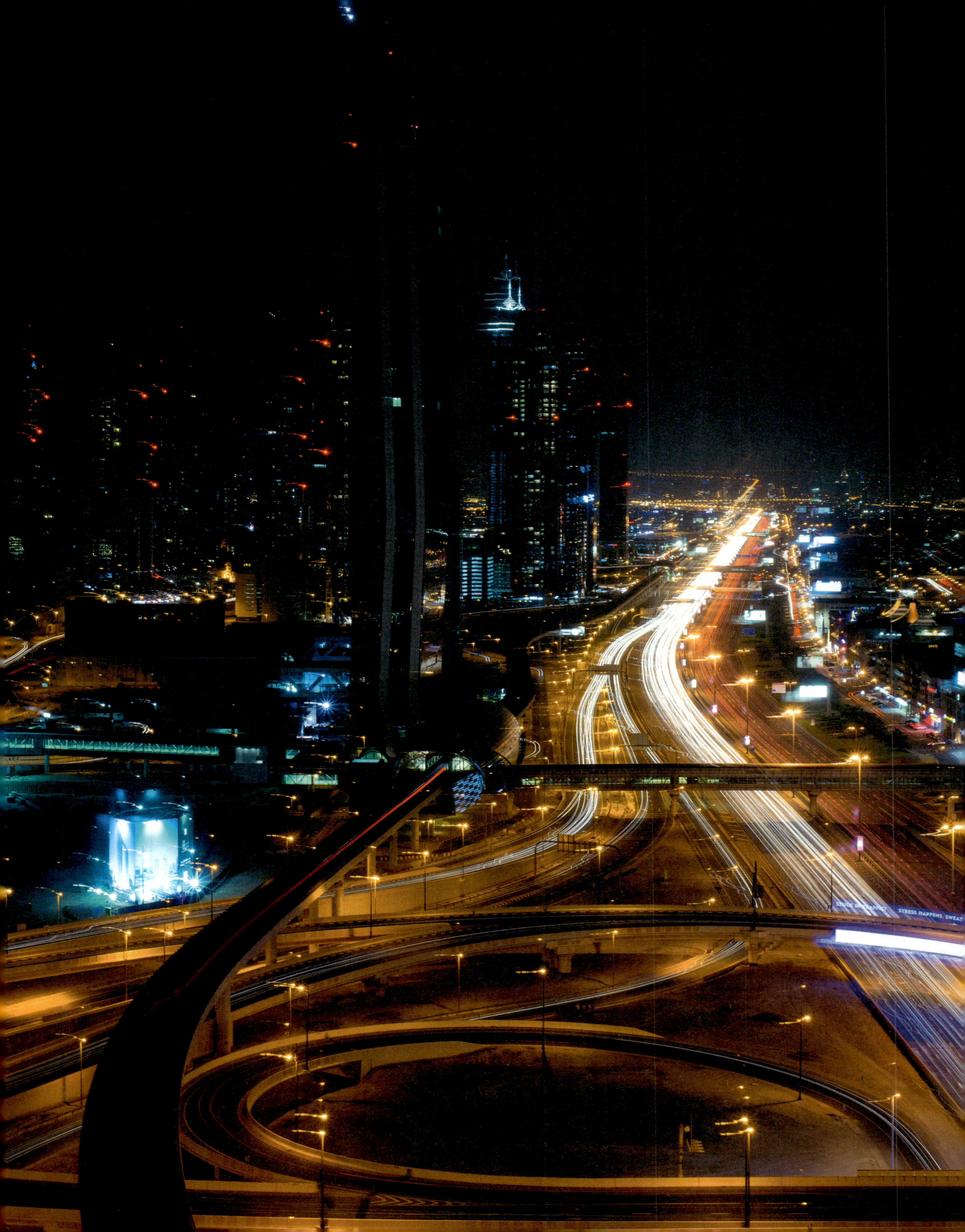
STRESS HAPPENS. SWEAT

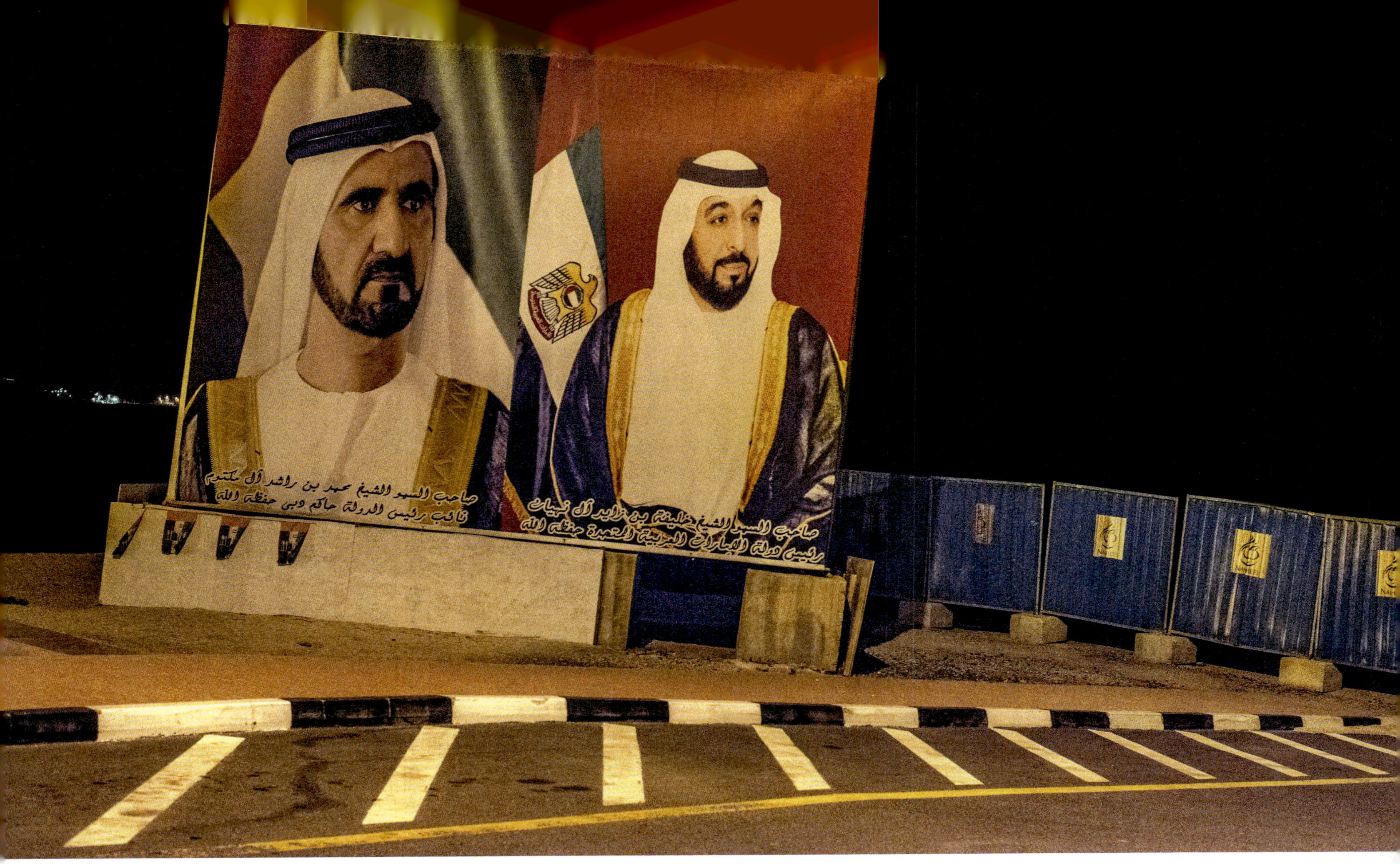
صاحب السمو الشيخ محمد بن راشد آل مكتوم
نائب رئيس الدولة حاكم دبي حفظه الله
صاحب السمو الشيخ خليفة بن زايد آل نهيان
رئيس دولة الإمارات العربية المتحدة حفظه الله

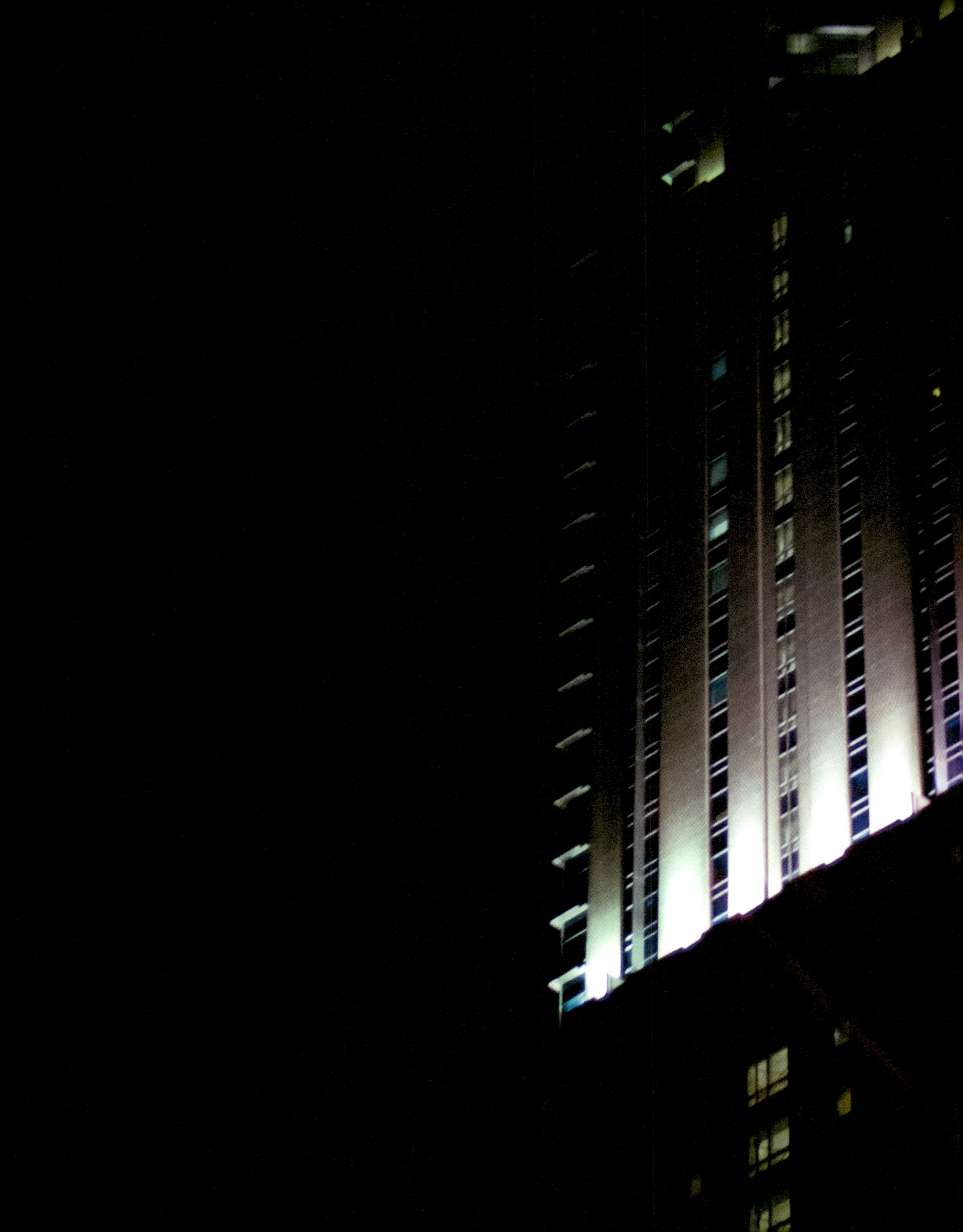

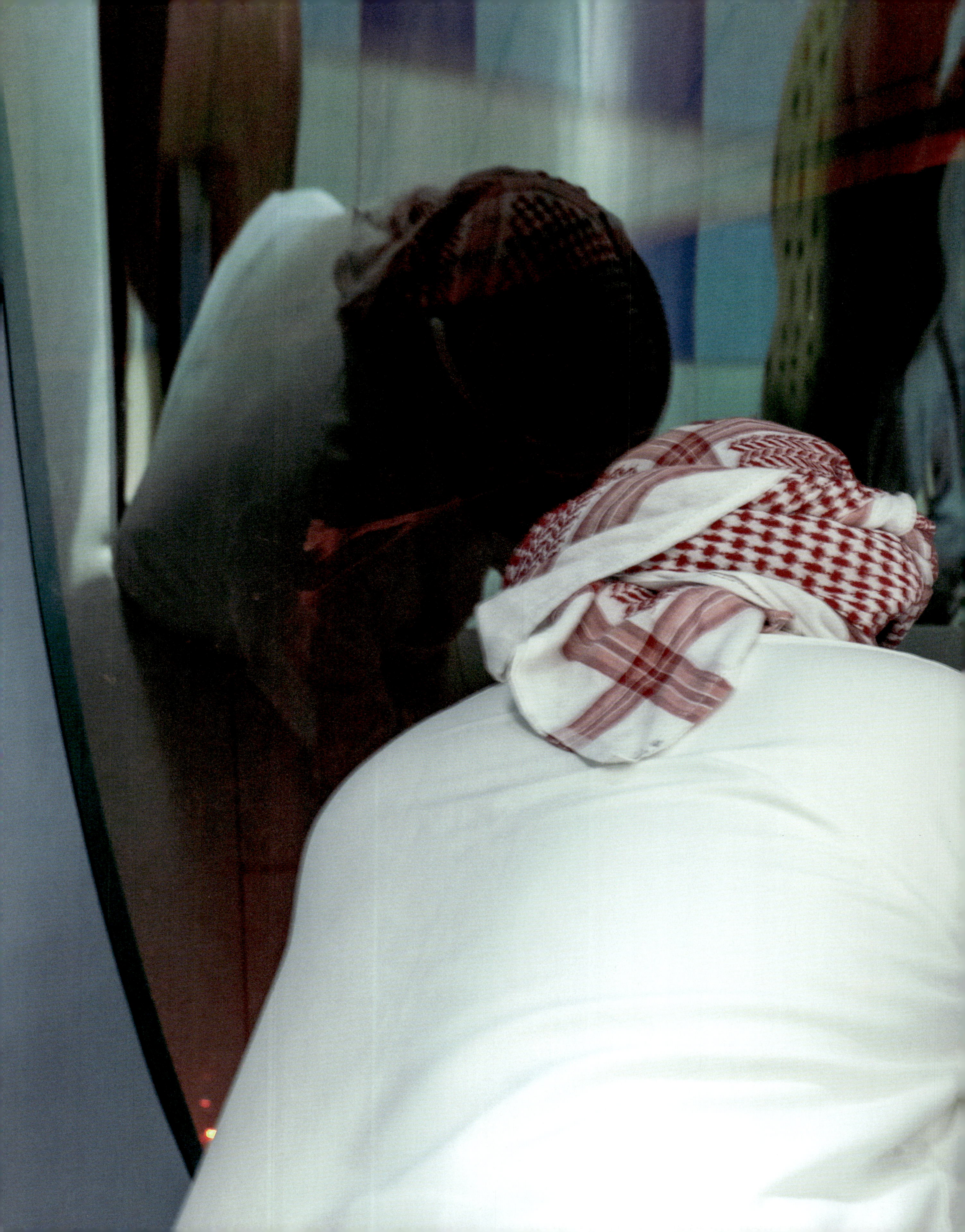

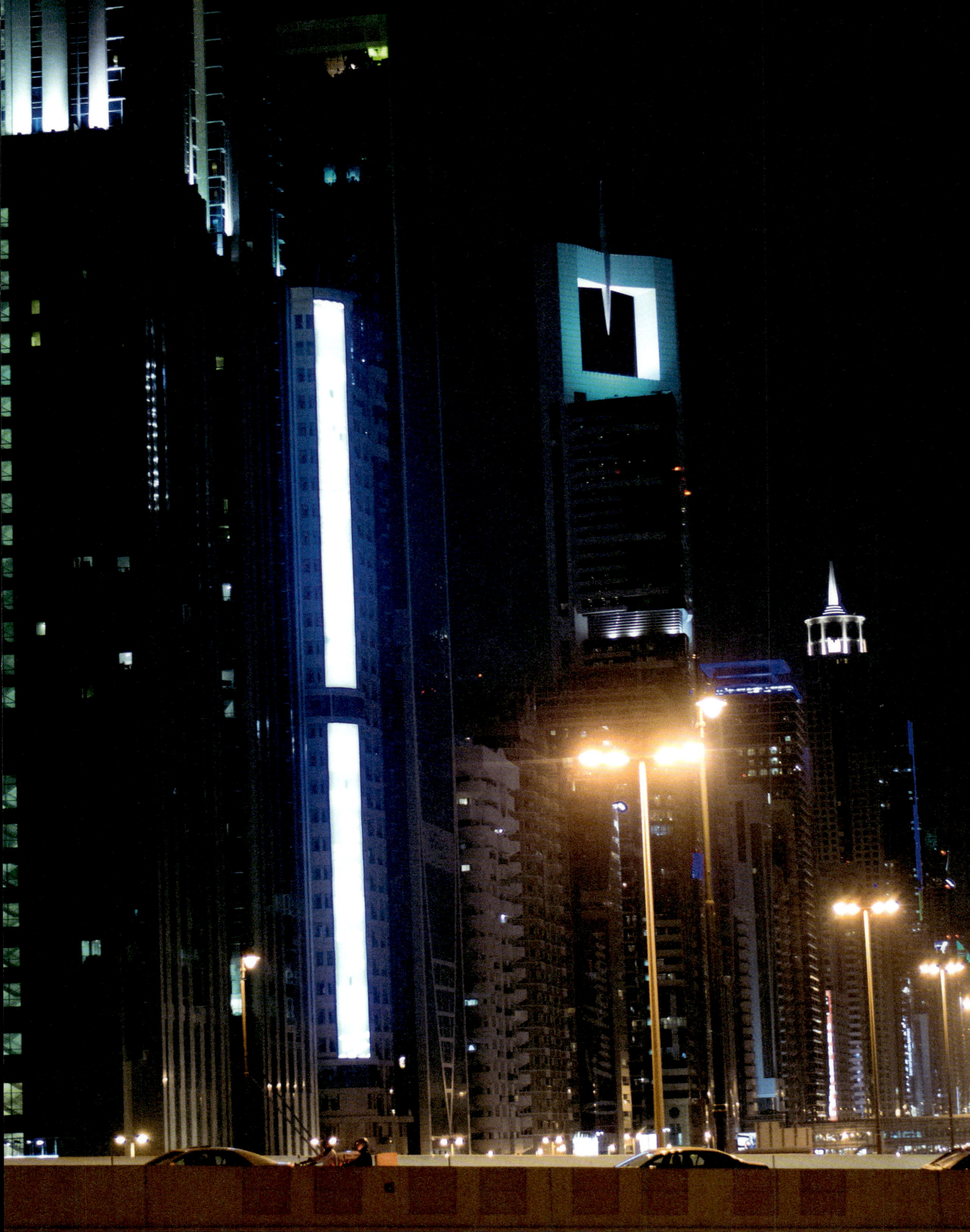

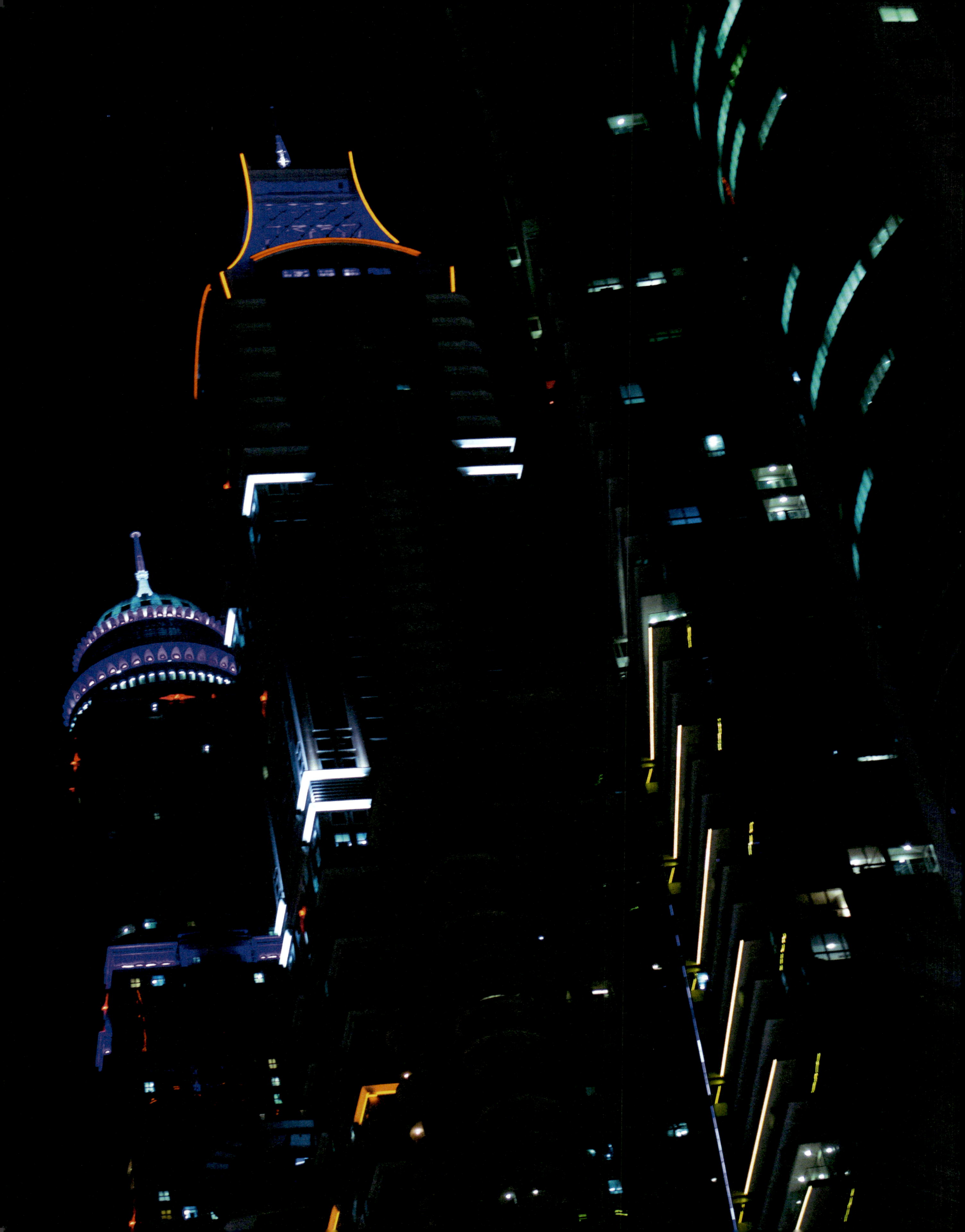

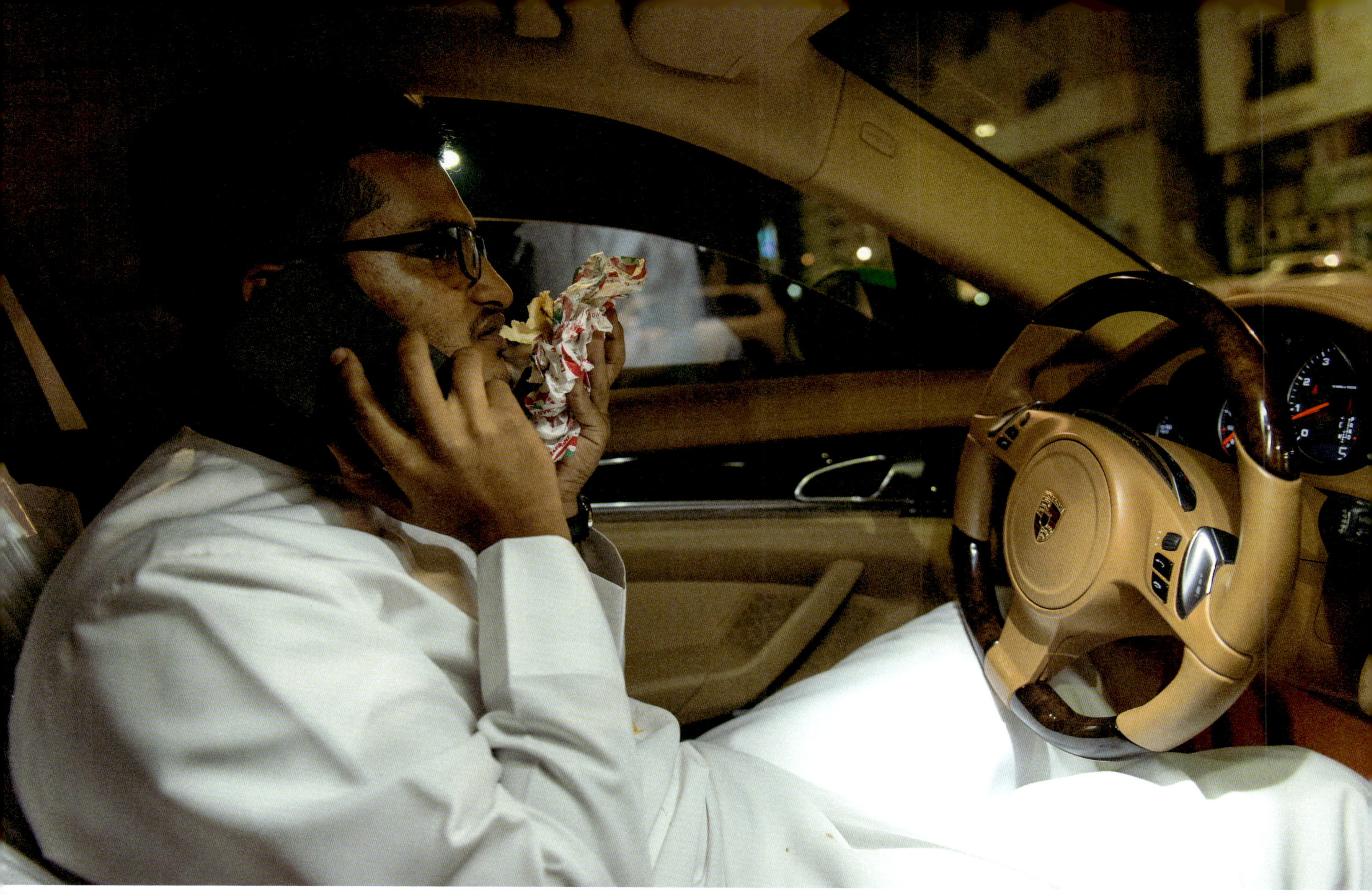

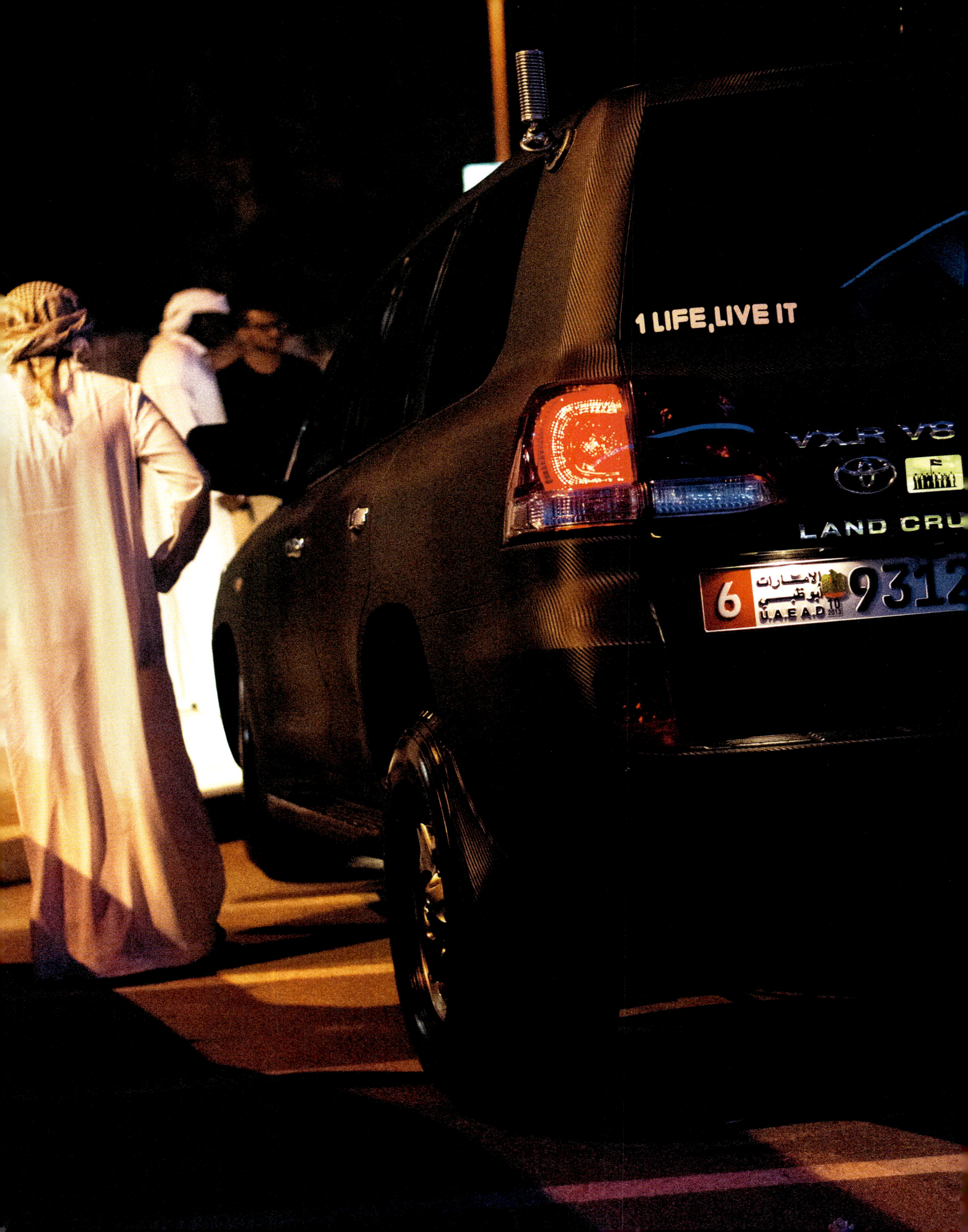
1 LIFE,LIVE IT
VXR V8
6
الإمارات
أبو ظبي
U.A.E A.D

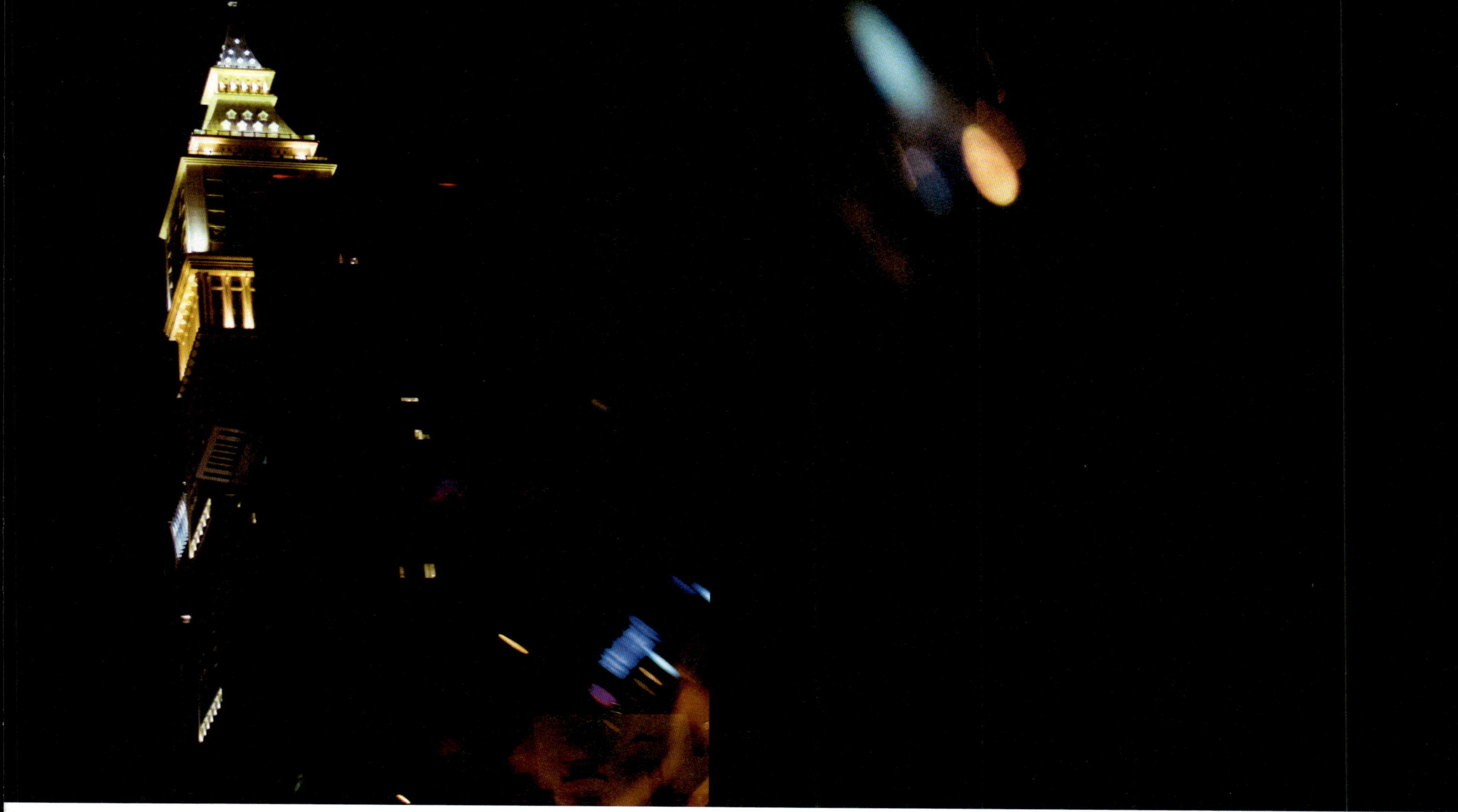

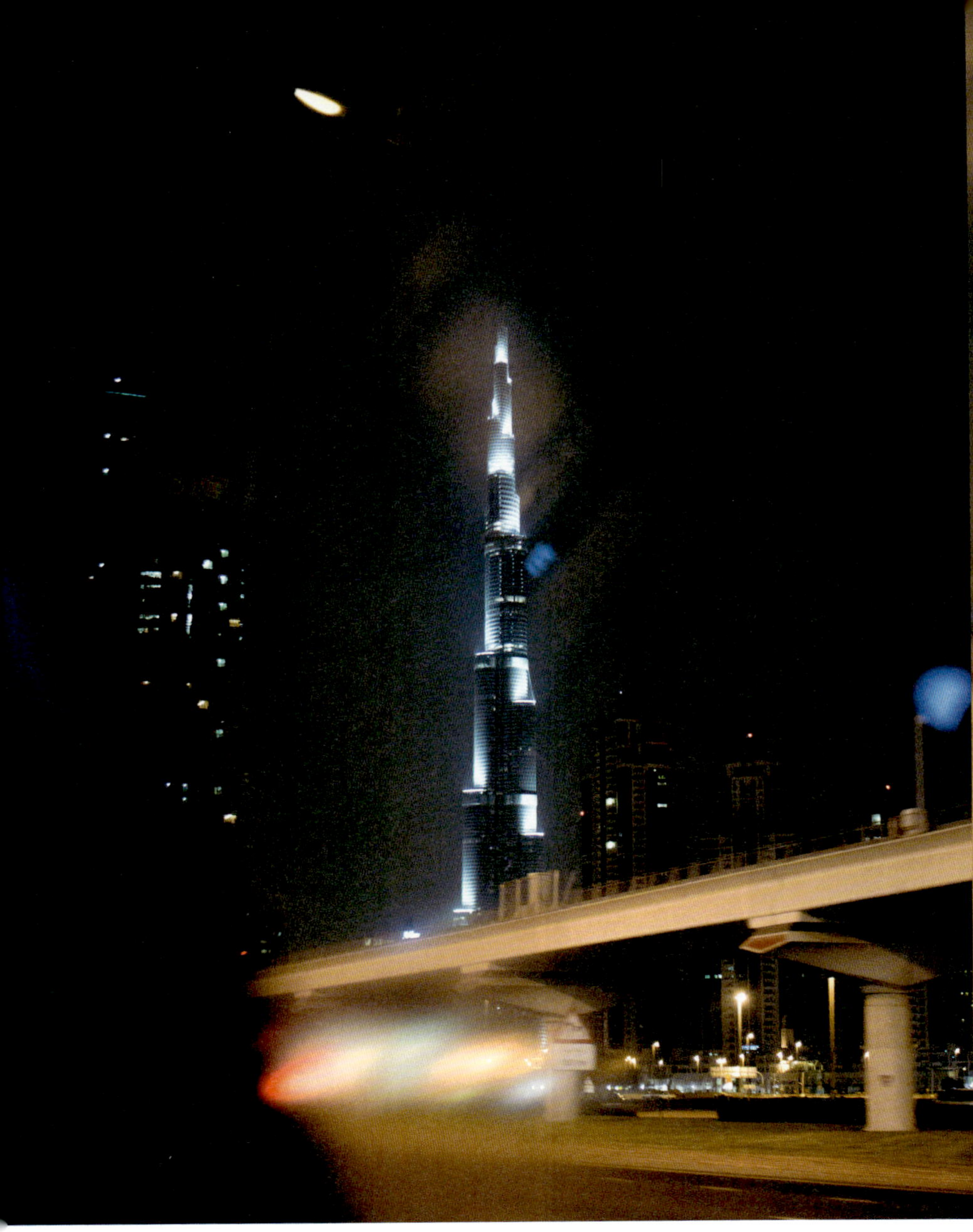

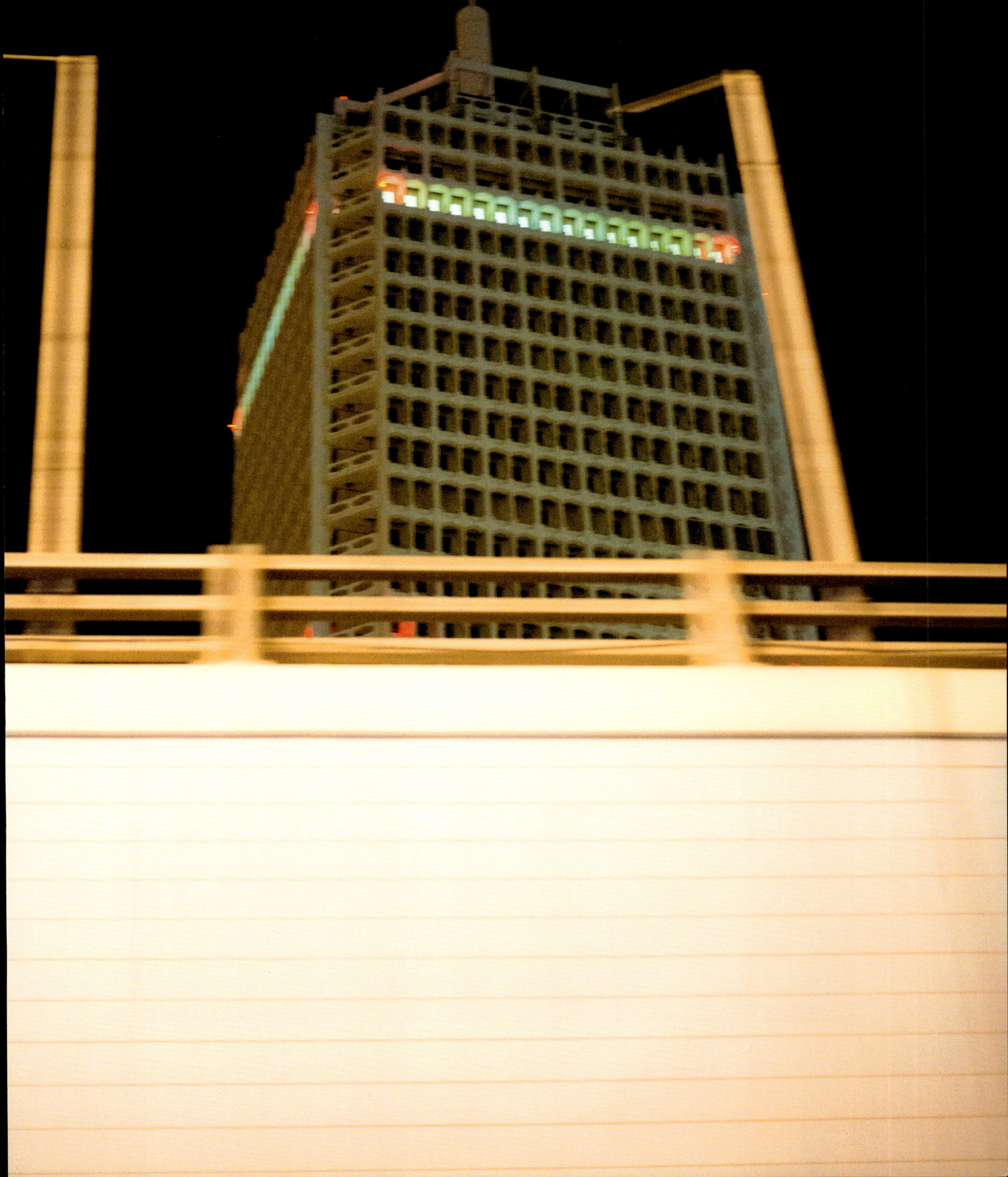

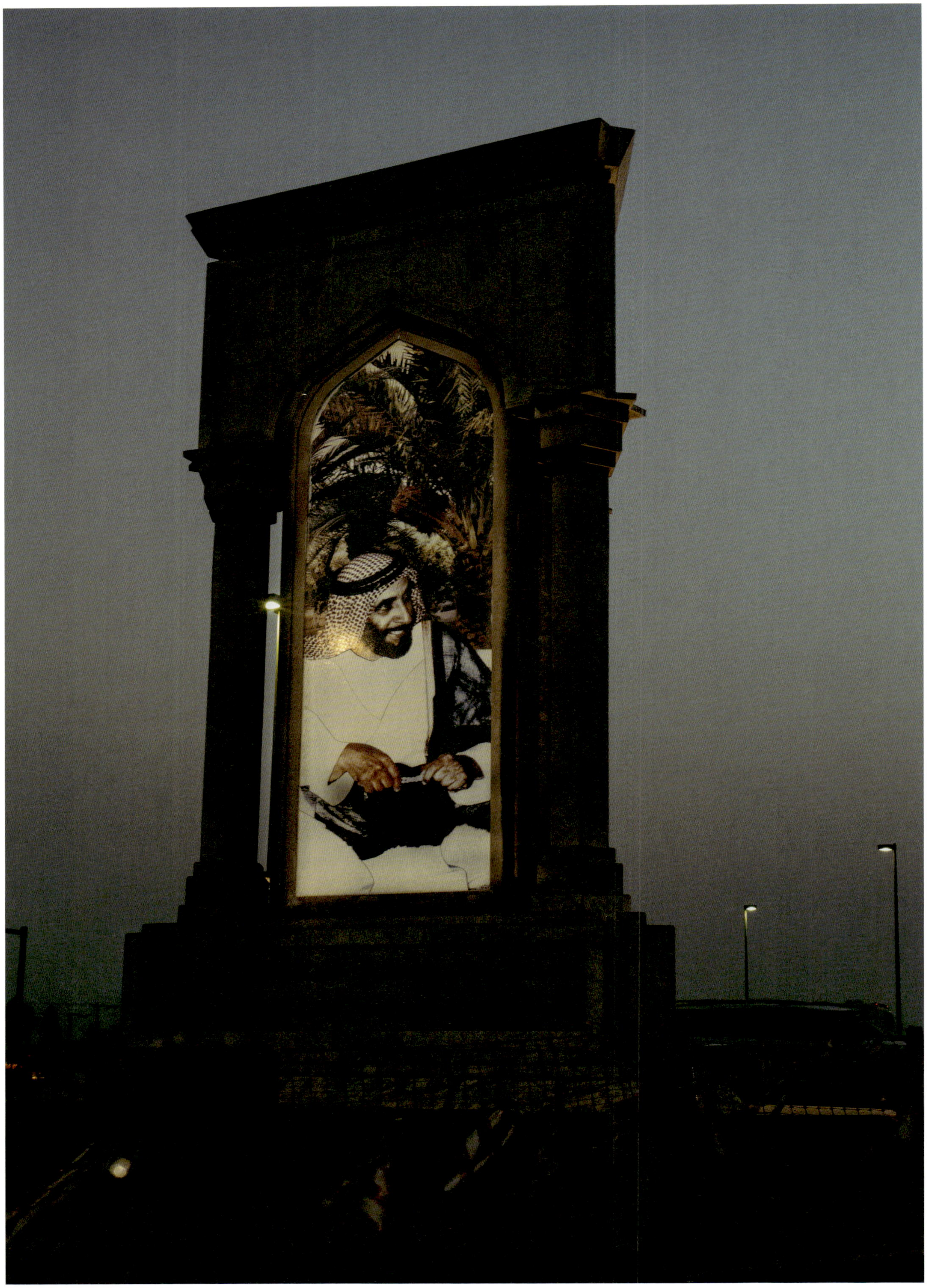

## FULLY FUELED

All photographs have been taken between 2012 and 2014 in and around Dubai and Abu Dhabi, in the United Arab Emirates. They document the nights of young Emiratis in their everyday life and on the 42nd National Day celebration.

## COLOPHON

Photographs: Basile Mookherjee
Concept, book design: Bureau DGC
Color seperation by Musumeci S.p.A., Aosta
Printed and bound by Musumeci S.p.A., Aosta
Paper: Magno Volume 100g
Cover: Symbol freelife E/E 49 country 250g
Font: 29LT Kaff
First edition: 800 copies



Edition Patrick Frey, Limmatstrasse 268
CH – 8005 Zürich
www.editionpatrickfrey.com
mail@editionpatrickfrey.ch



First edition: Edition Patrick Frey, 2016
ISBN 978-3-906803-15-9
Printed in Italy

## THANKS TO

Marina Coufopandelis, Eric Mookherjee, Le Nid, Inès Dalsoglio, Benjamin Lallier, Thaddée Lucan Clément Bonnetin, Sophie Delahaye

## SPECIAL THANKS TO

Jean-Vincent Simonet, Florine Bonaventure, Camille Audibert, Patrick Frey, Andreas Koller, Thomas Bellegarde, Héloïse Schwab,
علوي عبدالرحمن الهاشمي علوي عبدالله الهاشمي
سرور عبدالله المحرمي اسماعيل سعيد المسكري
علوي عبدالله الهاشمي علوي عبدالرحمن الهاشمي

## DISTRIBUTION

Switzerland:
AVA Verlagsauslieferung
CH – Affoltern am Albis
ava.ch

Germany, Austria:
GVA Gemeinsame Verlagsauslieferung
D – Göttingen
gva-verlage.de

France, Luxembourg, Belgium:
Les presses du réel
F – Dijon
lespressesdureel.com

United Kingdom:
Antenne Books
GB – London
antennebooks.com

Japan:
Marginal Press,
JP – Tokyo
marginal-press.com

USA:
RAM publications + distribution
USA – Santa Monica
rampub.com

Australia, New Zealand:
Perimeter Distribution
AU – Melbourne
perimeterdistribution.com

Rest of the world:
Edition Patrick Frey,
CH – Zürich
editionpatrickfrey.com